VALLEYS IN
TRANSITION

The Editors would like to thank the following for their assistance and co-operation.

The Aga Khan Foundation

DFID (Department for International Development)

Canadian International Development Agency

VALLEYS IN TRANSITION

Twenty Years of AKRSP's Experience
in Northern Pakistan

Edited by
Geof Wood, Abdul Malik
and
Sumaira Sagheer

OXFORD
UNIVERSITY PRESS

OXFORD
UNIVERSITY PRESS

Great Clarendon Street, Oxford OX2 6DP

Oxford University Press is a department of the University of Oxford.
It furthers the University's objective of excellence in research, scholarship,
and education by publishing worldwide in

Oxford New York

Auckland Cape Town Dar es Salaam Hong Kong Karachi
Kuala Lumpur Madrid Melbourne Mexico City Nairobi
New Delhi Shanghai Taipei Toronto

with offices in

Argentina Austria Brazil Chile Czech Republic France Greece
Guatemala Hungary Italy Japan Poland Portugal Singapore
South Korea Switzerland Turkey Ukraine Vietnam

Oxford is a registered trade mark of Oxford University Press
in the UK and in certain other countries

ISBN 978-0-19-547327-8

Second Impression 2007

Typeset in Adobe Garamond Pro
Printed in Pakistan by
Kagzi Printers, Karachi.
Published by
Ameena Saiyid, Oxford University Press
No. 38, Sector 15, Korangi Industrial Area, PO Box 8214
Karachi-74900, Pakistan.

CONTENTS

page

List of boxes vii
List of figures ix
List of tables xi
List of authors xiii
Acknowledgements xxiii
Foreword xxvii
List of abbreviations xxxi
Glossary xxxvii

Introduction: The Mutuality of Initiative 1
Geof Wood
1 Ethnographical Context 32
Geof Wood
2 Sustaining Livelihoods and Overcoming Insecurity 54
Geof Wood and Abdul Malik
3 Gender and AKRSP—Mainstreamed or Sidelined? 120
Aalya Gloekler and Janet Seeley
4 Community Infrastructure 196
Abdul Malik, Ali Effendi, and Muhammad Darjat
5 Natural Resource Management 226
Marc Aljoscha Gloekler
6 Enterprise Development 259
Fatimah Afzal
7 Micro-Finance 315
Maliha H. Hussein and Stefan Plateau
8 Collective Action: The Threatened Imperative 369
Geof Wood with Sofia Shakil
9 Working with Government: Close But Never Too Close 426
Adil Najam

10 The Way Forward: Fourth Dialogue 454
Izhar Hunzai

Annexures 493
References 499
Index 515

BOXES

2.1 An example of diversification: Gilgit region   69

3.1 WID and GAD   122
3.2 Women who make a difference (1)   143
3.3 Women who make a difference (2)   144
3.4 Women who make a difference (3)   156

5.1 Livestock trends in the programme area   244
5.2 Poultry specialist and businesswoman Shahida
     Numa of Princeabad Women's Organisation, Gilgit   246

· 6.1 Business development services (BDS)   301
6.2 Illustrative examples of business associations
     in the off-farm sectors   304
6.3 Illustrative examples of AKRSP's partnerships with
     commercial sector stakeholders   308

7.1 Issues and problems with VO banking   330
7.2 Comparison between the third co-operative
     congress and AKRSP   339
7.3 Growth in savings   358
7.4 The three stages of MFIs   361

FIGURES

2.1 Livelihoods needs / AKRSP strategy   56
2.2 Changing patterns of socio-economic stratification   58
2.3 Economic stratification of households over the last decade   59
2.4 The impact of accessibility on incomes   77
2.5 Sensitivity of head count index to changes in incomes   91
2.6 Components of the institutional responsibility matrix   104

4.1 Infrastructure maintenance matrix   220

5.1 The livelihood system in Northern Pakistan in transition   228
5.2 Resource management by institution   255

6.1 Collective marketing (1983–1997)   279
6.2 BDS market development paradigm   300
6.3 Increasing outreach through interest groups   305

7.1 Comparative analysis of AKRSP's model of sustainability with other NGOs   341

9.1 AKRSP–Government relations: a policy map approach   437
9.2 AKRSP–Government relations: a 'Four Cs' approach   439

TABLES

2.1 AKRSP's target households   57
2.2 Trends in per capita incomes (Rs: base year 1991)   63
2.3 Trends in poverty: percentage below the poverty line   64
2.4 Measures of poverty for the programme area   64
2.5 Primary occupation of male workforce and average
     incomes (%)   69
2.6 Inequality in the programme area   70
2.7 Sensitivity of poverty to changes in the poverty line (%)   92

3.1 Number of male and female staff by grade in 1996,
     2000 and on 31 March 2003   152

4.1 Productive physical infrastructure projects by region
     (as of December 2002)   202
4.2 Infrastructure portfolio by sector and region
     (as of December 2002)   202
4.3 Summary of WO infrastructure projects
     (as of December 2002)   204

5.1 Per household farm incomes: programme area and
     the regions 1991–2001 (Rs)   237
5.2 Percentage share of per household farm income:
     programme area and the regions 1991–2001   238
5.3 Water channels at Khyber village   240
5.4 Number of livestock in the programme region
     (excluding Astore) by type in 1986   244
5.5 Average livestock holdings per household in the
     programme region (excluding Astore) in 1997   245
5.6 Number of rural households in the 1998 census   245
5.7 Livestock holdings and growth rate between 1986 and
     1997 in the programme region (excluding Astore)   245

TABLES

6.1 Trends in average annual household farm and off-
farm incomes in the programme area (Rs, 1991–2001) 263
6.2 Collective marketing (1983–1997) 277
6.3 Cumulative achievements in enterprise development:
programme area and the three regions
(as of December 2002) 285
6.4 People benefiting from the projects/year
(as of year end 2002) 289
6.5 Number of local intermediaries assisted 303

7.1 AKRSP's savings and loan products 1982–2001 328
7.2 Analysis of outreach and significance of financial
sources for credit (percentage distribution) 351

AUTHORS

Geof Wood
Professor Geof Wood is Head of the Department of Economics and International Development and Director of the Institute for International Policy Analysis at the University of Bath. He is on the editorial board of the Bulletin of Concerned Asian Scholars and the Journal of International Development. He has directed the DFID research project 'Systems for Coordinated Poverty Reduction'; co-directed the Urban Livelihoods Study in Bangladesh; re-strategised social development in the Aga Khan Rural Support Programme in Pakistan; co-directed the Social Policy in Developing Countries research programme, and is thus a lead author with Ian Gough for *Insecurity and Welfare Regimes in Asia, Africa and Latin America* (Cambridge: CUP 2004); participates in the ESRC funded Wellbeing in Developing Countries research programme at Bath; has been part of the World Bank team on social development indicators; and part of the advisory team for the ILO 2004 *Economic Security for a Better World* report. He continues to provide strategic TA inputs into PROSHIKA in Bangladesh from 1979. He has worked extensively with DFID and Scandinavian donors, leading various appraisal and review missions. Overall research interests lie in social development, governance, agrarian change in South Asia, irrigation and water management, the analysis of rural and urban livelihoods, micro-finance, with particular focus on Bangladesh, India, Pakistan and Afghanistan. Recent publications include 'Prisoners and escapees: Improving the institutional responsibility square in Bangladesh', *Public Administration and Development* (2000) 20: 221-37; 'Introduction: Securing Livelihoods in Dhaka Slums', *Journal of International Development* (2000) 12 (5): 669-688 (with S. Salway); 'Desperately Seeking Security' *Journal of International Development* (2001) 13: 523-534; 'Staying Secure,

Staying Poor: The Faustian Bargain', *World Development* (2003) March.

Izhar Ali Hunzai

Izhar A. Hunzai currently serves as the General Manager of Aga Khan Rural Support Programme (AKRSP). Starting his professional career with AKRSP in 1984, Mr Hunzai went on to head the Aga Khan Culture Services in 1996 and rejoined AKRSP in 2003 after working with the International Water Management Institute(IWMI) in Colombo for five years. During his long association with the development sector, Mr. Hunzai has contributed content to various international conferences. His academic qualifications include a degree in International Development from Cornell University and a masters degree in International Relations from Karachi University.

Abdul Malik

Graduating in Agriculture Economics from University of Agriculture Faisalabad (1996) and then going on to acquire a masters degree in Business Administration from Lahore University of Management Sciences (2001), Abdul Malik is associated with the Aga Khan Rural Support Programme since 1997. He has served in various capacities in the Policy and Research section of AKRSP, and is currently, responsible for looking after the Monitoring and Evaluation department. During his professional association with AKRSP, Mr Malik has mainly worked on impact assessments and evaluation studies of varying scope. His particular responsibilities include designing and conducting large scale household socio-economic surveys of the Northern Areas and Chitral (NAC); impact assessment of programme interventions such as Natural Resource Management; and writing analytical notes on emerging issues in AKRSP. In addition to this, Mr Malik has also provided consulting services to various agencies with a special focus on programme evaluation, poverty analysis, and designing of monitoring and evaluation systems. In recent years, Mr Malik has mainly worked on the issues of poverty and livelihoods in the Northern Areas and Chitral. He has played a major role in the implementation and synthesis of the Northern Areas Participatory Poverty Assessment commissioned by the Government of Pakistan with assistance from DFID. His other contributions to the poverty debate in NAC include a paper in progress on chronic poverty, and a chapter on economic transition in Hunza.

Fatimah Afzal

By most traditional standards, Fatimah has followed a very non-conventional professional trajectory. After four years in investment banking and management consulting, she changed career tracks, choosing to leave the corporate sector to explore the emerging social development arena in Pakistan. Fatimah has special interests in enterprise development programmes and as an independent/free lance consultant, she works on a variety of other projects. After completing a post-graduate degree in International Relations from the Quaid-e-Azam University, Islamabad in 1987, Fatimah joined an agricultural research project of the USAID. In 1992, she earned a graduate degree in business management from the Lahore University of Management Sciences (LUMS) and began her career in the corporate sector with an international investment bank, and subsequently joined Coopers & Lybrand Management Consultancy (presently PriceWaterhouseCoopers International). Fatimah has broad based experience in financial analysis and management of credit, investments, equity placements, and underwriting. Her experience also extends to more diverse and complex organizational management, marketing research and business mobilization issues. Asia Foundation's Pakistan NGO Initiative (PNI) provided Fatimah with an opportunity to utilize her professional and academic background in the development sector. As the programme officer for the Pakistan NGO Initiative (PNI), Fatimah traveled extensively across Pakistan, acquiring familiarity with a range of development organizations, in particular those engaged in micro-finance programmes. More recently, as part of the Enterprise Development Programme team at the Aga Khan Rural Support Programme (AKRSP), Fatimah drew on her corporate sector background and understanding of policy issues and constraints germane to the development sector, to help develop a market based orientation of the programme. Fatimah was invited by the Aga Khan Foundation, Canada to present AKRSP's enterprise development initiatives for women at some of the premier universities across Canada, as a guest speaker for the University Seminar Series. Presently, Fatimah is based in Rawalpindi.

Muhammad Darjat
Muhammad Darjat is a freelance consultant. He joined AKRSP as a consulting Engineer in April 1983 and left in 1995 when he was Programme Manager, Community Infrastructure Programme.

Ali Effendi
Ali Effendi is currently working as Programme Officer at the RTI funded Education Sector Reform Assistance Programme (ESRA). He has remained associated with AKRSP Chitral for about two and a half years during 2000–03.

Maliha Hussein
A graduate of Punjab University, Ms Hussein obtained her M.Sc. in agricultural economics from Michigan State University and a certificate in international law, economics and politics from Somerville College, Oxford University. She is a Director of the Pakistan Poverty Alleviation Fund and is the Chairperson of the Gender and Water Alliance, a network of 133 organisations and individuals from around the world and an Associated Programme of the Global Water Partnership. Ms Maliha H. Hussein currently works as an independent development consultant. She was the first woman to join AKRSP in 1983 when she was appointed the Programme Officer, (Monitoring, Evaluation and Research, AKRSP, Gilgit)and coordinated the Women-in-Development programme in the area from 1986–1988. Her experience includes policy and institutional analysis, strategic review, socio-economic research, gender assessments, project design and review and monitoring and evaluation. She has experience in a broad range of sectors including agriculture, irrigation, forestry, micro-finance, rural development, health, education and water. She has worked in India, Bangladesh, Jordan, Yemen, Tajikistan, Kyrgzstan and Mozambique and has

extensive consulting experience with all the major multilateral and bilateral agencies including the World Bank, the Asian Development Bank, International Centre for Integrated Mountain Development (ICIMOD), International Institute for Environment and Development (IIED), the International Irrigation Management Institute (IIMI), the World Food Programme, the Global Water Partnership, UNIFEM; the International Fund for Agricultural Development (IFAD), the Aga Khan Foundation, bilateral aid agencies of Netherlands, Canada, Switzerland, Norway, United Kingdom, USAID; development projects, NGOs, and international consulting firms.

Aalya Gloekler

Aalya Sadiq Gloekler received her B.Sc. in Business & Economics with a minor in literature from Sophia University in Tokyo, Japan in 1987. After working for about three years in research with several market research and business management consulting firms in Japan from 1987 to 1990, she studied for a Diploma and then her M.Sc. in sociology at the London School of Economics in 1990–1992. After her post-graduate studies, she also studied German for a year in Munich University. She joined AKRSP in 1994 as WID Consultant. Since then she worked with AKRSP in various positions. Some of her achievements within AKRSP were the initiation of the first adult literacy centres and Traditional Birth Attendants training in the Baltistan region; the establishment of a new section focusing on social development issues in the Gilgit region, design and implementation of pilot poverty alleviation projects in the Gilgit region and formulation of gender policy for AKRSP. Besides working with AKRSP, Aalya Gloekler worked as a consultant with UNDP for the formulation of the Mountain Areas Conservancy Project in 1997. In December 2000, she left her position as Coordinator Social Development at the AKRSP Core Office to work as a free-lance consultant in gender and social development.

Marc Aljoscha Gloekler

Marc Aljoscha Gloekler worked for AKRSP between 1994 and 1996 as Social Scientist and Social Research Coordinator at Baltistan and Gilgit. Between 1997 and 2002, he was working as a Monitoring and Evaluation Advisor and Rural Sociologist for IUCN in Gilgit. He is now working as a freelance consultant based in Islamabad. Graduating from Sophia University, Tokyo, in Sociology and Anthropology he obtained his Masters in Anthropology and Development from the School of Oriental and African Studies, London.

Adil Najam

Dr Adil Najam is an Associate Professor of International Negotiation and Diplomacy at the Fletcher School of Law and Diplomacy, Tufts University, USA. He holds a Bachelors degree from the University of Engineering and Technology (UET), Lahore, Pakistan; two separate Masters degrees from the Massachusetts Institute of Technology (MIT), Cambridge, USA; a Specialization in Negotiation from the Program on Negotiation at the Harvard Law School; and a Ph.D. from MIT. His areas of research include nonprofit studies (especially the policy role of NGOs in developing countries) sustainable development, international environmental policy, development politics, multilateral negotiations, global governance, international negotiation, and conflict resolution. He has taught and published in all these areas in the leading journals of these fields. Dr Najam serves on the editorial boards of the leading journals and also serves on the boards of the Pakistan Institute for Environment–Development Action research (PIEDAR); The Center for Global Studies, University of Victoria; and the Fredrick Pardee Center for the Study of the Longer-Range Future. He has held research fellow positions at MIT, Harvard Law School, Yale University, Boston University, and the Institute for Applied Systems Analysis (IASA) in Austria. He is currently a Visiting Fellow at the Sustainable Development Policy Institute (Pakistan) and an Associate at the International Institute for Sustainable Development (Canada). He has worked extensively around the developing world on issues of public policy, including on the Pakistan National Conservation Strategy and on the President of Pakistan's Task Force on Human Development.

Janet Seeley

Dr Janet Seeley is a lecturer in Gender and Development at the School of Development Studies, University of East Anglia, Norwich. She is also a member of the Overseas Development Group at UEA with which she carries out consultancy and research assignments. Since joining UEA in 2000 she has undertaken assignments in Bangladesh, India, Nepal, Pakistan and East and Southern Africa. Dr Seeley has a BA Hons. in Geography and Anthropology from the University of Durham and an M.Phil. in Social Anthropology from the University of Cambridge. She also has a Ph.D. in Social Anthropology, on 'Social Welfare in Urban Kenya', from the University of Cambridge. Dr Seeley was formerly a DFID Social Development Advisor, and was actively involved in the development of DFID-funded rural livelihoods projects in India. She has also worked with DFID on long-term assignments in Nepal (as a socio-economics advisor in the Ministry of Soil Conservation and Forests and as a Social Anthropologist with an agricultural research centre), and in Uganda (as the Senior Social Anthropologist with an HIV/AIDS research programme). Dr Seeley has been associated as a Social Development/Gender Consultant with the DFID funded AKRSP Programme (M&E Capacity Building Programme: 'Gender Appraisal, Social Analysis and Evaluation') for the last three years. She continues to work with rural livelihoods projects in Bangladesh, Nepal and India and has recently undertaken research on gender-specific aspects of HIV/AIDS impact mitigation and rural livelihoods in Uganda, Malawi, Tanzania, Zambia and India and on Migration and Sustainable Livelihoods (SL). She is particularly interested in the practical application of the SL approach, including creating links to health interventions and social protection, and the development of the approach to more effectively reach different disadvantaged groups.

Sofia Shakil

With a BA in International Relations and Politics from Sophia University, Tokyo, Japan, Sofia attended the London School of Economics, University of London, England in 1992–93 for a M.Sc. degree in Economics, specializing in the economic development of Japan with an emphasis on the comparison of the Japanese pattern of growth to other Asian economies. In 1996, she was awarded the Robert S. McNamara Research Fellowship by the World Bank. She has been associated with the Aga Khan Rural Support Programme (AKRSP), Gilgit from 1996 to 1998. She has also worked with the World Bank education team in Islamabad on program lending in the social sectors and in education from 1999–2001, and continues to work with the Bank's human development team on education projects.

Sofia has undertaken extensive work in the area of early childhood education/development in Pakistan. Her long-standing work with AKF, and recently with JICA, in this field has provided new insights for the ECD sector in Pakistan. She has also served as a technical resource on public private partnership issues in the social sectors, with recent work for AKDN in this area for whom she prepared case studies to document and analyze partnerships for the delivery of education sector services, using the experience of the AKDN in Afghanistan, India and Pakistan. She also facilitated policy dialogues on public private partnerships in the social sectors and health for DFID. She headed the Public Private Partnership component during the start up phase of the Save the Children (USA)–Research Triangle Institute for the Education Sector Reforms Assistance (ESRA), a USAID funded program to support the Government of Pakistan's Education Sector Reform efforts. Currently, in addition to continuing her work in the area of early childhood development, Sofia is engaged with the World Bank on an education reform program in Punjab.

Sumaira Sagheer

Sumaira Sagheer joined AKRSP in 2001 as communications specialist with substantial experience of serving both the private and public sector. Since then, she has spearheaded the communications and outreach portfolio at AKRSP, working through a variety of media genres and outreach programmes, while playing an ambassadorial role in promoting organizational objectives through networking and collaboration with international partners and local authorities. She was the coordinator for the International Year of Mountains (2002) facilitating AKRSP's participation in the BISHKEK Global Mountain Summit. Later in 2003, she successfully led the design and organization of the international conference, 'Lessons in Development–The AKRSP Experience' aimed at sharing a synthesis of twenty years of development.

Before joining AKRSP, she was Information and Outreach Specialist for the UNDP. Her earlier experience includes freelance consultancy work with development projects as a communications expert, and senior positions in advertising agencies. She is a Fellow of LEAD International, a global network of individuals and non-governmental organizations committed to sustainable development.

Sumaira has a Master's in English Literature from Kinnaird College, Punjab University, Lahore. In late 2004 she left to pursue a postgraduate degree in Global Media and Postnational Communication at the School of Oriental and African Studies, London. She has a strong interest in understanding the role of mediated communications for democratization and policy advocacy, particularly in the South, under the complex dynamics of globalization.

ACKNOWLEDGEMENTS

This is a book about poverty focused development in northern Pakistan. While the book leans heavily on research and analysis, it also symbolises the culmination of the efforts of many individuals and organisations. For most of them, putting together this manuscript has been more than a labour of love, and they deserve more than a mere listing in the bibliography.

The editors would like to thank the Department for International Development (DFID) of the UK Government for their generous support. This was a partnership which went well beyond the provision of funds, offering supporting dialogue. We also owe special gratitude to the Aga Khan Foundation for facilitating and supporting such initiatives.

There are many colleagues who have made significant contributions. We are immensely grateful to Stephen F. Rasmussen, the former General Manager of the Aga Khan Rural Support Programme for initiating the Lessons Learned Exercise which eventually turned into the material for this book. He also patiently provided a sounding board for the analytical insights presented in the book.

We also owe special thanks to Steve Jones, Sustainable Livelihoods Specialist, DFID, for his crucial assistance at an early point in the project; and to the participants of the preparatory workshop held in November 2002 in London, where consensus was reached on publishing this book.

The papers presented in this volume were written through the dedication of many scholars and experts drawn from the national and international academia and development community. We are grateful to all the authors and co-authors: Abdul Malik, Aalya Gloekler, Adil Najam, Ali Effendi, Aljoscha Gloekler, Darajat, Fatimah Azfal, Prof. Geof Wood, Izhar Ali Hunzai, Dr Janet Seeley, Maliha Hussain and Sofia Shakil, all of whom held a series of scoping missions and substantive sessions with local actors in the Northern Areas and Chitral and further engaged with experts in rural development in Pakistan. Thanks for their dedication in enduring long weekends and evenings tapping away at the keyboard.

The results of these analyses were initially disseminated at the conference: 'Lessons in Development—The AKRSP Experience', which was held from 15–16 December 2003 in Islamabad, Pakistan, organised by AKRSP. We thank CIDA and DFID for generously supporting this event; and all the participants who further substantiated the relevance of this project by sharing experience from Central Asia, Afghanistan and South Asia.

Our great thanks go to Prof. Geof Wood, University of Bath, UK, for being an encouraging, flexible and yet a sufficiently pressing editor; and for all the valuable advice and guidance he gave on compiling the structure and contents of the manuscript. The book was authored under his supervision. He opened many doors and provided frequent encouragement to everyone even when he disagreed with some of their ideas.

We would also like to acknowledge the relentless support by Elizabeth Graveling, University of Bath for compiling the manuscript, managing the bibliography and successfully tracking down several references which were otherwise missing in the drafts.

Any discourse of this sort also depends on critics. Our special thanks go to David Marsden, Social Development Specialist at The World Bank, and Dr Akbar Zaidi, Freelance Social Scientist, for having so willingly taken on the task of reading and reviewing the manuscript.

We are particularly grateful to all our friends and colleagues who gave valuable suggestions and comments: the staff, management and Board members of AKRSP. And those staff in AKRSP who collated most of the information and data, contributing their time and talents.

The editorial team owes special gratitude to Izhar Ali Hunzai, General Manager, AKRSP for his patience, valuable support and encouragement that led to the successful completion of the manuscript.

Finally, and perhaps most significantly, we are indebted to the communities of the Northern Areas and Chitral, for their active participation in helping to constitute and make this knowledge-base available to a wider audience. The book is a vivid reminder of this legacy.

Sumaira Sagheer
Abdul Malik
Geof Wood

Islamabad and Bath.

FOREWORD

In 2003, the Aga Khan Rural Support Programme (AKRSP) celebrated 20 years of development effort in northern Pakistan, an important milestone for any development programme. Few such programmes have reached this age and few have maintained such a focused approach—in this case one that is based on the participation of local people in setting and controlling their own agenda by establishing and strengthening village-based development organisations.

His Highness the Aga Khan created AKRSP in 1982 with two specific objectives in mind. The first was to help double the incomes of rural people living in the remote mountain valleys of Chitral and the Northern Areas of Pakistan. The second was to develop and test an approach to rural development that could be adapted by other organizations to address similar development challenges elsewhere. At the time, these objectives seemed overly ambitious to many—given the mountainous, isolated and backward nature of the areas where AKRSP chose to work, in addition to an uneven track record in rural development efforts worldwide.

It is gratifying that AKRSP played a key role in accomplishing both of these. Over the last two decades, the income levels in AKRSP project areas have risen several fold resulting in a significant catching up with income levels in other parts of the country: local incomes that were one-third of the national per capita average in the 1980s climbed to two-thirds of the national average by 2001. More importantly, despite many disadvantages associated with the geographical remoteness, severity of climate and vulnerability to natural disasters of the region, the proportion of population living below the nationally defined poverty line has been reduced dramatically in the Northern Areas and Chitral and is now at par with the rest of the country. While AKRSP cannot and does not claim sole responsibility for these achievements, it rightly deserves substantial credit for its role among other major actions such as the government's building of the Karakoram Highway.

AKRSP's rural development model is now well established both in Pakistan in the form of a robust network of rural support programmes, many of them with funding and political support by successive governments in Pakistan, and in several countries of Asia and Africa where the Aga Khan Foundation and the UNDP each have established similar programmes. These achievements are well documented and recognized by scholars, development practitioners, donors and international organizations, including four independent evaluations by the World Bank's Operations Evaluation Department: the most recent of which—<u>The Next Ascent: An Evaluation of the Aga Khan Rural Support Programme, Pakistan</u>—'looked at both the period since the last, 1995 evaluation and the full period since program initiation in 1982.'

This book, on lessons and experiences accumulated by AKRSP over a period of nearly two decades, attempts to capture some of the critical approaches, functions and processes that contributed to its success. It has its origins in an International Workshop: *20 Years of Lessons Learned by AKRSP*, held in Islamabad in December 2003. In preparation for that workshop, AKRSP commissioned a series of studies, some that traced the evolution of the Programme's approach to various activities such as natural resource management and social organisation, and others that looked more closely at the lessons that could be drawn from that experience. Several of these studies were presented and discussed in the workshop, and these were then restructured and improved in light of those discussions.

This publication is neither a complete history of AKRSP nor a thorough evaluation of its impact. Rather it is more an eclectic set of perspectives on AKRSP's experience. It brings together the views of several international scholars and academics who have observed AKRSP and provided critical intellectual input to its approach over the years, the views of practitioners who were actually associated with the day-to-day management of AKRSP at different stages, and also the views of those who have tried to adapt this approach in other geographical settings. The combined effort has resulted in critical analyses of selected successes and shortcomings of the AKRSP experience. It is intended for students, scholars and practitioners of rural development as well as for international donor agencies and governments interested in specific or generic lessons. It is also a tribute to the hard work and resilience of the communities in Chitral and the Northern Areas with whom AKRSP has worked and shares its successes of the last 20 years.

The Workshop was a joint endeavour between AKRSP and two of its long standing partners, the Department for International Development (DFID) of the United Kingdom and the Canadian International Development Agency (CIDA), which have been important donors to AKRSP, together with other funding agencies.

The Aga Khan Foundation is pleased to share these practical lessons with the international community. It hopes that this contribution will improve our understanding of rural development and enrich our collective ability to address the remaining complex and pressing challenges of rural poverty and community renewal in the developing countries.

Tom G. Kessinger, General Manager
Aga Khan Foundation

ABBREVIATIONS

AA	Agro-ecosystems Analysis
ADB	Asian Development Bank
AK	Aga Khan
AKCSP	Aga Khan Cultural Services Programme
AKDN	Aga Khan Development Network
AKES	Aga Khan Education Services
AKESP	Aga Khan Education Services Programme
AKF	Aga Khan Foundation
AKFED	Aga Khan Fund for Economic Development
AKHS	Aga Khan Health Services
AKHSP	Aga Khan Health Service, Pakistan
AKRSP	Aga Khan Rural Support Programme
AKRSP–NLH	Aga Khan Rural Support Programme–Agriculture University of Norway
AKS	Apna Karobar Scheme
ALF	Agricuture, Livestock and Forestry
APDP	Accelerated Professional Development Programme
ASCA	Accumulated Savings and Credit Association
ASA	Association for Social Advancement
AWID	Association for Women's Rights in Development
BAMA	Baltistan Apricot Marketing Association
BDS	Business Development Service
BGA	Baltistan Gems Association
BRAC	Formerly known as Bangladesh Rural Advancement Committee
CA	Commission Agent
CADP	Chitral Area Development Programme
CAMAT	Chitral Association for Mountain Area Tourism
CEDAW	Convention on the Elimination of all forms of Discrimination Against Women
CBO	Community-Based Organisation

CEO	Chief Executive Officer
CGAP	Consultative Group to Assist the Poor
CIDA	Canadian International Development Agency
CIMMYT	International Maize and Wheat Improvement Center (Centro Internacional de Mejoramiento de Maiz y Trigo)
CRDB	Co-operative and Rural Development Bank
DAB	District Advisory Board
DAC	Development Assistance Committee
DAMEN	Development Action for Mobilization and Emancipation
DFI	Development Finance Institute
DFID	Department For International Development (UK Government)
DFO	Divisional Forest Officer
DFP	Dry Fruit Project
ECP	Enterprise Credit Programme
EDC	Enterprise and Development Consulting
EDPYME	Entidad para el Desarrollo de la Pequena y Microempresa (Entity for the Development of Small and Micro-Enterprises)
EE	Eagle Enterprise
ERR	Economic Rate of Return
ESC	Enterprise Support Company
FA	Field Accountant
FACET BV	Financial Assistance, Consultancy, Entrepreneurship and Training
FANA	Federally Administered Northern Areas
FAO	Food and Agriculture Organisation
FFP	Fondos Financieros Privados
FHIES	Farm Household Income Expenditure Survey
FINCA	Foundation for International Community Assistance
FMFB	First Micro-Finance Bank
FMU	Field Management Unit
FWB	First Women's Bank
FWO	Frontier Works Organisation

GAD	Gender and Development
GADO	Garam Cheshma Area Development Organisation
GAMA	Gilgit Apricot Marketing Association
GBPS	Graduates Business Promotion Scheme
GEF	Global Environment Facility
GM	General Manager?
GOP, GoP	Government of Pakistan
GQAL	Gender Quality Action Learning
GRC	Gender Resource Centre
GSP	Gender Support Programme
GTZ	German Government Development Agency (Gesellschaft für Technische Zusammenarbeit)
ha	Hectare
HRD	Human Resource Development
HTS	Huntings Technical Services
ICA	International Cooperative Alliance
ICIMOD	International Centre for Integrated Mountain Development
IDS	Institute for Development Studies
IFAD	International Fund for Agricultural Development
IIED	International Institute for Environment and Development
IK	Idara-e-Kisan (Organisation of Farmers)
INWID	Information-Sharing for Women in Development
IO	Investment Organisation
IPRP	Innovation for Poverty Reduction Project
I-PRSP	Interim Poverty Reduction Strategy Paper
IRM	Institutional Responsibility Matrix
IRR	Internal Rate of Return
IRS	Institutional Responsibility Square
IUCN	World Conservation Union (formerly International Union for the Conservation of Nature)
JMM	Joint Monitoring Mission
KADO	Karimabad Area Development Organisation
KKH	Karakoram Highway
KNP	Khunjerab National Park
KPP	Khushal Pakistan Programme

KVO	Khunjerab Village Organisation
LB&RD	Local Bodies and Rural Development
LDC	Less-Developed Country
LDO	Local Development Organisation
LFO	Legal Framework Order
LLE	Lessons Learned Exercise
LUMS	Lahore University of Management Sciences
MACP	Mountain Areas Conservancy Project
MER	Monitoring, Evaluation and Research
MFI	Micro-Finance Institution
MFU	Multi-Donor Facilitation Unit
MOWD	Ministry of Women's Development
MSE	Micro and Small Enterprise
MSME	Micro, Medium and Small Enterprise
MT	Master Trainer
MTR	Mid-Term Review
NA	Northern Areas
NABARD	National Bank for Agricultural Research and Development
NAC	Northern Areas and Chitral
NACCI	Northern Areas Chamber of Commerce and Industries
NACHIS	Northern Areas and Chitral Household Income Survey
NACIHS	Northern Areas and Chitral Integrated Household Survey
NAPWD	Northern Area Public Works Department
NARC	National Agricultural Research Council
NCSW	National Council for the Status of Women
NCW	National Council of Women
NDFC	National Development Finance Corporation
NDO	Nonhihal Development Organization
NGO	Non-Governmental Organisation
NORAD	Norwegian Agency for Development Cooperation
NR	Natural Resources
NRM	Natural Resource Management
NRSP	National Rural Support Programme

NSS	North South Seeds
NWFP	North West Frontier Province
ODA	Overseas Development Agency?
OED	Operations Evaluation Department (World Bank)
OLL	Orix Leasing Limited
OPP	Orangi Pilot Programme
P&R	Policy & Research
PARC	Pakistan Agriculture Research Council
PCI	Per Capita Income
PCSIR	Pakistan Council for Scientific and Industrial Research
PDA	Population and Community Development Association
PLS	Profit and Loss Sharing
PM	Programme Manager
PPB	Participatory Plant Breeding
PPI	Productive Physical Infrastructure
PPP	Pakistan People's Party
PRA	Participatory Resource Appraisal
PRIF	Pre-Investment Feasibility
PVS	Participatory Varietal Selection
RMT	Regional Management Team
ROSCA	Rotating Savings and Credit Association
RPO	Regional Programme Officer
Rs	(currency)
RSP	Rural Support Programme
RSPN	Rural Support Programme Network
SAHAJ	Name of an NGO in India
SANGAT	South Asian Network of Gender Activists and Trainers
SAP	Social Action Plan
SD SCOPE	Social Development System for Co-ordinated Poverty Eradication (DFID series of papers)
SDC	Swiss Agency for Development and Cooperation
SHG	Self-Help Group
SIP	Small Infrastructure Project
SME	Small and Medium Enterprise

SMEDA	Small and Medium Enterprise Development Authority
SO	Social Organiser
SRSP	Sarhad Rural Support Programme
TBA	Traditional Birth Attendant
TDC	Training and Development Centre
TLP	Training and Learning Programme
ToP	Terms of Partnership
TOPs	(Name of Pakistani beverage company)
TSP	Target Strategy Paper
TWF	Tropical Whole Foods
UK	United Kingdom
UN	United Nations
UNDP	United Nations Development Programme
UNFPA	United Nations Population Fund
UNICEF	United Nations (International) Children's (Emergency) Fund
UNRISD	United Nations Research Institute for Social Development
USA	United States of America
USAID	United States Agency for International Development
VC	Village Council
VCC	Village Cluster Council
VDO	Village Development Organisation
VI	Village Institution
VO	Village Organisation
VOB	Village Organisation Banking
WAD	Women and Development?
WAF	Women Action Forum
WASEP	Water and Sanitation Extension Programme
WID	Women In Development
WIRFP	West India Rainfed Farming Project
WO	Women's Organisation
WOCP	Women's Organisation Credit Programme
WTO	World Trade Organisation
WWF	Formerly known as the World Wide Fund for Nature

GLOSSARY

Artis	traders/middlemen
Baitul Mal	Public treasury of an Islamic government
C-591, C-278	variety of wheat
Chakwal 86	variety of wheat
Chowkidars	watchmen
Dehi	rural, village
Dirk	variety of wheat (= *Kuruto*)
Ghee	clarified butter
Gujar	pastoral nomadic ethnic group
Haiti	clan
Harijan	name given to untouchable outcasts by Gandhi, meaning 'children of God'
Imamat	apex religious authority within Ismaili sect
Imambargahs	Shia places of worship
Islahi	reform
Jamatkhana	Ismaili place of worship, also functions as community centre
Jati	sub-caste, literally reference to birth origin
Jirga	council of respected elders
Kanal	measurement of land area, 1 hectare = 20 *kanals*
Kisan Sabha	literally 'farmers' movement', created as part of the struggles for independence against the British Raj and increasingly connected to Congress
Kuruto	variety of wheat, literally 'small ears' (= *Dirk*)
Lodging	the bending of wheat plants when they cannot support their own weight any longer
Maalia	payment in the form of livestock and/or agricultural produce, demanded by the princely states for the use of newly developed infrastructure
Mohallah	geographically defined sub-section of a village, often clan-based and likely to have its own religious centre

Mullah	Muslim clergy
Naib Nazim	Deputy Chair of District Council
Nazim	Chair of District Council (directly elected position)
NR 152	variety of wheat
Numberdar	appointee of the feudal authority to collect local taxes (cash or kind) and maintain order
Pak-81	variety of wheat
Pathan	familiar name given to Pashtu-speaking people from the North West Frontier Province
Patwari	local feudal official charged with recording land occupancy and therefore rent and tax obligations
Purdah	veil or curtain (Muslim female seclusion)
Rajaki	traditional system where every household in a village contributes labour for collective work
Shegaste	variety of wheat
Sheikhs	Muslim clergy
Shu	woollen windproof fabric produced in Chitral
Subadar	non-commissioned officer rank in army
Tehsil	administrative unit below the district level
Thana	police station
Vulfin	Japanese variety of wheat
Yardoi	traditional system of households sharing labour for large-scale activities
Zakat	formal or semi-formal obligations among Muslims to contribute funds locally or nationally for welfare purposes
Zamindari	tenure-holding class of landlords favoured by the British colonial occupation

Introduction: The Mutuality of Initiative

Geof Wood

This book has its origins in the practice of rural social mobilisation over the last two decades in the mountains of northern Pakistan. It represents a reflective account of the work of the Aga Khan Rural Support Programme (AKRSP), formed in 1982 to address the widespread poverty and vulnerability in the remote mountain valleys of the Karakoram and Hindukush systems. But the book claims to be more than an evaluation of that experience.[1] It offers analysis across a wide range of contemporary themes in poverty-oriented development, and thus intends to be useful to a broad range of stakeholders beyond the confines of mountains, and South and Central Asia. At the same time, it has the comparative advantage of unprecedented critical access to a single programme and its evolution over many years. Some of the authors in this book had operational responsibilities during this period, others of us had the privilege of parallel analysis and capacity building of staff through exchanges of ideas, debates, research and joint reflection on praxis. All of us have been 'trusted' with the reputation and legacy of a remarkable development organisation: remarkable not only because of its pioneering status in participatory rural development world-wide; but also because of its openness to the critical attention of outsiders. Having personally worked extensively across the subcontinent in similar organisations (i.e. the NGO rural development sector), the capacity for critical self-reflection in debate with outsiders is unsurpassed. Some might observe that this has gone too far, and is harming the clarity of purpose in the organisation. Others, though, see this as an exemplary and necessary process of staying in touch with changing realities.

Valleys in Transition contains the strong theme of 'values in transition'. In the sense that no man is an island, so the pursuit of poverty reduction and improvement in the livelihoods of even remote mountain peoples does not occur in isolation of many other processes of change. For the people themselves, their reality is not static culturally, socially and materially. Some of that change might be attributed to the impact of AKRSP, but much of it can be attributed to other forces as indicated at various points in this book. For the organisation, it has been continuously exposed not only to the changing realities of its target population, but also to the changing discourses about development over the last twenty years. Thus, at many points of contact and interface between the direct and indirect stakeholders associated with this process, there has been dialogue: a creative tension as values and principles are confronted by others. Indeed 'dialogue' has been a central concept of the organisation–client interface, but it extends to the interface between its staff and advisors associated with donor funding. Interestingly, and perhaps uniquely, there has also been a dialogue within staff, between those from the region and those recruited from 'down-country' whose 'superior' educational opportunities at the beginning of the programme gave them a competitive edge in relevant competences. 'Down-country' retains both sacred and profane meanings within the cognitive maps of locals: the source of ideas, resources and opportunities, alongside a repository of threats associated with the dominant culture of the plains. But 'down-country' has also been the means of access to the 'global' dimension via personal education, exposure to cosmopolitan cultures and communications. Thus, a feature of the area is that many in the population (from across different social classes) manage their lives in parallel universes. They speak multiple languages. They migrate both physically, but also in their minds, back and forth through cultural windows, adjusting behaviour accordingly.[2] They are instrumentally rational (strategising, planning and investing) as well as value rational and patrimonial (in the sense of strong attachment to traditional norms). They are equally at home in markets and non-market forms of resource allocation. For the educated locals, 'Gotham', Gilgit or Gulmit is almost seamless, aided by the satellite and the internet.

Thus, if there was ever the idea of modernity entering the terrain of backwardness, embodied in the notion of rural development as a catalyst for change within passive, dependent communities—such illusions are quickly dismissed by the mobility of minds. Such understanding redefines notions of participation and ownership, and social agency. In other words, the initiative for change does not lie exclusively with a modernising organisational presence such as AKRSP. Instead there is a real notion of partnership, with much greater equity between the organisation and its clients than usually imagined. When the first General Manager of AKRSP, Mr Shoaib Sultan Khan, says that he owes his reputation for supporting rural livelihoods to people in the local communities, it is because he is acknowledging the balance of dialogue, and the mutuality of initiative and risk. The implications are far reaching. The story of twenty years of rural development in this area is a tension between a model of social mobilisation[3] on the one hand, and forms of local, indigenous social agency, on the other, adapting to change in values and aspirations through various re-workings of that social mobilisation model. These 're-workings' draw both on collective action traditions prior to AKRSP's appearance and upon the evolution of livelihoods options as opportunities open up and socio-economic change re-defines ideas about community. Re-working the model is precisely evidence of that mutuality of initiative, and in that sense to be celebrated.

CATALYST AND CLIENT: THE TENSION BETWEEN EXPERTISE AND SOCIAL DEVELOPMENT

Fashions in development change, and so does the way we write about the phenomenon. We have the problem of the historian: whether to apply contemporary or retrospective paradigms. Certainly the criteria of judgement about the quality of development has changed significantly over the years. Indeed, one might almost say that the history of development studies coincides with this period, given that the 1960s and '70s were still dominated by ideas of top down planning and technical expertise. The formation of AKRSP coincided, for example, with Chambers' *Rural Development: Putting the Last First* (1983) and the marking of a more populist agenda about the value of indigenous knowledge and participation. The rhetorical trick was to reconcile the ongoing case for an external catalyst with respect for grassroots institutions. Chambers, with his later *Participatory Rural Appraisal*, gave us the vocabulary for managing the switch from the expert-led Rapid Rural Appraisal of the early 1980s, a switch which mirrored Chambers' own applied career from District Officer to development anthropologist. But his populism was itself building upon an already well-established tradition, or genealogy, from liberation theology in Latin America, via the conscientisation of Paulo Freire (1970) to the empowerment agendas of post-liberation NGOs in Bangladesh. The latter's poverty targeting in Bangladesh was, ironically, a rejection of the technical farmer bias of the pre-liberation Comilla model which effectively excluded the growing numbers of rural landless and women. Thus, AKRSP's continuation of the Comilla legacy could be regarded as an improvement, in the context of contemporary paradigmatic shifts towards 'participation'. However, the mountains of northern Pakistan are not the socially divided plains of down-country in the subcontinent. Thus, a modified version of Comilla in which the Krishi Samabaya Samitis became Village Organisations, but with more dialogue and conditionality about grassroots involvement and ownership, brought together top down with an element of bottom up.

Over these two decades, development writers have become more sceptical about the claims for bottom up. They have deconstructed the populist, participatory rhetoric,[4] deploying the 'structuration' arguments of Anthony Giddens, and in particular the 'actor-oriented epistemological perspectives' associated with Norman Long and his colleagues at Wageningen. Such perspectives have been concerned with an analysis of the interface between clients and organisations, recognising agency on both sides of the divide and the mutually constraining influences of their respective contexts. In this process, knowledge as a social phenomena is itself understood as contested and negotiable within the exchanges and relationships of respective protagonists over extended time periods. Hence the critical deconstruction of indigenous knowledge and farmer first slogans, as in the 1992 collection of essays edited by the Longs: *Battlefields of Knowledge*. It is worth reflecting upon the sapping effect of the populist de-professionalisation agenda, associated with Chambers, during this last decade, prior to its recent disintegration as a paradigm of practice and understanding. The challenge to science, rationality and expertise implicit in this populism has been corrosive in denying constructive roles to outsiders, with the logical implication of poor people having sole responsibility for their own condition, including poverty. This, of course, amounted to an insidious removal of political economy from explanations of the reproduction of poverty, absolving rural elites and urban capitalists locally and globally from their exploitative, rent-seeking behaviour. I am not suggesting that the populists intended to blame the poor for their poverty, but it has certainly been the logical outcome of their epistemology. Thus, even the most empowerment driven organisations, like PROSHIKA in Bangladesh, accept that even after 25 years of social mobilisation, the rural poor still need the organisation of external catalysts. The reasoning is simple: the poor (rural or urban) do not comprise natural solidarities in class divided societies, since these inequalities oblige the poor to compete among themselves for opportunities granted by the classes over them.

Fortunately, despite the efforts of successive donors to the contrary (including OXFAM in the early days), AKRSP never completely succumbed to the populist challenge. It has retained throughout a belief in the value of technical expertise and scientific knowledge in the raising of production frontiers. But perhaps more importantly, beneath its own attempts to engineer democratically run VOs, it has not attempted in practice to intrude too heavily in the local ways of getting things done, collectively. In other words, it has balanced a less extreme idea of participation with the principle of leadership from itself as well as from among the stronger families and activists locally. Thus, the appearance of imposition is modified by the practice, with both organisation and client in effect putting their respective institutional cultures on the table. This has occurred through interactionist processes of learning about each other, enabling adaptive behaviour and recognition of boundaries of possibilities. Perhaps a key test of this process has been AKRSP's stance in non-Ismaili areas. As an institution within the Aga Khan family of development agencies (the Aga Khan Development Network—AKDN), the association of AKRSP with the Ismaili community is strong. But while the motivation for an AK institutional presence in an area may be prompted by the presence of a significant number of Ismaili villagers, AK agencies seek to work even handedly with all groups and sects in the locality. For northern Pakistan, this means other Islamic sects: Sunni and Shia. However it would be naïve to think that the organisation-client relationship has the same intensity as for the Ismaili communities, where loyalty through the Ismaili Jamaat is assured. Nevertheless, AKRSP has managed to work both in Southern Chitral which is predominantly populated by Sunni clans, and in Baltistan which is predominantly Shia. In both of these areas, AKRSP has adapted its modes of participation in the local communities to local realities which can sometimes be hostile, and sometimes sufficiently strategically aware of the resources on offer to accept AKRSP support. Particular difficulties have been over issues of microfinance and gender, where compliance to the AK version of modernity has been more difficult to achieve. But the culturally reinforcing link between the practices of the Ismaili *Jamaatkhana* and the VOs has been absent too, in these relationships to other sects.

This continuous tension between expertise and social development, which is found across grassroots development work globally, has been manifested in different organisational phases of AKRSP over the years. The initial emphasis upon social organisation as a strengthening of community capacity to create new forms of collective physical and financial capital was reflected in the primacy of the social organiser as the key point of contact between organisation and client. The role of technical expertise was located at one remove from the locality and situated in regional headquarters as a backstopping function—to be called in at key moments of need in the dialogue process. As the complexity and density of the programme evolved, so the need for technical expertise expanded alongside the challenge to bring technological innovation into closer calibration with institutional practices and possibilities. In other words, technical specialists in different sectors (engineers, livestock, agriculture and horticulture, as well as microfinance) needed more direct exposure to grassroots realities as the basis for grounded innovation, rather than relying upon the social brokerage of the social organiser. In effect, this meant a mainstreaming of social organisation across the programme, in which ironically social organisers lost their *primus inter pares* position. This organisational density of presence was expressed from the mid-'90s in the Field Management Units, which operated with technical staff at the sub-regional level, where previously social organisers had enjoyed a monopoly of presence. More recently, a change in funding levels and re-orientation of the programme away from the intensity of operational functions towards strategic, advisory services has again removed technical expertise from a proactive to a demand-led participation with local communities.

The Discourses of Rural Development: Pre-Colonial to Modern Times

These organisational developments within AKRSP reflect wider changes in the evolution of rural development discourse over a longer period. By situating AKRSP's evolution within this wider discourse, we can demonstrate AKRSP both as a learning organisation and as a significant contributor to more universal changes in the way that rural development is conceived. Looking over the history of rural development 'fashions and phases', it is remarkable how AKRSP has interacted with so many of them. The list can be quite substantial, as I discovered when presenting an overview seminar on this history recently.[5] For AKRSP it is definitely worth starting with the notion of '**hydraulic society**' associated with Wittfogel's 'Oriental Despotism' and Marx's 'Asiatic Mode of Production'. This was essentially a system of feudal control over labour to create, maintain and operate community and inter-community infrastructure. Nowhere was such a system more evident than in the Northern Areas and Chritral, where for the past few centuries until the recent 1970s the ruling families in these statelets controlled the movement of labour to ensure that local canal-based irrigation systems from glacial and snow melt sources would maintain subsistence production with an element of surplus tribute to themselves. More recent traditions of colonial management have also influenced AKRSP when considering the emphasis placed upon improving the productivity of agriculture as part of a strategy of converting roaming and therefore 'uncontrollable' pastoralists into peasant agriculturalists, and recognising the contributing investment in rural works (i.e. infrastructure), often as part of a seasonal relief function.

Leaving aside the era of 'primitive socialist accumulation' which does not apply to such a precarious subsistence economy, the relevance of a **community development** discourse is clear. There are several strands here, though for the subcontinent Gandhian notions of village republics have been overarching in the post-Partition period. In India, this was reinforced by the report of the Balwantra Commission in 1958 and the demonstration effects across borders to West and East Pakistan into the formation of the Comilla and Peshawar Academies, with a combined emphasis upon community and the Raiffesian cooperative tradition. The military regimes of Pakistan relied heavily upon this tradition through Village Aid and later Basic Democracies as an attempt to build a political constituency. In many ways, these community based approaches retained a naivety, stemming from the Gandhian juxtaposition of village and landlord, without acknowledging the realities of power and inequality at the village level itself.[6]

Certainly this community 'platform' spawned further parallel rural development traditions of **agrarian reform**, **agricultural modernisation** and **self-reliance**, all of which have been reflected in AKRSP's experience. The abolition of feudal statelets from the late 1960s into the '70s re-arranged the tenancy status and obligations of ordinary farming families in the programme area and provided the opportunity for institutional reform through the formation of Village Organisations, organised on cooperative lines, to fill the 'institutional vacuum' left by the abolition.[7] This was reinforced by the language of self-reliance so prevalent across the subcontinent in the *Sarvodaya* and *Shramdana* movements of Sri Lanka; the Comilla, Ulashi and Gram Sarkar models of post-liberation Bangladesh; and the *panchayati raj* traditions of India. These institutional reforms were the vehicle for the agricultural modernisation associated with the technologies of the 'Green Revolution' in the pursuit of improvements in the productivity of labour and land as the basis of self-sufficient food security. This has been a strong imperative in the programme area because of its overall vulnerability to seasonal food shortages, with a history of annual famines in the spring and early summer before the first harvest, in the context, initially, of weak access to down-country sources of food.[8] Of course, the Green Revolution technological 'package' entailed a transformation of 'peasant' into 'farmer', i.e. into 'rational economic man' supported by public sector infrastructure, input subsidies, credit and technical assistance through 'extension', alongside the biological, chemical and mechanical innovations. In many ways the '70s and early '80s embodied a contradiction between the rhetoric of self-reliance and the top down, catalyst approaches of external, science based expertise. The populism of Chambers, noted above, became part of a wider resolution of this contradiction by reacting against the application of laboratory derived science to farming systems which were perceived as failing in realising their productivity ambitions.

Thus we enter the **farm systems** era based upon observing farmer practices (including rotation cycles) and situational field trials, with an emphasis therefore upon adaptation rather than imposition and replacement. Given the continued prominence of chemical based agriculture in the subcontinent, the farm systems approach was not a complete inversion of the outsider-insider relationship, but certainly ambitions were adjusted towards sustainability, as signalled in the preference for improved varieties rather than high yielding ones. 'Farm systems' evolved as 'indigenous knowledge' and 'appropriate technology', with corresponding outsider methods of knowledge creation such as Rapid Rural Appraisal and Participatory Rural Appraisal pioneered by Koen Khan University in NE Thailand, thereafter popularised by Chambers. AKRSP was certainly in the forefront of this participatory tradition, although it has also shared in the more recent critiques of the fetishism associated with it. In other words, it maintained attached, throughout the rise and fall of the tradition, to the catalyst principle, seeing the need for dialogue and iterative learning between outsider and insider knowledge. Thus, it was committed to employing professionals with detailed technical knowledge in the agricultural and natural resource sectors, and did not seek to de-professionalise their expertise. Although such technical professionals were later brought into the mainstreaming of social development across the organisation, their technical knowledge was seen as a key resource and continues to be valued in AKRSP's present incarnation as a leaner more consultancy oriented organisation, with the catalyst principle even more dominant.

By coming into being in the early eighties, AKRSP was clearly riding the crest of the **participation** wave. And it was possible to surf this tradition fairly uncritically until the mid-nineties, when the World Bank's own 'take' on the theme moved the agenda from empowerment to cooption.[9] For AKRSP, the theme of participation was central to its concept of mobilisation, or **social mobilisation**. At the same time, it is important to acknowledge the difference between the AKRSP version of 'mobilisation' and its meaning elsewhere in the NGO world both in the subcontinent and further afield. Thus, from the mid-seventies, especially in newly liberated Bangladesh, emerging NGOs such as BRAC and PROSHIKA had adopted elements from the peasant mobilisation experiences of the Long March in China, the liberation theology, Freirian teachings in Latin America and the urban movements of the Philippines, merging them with the *Kisan Sabha* and other movements from the repertoire of India's independence struggles. The social mobilisation that arose from this context emphasised struggle with oppressive classes over rights and resources, based upon poor people's solidarity and organised social action to change relationships and structures, initially at the local level—the most immediate site of oppression. Although it could be said that there was a long term target for the creation of social capital in these struggle/ empowerment NGOs, the more immediate and medium term goals were on the creation of effective, countering social resources among the poor through the creation of solidarity groups essentially based on the principle of class.

The AKRSP approach to social mobilisation differed from this in several respects. To explain these differences it is necessary to refer briefly to the socio-economic characteristics of northern Pakistan, though chapters 1 and 2 offer much more detail. Unlike the plains agriculture of 'down-country', the mountain regions were not in the early eighties characterised by significant gradations of inequality stretching into the villages, with locally oppressive patron classes of landlords, moneylenders and monopoly employers. Outside the narrow apex of ruling families, clan and sect divisions at the village level were better understood as vertical segmentation rather than horizontal segmentation: in other words similarly composed groups sometimes in conflict and sometimes cooperating, rather than stratified classes with opposing interests. But these groups outside the ruling families were all poor and vulnerable, albeit to differing minor degrees. Thus AKRSP considered itself to be working with the whole community, not a class-based sub-set of it needing to be mobilised in opposition to other groups or classes in the village. Therefore support for social resources (i.e. higher productivity relationships and networks) coincided with support for the development of social capital in the more abstract sense of well-functioning institutions for the use and access of all members in the community. Where conflict resolution became part of the agenda, it was resolution between equally resourced or under-resourced groups/identities competing for scarce material resources and opportunities. Thus social mobilisation was about bringing the whole community (at whatever level of definition) together for mutual benefit (i.e. improved security or reduced vulnerability) via: the pooling of infrastructure investment (productive physical infrastructure); collective receipt of extension advice and physical packages to agriculture, horticulture and livestock; and later the sharing of liabilities via credit and savings.

Thus the **objectives of AKRSP were the creation of enhanced physical, financial and social capital** among all members of the community. The 'fight', in the initial analysis and early years, was against the common 'enemies' of extreme climate, poor physical infrastructure, low productivity of the local natural resource environment, absence of cushioning in kind or cash, vulnerability to hazards and shocks, and the withdrawal of ruling family patronage without adequate substitution from the state either due to geopolitical uncertainties (the Northern Areas in relation to the Kashmir dispute with India) and/or to remoteness (i.e. Chitral having only summer and autumn access to the rest of NWFP). In the chapters that follow, chapters 2 and 8 in particular focus upon the extent to which these original principles of social mobilisation remain relevant to the changing conditions and needs in the societies of the Northern Areas and Chitral. At the same time, it can be observed that these 'whole community' principles are being applied to the very different socio-economic contexts of the more class divided village communities in the plains of 'down-country', through the proliferation of the Rural Support Programme model to the provinces of Punjab, NWFP, Balochistan and very recently Sindh. Meanwhile, the rural development fashions continue, and AKRSP has broadened its own model of social mobilisation to embrace them.

Although it is difficult to follow a strict chronological order in presenting these themes in rural development, by the end of the eighties AKRSP was recognising the **particular situation of women** within its overall analysis of mountain poverty. Thus alongside the formation of Village Organisations, it begun to create Women's Organisations and to recruit more female staff to interact with such groups. The stages of thinking within AKRSP about women's livelihoods is analysed in chapter 3, tracking the evolution of programme interventions. Again AKRSP represented wider discourses about women, moving through the now classic phases of Women in Development (WID) to Gender and Development (GAD). But the flavour of debates and struggles over gender has been much richer than the WID to GAD sequence. The 'protagonists' have been: professional female staff from 'down-country'; more recently recruited female staff from the communities in the Northern Areas and Chitral; a critical mass of interns from the USA and UK, often themselves of Asian origin; village women themselves, especially strong mothers and mothers-in-law,[10] but also some younger, more educated daughters benefiting from the Aga Khan Education Services and school attendance; representatives of gender discourse among donors on review missions and other studies; and some males across these categories.

The arguments have been varied: the variations of patriarchy between the different sects; the impact of female education on gender relations; the gender value of extending work opportunities to women in terms of double day and control over decisions and income; the substitution of male farmers by female farmers in the context of annual and seasonal migration by males, with implications for the male extension bias in the programme; the real functions and meaning of *purdah* in its range of forms; the clash between donor driven secular feminism and the more pragmatic, locally informed caution of female staff in the context of male conservatism; the gender relations between staff in both programme priorities as well as equity of opportunity and promotion. Some of the most intense and heated debates within AKRSP have been on these issues, far into the night, clustered around fires and paraffin stoves. A key, specific, dimension of these exchanges has been the range of sectarian variation between Ismaili traditions and Sunni and Shia communities. Sometimes more formally educated down-country female staff came from the more conservative sects in contrast to the locally recruited staff, many of whom are Ismaili. This certainly confused the simple modernising catalyst principle that outsiders were more progressive. At the same time, the sometimes hectoring stance of donor females grated badly upon local sensibilities, with local female staff feeling misunderstood and indeed disempowered as a result.

Of course **microfinance** has come to dominate poverty-focused rural development strategy increasingly over the last twenty years. Interestingly enough, the motivation for microcredit and microfinance in AKRSP differed from elsewhere in the 'plains' agrarian political economies of South Asia. This difference represents an important point of contrast between both AKRSP and its offspring in the Rural Support Programme movement in Pakistan and other non-governmental rural development initiatives in the region. If the claim is accepted that the microfinance movement had its origins in Bangladesh, then its main motivation was to overcome usurious and exploitative relations between patron-moneylenders and their poor clients among the tenant, sharecropping classes of the peasantry. It was a radical, progressive intervention to alter the power balance at the local level in a hostile political economy. As the realisation about the extent of rural landlessness grew in the late seventies in Bangladesh, so it was understood that there were classes of the poor who could not even access such credit from local moneylenders because their extreme poverty implied no collateral worth having to the money lender. Thus microcredit was also a dimension of decommodification,[11] in the sense of introducing institutional forms of credit to compensate for the exclusion from even usurious credit markets!

By contrast, the entry of AKRSP into microcredit, and later microfinance more widely, had different origins and motivations from these attempts to redress inequality. Given the overall geographical conditions of poverty below the apex of ruling families, there was a pervasive shortage of financial capital among most of the semi-pastoralist farmers. As a result, there was no capacity or 'slack' in a family's livelihoods portfolio to insure themselves against shocks and hazards via savings, or to invest in other forms of capital and resources (whether raising agricultural productivity, children's education or down-country migration for employment) through use of credit. With little collateral on offer, the social collateral, group liability formulae of microcredit elsewhere in the subcontinent was adopted. The story of the growth of microfinance in AKRSP is told in chapter 7 by Maliha Hussein, who was closely involved in the early development of microfinance in AKRSP, and by implication thus for Pakistan as a whole.

It is a story of mixed messages, which we have come to expect from experience elsewhere. First the expansion of microcredit into a broader agenda of microfinance; second, the real function of such programmes in terms of support for development or welfare; third, therefore, the role of such credit for consumption smoothing and liquidity management in highly seasonalised environments, increasingly characterised by winter outmigration of adult male labour; and fourth, the market distortion effects of subsidised finance inducing forms of investment and economic behaviour, which cannot be absorbed under local market conditions. In the Northern Areas and Chitral, there has also been an issue of the pattern of participation in microfinance products on a geographical/ sect basis, with some evidence of borrowing and savings activity concentrated in areas where AKRSP enjoyed most cultural support. Since the late nineties, a wider, global, microfinance debate has raged over the sustainability and institutionalisation of financial services to the poor (i.e. those self-selecting into such programmes, due to their exclusion from the formal banking sector). Unlike other NGOs in the subcontinent who have either become full-time MFIs, or who have used returns from microfinancial services to fund the social development side of their programmes, AKRSP has struck out down another route. It has spun-off its microfinance operation into a separate bank, the First Microfinance Bank, headquartered in Islamabad but, so far, having the bulk of its current 21 branches in the original programme area. With other rural support programmes and NGOs also present in the sector with their own institutionalised services, poverty-focused banking in Pakistan is in the early stages of evolution. Will the First Microfinance Bank be successful in spreading its business beyond its initial programme area and thus return a premium to AKRSP as its major shareholder, or will other competitors quickly appear if the demand and market is strong enough? In the meantime, AKRSP has significant capital locked up in the enterprise, and thus has to look elsewhere for sustainable sources of income to fund its other, non-microfinance activities.

Currently, AKRSP is a site for a number of criss-crossing debates about strategic priorities which again reflect broader trends in development and rural development thinking, particularly in the pursuit of sustainability. Certainly there is a **growth perspective**, arising out of one part of the financial services experience embracing attempts to move beyond the 'micro' lending approach into support for more significant business development. This mirrors the rise of the **small enterprise movement** elsewhere in development discourse, and interestingly has been adopted by even more radical NGOs such as PROSHIKA in Bangladesh. This is a recognition of both demand and the opportunity to support potential entrepreneurs, rising from the ranks of the poor, who remain excluded from the normal loan finance available from the orthodox banking sector, partly due to weakness of collateral. Although the mountain areas of Northern Pakistan have limited comparative advantage, they do nevertheless have opportunities in fruit and nut production with related processing. Upper elevations support the prospect of virus free potato production. Under improved overall geopolitical security conditions, there is a 'peace dividend' through tourism. Improved communications offer more trading possibilities with China and Central Asia. Improved road access may, controversially, increase the prospect of external capital for mining (e.g. marble, semi-precious stones). AKRSP has experimented with some of these opportunities, and this is recounted in chapter 6. There has been a tendency to be supply driven with inadequate attention to market analysis, which has been the Achilles heel for these mountain settlements. Behind this 'growth' perspective, through supporting larger-scale enterprise, there lie deeper arguments about reducing poverty. Is it really possible to expand the local, mountain economy as the main instrument of poverty reduction given the geographical and human capital constraints always associated with remote regions, with low productivity and multiplier effects with limited backward and forward linkages? Or is this unduly pessimistic, in effect, a self-fulfilling prophecy?

The economic alternative to the optimistic growth approach is to secure sustainable subsistence in the region through a combination of locally sustainable resource management and remittance income from external activity in higher productivity markets through migration. This certainly brings into play the issues discussed in chapters 4 and 5 of this volume, respectively **community infrastructure** and **natural resource management**.

Both of these themes embody principles of symbiosis between humans and other features of the local environment. Neither are purely conservationist in the sense of privileging the natural environment at the expense of human needs. Both are concerned to achieve some sustainable balance between the development of the surrounding environment, especially in the maintenance and creation of renewable resources of energy and essential materials for local subsistence. Both are concerned with the creation of enhanced public goods, and both require the values of community and collective action as the basis of success.

The development of **community infrastructure** was pursued through grant aided Productive Physical Infrastructure projects (PPIs) from early on in the inception of AKRSP. While there has been much debate within AKRSP about the merits of grant aided support in reproducing a dependent clientele among the local population (i.e. setting up over-generous long term expectations about subsidies, thus making the later moves towards greater cost recovery more difficult to achieve), there can be little doubt that this has been the major success story of the programme, producing the greatest multiplier effects. Although much of this PPI investment has been an extension and enhancement of traditional technologies in irrigation and communications (namely improved channels, roads and bridges) there have been dramatic effects upon local communities in terms of livelihoods options, land productivity, and access to markets and services.

As a simple reminder, I recall a community in upper Yarkhun valley in upper Chitral on the 'wrong' side of the river (i.e. the opposite side from the road communication to Mastuj sub-divisional headquarters and other destinations beyond to the south) which was cut off for much of the year. And when able to cross, it was winter (rivers low, occasionally iced up) and the passes blocked out of Chitral district, thus foreclosing seasonal migration down-country. Without access, unnecessary deaths through lack of medical treatment and seasonal famines were the norm. The new bridge has changed all that, not only for this village but for the entire upper Yarkhun valley into Lasht, Borogil and beyond. Additionally any visitor to the region can also see the improved irrigation channels, bringing more reliable water to thousands of plots and farms, both securing and extending the main growing season, thus insuring against late springs and early autumns. Erstwhile deserted alluvial fans have, as a result, been settled more extensively; land developed; walls built; and field water courses laid out. Local residents can point to previously barren hillsides now benefiting from channels located higher up the hillside and enabling 'below-channel' tree planting which combines forest products with land stabilisation. A more recent addition to these PPIs, over the last decade has been the micro-hydels, delivering key lighting to the dark nights of remote villages as well as stimulating access to satellite TV. The initial investment was in Chitral, though this has now spread. It has heralded in some cases a re-awakening of collective action and apparently dormant Village Organisations (see chapter 8). The terms of partnership between AKRSP and the local communities over micro-hydel installations has certainly devolved more responsibility onto the communities themselves for complex operation and maintenance.

Natural resource management, conceived in the realm of public goods beyond a family's own farm, has been the other platform of local sustainability. In a semi-pastoral society with traditionally limited access to external opportunities, the reliance upon a broad range of natural resources is a key part of the livelihoods portfolio. The argument is made both in chapter 5 as well as chapter 8 that 'resource-hopping' has not really been an option for these mountain households, since the exit options are precarious, uncertain and insecure. Thus even families with strong evidence of outmigration and remittances will not entirely turn their backs upon the local natural resource base. Its conservation is a form of insurance against hard times occurring elsewhere, down-country. Livestock, for example, performs this function. For many families it is a form of saving or insurance, a stock to be used when hazards or shocks need to be faced, such as weddings (hazards) or medical expenses (shocks). This explains the apparent paradox of families seeking to maintain large herds of goats, sheep and cattle beyond their reasonable and seasonal consumption needs. It is not just a matter of prestige and status, though the existence of such proxy savings and insurance may represent a form of symbolic capital. Of course, in mountain societies, livestock cannot be maintained without the availability of pasture beyond the farm plots, and especially pasture which is available when crops are in those plots. Thus pasture management becomes a further key dimension of natural resource management requiring many key features of common property management systems. 'Tragedies of the Commons' have to be avoided. The sustainable management of pastures, some of them 'high pastures', is thus an essential element of local survival and insurance, at a collective level.

Although not connected to livestock in the same way, forest areas also fall into this category of common property management, with wood required for heating as well as construction and other farm needs. Although paraffin and even bottled gas has entered the society, it is by no means pervasive, and of course difficult to distribute into remote settlements anyway. The demand for wood products is clearly evidenced by de-forestation and the movement of wood up and down the valleys, according to localised patterns of demand. Cases of conflict and collaboration over forest management are described in chapter 5, and explored for their collective action implications in chapter 8. The role of AKRSP has been to understand patterns of conflict and depletion, to seek resolution of conflict and sustainable institutional management solutions between different sets of interests, and to provide support for re-forestation where possible, though there are technical constraints in the replacement of long established, but depleted, natural forests.

POVERTY TARGETING: A CHALLENGE TO COMMUNITY?

But as AKRSP has evolved over the last two decades, it has also engaged with strategic priorities in two further dimensions, both of which reflect contemporary development dilemmas: **poverty targeting and social protection** on the one hand; and its role in **relation to government** on the other. The first of these issues has been the subject of intense debates since the mid-nineties when it became clear that the mountain societies of Northern Pakistan were not static in their post-feudal social structure. Significant changes had occurred from the late seventies, and indeed some of these changes from the early eighties could themselves be partially attributed to AKRSP's own efforts. Poverty targeting emerged through the analysis from the mid-nineties onwards of increasing social and economic differentiation between households, villages and valley locations. The early assumptions of relative socio-economic homogeneity outside the ruling clans needed to be replaced by an acknowledgement that some families had benefited considerably from various sources of development by the mid-nineties. While AKRSP itself is one of these sources, improved overall communications, other parts of the Aga Khan Development Network and the intense presence of the army were also other sources of this change. This process is described and analysed in chapter 2 of this volume.

During this period from the mid-nineties, AKRSP focused more of its attention upon social development, reflecting upon strategic and institutional options as an autocritique of its productivist approaches up to that point. In 1996, it commissioned a report from me on its organisational strategies, which was presented as 'Avoiding the Totem and Developing the Art'. This report, derived closely from the analysis presented to me by staff through dialogues with them, argued for less formulaic rigidity in its organisational vehicle (i.e. the Village Organisation), a closer look at the functional value of ongoing 'indigenous' institutions, and the increasingly differentiated patterns of need appearing in the society. The follow up was a series of six repeated courses in social development for many of the professional staff in AKRSP, AKDN and even some down-country RSPs. This became known as the Training and Learning Programme in Social Development, or TLP for short. This programme was unique in being conducted *in situ*, drawing upon village studies and household profiles, as well as assignments which reflected particular local issues and/or staff specialisms.

From this experience, the understanding of differentiated forms of poverty was systematised by distinguishing between upper, middle and lower geographical elevations, alongside variable access to feeder roads and growth pole centres, as well as between different households even within otherwise coping localities. This provided the basis for poverty targeting through a range of safety nets and social protection. These experiments represented a departure from the erstwhile productivist emphasis, and expanded conventional approaches to rural development in line with wider discourses globally. In particular, the strategic thinking involved an analysis of religious based institutions in the *mohallahs,* alongside the Village Organisations and other spin-offs, for their capacity to administer welfare to selected, very poor households. It also explored ways to strengthen the normative basis of rights and entitlements to welfare beyond the prevalent forms of personalised preferentialism. Since these institutions had a reasonable track record of collecting funds from the coping and improving families for redistribution as welfare, reinforced by Islamic injunctions, so caution was required not to swamp these forms of local social capital with well meant external funds. Nevertheless, the sustainability questions were asked, alongside the ethical question of expecting near poor families to have the responsibility for the welfare of other poor families in the locality given that families had cultural obligations to commit scarce funds as a proportion of income to their respective *jamaats.*

Connecting to Government: Finding the Support Role

AKRSP's relation to government, discussed via an elegant model in Adil Najam's chapter 9, clearly has both a specific context as well as being part of a wider, global debate about state-civil society-NGO relations. In many ways, until the late nineties, AKRSP was the only rural development catalyst in these mountain societies, with resources far superior to those provided either through the federal, provincial/district allocations (as for Chitral within NWFP) or through the specially administered Northern Areas, held in political limbo by the stand-off with India over Kashmir. Under these conditions, reinforced by the prestige of His Highness, the Aga Khan, and the formal backing of successive governments in

Islamabad, local political and governmental authorities looked to the AKRSP to deliver the main development resources and extension to the local communities. This dominant development responsibility introduced another 'player' in the citizen relationship between local communities and 'their' governments, locally and nationally. It certainly induced triangular relations between AKRSP staff, local representatives (in successive versions of local government) and rural people, with local political actors keen to gain credit in their constituencies for the projects adopted by AKRSP. This prominence also guaranteed that AKRSP would be the object of political competition and criticism. In other words, it was public property and its internal affairs as well as policies and strategies came under scrutiny. It was, of course, a key employer of professionals and other support staff (crucially, the jeep drivers) in the area. Its personnel policies were therefore also a matter of public debate, with fathers and uncles keen to have their junior relatives employed.

Najam's chapter reflects on these different dimensions of the relationship: cooption, cooperation, collaboration, competition and conflict. Clearly, these have not operated in some strict sequence, but get activated by different stakeholders at different times as well as simultaneously. Local community elders and their representatives seek to coopt AKRSP to their local interests and projects. AKRSP is seeking their cooperation in return for its agenda of packaged interventions and the accompanying behavioural principles (such as democratically run meetings). But at the same time, AKRSP's programme priorities (for example in the allocation of engineering, infrastructure projects) may clash with other competing demands. But all the time, there has been an issue of authority expressed as a local desire, whether through local government institutions or the *jamaat*, to limit the autonomy of the resource privileged actor. These relations too should be understood as part of the participation agenda, and perhaps better construed as the mutuality of initiative. One might argue that institutional and developmental sustainability in these mountain societies can only be achieved by a weakening of AKRSP's position in relation to these other forces. This is now happening by default, as donor funds recede and the microfinance operation has been transferred to the First Microfinance Bank, not yet returning on shares.

However, the agenda has significantly moved on in the relationship between government and the NGO sector both globally, nationally and locally. Globally, the concerns about the weaknesses of neo-liberalism embodied in the Washington consensus have been replaced by a post-Washington consensus in which the state is regarded as a necessary but of course not sufficient condition of developmental success. Thus the alliance between between neo-liberalism and NGOs (as representatives of private sector solutions in the redistribution and welfare business) is being questioned. Has the 'franchise' model of leasing state functions in the social sectors to NGOs come up against the governance and accountability arguments? Has the danger of producing states without citizens (Wood 1997) been realised, in the sense of a severing of the link between governmental performance and accountability to citizens, since their statutory services are being supplied outside the state? In other words, by-passing the state via NGO services undermines precisely those principles of good governance so espoused by the international agencies. The question for AKRSP, in the context of these discourses, is whether it should continue to be the dominant, catalytic, force for rural development in the Northern Areas and Chitral valleys of Northern Pakistan?

In many ways, the decision to 'retreat' has been taken out of AKRSP's hands by a reduction in donor support for a continuation of the earlier levels and scale of direct operational activity. This reduction in support has itself been a function of this wider shift in development discourse towards a return to the 'necessity of the state' in national and local development activities. Thus AKRSP's donors have been urging it to work more closely in support of the strategies in post-1998 Pakistan to enhance the powers of local government as part of a decentralised return to democracy. There are ironies here, not lost on a wider audience, of a military regime pursuing such an agenda, and gaining donor support. In other words, the traditional alliance between military regimes and NGOs, found so frequently elsewhere in the subcontinent, and more widely, is actually being reinforced here via the democracy argument!

Whatever the contradictions, AKRSP has certainly adopted the device of moving itself from a position of primary operational responsibility for rural development in the region towards a more indirect, support role for local government and their constituents. This is a crucial shift of stance, and actually resented by many of the villagers, who prefer the old AKRSP model of direct intervention. They saw AKRSP as the institutionalised source of their support in the region rather than any of the sequence of tried and usually failed local government experiments. However, the difference now is that AKRSP has little option but to follow this route, since the interventionist option has been undermined by the withdrawal of much donor support in favour of the formal (local) government option, wherein donors argue that true good governance and accountability can be achieved. In many ways, this outcome has been a constructive crisis for AKRSP. It has forced it to consider a new path, to become more advisory both to government and incipient private sector initiatives rather than trying to substitute for both of them.

The New AKRSP: Public-Private Partnership

Thus AKRSP is now in a position of **changing its mission to one of support for decentralisation initiatives on the one hand, and support for a growth, market-oriented, private sector path of development on the other**. In doing so, it is conforming to a further 'global' model of private-public partnerships, in which private sector companies are commissioned by government to perform tasks for it, under its budgets. A clear example of this in Northern Pakistan has been the recent 'privatisation' of AKRSP's erstwhile engineering activities. By downsizing its staff (in engineering and other sectors), it is holding on to some key 'advisory' staff while encouraging other released staff to set up companies (with initial AKRSP support) to compete for tenders under local public sector initiatives such as roads and bridges. At the same time, it is encouraging its clientele among the Village Organisations to participate in the local '*dehi*' and district councils,[12] and indeed to use their experience of village and cluster[13] leadership to take on a leadership role in these new decentralised institutions. The social mobilisation theme of AKRSP has always emphasised the role of village activists as local leaders and catalysts for change alongside the themes of participation and democratic process, so the government led decentralisation process represents an opportunity to mainstream these roles into the local body politic. In this new stance, there are also risks for the AKRSP social mobilisation legacy. While on the one hand, we learn from Najam in chapter 9 that AKRSP never had a social mobilisation mission to challenge and confront government and its ruling practices (i.e. whether military and unrepresentative, or civilian, but nevertheless problematic on democracy and governance issues), there are dangers in becoming too close to the contemporary strategy of decentralisation.

Successive military regimes in Pakistan, and also Bangladesh, have typically experimented with various forms of decentralisation in order to legitimate their regimes and provide a route back to some form of democracy, preferably under their leadership. The strategy of the present government in Pakistan has been derived from an attempt to 'clean-up' the corruption so strongly associated with the political class of whatever political party affiliation, by focusing upon a 'new breed' of local actors.[14] In the present circumstances of the early twenty-first century in Pakistan, the particular problem is the conflict of interest between established patterns of federal-provincial-district administration and the current greater emphasis upon the powers of elected local government representatives. Although there were previously elected Chairman of Districts and Unions,[15] they had very limited powers in relation to the erstwhile delegated powers of District level officials (crucially the Deputy Commissioner) from the Provincial centres. Given the history of government in Pakistan, there can be no guarantees that the present arrangements will survive a change of regime. At the same time, it is hard to imagine that this current experience of representative local government will be easy to dismiss by any future regime, unless it is done so by starving local authorities of budgets.

The other half of this revised 'advisory' mission is support for economic growth in these mountain societies via expanded market activity in production and trading. In the sense of supporting farmers, AKRSP has always been supportive of the private sector. But initially of course that was directed at a strengthening of subsistence agriculture to reduce vulnerability and increase security, as noted above. Commercial farming has mainly developed through cash crop potato production and various experiments with fruit processing. The growth model is undoubtedly a challenge in geographical areas where the economies of agglomeration are difficult to achieve. Where are the really significant drivers for economic expansion that will act as multipliers across the whole regional economy? No doubt, under changed geopolitical conditions, tourism would be such a driver, and there is evidence that the internal Pakistani market is expanding as their travel options overseas becomes more problematical. Further improvements in communications infrastructure will not only assist tourism, but also other possibilities such as the mining of semi-precious stones and the quarrying of marble. A further opening of trade routes to China and Central Asia, and perhaps the opening up of all-season communications to Chitral from the South, will also be significant in stimulating cross border trade. However, the growth path for these mountain areas may have to be a more subtle combination of local activity and migration/remittance packages in which the welfare and social protection needs of the local communities are not solely reliant upon the low equilibrium economic conditions of remote mountain regions.

CONCLUSION: MUTUALITY OF INITIATIVE BETWEEN AGENCY AND CLIENT

Looking across the arguments in the following chapters, the reflective research undertaken for this volume leads us to the following set of conclusions from the experience of AKRSP over the last twenty years in the mountain areas of northern Pakistan. The poverty target has clearly changed in character. The profile of livelihoods options for many client families has changed from exclusive dependency upon local natural resources, comprising farm plots, livestock and forest products. The socio-economic differentiation arising from a wider array of livelihood options requires a plurality of responses, and in particular a recognition that the fulfilment of needs now lies beyond the confines of support for farming. Considering the position of women in such societies, the western feminist agendas, which emphasise equality rather than equity of treatment and status, sit uneasily upon subsistence, patriarchal societies. This is especially the case when the gender relations arising from such peasant, semi-pastoral, subsistence conditions are mainly codified via religious-based cultures and values, under conditions of high illiteracy and poor education (for males as well as females). Thus the discourse shift among donors from WID to GAD remains a rhetorical donor fashion rather than a reality owned and internalised by local development leaders. Local staff, charged with responsibility for promoting the interests of women, realise that they have to move more cautiously and subtly so as not to expose vulnerable women to more domination within their households. This entails a basic dialogue with males over patriarchy, and an exploration of the room for manoeuvre in the consciousness and interests of local women: consciousness which may not always be false.

The central catalyst for change has been the principle of social mobilisation, but the term needs to be deconstructed for its different objectives. The creation or evolution of village level organisations (the Village Organisations, and later Women's Organisations) is clearly essential for reducing transactions costs of the delivery and extension interface between catalyst agency and client. That has been understood world-wide. But the object of social mobilisation has also been to share the responsibility for action between agency and client, by adding to the capacity of clients via collective forms of organisation as well as in individual skills and competences. It is a mature agency that understands that collective action is an historical imperative in situations where clients are heavily dependent upon local natural resources and each other for survival, which is the case *par excellence* in remote mountain communities with high seasonality and problematic access to external resources and services. However, it has also always been the case that collective action is challenged by intra-group dynamics, by new forms of jealousies and conflict, by increased exit options for more successful families and local leaders, by the extent and intensity of livelihoods dependency on particular local resources, and by over-exclusive identities (whether religious, ethnic-linguistic, or clan/kinship) which restrict the limits of mutuality and moral responsibility for each other. Inclusive social mobilisation models come up against these hard social facts. Also the original basis of mobilisation around the narrower objectives of improved farm subsistence can increasingly exclude those whose livelihoods are following a different path of activities and incomes.

But it also appears that while the early leverage and incentive approaches, via grants for infrastructure, produces some loyalty and compliance to prescribed institutional arrangements such as the rules of conduct within Village Organisations, when those grants disappear, so do the incentives for compliance to the original model. This is witnessed in the bifurcation and sometimes disappearance of the originally created Village Organisation. However, as argued in chapter 8, the survival of originally created Village Organisations is not the only measure of institutional success or sustainability, since there is plenty of evidence that the culture of forming organisations to pursue collective interests has been established among local people, so that other manifestations of social capital appear. An agency like AKRSP also has to acknowledge that it is not the only player in the institutional landscape for its clients. Rural clients perceive a wider array of institutional possibilities through which to pursue their interests than those prescribed by a single organisation, even one so closely associated with their own religio-cultural base. Thus clients, as dynamic, thinking, flexible actors can adapt the presentation of their needs and interests to the values and priorities of a range of different potential service providers. In other words, exclusive loyalty to one's own agency model cannot be assumed. And of course, as that institutional landscape becomes more crowded (i.e. more local government, more NGOs) so the agencies themselves have responsibilities to collectively present as rational a catalytic framework as possible to rural clients. In this context of increased competition to AKRSP's erstwhile virtual monopoly as a development catalyst in the region, the 'rights' of different intervening agencies needs also to be clarified both between themselves and in relation to government, especially when government itself is under-resourced and weakly legitimated to its constituency.

There are two final key points to make, before the reader embarks upon a tour of the following chapters. **Firstly**, the differentiation of types of poverty, both in the experience of it as well as the explanations of it, requires the twin principles of economic growth and social protection. In other words, a poverty-focused strategy needs to deal with long term inclusion via the expansion of economic activity to enlarge livelihood choices for more people. But at the same time, it needs to deal with the short term exclusion of those unable through structural conditions or idiosyncratic reasons (see chapter 2 for this discussion) to participate adequately in the present or projected economy. This has to be achieved via safety nets as well as sustained welfare transfers for the persistently poor who are unable to help themselves. To the extent that socio-economic changes imply a shrinking of moral responsibility within extended families, then other collective action or agency mechanisms have to be found to fulfill these functions. **Secondly**, given that AKRSP defined itself as supporting the enhancement of physical, financial, human and social capital, the key analytic question for any agency is which category of capital represents the key constraint in any particular situation, and which is valued most highly in terms of need by the local population. Since all of these 'capitals' need to be functioning well, in a positive equilibrium for people's livelihoods to be secure and improving, then identifying the key one with the most positive multiplier implications for the others becomes the crucial basis and criterion of successful support by outsiders for insiders. It is the mutuality of initiative between agency and client, rather than the populist, participatory rhetoric, which achieves this. I believe this to be the main lesson from the last two decades of ASKRSP in Northern Pakistan.

NOTES

1. The World Bank has conducted a series of five yearly evaluations, the most recent one in 2000 entitled 'The Next Ascent'.
2. For women, this can be very obviously observed in the 'dress and contact' dimensions of *purdah.*
3. Brought from an institutional genealogy in the European cooperative movements and evolved by Akhtar Hameed Khan first in Comilla (now in Bangladesh) and later in the Orangi urban projects of Karachi.
4. See, for example, the essays in Cooke and Kothari (Eds) (2202) *Participation: The New Tyranny*
5. To the cooperative consultancy group 'Mokoro' in Oxford in April 2001.
6. It might reasonably be argued that Gandhi was deliberately naïve in order to bring about a basis of rural solidarity to confront the alliance of landlord classes and colonial regimes.
7. Of course, this notion of a 'vacuum' is contested, given the array of continuing indigenous institutions around religious centres, groups of household elders and irrigation management in particular. See chapter 8 'Collective Action: The Threatened Imperative' for further comment on this.
8. Access has steadily improved with the completion of the Karakoram Highway and feeder roads, and the availability of subsidised wheat.
9. The Bank produced its key document on participation in the early nineties.
10. See the interesting Ph.D. thesis on women's participation in rural development programmes in Nepal by Ava Shrestha (1994) for a good analysis of the power relations between women which determine this participation.
11. This term is borrowed from Esping-Andersen in *Three Worlds of Welfare Capitalism* 1990, Cambridge and Oxford: Polity Press. It refers to limiting the pure effects of the market (i.e. commodity relations) through regulation and public re-distribution.
12. These names vary according to whether the location is in the federally administered Northern Areas, or the provincially administered district of Chitral.

13. A cluster in AKRSP language is a group of villages, usually in the same valley with various infrastructure and natural resource interests in common, requiring common management between villages.
14. Some observers have argued that this is a fanciful ambition with ongoing strong kin connections between the new and old breeds!
15. The primary administrative level below the District and Sub-Division.

1

Ethnographical Context

Geof Wood

Topography and Natural Resources

The area has to be understood as a part of the mountain desert systems of Central Asia. It is characterised by: extreme variations in summer and winter temperatures; significant light and shade variation, affecting photo-periodic cropping in terms of heat, length of day and length of season; very low levels of direct precipitation onto the alluvial fans of the valley bottoms; regular winter snowfall at higher altitudes; a large concentration of the world's glaciers; mixed agriculture, horticulture and livestock farming systems, concentrated into the alluvial fans; net deforestation after afforestation is accounted for; fragile high summer pastures and constrained lower altitude grazing; and essential irrigation provided by surface water channels, sourced from glacial melt. It is an area of gentle rather than steep terracing, since the steep hillsides are quickly barren. People live at varying elevations, which determine the productivity of their small, terraced farms. Although most families were settled in agriculture, they are also semi-pastoral with livestock representing a significant component in their subsistence. Common grazing areas are open in the summer months in small, upland plateaux and herds have to be moved into these high pastures away from village fields. In the upper elevations, farms are single cropped; and double cropped in the lower. There are intermediate areas, where the second crop may not ripen and is grown mainly for winter fodder. The historical conditions of remoteness determined lower agricultural activity during the winter, a requirement to store food and fuel in the autumn for use during the winter, and fewer off-farm employment opportunities. Diet and nutrition levels were therefore highly seasonal with the greatest stress experienced during the end of winter/spring period before the first summer harvest appeared. Women and children were especially vulnerable at these times under near-famine conditions. Dwellings tended to be clustered for mutual protection, with some contemporary evidence of residential overspill onto erstwhile cropping land. Under these conditions there has been a high, though declining, dependence upon local natural resource management, especially water. Indeed, until two decades ago, these communities were almost entirely dependent upon local natural resources, with some element of trading in order to acquire non-local goods.

PRINCELY STATES AND POLITICAL IDENTITY

The three main areas in this Karakoram–Hindukush region (Ghizer–Gilgit-Hunza, Baltistan and Chitral district of NWFP—usually referred to as the Northern Areas and Chitral [NAC]) were princely states surviving beyond the partition of British India into the mid-1970s. This is the arena of the Great Game, in which the British deliberately created a mountainous bulwark to defend its Indian empire against incursion from the Russian Empire. Political Agents were posted from the late Nineteenth Century offering a combination of stick and carrot to local rulers to ensure adequate loyalty to turn them away from Russian and Chinese suzerainty. The Wakki clan territory was allocated by the British and Russians to Afghanistan as the Wakkhan Corridor (running west–east to the source of the Oxus across the 'top' of the Chitral and Ghizer valleys) to act as a buffer between the two Nineteenth Century superpowers. This now represents the strip of territory between Pakistan and Tajikistan, held by the non-Pashtun, erstwhile 'Northern Alliance', clans of Afghanistan in contrast to the Pashtun tribes, south of the Panjshir valley. This territorial settlement, arising from the Great Game, also functioned to sever the historical trading links between Chitral and states in Central Asia, compelling Chitral to ally itself more closely to Kashmir to the east, and the British Empire to the south. The former ruling families in the different valleys retain some influence in their respective areas, though perhaps more so among the Mehtars of Chitral than elsewhere. But even here in the Mastuj sub-division of Chitral, recent Union elections did not return the son of the prominent noble. Since the areas are almost entirely populated by Muslims from different sects, they opted for Pakistan at the time of Partition in 1947, with the East and Southern boundaries of Baltistan representing the UN line of control with Indian occupied Kashmir. Thus again within the region, many of the trade and cultural routes though to Ladakh and Srinagar were severed, as the area had to re-orient its communications through the Indus valley to the down-country Pakistani cities of Islamabad (the new capital created from 1967), its neighbour Rawalpindi, Lahore, and, for Chitral, Peshawar. Connections from all parts of the NAC region to the commercial capital of Karachi on the southern coast are significant for education and employment.

Since the Baltistan and Ghizer/Gilgit/Hunza areas are considered to be part of disputed Kashmir, successive Pakistan governments have been reluctant to absorb these areas into mainstream national politics through fear of weakening, *de facto*, their demand for a plebiscite for the whole of Kashmir with the three options on the agenda of independence, opting for India or opting for Pakistan. As a result, these areas, collectively known as the Northern Areas, have special governance arrangements outside the federal system (i.e. local councils with limited powers, an appointed Minister rather than democratic representation at national level, local rule by civil officials) and a high army presence operating continuous, quasi 'martial law'. Although the population of the Northern Areas is entirely Muslim, three main sects are represented plus smaller ones. Thus Baltistan is mainly populated by Shia, with some Noorbakshi, and since the Iranian revolution of 1979 the area has even been nicknamed as 'little Iran'.[1] There are also significant connections to the Shia population of Kuwait. The 100 mile-long Hunza valley is mainly populated by Ismaili sects, who have brethren scattered in Gilgit, Ghizer and upper Chitral, as well as in the central Asian, 'Badakshani', states to the north. But there are also Sunni sects in these areas too, with some Shia sects in lower Gilgit. Also below Gilgit, extending south towards Astore and the rest of Diamer district, Sunni traditions are particularly strong and conservative.

Chitral to the west, by contrast, is formally integrated into the federal system as a district of the North West Frontier Province (NWFP), and returns members to the Provincial Assembly and the National Assembly (when they have not been suspended by martial law). However, the area also faces uncertainty and insecurity, derived partly from the instability of its neighbour, Afghanistan and the consequent influx and now departure of Afghan refugees; partly as a cultural, ethnic and religious frontier between Pashtun (or Pathan) and Chitrali, and between Sunni and Ismaili sects, with the Sunni concentrated in the lower half of the district and the Ismaili in the upper half (though with some Sunni dominated valleys like Turkho); and partly because it is separated from its nearest southern neighbouring district, Dir (strongly, even fundamentally Sunni), and through Dir access to 'down-country' and Peshawar by the 10,000 feet Lowari Pass, which is impassable during the 6-7 winter months. Indeed, during these months, the only road access is through the Kunar valley which runs into Afghanistan before re-connecting to Pakistan via the Nawa Pass.

LANGUAGE AND SECTS

Identity and solidarity, which are so important as ingredients of survival in these remote areas, are also features of kinship, clan and language. Thus, alongside these differences of sect (and some villages can be mixed between different sects), linguistic groupings are significant. The primary language for most inhabitants is quite localised. Most people in Chitral speak Khowar, sometimes referred to as Chitrali, regardless of sect, clan and location. Thus despite the sharp Sunni/Ismaili contrast in settlement between lower and much of upper Chitral respectively, the virtual common language of

Khowar has been cited as an important ingredient of cohesion and sense of Chitrali identity—even to the point of nationhood, though that is probably far-fetched. In a sense, language and sect compete as the basis for identity, with a fear among the fervent Chitrali that sectarian division will win with the Chitrali Sunni increasingly identifying with their sectarian brethren in the fundamentalist Dir District to the south, over the Lowari Pass. Thus both external and internal events can increase inter-sect hostility for periods of time.

In Gilgit/Astore/Nagar/Hunza (including the sub-region of Ghizer to the west), three sects (Ismaili, Sunni and Shia) are represented, alongside distinct language groups. Thus, to the west in Ghizer, Ismailis numerically dominate with pockets of Sunni, all speaking Khowar (despite the Hindu Raj mountain barrier between themselves and the Khowar speakers of Chitral). This 'extension' of Khowar-speaking populations to western Ghizer can be explained by formal control over the area by branches of the Mehtar ruling family from Chitral until the British brought the area under Gilgit. Indeed, the 'Raja of Iskoman' in western Ghizer to this day retains close kinship ties with the descendants of the Mehtar families. From Ghizer, eastwards towards the valleys around Gilgit, the language becomes Shina, spoken by a mix of Ismaili, Shia and Sunni (with some Sunni more recently migrated from Swat and other areas of NWFP, having Pashtu as their original language). There are some entirely Shia valleys like Bagrote. Astore is predominantly Sunni. Moving north from Gilgit, Nagar is Shia with Shina spoken alongside Burushuski in its northern edge. Further north is Hunza, entirely Ismaili and speaking Burushuski, until the uppermost areas bordering the Wakkhan Corridor and back west across the north of Ghizer where Sunni Wakki speakers live. In Baltistan, to the east, nestled between the Himalayan and Karakoram ranges, there is again the virtual unifying language of Balti, coterminous with the Shia sect to which more than 90 per cent of the population belong.

These distinct linguistic regions have to be understood as primarily geographical in explanation rather than reflecting social or religious categories. For example, depending precisely where you live in Ghizer, regardless of being Sunni or Ismaili in this mixed sect area, you will either have Khowar or Shina as your first language. Likewise, Shia Nagar and Ismaili Hunza will both speak Shina at the lower, southern end of the valley and Burushuski further to the north. For all of these groups, the more mobile family members due to status, education and other necessary migration will have some knowledge of neighbouring languages. And if their movement is further afield, then many will share Urdu as a second language. Inherently there is a strongly gendered pattern to familiarity with other than a primary language, as well as reading and writing. Certainly, among the more educated, and those with exposure through army recruitment or down-country labour, Urdu is spoken widely (though it may only be read by a smaller subset). English is only spoken by a tiny, educated elite. To conclude, in some areas, common language cuts across other divisions, while in others language and sect identity coincide, thereby reinforcing an enhanced sense of exclusiveness.

Thus among a small total population of approximately one million people, there is significant segmentation of identity and social networks through which livelihoods are pursued and poverty experienced. As is to be expected in high mountainous areas with poor infrastructure and communication, the 'valley' is a key component of this segmentation, reflecting centuries of migration and specific settlement. Comparisons of living standards and opportunities are frequently made between these identities which are often manifested as jealousy, mutual suspicion and distrust. In this sense, conflict is always just beneath the surface (when it has not actually erupted) and support agencies (government and non-government) are frequently accused of bias and capture by opposing groups. In other words, in the context of scarcity, vulnerability, fragility and precariousness of opportunities and survival, competition is intense and cooperation at a premium. Social and cultural resources acquire enormous importance as routes to security, including the defining of rights to key natural resources such as water.

Religious identity thus clearly remains a strong binding force. All three of the major sects of Islam prevalent in northern

Pakistan—Sunni, Shia Ithnashari, and Shia Ismaili—have a profound sense of belonging in and to the area. The Ismaili tradition of community is strong, and manifests itself around a strong sense of responsibility to contribute towards the community. For example, the widespread contribution of about ten percent of one's income by Ismailis to the Imamat is an institutionalised way of contributing towards the development of one's community. The expectations of the Ismaili community towards a programme that bears the Aga Khan's name are thus significant, attracting strong institutional loyalties. But Sunni and Shia traditions are also very strong in this region.

KINSHIP AND CLAN

Overlaid across these broad ethnic and sectarian differences in the NAC region is a complex kinship system in which families are essentially grouped into identifiable clans. While they are broadly coterminous with sectarian divisions, there are instances in which clans might straddle sects due to sporadic conversions and inter-sect marriage. Again these clans are mainly endogamous, but not exclusively so. Generally within Muslim society, marriage within small kinship units is quite common including cross-cousin marriage, thus reinforcing a general practice of clan endogamy. A large village will typically be divided into *mohallahs* (each *mohallah* with its own religious centre), which are most probably of a single sect (where the village is a mixed sect). In single sect villages, these *mohallahs* may themselves be coterminous with a clan but even this is difficult to generalise with different clans from the same sect living closely together. A village may typically comprise five to ten distinct clans. Historically, these clans may have been associated with particular occupations, thus resembling a caste/*jati* structure though with a much reduced sense of pollution: ritual or real. Currently these occupational distinctions have receded, although in some areas some clans retain a higher political and social status than others, derived either from being part of the ruling clan (e.g. Kators in Chitral as the clan name of the ruling Mehtar family) or being favoured with administrative office by the ruling families. Such clans retain a certain dominance in village affairs, partly based on lingering respect, partly based on superior assets arising from this ruler association, and partly due to inter-linked superior education with some clan members holding secure, professional jobs.

Before the reader becomes over-frustrated with this, still superficial, ethnographical tour of the region, there are some preliminary conclusions to be drawn which impact upon other arguments in this volume. The 'frontier' characteristics of the NAC region have constituted a history of dynamic settlement reflecting: invasion (the genetic outcomes of the presence of Alexander the Great in the region can still be seen); trade movement; local migration due to squabbles or pressure on fragile resources in nearby areas; and induced migration by order of ruling families to settle new alluvial fans and thereby bring them under control for revenue purposes as well as extending political territory in competition with others. In most villages of our fieldwork, informants will invariably trace their ancestry to somewhere else within the region. Combine this history of settlement with the topography, in which valleys and sub-regions can be relatively inaccessible from each other, and the socio-cultural heterogeneity and diversity can be appreciated. With a slow but steady increase in communication via road links, some of this diversity might reduce—to be discussed below. However, with this settlement legacy, we encounter an area which was characterised by cross-cutting ties and fission-fusion as the basis of order and disorder, in which people simultaneously inhabit parallel, contingent communities, variously active or passive according to circumstance, within a framework of feudal authority which had set limits to local conflict as the basis for competition between larger, aggregate socio-political units. Thus we have a social basis for collective action, which is partially induced by feudal authority, and partially underpinned by the principle of contingent community (see Streefland et al. (1995), for further elaboration of some of the above description, though most of what is presented here is based on our own primary fieldwork).

THREE KEY EVENTS: ABOLITION OF PRINCELY STATES; NEW ROAD COMMUNICATIONS; AND AKRSP

Chronologically, in recent times, the political system of princely states (statelets) across Chitral, Ghizer, Hunza and Baltistan was dismantled in the mid-1970s by Z. A. Bhutto and the Pakistan People's Party, as the government of Pakistan, signalling a decline (but perhaps not complete removal) of influence of Mehtars, Mirs and Rajas and their intimate clans with their superior landholdings and retainers. For Chitral, this change of status occurred a little earlier, in 1969, under General Yahya Khan, when it became an administrative district of the North West Frontier Province, with royal privileges formally abolished in 1972. However, the formal liberation of peasant–pastoralist clans from labour and rental obligations to their lords did not place them under the development authority of an effective alternative government. This was the rationale for the creation of the Aga Khan Rural Support Programme (AKRSP), intended as a secular intervention, but triggered by the presence of Ismailis in the NAC. Later in the '70s (1978) the Karakoram Highway (KKH) was completed which linked Islamabad to the Chinese border via Chilas, Gilgit and Hunza. This all-season highway thus also eventually improved communications to Baltistan, Nagar and Ghizer via link roads. Chitral remains enclosed for approximately six winter months of the year with the Lowari to the south and Shandur pass to the north-east impassable due to snowfall. Though it is worth noting that before the KKH, Chitral was actually relatively more accessible than the Northern Areas, and thus an important trading route into the Northern Areas via the Shandur Pass. The KKH has had a significant impact upon economic, social and cultural variables in the Northern Areas. Thus from the mid-'70s to the early '80s, these three events were significant in changing the livelihoods, status and opportunities for ordinary people in the NAC: abolition of princely states; opening of the KKH; and the introduction of AKRSP. Some additional factors are also relevant. The ongoing dispute with India over Kashmir (of which Baltistan and Gilgit/Hunza were formally and formerly components) requires a large-scale, continuous army presence with particular impact upon infrastructure and local employment. Also, other components of what is now the Aga Khan Development Network (AKDN) have operated in the area: the Aga Khan Education Services (AKES) and the Aga Khan Health Service, Pakistan (AKHSP). More recently, other dimensions of the network have also evolved in the water and sanitation, housing and cultural (restoration) sectors. And, of course, other dimensions of government and civil society (especially through networks of religious institutions) have become more prominent.

This severely summarised institutional and social history of the NAC provides the context over the last two to three decades for the experience of poverty and livelihoods, and the changes which have occurred. Thus in the early '80s it was reasonable to describe the whole area as poor, with minor exceptions among some elite classes, and minor variations in the productivity of the local natural resource base, depending on remoteness and elevation. Livelihood options outside agriculture, horticulture (especially fruit and nuts), pastoral management and some army-related employment simply did not exist. Obviously, the building of the KKH provided some opportunities for locally employed road construction labour. Other infrastructure labour for irrigation channels, dirt roads and tracks had traditionally been mobilised by the princely authorities in lieu of cash rents for cultivable land and rights to common property resources (grazing, forests and so on). The time gap between the dissolution of these authorities and the arrival of AKRSP was described (by AKRSP leaders) as an institutional vacuum in which the quality of public infrastructure declined. This was not entirely accurate, with many local, *mohallah* and mosque-based groups continuing to manage local water distribution, some localised maintenance, and high pastures.

LIVELIHOODS IN THE EARLY EIGHTIES

In the NAC, 25 years ago, all areas were inaccessible. And 30 years ago, most areas were only just emerging from a series of small-scale, feudal political systems in which labour power was significantly controlled by local, aristocratic clans and royal lineages. This combination of remoteness and subservience defined to a large extent the livelihoods systems available to the local population, and also ensured the reproduction of widespread poverty. Human lives were precarious and the physical environment was fragile. With these conditions, it was possible to conclude that all but a tiny minority were poor. It was also possible to conclude that the patterns of livelihoods for most families were also similar to each other and heavily reliant upon local natural resource management either at farm level or in a common property sense. There was some recruitment into the armed forces and local militia units (such as the Chitral Scouts): to the ranks for those from peasant families; and to officer grades for some sons from the small minority of educated, literate aristocratic clans. Secondary and further education had been obtained down-country, requiring laborious travel and long absences. This gave the small elite class national exposure; sometimes cosmopolitan, albeit English speaking, missionary schools and colleges were involved. We make this observation in order to alert the reader to the paucity of local human capital for development purposes and the subsequent prominence given to non-local staff from down-country for administrative and leadership purposes in both government and non-government services.

Peasant Subsistence Economy

Under these conditions, livelihoods could classically be understood within the framework of a peasant subsistence socio-economy—very hand to mouth. Farmers produced primarily for their own consumption and committed their labour in a drudgery averse manner (Chayanov 1966), driven by the particular dependency ratios in their joint families. Indeed, demographic differentiation (Ellis 2000a, 2000b) was more significant than class differentiation (see next paragraph). Trade of farm produce was local and seasonal, barely petty commodity production. There were no commercial surpluses, so that petty trade accelerated in the immediate post-harvest periods when non-farm goods were purchased (e.g. clothes, utensils and other such survival necessities) from local bazaars or peripatetic traders. There was a high opportunity cost to these purchases in terms of adequate food stores until the next harvest. Livestock use functioned as an important consumption smoother and insurance, providing meat and wool alongside dairy products. Over-consumption of livestock, induced by seasonal necessity, could result in critical herd depletion. At the same time, scarcity of winter fodder could induce non-sustainable slaughter. Although people mainly lived in joint, extended families which offered some scope for risk spreading and energy pooling between a larger number of family members, there were also persistent pressures for nucleation in order to resolve resource and consumption disputes between inheriting brothers and their immediate kin, especially after the death of the patriarch. With low life expectancy, the frequency of farm (land, livestock and productive assets) division was more intense, producing continuous fragmentation of holdings and increasing the transactions costs of cooperation (e.g. sharing of labour and bullock power, or water sharing) even between close blood kin.

INEQUALITY: STRATIFICATION RATHER THAN HOSTILE CLASSES

Interestingly, in comparison with other agrarian systems in the non-mountainous areas of South Asia, one classic feature of peasant life was largely missing, especially after the mid-'70s: namely the dimension of class. This is a complex issue to summarise. Obviously, in the princely era, there was formal hierarchy in a classic feudal sense of control over labour (i.e. the scarcest factor of production, rather than control over land directly, which is a common misconception about feudalism). In that sense, a key condition of peasant society was fulfilled: namely subservience and contributions of rent/produce to a dominant outsider in return for protection, security and the authoritative mobilisation of public goods labour (i.e. oriental despotism or the Asiatic mode of production) (Shanin

1972; Wittfogel 1957). These princes in turn often owed tribute to more distant protectors (variously from Central Asia, China and kingdoms/empires to the south and west during earlier centuries) under suzerainty arrangements. It was also clear that these local princely rulers operated through a blood-related clan network supplemented by the practice of fostering out their male children, thereby creating adoptive kin relations as well. These clans and families would hold prebendary titles to land in dispersed localities and perform *patwari* functions.[2] In this sense, a superior class over the ordinary peasantry existed. However this superiority was more evident in terms of favoured, dependent status rather than expressed as significantly higher standards of living, education and so on, except for a few. The dissolution of the power of their patrons removed, to a considerable extent, this source of status. Thus, at the beginning of the 1980s, the societies of NAC were more characterised by vertical clan segmentation, as described above, rather than horizontal segmentation of a class exploitative kind.

Thus the experience of poverty and precarious livelihoods was less attributable to entrapment in oppressive class relations with all the negative psychological characteristics of powerlessness and alienation in relation to local landlords, moneylenders and their bureaucratic allies in government, than elsewhere in South Asia. Likewise, although some clans enjoyed superior status either through their connections to princely ruling families or through religious functions and deference (e.g. Syeds), there was no caste system as such to differentiate people horizontally, no strict delineation of occupations on a ritual pollution scale, and therefore no transfer across of such status into a legitimation of economic class differentiation. This is not quite the whole story, with subtle differentiations acknowledged locally, such as the social inferiority of the Dom (Musician) clans in Karimabad, Hunza as well as in Chitral. Other differences may result from precise locations of settlement (good land, nearer water sources, sunlit rather than shadowed valley sides, migration history, minority sect status in a mixed village and so on). However, these differences were sufficiently diversified and idiosyncratic for any clear sense of class relations to emerge in the early '80s. Indeed, it is still the case, two decades later, that while there may be marked increases in inequality and social differentiation (see below), these have to be understood as class **differences** (stratification) rather than as exploitative class **relations**.

CENTRALITY OF THE FAMILY

Within these social, cultural and economic aspects of peasant subsistence arrangements for the pursuit of livelihoods, the circumstances of the family and the relationships within the family are central. Independent of cultural and social practices associated with Islam, these are strongly patriarchal and virilocal societies. Adult male social dominance within families is a universal norm, rarely challenged from within the society. Patriarchs and elder sons/brothers both represent the family in wider social forums (*mohallah* and village meetings, meetings with outsiders, common property management activity through indigenous religio-social institutions such as the *jamatkhana* (for Ismaili), mosque (for Sunni) and *imambargah* (for Shia) and have acknowledged responsibility for resource use and allocation within the family. Of course, real relations within families depart from these norms in a variety of subtle ways, and especially when considering trends over the last two decades. Thus, it would be a mistake to think of women as entirely without power, simply because they are more confined to the private domain rather than the public (for a discussion of this in Bangladesh, see White 1992). Elderly informants tell me of impressively powerful women among the Mehtars during the Nineteenth Century, influencing military strategy and acting as strong regents over their 'minor' sons when they became formal rulers. It would also be a mistake to generalise across the sects, with women traditionally having more public community level interaction in Ismaili communities through greater and culturally accepted participation in the *jamatkhana*, festivals and inter-household occasions (such as marriages and other *rites de passage*). Men and women negotiate between themselves many aspects of livelihoods management in terms of: land management priorities; buying, selling and use of livestock as well as management of fodder and grazing; commitment of family labour to public goods development and maintenance; allocation of scarce family funds to social protection charitable donations; rationing consumption of subsistence products; purchase of non-farm essential items; choice of marriage partners for children or younger siblings; cutting and planting of trees; storage of fuel, food and fodder; division of joint family assets. Women also trade with neighbouring women, exchanging essential items (such as small amounts of sugar, *ghee* or maybe eggs and fruit) and sharing forms of domestic labour (clothes washing, child care, house maintenance). They also meet by water courses for clothes washing or collecting water, and exchange information about health, or other family pressures. Thus, mutual female support outside the confines of the extended family is not absent, though obviously some households are stricter in a *purdah* sense than others and local paths between houses must be seen as secure and non-shaming.

The Position of Women

Notwithstanding these caveats, there can be little doubt that despite their observable contribution to family subsistence through productive labour both domestically and on the farm (weeding, threshing, carrying, livestock management), women were and continue to be of inferior social and cultural status to men, and are tail-enders for quantity and quality of food. As daughters, they are socialised into domestic labour and reproductive expectations and traditionally receive little other human capital investment (literacy rates for women in the NAC still remain at a staggeringly low 4 per cent). Although there are varying practices of brideprice and dowry across the NAC, virginal brides are essentially traded between families ensuring the essential principle of unambiguous paternity as the basis of agnatic inheritance in a patrilineal system. The general practice of *purdah* is derived from this basic logic of peasant reproduction in which land and livestock is the only productive inheritance, with the labour of children socialised and harnessed accordingly. In this sense, ironically perhaps, the richer the family by reference to land and livestock, the more important is conformity to *purdah*. The poorer the family, the more the woman has to labour outside the homestead, and the more shame and status loss is incurred. In this sense, productive contribution does not map onto positive status as in the WID[3] assumption. It is successful reproduction in richer families which offers more status and less shame, and more honour for the family enabling it to be more successful in public/community forums. Do the women of such families therefore have more personal power in gender relations within their families and, for Ismailis, in the limited public domain of the *jamatkhana*? Clearly, the experience of poverty for poor women contains these dimensions of status, power, shame and honour. In addition, it is important to disaggregate the experience of women in other ways too. The demographic position within the family can be significant, with junior daughters-in-law and unmarried mature daughters the most vulnerable, and successful (in reproductive terms) mothers and mothers-in-law (in extended joint families) the most powerful (for a discussion of these issues in Nepal, see Shrestha 1994).

Although the above description of female livelihoods and poverty experience owes much to the logic of peasant subsistence arrangements, this 'materialist' logic receives a cultural reinforcement from Islam in NAC.[4] But that cultural reinforcement is expressed in different ways between the sects, and is also affected by the poverty/wealth status of the individual family as well as other factors like education. It is generally understood that the Ismaili communities are less formally restrictive of their women than Sunnis, especially in Sunni-only areas like lower Chitral or Astore/Chilas. Shia in Baltistan operate strong *purdah*, while some Shia in Nagar have become less restrictive, possibly influenced by their Ismaili neighbours and the Ismaili community support for female education.[5] With the partial exception of the Ismaili community due to the long existence of Diamond Jubilee Schools, the consequences of this restriction for poor women (i.e. most women) was a complete inability to represent their interests in the society, leaving them vulnerable to patriarchal management and powerlessness. Their livelihoods experience was concentrated upon subsistence reproduction (biological, labour and social) within the family.

DEMOGRAPHIC RATHER THAN SOCIAL DIFFERENTIATION

In these peasant subsistence circumstances found in the early 1980s, there were few significant off-farm opportunities for the pursuit of livelihoods. This absence of economic diversification and alternative sources of income and subsistence brought the centrality of landholding and family survival together in systems of multiple inheritance and continuous processes of farm fragmentation. This was only partially relieved by low technology irrigation development which offered possibilities of bringing hitherto uncultivable land into production and increasing the productivity of land through double cropping. A peasant family farm is essentially an inter-generational bargain, in which children's labour is controlled by adults in exchange for inheritance, with young adults eventually taking welfare responsibility for ageing parents. The livelihoods experience is thus captured by a three generation model of children, parents and grandparents in an extended, usually joint, structure (Collard 2000). The dependency ratio of working family members to non-working members thus crucially determines labour inputs and subsistence levels. Thus any differentiation between peasant families in the society had to be understood as demographic rather than social. This form of differentiation is affected also by the sex composition of children in the family—fewer sons meant less fragmentation in the next generation and a higher prospect of future adequate subsistence, though more daughters in a dowry system meant a predictable loss of assets to make a good marriage, while too many sons in a brideprice system could have the opposite effect. A high probability of infant mortality tempted families to overcompensate, further adding to the fragmentation process.

CONCLUSION

In summary, the key experience of poverty and livelihoods in the early '80s was lack of choice and entrapment in a low productivity, low-level equilibrium trap environment in which the main objective for individuals and families was simple reproduction rather than any prospect of expanded reproduction. All dimensions of capital were weak, though partially compensating personal social resources were idiosyncratically strong for some families whether through the demographic conditions of the family (as above) or through linkages to stronger clans (further above). Women had still less choice than men, though their circumstances could be substantially attributed to the lack of choice for men also. However, that observation leads to a crucial question of gender analysis when reviewing the intervening period from the early 1980s to the present day. Put starkly: do women remain without power and choices even if the choices for their menfolk have expanded?

Additional changes have occurred in the region which are not the primary focus of this volume, but which have nevertheless altered to some extent the social conditions under which people are pursuing their livelihoods. Social sector investments by other parts of the Aga Khan Development Network, especially in education and health, have occurred alongside and sometimes prior to AKRSP's own interventions. Thus the Aga Khan Education Services built upon earlier origins in the AK Jubilee Schools from the 1950s. These schools undoubtedly contributed, along with some other public and private sector schools in the expansion of knowledge and information in the society, and provided the platform for some boys, especially, to move on to higher education down-country. Not only did these young men themselves gain professional careers both further afield and locally, but they acted as crucial role models for a following generation, leading to more down-country migration for education and subsequent diversification of incomes. They also represented a wider exposure to information and ideas which challenged some of the local traditions, norms and power structures. In other words, they were early catalysts for later development. As the Aga Khan Education

Service evolved, so it focused more upon education for girls as part of a deliberate programme of affirmative action. This has led to a more recent development of educated females seeking professional careers, thus mirroring the early steps taken by young men in the previous era.

Likewise, the Aga Khan Health Services, alongside other improvements in health provision and access to it, has been significant in changing the livelihoods and vulnerabilities of poor households. The proliferation of community level hospitals and clinics has significantly reduced maternal and infant mortality, as well as the more simply treated but previously fatal illnesses of adult income earners. This has improved the overall security, and sense of security, of households across the region. It is now interesting to see some shift from the curative to preventive health model, with greater emphasis also upon water and sanitation investments by AKDN. These social sector interventions by AKDN have themselves constituted a role model for other government-led programmes, and have changed and enlarged the expectations that local people have for services more generally. Both education and health services have also had internal migration effects, since these services are typically located in what become growth pole centres (partly as a result of their presence). Thus we see young families migrating to such centres to access education for their children, and later on in their domestic cycle, bringing down aged parents from remoter, upper elevations in order to use health services. They are therefore contributing to a demographic, spatial re-structuring of the society.

Finally, it would be unwise to complete this background, contextual chapter without referring to heterogeneity and conflict. Although there has been the presumption of relative socio-economic homogeneity of households below the ruling families at the outset of AKRSP's time in these societies, we will see in the following chapter arguments and evidence about increasing socio-economic differentiation over the last two decades, partly as a result of development and the success of some families. Unlike the class-divided political economies of down-country Pakistan as well as further afield in the subcontinent, conflict in these mountain societies has been less in terms of class exploitation. Rivalries of other kinds have emerged, perhaps more strongly over the period. These are often understood in identity terms between geographical areas, overlaid with ethnic, linguistic and religious differences. Sometimes the intensity of these local identity based rivalries have been a reflection of events in a wider domain. Many in the Northern Areas recall the events of 1988, when armed groups of Sunni followers, urged on by some elements in the then national government, came north into the valleys south and west of Gilgit to attack Shia communities. This reflected Sunni/Shia tensions elsewhere in the country, as the minority Shia communities were apparently gaining political and economic ground after the 1979 revolution in Iran. Their rise in confidence was perceived as a threat to Sunni dominance, and Shia communities were attacked, leaving many dead and injured. The heartland of Shia identity in the Northern Areas, Baltistan, was never reached by these forces, but certainly their overall political vulnerability encouraged an intensification of the subsequent link between Shia and Ismaili brethren in the form of more investment in Baltistan by AKDN.

Other conflicts with sectarian/ethnic overtones are also evident. There has always been the charge from the early days of AKRSP by non-Ismaili communities that AKRSP and other parts of AKDN have favoured the Ismaili areas of settlement over Sunni ones especially. There is a difficulty here, since AKRSP certainly has more cultural capital in Ismaili areas, with the *jamat* encouraging, even ordering, cooperation with AK programmes. It is thus always tempting to work more in localities which offer a more favourable response to ideas and initiatives. Over time, this has resulted, for example, in the Sunni communities of lower, southern Chitral distrusting AKDN's intentions. This was reinforced during the late eighties into the early nineties by some police and military officers embarking upon a programme of mosque construction and upgrading, bringing fears among the northern Chitrali, predominantly Ismaili, population of a 'march' of Sunni fundamentalism into their areas. Dir district, immediately to the south over the Lowari Pass was long associated with a more conservative Sunnism.[6] An incident in August 1999 brought all this out into the open, when a murder between two close relatives (the victim had converted to Sunnism from Ismaili) over land was interpreted by the Sunni communities as a sectarian counter-attack. All offices of AKDN were closed for a while, with AKRSP taking the main criticism, as local mullahs mobilised their communities to protest. Apart from these two obvious events (i.e. 1988 and 1999), conflicts simmer below the surface as communities watch each other warily. There is always a strong army presence on the streets and in the bazaar at the Shia festival of Muharram, for example. But any major religious occasion can be the opportunity for tension.

With such diversity of identity in language and sect across these valleys, it is not surprising that latent conflict and some pervasive sense of competition will occur when additional resources are introduced into resource scarce environments. People with precarious, subsistence livelihoods have always understood the zero-sum game aspect of living in a situation of fixed, finite resources where gains by some must, by definition, be at the expense of others. Yet the collective reliance upon the sustainable management of these precarious local resources has also historically held some of these conflicts in check. The challenge is when new resources appear, initially as cargo, so the old zero-sum game rules of restoring equilibriums get misapplied, since the nature of competition now relies more upon accepting new ideas, initiatives and risks. New forms of jealousies arise when one community is seen as getting ahead, not necessarily at the expense of others since the pot of resources has expanded, but getting ahead, nevertheless. Or moving out of traditional lowly, marginalised status, as for the Shia communities prior to 1988. Such a picture fits into a pattern observed elsewhere in the subcontinent and further afield, when new resources and 'progress' stimulates new forms of conflict.[7]

NOTES

1. It used to be nicknamed 'little Tibet'.
2. This refers to the recording of holding rights for tax, rent and other obligations such as labour or tribute in kind.
3. Women In Development.
4. It receives cultural reinforcement from Hinduism in other parts of South Asia.
5. As reported by Shia informants from Nagar.
6. Indeed, Dir was a definite source of recruitment for the Afghan Taliban in their struggles against the Northern Alliance, and the US led invasion in 2001.
7. See for example the classic study by R. Nicholas on village factions in West Bengal (1963).

2

Sustaining Livelihoods and Overcoming Insecurity

Geof Wood and Abdul Malik

INTRODUCTION

In the mountain regions of Northern Pakistan, poverty continues to blight the prospect of sustainable livelihoods for much of the population. For the last 20 years, the Aga Khan Rural Support Programme (AKRSP) has sought to contribute to the reduction of poverty in the region. Mountain areas present a series of special challenges to their residents, and to the agencies which try to support sustainable livelihoods. This chapter describes these challenges and reviews the experience of AKRSP, as a key support agency. In addressing the creation of sustainable mountain livelihoods, the chapter offers wider regional and theoretical significance than an account of these themes solely in the region of Northern Pakistan.[1] The chapter argues that AKRSP features initially as only one element in a wider story and institutional landscape. It describes the conditions of poverty and livelihoods at the beginning of the AKRSP period, followed by an analysis of trends over the last 20 years. It then offers a reflective analysis of AKRSP's role in poverty reduction and support for sustainable livelihoods, before concluding with a further analysis of the implications of the NAC–AKRSP interface for poverty reduction and sustainable livelihoods in other mountain areas. Some of the analysis is based empirically upon the Northern Areas and Chritral Household Income Survey (NACHIS), which is the main monitoring and evaluation database created by AKRSP's Monitoring and Evaluation Section.

No chapter of this kind can be exhaustive of description or the application of the many different ways of approaching the analysis of poverty and livelihoods. We are pursuing a particular argument with reference to the policies and strategies of a key intervention agency (AKRSP) which, over 20 years, has had the objectives of poverty reduction and improvement in sustainable livelihoods. The argument operates within the parallel processes of changing ground realities in AKRSP's programme area and the evolving global discourses about poverty and livelihoods over the last two decades. It suggests that in its first period (i.e. the eighties) households across the whole programme area (NAC) could be regarded as poor in terms of public goods and family resource endowments. Thus, a non-targeted, inclusive approach based on infrastructure and resource development would address the crucial needs of most households in the region and contribute to poverty alleviation for all. However, by the second period (i.e. nineties to present day), greater socio-economic differentiation and inequality limited the social utility of these mainstream rural support activities to graduating households, leaving other, poorer households effectively excluded from provision relevant to their evolving circumstances. Considering the following diagram, line A represents the continuing poor and their livelihood needs over the last twenty years; line B represents the pattern of livelihoods needs for graduating people over the two periods; and line C represents the successfully diversified and graduated people. The shaded area between line A and C represents the AKRSP's strategy in the two periods. The diagram offers an argument that in Period I, AKRSP's strategy was addressing all categories of household in the programme area by offering a portfolio of activities e.g. irrigation channels, land development loans, distribution of improved plants, which were tightly aligned to the livelihood needs of the people (represented by dark shaded area in Period I). However, despite the breadth of its portfolio (represented by the breadth of shaded area in Period II), mainstream AKRSP strategy has remained more relevant to graduating households in Period II, and lost its full contact with the continuing poor. At the same time, AKRSP's strategy has also become less relevant to the needs of successfully graduated people.

Figure 2.1. Livelihoods needs / AKRSP strategy

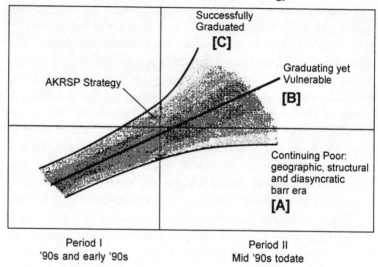

In other words, AKRSP's non-targeted approach was very relevant at the time of its inception because most of the people in the NAC were poor and were following similar livelihood strategies. But by the second period, it became less relevant in the context of changing socio-economic differentiation across the programme area. The table below shows that those who are associated with AKRSP today are largely non-poor e.g. 67 per cent in 2001 compared to 47 per cent in 1994. It shows that the target for AKRSP has been closely representative of the poor /non-poor distribution in the programme area as a whole rather than particularly focused upon the poorer category. This would indicate that AKRSP was not specifically targeting the poor. Had that been the case, the percentage of poor households in AKRSP's membership should have been higher than that of the programme area.

However, this argument should be qualified. It must be recognized that the improvement in the percentage of non-poor is based upon the national poverty line. Later in this paper, we show that minor adjustments to poverty line assumptions and income sensitivity changes the picture dramatically, significantly increasing the proportion of poor and vulnerable people. Thus the above diagram would tilt rightwards on its axis and have profound implications for how the clientele of AKRSP is identified and its needs addressed.

Table 2.1. AKRSP's target households

	1994	1997	2001
Poverty in programme area (%)	54	45	34
Poverty in member households (%)	53	40	33
AKRSP-covered households in the sample (%)	63	71	73

Source: Data from Household Income & Expenditure Survey Series, AKRSP.

Even using the national poverty line assumptions, the data above clearly indicates a significant category of the continuing poor. This has influenced the way in which AKRSP has perceived the limitations of its initial approach (i.e. its original strategy of supporting rural infrastructure and the natural resource base). It has led to a recognition of the changing forms of poverty and livelihoods and the need to include additional poverty-focused strategies which depart from its original conception. If we then recognise that poverty and vulnerability may be even more significant than revealed in the data above (based on the national poverty line) then the limitations of AKRSP's mainstream approach become more acute.

A further way of expressing changing patterns of need for livelihoods support over the last two decades is in the following schematic representation of stratification in the NAC. Thus, up until the beginning of AKRSP's presence in the NAC, the society crudely comprised a narrow (literate) elite of ruling families and their immediate kin and a large mass of undifferentiated peasantry/ semi-pastoralists. After two decades of change, brought about by many influences in addition to AKRSP, that picture changes. There is a continuation of a narrow elite, though its power base has changed. But now there is a clearer differentiation of the remaining population into: a small professional class based on expanded literacy and education; a larger 'graduating' class of successfully diversified farmers (with a significant proportion of off-farm incomes, sometimes through services and other skilled employment); and a class of continuing poor peasants, highly vulnerable, with precarious off-farm diversification through casual manual labour. This changing pattern of stratification has several implications. First, that the society has differentiated and become more unequal as it has progressed overall. Second, therefore, that in effect a Pareto Optimum outcome has been achieved in which everyone has done better, but some much more than others. Third, that the livelihoods dynamics of particular families (perhaps in any society without widespread safety nets and social protection) produces both chronic, extreme and churning forms of poverty requiring respectively sustained welfare transfers or temporary safety nets. And fourth, that vulnerability (in the absence of universal, statutory social protection) remains widespread, rather than just confined to the continuing poor, since even successfully diversifying farming families can find that employment or business conditions change dramatically in a precarious mountain economy.[2]

Figure 2.2. Changing patterns of socio-economic stratification

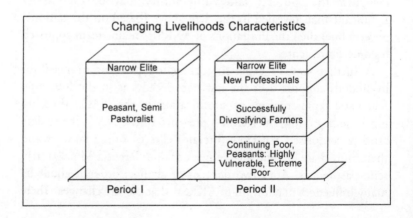

This increasing stratification and its subsequent impact on the livelihoods outcomes can be seen in the following figure drawn from the quantitative evidence collected over the last decade. When we compare the distribution of households around the mean incomes of 1991, we find that a greater proportion of households were falling in the upper income group[3] in 2001, compared to a smaller proportion found in the same bracket a decade ago.

Figure 2.3. Economic stratification of households over the last decade

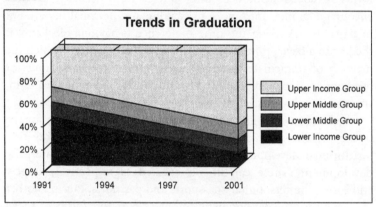

Source: Data from Household Income & Expenditure Survey Series, AKRSP.

While not pretending that the picture is as simple as the above diagram, it does draw attention to the policy and strategic options facing AKRSP, either on its own or together with other agencies in the Aga Khan Development Network (AKDN) as well as government, other NGOs and 'indigenous' philanthropic institutions (often via religious injunction and organisation). Certainly the combination of continuing poverty for some and vulnerability for most, with the ever present threat of poverty, has led AKRSP into a policy debate about its strategic options. If we introduce the language of passports and buffers,[4] the above diagram would suggest that AKRSP as a major development player in the region has been successful in offering some rural clients passports to graduation out of poverty (if not vulnerability) as they move from Period I to Period II through land enhancement, infrastructure, productivity enhancing packages and other public goods. However, it remains a question whether it has been able to offer buffers to prevent families from declining still further into poverty over the period through safety nets and social protection as well as public goods such as improved access to medical centres or employment opportunities (e.g. via relevant vocational, off-farm training). The connection between buffers and passports must also be acknowledged. To the extent that buffers (in effect, through various forms of social insurance) offer longer term security, so they encourage families into more risk-taking and personal investment in passports. Altering the time preference behaviour of clients is the key to a development breakthrough in the region, in which the meeting of immediate, practical needs creates the conditions for overcoming uncertainty and discounting, leading to longer term, strategic investments.[5] This is the welfare/development link.

These arguments map well onto AKRSP's current vision for the future, which is captured in three main organisational priorities: institutional development, resource development, and enterprise development. These can be represented as respectively largely addressing: buffers, buffers/passports and passports. Put in another way, institutional development embraces post VO forms of social mobilisation and collective action which includes poverty targeting and the development of new social insurance, safety net and social protection 'products' (either through microfinance or local philanthropy in the absence of any prospect of meaningful state cover). Resource development represents a continuation of mainstream support for the natural and infrastructural resource base of the society, which underpins more market oriented forms of economic development as well as public goods. And enterprise development speaks for itself as the stimulation of more economic activity in the region in order to expand profits, investment, employment, and savings in order to reduce dependency upon precarious donations (international as well as national and local). Clearly there is a strong 'trickle down' assumption in the enterprise development dimension, thus acknowledging that not all passports are equal: a Pareto Optimum choice in other words. However, this implied divorce between equality and poverty is partially offset in strategic terms by the presence of, provision of, or support for buffers.

As we pursue this argument through the following account of poverty and livelihoods in the region, there is a further uncomfortable process to consider. In the account which follows, migration in various forms has been a crucial livelihood option providing complete exits for some families from the region as they pursue their livelihoods in more favourable economic environments, and partial exits for others, either from the region or from the more difficult and less productive geographical parts of it. However, we might ask the question, why has there not been more out-migration from such a hostile environment for successful livelihoods? This is a general question for remoter, mountain regions, especially those considered to be mountain deserts to a large degree. Has the support for rural clients over the last two decades had the perverse effect of slowing up processes of out-migration and maintaining the population in an ultimately untenable environment for contemporary global standards of living? Has the continuation of the Mir and Mehtar traditions of investing in new land development and settlement in effect held the population in a low-level equilibrium trap, when a promotion of out-migration might have offered more opportunities for personal development? In other words, has the development of the region been at the expense of the underdevelopment of its people?

This stark, unpleasant question has the virtue of drawing our attention to other aspects of livelihoods and indeed broader dimensions of quality of life in which aspects of material poverty (as observed by outsiders) are traded off against other virtues of continuing to live in one's home territory: social and cultural inclusion, entailing effective informal, local rights;[6] non-discriminatory behaviour by economically dominant classes; opportunities for risk-spreading between agriculture and pastoral options; the prospect of economic take-off through political settlement and trade expansion; close kin solidarities; as well as the perceived dangers of trying to compete successfully in alien localities without established social and cultural resources close to hand.[7] Indeed the strength and attraction of these social resources does underpin a wider, social capital conducive to the creation and maintenance of public goods through which joint projects can and have been very successfully achieved. In this sense, it is interesting to reflect that while Period II (above) may reveal a more complex class stratification, we should not confuse this with class relations. While there is evidence of differentiation and inequality, and certainly an exercise of social power through the quality of personal networks, these are not societies characterised by landlord–tenant, money lender–borrower exploitation as is found elsewhere in South Asia. The sense of social and cultural inclusiveness is an antidote to the idea of alienation, and has certainly supported strong participation in programmes and resources offered by AKRSP, although that generalisation has to be qualified by the variation in cultural attitudes by sect difference, as indicated in Chapter 1. All these social and cultural factors around the theme of identity go some way in negating the harsh 'underdevelopment' question.

POVERTY TRENDS OVER THE LAST TWO DECADES

The experience of poverty and livelihoods has clearly not remained static over the last two decades from the beginnings of AKRSP in the early 1980s. In considering these changes, it is not the intention yet to attribute causation to AKRSP's interventions but to recognise that other 'primary drivers of change' have also been in play, such as the Karakoram Highway and link roads, the strong army presence in parts of the NAC, government performance (including law and order), the presence of other development and welfare agencies (including therefore the philanthropic ones), the influx of Afghan refugees (especially in Chitral), some, often sporadic and short lived, increases in tourism (always threatened by overall security conditions). It is also true that some of these drivers for change have met their own resistance, so the process has to be understood dialectically rather than in simple, linear, terms of modernisation. And again, we have to be wary of generalisation even over such a small population due to the diversity noted above.

The quantitative evidence offered below indicates that there has been a phenomenal growth in the incomes of the people in NAC, with per capita incomes more than doubling over the last twelve years (see Table 2.2 below). This growth further indicates that there has been a significant catching up with the national economy. It is estimated that incomes have increased from about one third of national average per capita incomes (PCI) in 1991 to about two thirds of the national PCI in 2001. The issue is whether this average growth has been evenly distributed across the region. For example, this catching up was even higher in the growth poles of the Northern Areas such as Gilgit, where per capita incomes were at 70 per cent of the national PCI averages in 2001.

Table 2.2. Trends in per capita incomes (Rs: base year 1991)

	Gilgit	Chitral	Astore	Baltistan	Programme
1991	3,134	3,233	2,850	2,384	2,939
1994	4,769	4,312	2,790	3,407	3,976
1997	6,074	4,337	3,684	4,771	4,851
2001	7,402	4,886	4,870	6,078	6,198

Source: Data from Household Income & Expenditure Survey Series, AKRSP.

While the evidence suggests that a majority of households in NAC have benefited from this income growth even using the national poverty line assumption, 34 per cent of the population is still below the poverty line (certainly an improvement from the 80 per cent below the poverty line when AKRSP started its operations).

Table 2.3. Trends in poverty: percentage below the poverty line

	Gilgit	Chitral	Astore	Baltistan	Programme
1991	62	68	64	76	67
1994	38	51	72	65	54
1997	35	50	62	43	45
2001	29	42	38	34	34

Source: Data from Household Income & Expenditure Survey Series, AKRSP.

Thus, while there has been a considerable overall reduction in the incidence of poverty in the programme area, it can be clearly seen from the table above that there have been differential gains in poverty reduction across the region. Furthermore, for regions like Chitral which started more or less at the same poverty level in 1991, the reduction in poverty has been very slow vis-à-vis other regions in the programme area. Some of the reasons behind these differential gains in poverty are discussed in the later sections. It is important to note that the head count ratios given above do not tell the full story, therefore some additional measures of poverty have been presented in the table below:

Table 2.4. Measures of poverty for the programme area

	Head count Index (%)	Depth of Poverty	Intensity of Poverty	Severity of Poverty
1991	67	0.53	0.36	0.75
1994	54	0.49	0.27	0.55
1997	45	0.42	0.19	0.41
2001	34	0.38	0.13	0.27

Source: Data from Household Income & Expenditure Survey Series, AKRSP.

All the measures of poverty, including depth (Poverty Gap), intensity (Poverty Gap Index), and severity (Sen's Poverty Index) show a decline in the incidence of poverty in the programme area. Simply put, not only has there been a reduction in the number of people living below the poverty line, but the consumption levels of the people still living below the poverty line have also improved over time. In other words, every one has gained something out of the growth witnessed in the programme area. However, the magnitude of gains in incomes and poverty reduction has varied across different regions and groups.

Nevertheless, three important things should be borne in mind while drawing conclusions from the income and poverty trends presented above. First, a large proportion (34 per cent) is still suffering from poverty. Furthermore, these estimates, as hinted at earlier, are based on the national poverty line (Rs. 650 per person per month in 1998–99 adjusted for inflation over time), which actually represents a fairly low level of consumption. If we increase the consumption levels to those of internationally accepted standards, the poverty figures for the area dramatically increase. Second, there is a significant variation in the incidence of poverty across geographic and social groups and these variations do have important implications for AKRSP future policy. Third, the poverty figures mentioned above talk about but one dimension of poverty: income poverty. From a multidimensional perspective of poverty, many other considerations are worth keeping in mind to do justice to the complex debate on poverty and livelihoods.

FACTORS AND PROCESSES AFFECTING LIVELIHOODS

Many factors have played their role in sketching this complex picture of poverty and livelihoods in the NAC. There are trends like improved communication, availability of new off-farm opportunities such as tourism, jobs in the public and private sectors, and increased access to social sector services which have positively affected the livelihoods of communities in the NAC. At the same time, negative trends such as degradation of natural resources, fragmentation of landholding, and price hikes on essential inputs and consumption goods have adversely affected livelihood outcomes. Trends like migration have had both positive and negative affects on livelihoods by enhancing access to new markets and opportunities on the one hand and increasing the vulnerability of those who are left behind on the other. The effect of these trends has varied across geographic, ethnic/social, and gender groups. The following paragraphs summarise some of the key trends and processes which have had important implications for the poverty and livelihoods experienced in the NAC.

Fragmentation of Farm Holdings

Perhaps the most significant process affecting all families has been the fragmentation of farm holdings and thus smaller holdings per household. With land as the essential inheritance entitlement and productive asset for sons (the rights of daughters to their father's land are usually transformed into movable assets at the point of the daughter's transfer to her groom's household), the principle of multiple inheritance of land among sons prevails. Multiple inheritance is sustainable in production and family survival terms as long as several conditions apply. First, infant mortality is high, producing fewer surviving sons. Secondly, when either new land is being brought into cultivation (via new irrigation channels) and/or migration (often at the feudal lord's request) to virgin cultivable land in the region continue to be an option. It is revealing, in interviews with village informants, that most report a migration history in their parents' or grandparents' generation, but very few have moved themselves. This shows the closing up of the rural–rural migration option, perhaps influenced by the prospect of reclamation of barren land via improved irrigation engineering in their residential locations. The multiple inheritance principle threatens to be unsustainable for survival when more sons survive as a result of improved access to medical services, improved nutrition (perhaps aided by remittance income) and extended life expectancy of parents (especially enabling fathers to take second, fertile, wives). The whole region has experienced population growth above the high rate for Pakistan over the last two decades. It is experiencing the classic demographic transition: a decline in mortality alongside retention of high fertility.

This fragmentation of farm holdings and reduction in land size per household has several immediate and obvious knock-on effects. First, it reduces the capacity of the household to survive from land and livestock alone. Second, it creates pressures for increasing the productivity of remaining landholdings per household, though this can lead to soil exhaustion and of course alters production input-output ratios. Third, it reduces the capacity to feed the same *pro rata* head of livestock per household member: partly due to increased pressures on common grazing in upper pastures, partly due to lower fodder levels from smaller holdings (unless partial double cropping has been introduced to compensate), and partly due to reduced common grazing around the village as land use is intensified for other purposes. Fourth, in reducing the farm based subsistence prospects per household, there is greater pressure to seek off-farm sources of income either within the local agrarian economy, other local employment options (e.g. connected to tourism), or further afield including down-country outside the region altogether. Fifth, this increases the need for education and training in other knowledge and transferable skills.

Positive and Negative Diversification

The NACIHS reveals clear evidence of the increasing significance of off-farm sources of income, though unevenly distributed across the wealth range. In 2001, households in the NAC drew more than 50 per cent of their total incomes from non-farm sources. The share of non-farm income was highest for the wealthiest group, i.e. the top 20 per cent of the population accounting for 65 per cent of total incomes compared to the bottom 20 per cent of the population which drew approximately 40 per cent of their incomes from non-farm sources. Poorer families remain more dependent on farm income, even though they also have smaller per capita holdings. A superior capacity to diversify out of farm based subsistence also has a positive inter-generational effect upon fragmentation by removing some sons from an inheritance share in holdings. The need and the opportunity to diversify out of farming (including livestock) have fortunately coincided. There is some co-variance with 'need' prompted by population growth, due to improved medical services and communications also providing 'opportunities' to access wider education and employment. Thus rural–rural migration has essentially been replaced by rural–urban migration, with 'urban' ranging between local growth poles, longer established regional centres, and further away, down-country. The partial exception to an urban destination is road construction and maintenance employment which has obviously been significant over the last 25 years, not only with the KKH but all the link and smaller feeder road development. It is important, then, to distinguish between varied forms of diversification away from reliance upon the farm. Stronger families have been able to diversify positively, having the resources and/or kin and other social connections to invest in education and assist sons (and occasionally and more recently daughters, especially in the Ismaili communities) into professional or business opportunities with a relatively high return. They in turn are able to repeat similar processes across their extended joint families (though see discussion on individualisation, below), thus reproducing strength (see Box 2.1 for an example from Gilgit region). Weaker families at the outset of these two decades could only negatively diversify through unskilled and low return construction or other manual work for males either in the region, or down-country. Clearly the income sources from negative diversification are valuable in the short term but have little longer term structural significance for taking the family out of poverty. These two contrasting trajectories for diversification out of farm based subsistence have wider implications for the coherence and solidarity of the communities, as further inequalities between families appear. These trends pose complex strategic and policy questions for external agencies like AKRSP which will be explored below.

Box 2.1. An example of diversification: Gilgit region

The evidence suggests that non-farm sources of income have gained considerable importance in the lives of the people in the NAC in general and Gilgit region in particular. However, the type and nature of diversification varies across valleys within the Gilgit region and evidence suggests that some communities have gained more from diversification than others.

Table 2.5. Primary occupation of male workforce and average incomes (%)

	Farming	Government Jobs	Private Jobs	Business	Skilled Labour	Unskilled Labour
Hunza	28	20 (92)[a]	16 (218)	11 (109)	16 (49)	4 (19)
Nagar	33	19 (57)	6 (28)	8 (130)	21 (50)	4 (25)
Punyal/ Ishkoman	45	28 (57)	6 (55)	1 (60)	11 (47)	6 (20)
Gupis/Yasin	41	25 (51)	4 (37)	4 (45)	14 (30)	7 (15)

[a] The numbers in parentheses are average annual incomes (thousand Rs) from each column.
Source: Malik and Piracha (forthcoming) 'Economic Transition in Hunza and Nagar Valley'.

The table above shows that in 2001 about 66 per cent of the total male workforce in Hunza had adopted the non-farm sector as their primary occupation. This was the highest proportion in the region. Furthermore, what differentiates Hunza from elsewhere in the region is employment in the private sector and self-employment (business). These are the two highest rewarding sectors within all the occupations adopted by people in the Northern Areas (see the figures in parentheses). In these two sectors (i.e. private jobs and business), the returns accruing to the workforce from Nagar and Hunza were higher than those of other valleys in Ghizer district (i.e. Gupis and Punyal). The overall trend in the table suggests that the valleys along the KKH (Hunza and Nagar) have experienced more diversification into the non-farm sector than those valleys away from the KKH (i.e. Ghizer).

Economic Inequality

As noted in the earlier sections, NAC was justifiably characterised as an economy of very low economic differentiation two or three decades ago. Most of the households were trapped in low-productivity, subsistence modes of farming and hence experienced persistent poverty. From the early nineties, we see a completely different picture where there is a clear economic differentiation among various population groups as revealed in the table below. Thus in 2001 (the latest figures available), approximately half of the incomes in the NAC accrued to the top 20 per cent of the population while the bottom 20 per cent of the population was only surviving on 6 per cent of the total incomes. Furthermore, there has been no major change in the distribution of incomes over the last decade (there was a slight improvement in the economic conditions of the bottom 20 per cent of the population whose share rose to 6 per cent from 2 per cent between 1991 and 2001).

Table 2.6. Inequality in the programme area (% of population in each income quintile)

	1991	1994	1997	2001
Lowest 20% households	2	4	5	6
Lower middle 20% households	10	10	10	11
Middle 20% households	16	16	16	15
Upper middle 20% households	23	23	23	21
Highest 20% households	49	48	46	47

Source: Data from Household Income & Expenditure Survey Series, AKRSP.

Two tentative conclusions can be drawn from the trends in inequality presented above. First, even when there was low differentiation in the economy two or three decades ago, there existed an extremely poor class (a class comprising of individual households across the programme area who suffered from idiosyncratic factors as well as groups of communities living in the remotest and marginalised areas) whose share has not significantly improved to date. Second, the increase in economic inequality has not been a linear process in the NAC. In other words, inequality sharply increased in the late seventies and throughout the eighties mainly due to the differential access of communities to emerging opportunities such as KKH and education in different localities. This geographic variation in the distribution of public goods, however, narrowed during the '90s as the marginalised areas received increased investment for infrastructure and other social protection measures. As a result of this narrowed gap in access to public goods across the regions, economic inequalities did not widen any further in the late 1990s but, in fact, started to improve.

Social Differentiation Arising from Off-Farm Diversification

The increasing reliance upon non-farm sources of income through diversification sets in motion significant processes of social differentiation, whether in the form of inequality or simply differences between families in the way that subsistence and livelihoods are pursued. Put simply, we might accept that in the past there were only minor variations between families in lifestyle. Neighbours (often therefore kin) had the same combination of agricultural and livestock management activities, and identical daily and seasonal patterns to their labour inputs and incomes. In other words, they were bound together by both residential proximity and similarity in the economic, social and cultural dimensions of their livelihoods. Durkheim referred to this as mechanical solidarity, derived from a low variation in the division of labour. Of course, there were some specialist occupations providing goods and services to the main peasant population (blacksmiths, potters, carpenters, mullahs and so on), but even these specialists were also peasants with land. By sharing their lives, places of worship and other *rites de passage*, households were bound together socially by the absence of differentiation between themselves: shared interests, shared customs and habits, shared values and beliefs, shared visions and aspirations. Any deviation from these would threaten unity and the basis of the necessary collective action to manage public goods and common property. These social conditions were an important basis for AKRSP's strategies of social mobilisation. Thus any structural shift from these conditions to greater social differentiation, through variation and diversity in lifestyles and livelihoods, challenges the institutional traditions of the society.[8] The issue for this chapter is the effect of this socio-economic differentiation upon livelihoods trajectories and the increasing complexity of poverty. Are people now poor in different ways from before? And is poverty less universal across the region and more specific? Certainly, some families in some areas have made progress in securing and enhancing their livelihoods while others have not. In travelling across the region, this differentiation is evident between valleys, between villages, and between families in villages. This differentiation has to be understood in terms of a set of interconnected variables: location and elevation, migration, communications, household demography, cultural attitudes, market penetration, access to social sector services, access to other infrastructural public goods, membership of successful common property institutions, inclusion in socially defined social protection and safety nets.

Geographical Differentiation: Centre-Periphery

Location and elevation have always been key determinants of life chances in the region. But the significance of the variable has been exacerbated over the last two decades. Thus it is necessary to have a centre–periphery conception of the geographical distribution of livelihoods across the region. Higher elevation settlement usually correlates with remoteness and inaccessibility, unless connected to the main KKH. Higher settlements are single-cropped areas due to the longer winter, and have always entailed some seasonal out-migration of males to lower elevation opportunities. Lower elevation settlements, more towards the lower opening of valleys to other valley bottoms, are more likely to be double-cropped with longer summer seasons. The topography is less steep, thus reducing erosion. A wider variety of subsistence and fodder crops can be grown. Irrigation water is available for longer, thus adding to the productivity of land. The marginally warmer climate (certainly over a longer part of the year) reduces the annual demand for wood fuel. Communications are better for casual employment and access to services. Educational facilities are nearer. Growth poles have emerged at the intersection of major valley bottoms, such as Gakuch in Ghizer/Punyal or Buni in upper Chitral. There are variations to these general patterns. Some upper valleys may attract tourists and therefore economic opportunities. Even some settlements lower down are disfavoured by shadow and reduced sunlight hours. Cultural flexibility to change and opportunities may also offset location constraints. Proximity to main highways is always an advantage.

Migration: Key Livelihoods Option

Migration options have been partially discussed above. The expansion of migration in various forms has obviously been the main livelihoods story of the last two decades. Most observers will highlight the increased traffic with towns down-country, outside the region altogether. Different communities in the North have built up particular connections and destinations down-country. Thus, for example, may Ismailis in Buni, Upper Chitral, travel to Karachi for work and education. Sunnis in Lower Chitral have more connections with Peshawar. Rawalpindi and Islamabad attract more communities from Gilgit and Nagar/Hunza to the north of the region. As noted above in the discussion about contrasting forms of diversification, down-country migration may represent progress for the family with a son, or occasionally a daughter, entering a secure, relatively well-paid profession (often within some branch of government), or a successful business. But for others, the migration may only reflect a coping strategy as family members enter precarious, unskilled employment. It is also now recognised that the household strategy of investing in education as access to down-country higher value employment is beginning to unravel, with over-educated, under-employed returnees to the region. Status considerations make such returnees (often supported by their status-conscious fathers) reluctant to re-engage in farm work.

However, migration as a livelihoods strategy is not only confined to the examples above. There has always been recruitment to the army and other para-military forces (such as the Chitral Scouts—primarily a border security force, under the command of gazetted army officers). Sometimes this service will be in the regional locality, but if recruited to the army then service further afield is likely, involving year long absences with short annual leave. The livelihoods and development significance of army or army-related employment cannot be underestimated. It represents a major source of off-farm remittance income into many families, and indeed may compensate significantly for the poor geographical location of those families, since army recruits from harsh localities can be the best qualification for the sustained hardships of mountain or desert warfare. But in addition to the army, there is also migration within the region, especially from the higher to lower elevations, and now markedly to growth poles. These migrations have become an important part of household livelihood strategy with inter-generational implications. The move to lower elevations, attracted also by enhanced employment opportunities, is often initiated by young adult males perhaps in conjunction with wives. They may have been able to acquire land through some ancestral claim, or because it is newly reclaimed land with unknown potential and therefore of less interest to the locals (for example a patch of land above Ayun in Lower Chitral, being settled by in-migrants from Mulko in Upper Chitral). They certainly offer themselves for employment as artisans, construction workers, or in the bazaar. They are certainly interested in accessing education for their children. And they are attracted by less harsh winters. Parents are initially left behind to maintain the original farm, with assistance from the migrant during the busy summer months. As parents become more dependent upon their migrated children, so eventually they also move down to lower elevations to join their adult children, and take on grandchild care roles. Whether this pattern of migration will eventually drain the upper elevations of population remains to be seen, though that prospect is certainly an important development policy consideration. Clearly the constraint to this kind of migration is determined by the absorption capacity of the lower elevations in terms of cultivable land and residential space availability, and employment opportunities. Of course, there is also internal migration to the larger towns such as Gilgit and Chitral, as well as the smaller growth poles.

While the varied forms of migration indicated above have clearly contributed positively to individual and family livelihoods through remittances or permanent re-location, it is interesting to reflect upon the condition of those who have not migrated, or who have no migrant dimension in their income portfolio. Have they been kept, artificially as it were, in the region, facing narrower choices, and reliant only upon the local natural resource base? Has the AKRSP support for the resource base retained them in the region when they might otherwise have migrated too? Also, those left behind tend to be weaker in social status and less skilled than those who have departed (temporarily, seasonally or permanently). How does this affect the quality of social institutions of collective action, for example? Is a significant and useful voice removed from the local society? Are those left behind therefore more vulnerable, more stigmatised as failures? And indeed, are those left behind enduring heavier workloads, especially women in female-managed households where the remittance income hardly compensates beyond spreading risk across more income sources.

Communications: differential isolation

To a considerable extent, the communications variable is represented by the road network. In the Northern Areas, this is dominated by the KKH and the metalled roads linked to it, with unmade feeder roads reaching beyond the linked ones. Although the KKH can be vulnerable to landslides (especially lower down in the Kohistan ravines), these blockages rarely last for more than a few days. Otherwise there is year round accessibility which has a profound effect upon people's livelihood options as well as market integration. A jeep, car or bus can travel from Islamabad to Gilgit in about twelve hours. (From Skardu to the KKH just below Gilgit and onto Islamabad is about 26 hours). A heavily laden truck might take three days. In Chitral, the Lowari Pass at the southern end of the district is closed for about six months of the year by snow. (There is a winter route via the Kunar river and Nuristan in Afghanistan, but this is currently very insecure for Pakistani travellers.) Within Chitral, a metalled road extends from Drosh in the South to Buni in Mastuj sub-division in the North. It is likely that this metalled road will soon reach Mastuj itself. Presently the unmade road between Buni and Mastuj, and beyond either northwards up the Yakhun valley or eastwards over the Shandur Pass is passable to jeeps in the summer, but the winter closes the Shandur Pass (and the link to Gilgit and the KKH) and can even make Mastuj occasionally inaccessible after a heavy snowfall at valley bottom level (approximately 7000 feet). Under these conditions, people have to plan for the winter both for out-migration (e.g. for males on down-country construction work, or movement to lower elevation growth poles) and/or for storage of fuel and food. The entire rhythm of the year is defined by these circumstances, and there is a combined psychology of siege and mutuality, which sets limits to levels of conflict and fission. The elite of Chitral do have winter access to Pakistan International Airlines flights in and out of the valley, but others would have to struggle over the passes on foot or with donkeys, and pick up transport on the South side of the Lowari in Dir. In the summer, Chitral to Peshawar is about twelve hours. In the summer over the last two decades until 2002, there has also been an influx of Afghans and their livestock from the passes to the northwest of the district from Afghan Badakhshan.

The impact of this differential access can be seen in Figure 2.4 below. The figure shows the comparison between AKRSP's member and non-member households in two different localities—Gilgit and Chitral districts. The Chitral district represents a case of low road access and the Gilgit district is placed under high road access. It should be noted that in these two districts, besides the difference in accessibility, per capita government spending also varies with Gilgit district receiving significantly higher per capita investment. The graph shows that there is a clear difference between per capita incomes of households in these two different localities (it should be noted that these two localities had very similar per capita incomes in the 1980s). In 2001, the per capita incomes of non-members were about Rs. 8,800 in Chitral district compared to Rs. 13,000 in Gilgit district. However, the incomes of Village and Women's Organisation (V/WO) members were higher at Rs. 15,000 and Rs. 25,000 for Chitral and Gilgit respectively. While many endogenous and exogenous factors may have contributed to this difference, road access seems to be one of the major contributory factors in this regard. It is interesting to note how increased government investment, particularly in large-scale infrastructure, enhances the effectiveness of development inputs given by agencies like AKRSP.

Figure 2.4. The impact of accessibility on incomes

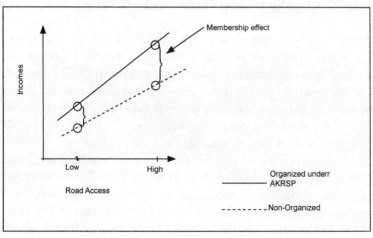

Source: Malik and Piracha (2003).

The impact of metalled roads cannot be underestimated. Before the late 1990s, Chitral town to Buni was five hours, with a further two or more on to Mastuj. Effectively, a short day's drive. Now it is one and a half hours to Buni and a further hour to Mastuj (the unmade road has been upgraded prior to metalling.) With the Mulko and Turkho valleys also linking to Buni (as a growth pole), these improvements are bringing much of Upper Chitral into much closer association with Lower Chitral and the district HQ. This is certainly facilitating product and labour market integration within the district, offering wider off-farm subsistence options. This reduces, for example, the need for families to accumulate full winter storage in the autumn, if remittances are providing income for purchases from other market centres during the winter season (assuming that traders have adequately predicted winter market demand and have brought in sufficient supplies). Obviously in the Northern Areas, this widening of off-farm livelihoods options is significantly assisted by the KKH and its linked roads, even into frozen Skardu during the winter.

Roads as Public Goods: Not Socially Neutral

As public goods, improved road networks do not equally impact upon the livelihoods of local residents. There have been many studies[9] demonstrating the uneven outcomes of roads. They are not socially neutral. And indeed, the outcome may not be Pareto optimality, if for example the external availability of mass priced supplies undermines local shopkeepers and puts them out of business, or if an 'export' demand for local produce sets off higher local subsistence prices. Farmers with adequate holdings and capital may make considerable (often short-term) gains from innovation (e.g. the production of table and seed potato for down-country traders) while other farmers cannot enter this market and perhaps in the end lose their land to an increasingly commercialised sub-set of farmers. At the same time, continuing the potato story, prices of inputs such as fertiliser and seed may move up as yield co-efficients decline and farm prices come down, with trader-buyers always having the option of re-locating their product sources to other competing areas. External traders ('Pathans' are often cited in this context) with superior down-country connections can displace local ones. Wages for localised construction employment (e.g. road maintenance) can be depressed by the ease of non-local in-migration and competition. And finally, some families have internal demographic structures (see below) which enable them to seize out-migration opportunities while others do not.

Media access: Broadening Horizons, Rising Expectations

Of course, 'communications' is not just about roads. Over the last decade, the rise of the satellite dish and telecommunications have enabled some families to access information and to be exposed to other cultures, values and lifestyles via the television. There is also internet access in some areas and for a privileged few (often those working in government or non-government agencies). Of course, any media that requires literacy (i.e. including newspapers with national news which are now more available in NAC) is immediately confined to a narrow elite and men in particular, given the remaining low levels of literacy. Education and training opportunities are similarly confined socially, especially if early primary schooling has not been sustained into secondary levels. The opportunity cost of secondary education, as well as its direct financial cost, precludes much of the population, even more so outside the Ismaili areas. Those families who have invested in education, or who have been within the catchment of Aga Khan Education Services (AKES) subsidised provision (i.e. especially for girls), have expanded their livelihoods portfolio as off-farm sources of income become more significant and necessary. However, recession in the down-country economy has reduced the range of employment opportunities for educated young men with potential negative local social outcomes as a result, including crime. Wider communications, particularly through the television (which is more widely accessible), also has the effect of reducing the monopoly of local elders and religious leaders over values, cultural principles and symbols. These influences can also affect relationships within the family, perhaps reducing the authority of male elders to direct work and allocate key opportunities. They also have an effect upon developing individualist perspectives and cognitions at the expense of collective ones.

Demographic Differentiation: Cyclical Fortunes or Stratified Outcomes

Although we are pursuing an argument here about socio-economic differentiation arising out of the increasing reliance upon off-farm income interacting with new opportunities, we also have to consider the impact of demographic differentiation upon this process. To the extent that we are observing a disappearing peasantry,[10] then the demographic composition of families interacting with change represents a key point of departure for their fortunes. Indeed, some would argue for peasant societies (Ellis 2000a, 2000b) that demographic differentiation is more significant, even offering the prospect of a cyclical process in family fortunes.[11] At its most obvious, the idea of destitution as captured in local languages usually refers to the absence of an adult working male with patriarchal responsibilities. We can certainly see a correlation between female-headed families and extreme poverty, despite some exceptions of positive diversification. But the issue of household composition goes beyond the presence or absence of a patriarch. Is the household nucleated or extended? If extended is it 'joint' with a number of co-habiting adult brothers, or simply three-generational? What is the composition of sons and daughters in relation to landholding and other property, and how do dowry or brideprice arrangements impact upon household fortunes with different gender compositions? On top of these variables, each household goes through a domestic life cycle in which its dependency ratio changes over time, requiring more or less labour input per unit of labour worker available, relative to consumption needs. The higher the consumer–worker ratio, the more labour input per worker required. Of course, the productivity of this labour (determined by its human capital content and market leverage), its location and its security will also matter in this calculation. A high productivity breadwinner may compensate for several lower value ones.

Characteristics of a Poor Family

What general conclusions arise from this complexity? Poorer families: are at a weak point in their dependency ratio; have a higher proportion of under-educated lower value workers; are net exporters of dowry due to the sibling ratio (involving net losses of fixed as well as transferable assets); are negatively diversifying, if at all; have fewer active members to spread across a wider portfolio of earning options thus concentrating risk; have over-dependency upon a single male, engaged in stressful manual work and thus always vulnerable to ill-health and reduced life expectancy. Such households might, as a result of these demographic constraints, find that they are weaker with respect to other resources including social and cultural ones—but more of that below. Basically such households can never save enough in the present to invest for the future, and so can never get onto a securer platform. They can never recover from the weak point in their domestic life cycle. However, this description also connects to the issue of poverty over time: is it chronic or transitory and churning? The issue for empirical analysis is whether generally we are looking at cyclical experiences of poverty (churning) or whether households are able to seize the opportunities at the top of the domestic life cycle (i.e. at the most favourable point in the dependency ratio) to graduate permanently? In other words, does demographic differentiation lead to churning of fortunes, or does it lead to sustained socio-economic differentiation with those households well-placed demographically when new opportunities arose gaining permanent rewards and advantage? The latter outcome is more likely, as some households get ahead through positive diversification and never look back. If demographic differentiation leads to socio-economic inequality in this way, then poverty reduction programmes have to take note.

Cultural Attributes of Poverty

We referred above to the relation between communications and changing cultural attitudes, but the relation between poverty, change and culture goes beyond this. Although cultural variables cannot be fully explored in this chapter, some observations must be made in the context of gender, religion and sectarian tradition over the last two decades. Bringing these elements together, are some households (other socio-economic variables being equal) more predisposed to innovate, experiment and take risks than others? In other words, poverty may be a cause of conservatism because the socio-economic circumstances of poverty require a substantial discounting of the future (Wood 2003), but to what extent is conservatism a cause of poverty? Or, are conservative households likely to be poorer than others? It is not the intention to be judgemental about values, beliefs and attitudes embodied within culture, with conservatism regarded negatively, rather to examine the relationship between conservatism and poverty.

Clearly there exists a varying receptivity towards change among the followers of different sects of Islam. There are the followers of branches of Islam who tend to judge the desirability of change in the context of fixed principles and prescriptions. By contrast, there are other more flexible branches of Islam, in which the relativity of means adjusted to contemporary realities and possibilities are continuously debated and advocated. This is most evident in the principle of His Highness the Aga Khan as the living Imam of the Ismaili community, with responsibility to offer prescriptions relevant to the present day, and to live out universal principles by his example. This is a kin based, descent role performing similar functions to nominated, selected and elected equivalent positions in other sects and confessional faiths. Perhaps the conclusion is that members of the Ismaili community are all led, to the extent of their individual abilities, in a way that embraces change, including access to literacy and education, as long as essential universal principles are maintained, while there is variation in other sects with a correlation between more fixed traditions and peasant-based societies characterised by low literacy levels.

Exposure to other Cultural Practices and Values

These variations do impact upon the social practices of patriarchy as well as attitudes towards human capital investment and risk taking. They also affect the degree of openness to external cultures and influences coming through 'communications' (including, therefore, market penetration), but also specifically coming through the army (as institutionally representative of the modern state in NAC), development agencies (including the values and priorities of external donors) and tourist visitors. The army offers many opportunities for training and skill development. It also represents another source of authority to local elders and religious leaders, thus permitting alternative loci of respect. Army commanders have to prove themselves to their men, so that the merit principle gets established. Service outside the immediate locality also obliges recruits to serve alongside other ethnic groups and to learn a tolerance for other ways of doing things. Empathy is an important principle of camaraderie. It has been interesting to observe the prevalence of retired ranks (*subadars*, *subadar-majors*, and so on) in activist and community leadership positions with AKRSP on their retirement from the army. They have internalised a more complete recognition of the agency's development agenda, and the rationality required to reach objectives and targets. The families with the highest army connections tend to be the more dynamic and progressive in the region. Obviously they eventually acquire the advantage of a lump sum pension to deploy (often, as it happens, in failed shop-keeping enterprises in locally saturated markets) which assists in the graduation from poverty as well as setting role models for younger male members. The development agencies in the region have been strongly associated with the Aga Khan Development Network (AKDN), so it is small wonder that the counterpart Ismaili community has been the most accommodating of its initiatives. Thus there has been a basic trust in AKRSP's 'superior' knowledge about development innovation. This has also transferred across into respect for other agencies (both the donors to AKDN, but also other NGOs such as the World Conservation Union (IUCN) or WWF) as well as some government initiatives—

for example the Chitral Area Development Programme (CADP) in Lower Chitral which was modelled on the AKRSP, but arising from the provincial government in Peshawar.

Expansion of the Labour Market

This combination of improved communications, demographic cycle opportunities and cultural attitudes all affect the way individuals, families and communities interact with the market and expanded market opportunities over the last two decades since AKRSP started. Although in a patchy, non-uniform way, significant parts of the society (socially and geographically) have moved beyond the petty commodity production and exchange of peasant societies to a more market-oriented economic culture. Perhaps most obviously, given farm fragmentation and the rising importance of off-farm incomes, the expansion of the labour market has been the most important. We referred above to a contrast between positive and negative diversification in this regard, correlated to educational levels and other wealth variables for a family, including its dependency ratio. There can be little doubt that an expansion of off-farm labour market opportunities both locally and down-country has differentiated the fortunes of local families, enabling some to graduate, either sustainably or for short periods of temporary additional income, while leaving others behind in poverty, and more vulnerable to family crises. Mobility and migration, along with skills levels, are the key variables in accessing different levels of value in these labour markets. With the exception of the 'proximity to KKH' variable, generally those in the more Northern, upper elevation areas of NAC could be expected to have the most problems in accessing both NAC and down-country labour markets. A further exception is army recruitment, noted above. However for Chitral and Gilgit/Hunza/Ghizer, these are predominantly Ismaili communities, and certainly many families in these communities have been culturally more ready to be mobile and to acquire new skills and thus enter wider labour markets. This gives some explanatory weight to the significance of cultural variables in graduating from poverty. Other remote communities in Astore or Nagar (respectively Sunni and Shia) for example have at best negatively rather than positively diversified. Baltistan, with a more unitary cultural system, displays the geographical access variable more clearly in accessing labour markets. One of the strategic conclusions from this kind of analysis, is that some communities require more investment in local natural resource based activities as a compensation for their greater labour market rigidity. Such investment may then connect them to other commodity markets.

New Commodity Markets: The Potato Example

Potato is a good example therefore of both commodity market expansion and comparative advantage for remoter, higher elevated areas where the high value seed potato is best ecologically situated to resist virus. However, the potato has also functioned as a differentiator between families. Those with appropriate land, family labour and capital to invest in high input production were able to secure significant incomes and wealth relevant to neighbours with a less favourable resource mix—at least in the short term until output prices fell while input prices for chemical fertiliser rose. This possibly short-term bonanza nevertheless enabled some families to move quickly ahead—purchasing residential land, building new houses, educating their children, and funding their entry into other business opportunities as well as down-country employment. Of course, families who financed these opportunities through debt have got into trouble when net returns on capital outlay declined, unless they have also been able to successfully default.

This example of commercialisation of agriculture and emergence of new cash crops such as potato needs to be seen in the context of government policy on agricultural subsidies. It is worth noting that the Northern Areas receive a substantial transport subsidy on wheat every year. As a result, people in the Northern Areas get wheat grain and wheat flour at more or less the same prices as one can get elsewhere in Pakistan. This subsidy works as an implicit incentive for the farmers in these remote valleys to grow more commercial crops like potato and other horticultural produce. One can argue that in the absence of this wheat subsidy and its reliable supply to the Northern Areas, farmers would have opted to grow cereal crops at their farms to enhance their grain security. Put differently, many households who were directly engaged in the Natural Resource Management (NRM) packages of AKRSP and other agencies could not have graduated, had there been no subsidy on wheat.

Tourism: Distribution of Opportunities

Other forms of market expansion have been less sharply divided between those included and excluded. Tourism, for example, certainly concentrates returns in the hands of the wealthy operators, often external to the local society (airlines, hotel chains, travel companies, transport operators). However there is also some trickle-down into local employment: porters, cooks, waiters, cleaners, laundry services, and so on. While international tourism has fluctuated according to global security events and is currently squeezed post-9/11, domestic in-country tourism may actually be on the increase. If tourism therefore remains and expands as a form of market penetration, then certainly a poverty focused agenda of redistributing the value added from tourism needs to be pursued. This is not a simple issue of promoting ecological tourism and building 'low tech' guest houses in poor, but beautiful localities. There has to be some synergy between the quality of facilities which attracts tourists in the first place and the spatial distribution of tourists themselves across the communities for exposure to a more local experience. Cooperation between larger and smaller 'providers' is therefore necessary in order to be more inclusive and to spread the livelihood opportunities from this market.

Market Integration through Trade: Imports and Local Produce

Clearly improved communications has brought more imported goods into the NAC: either from China to the North (despite various tariff restrictions still in force until the current World Trade Organisation (WTO) round is completed) or from down-country. The proliferation of goods in local markets has obviously provided expanded opportunities for retailing, with shops and bazaars appearing even in the remotest places. There is a process of market clearing occurring, with many of these shops going bust in over-saturated markets. Army pensions have functioned a little like microcredit in distorting local financial markets by artificially easing entry into a low absorptive retail market context. There has also been less convincing market integration through the expanded production of high value horticultural products in addition to potato discussed above. Obviously AKRSP has supported the expansion of fruit production through below channel land reclamation and nurseries, and through the introduction of processing and storage technologies. Transportation of produce for export out of the region remains a problem for fresh fruit, given communications constraints and the perishability/bruising characteristics of the product. Preserved fruits have been seen as the better option. While these options for farmers across NAC have been fairly inclusive, insofar as they are a meaningful addition in people's livelihoods, there is obviously again a bias towards those families who have superior access to the best fruit-growing land, and better communications access. Alongside fruit, there have been concerted efforts to expand seed production in vegetables for commercial sale both within the region and externally down-country through the 'North-South Seeds' company. Market integration through livestock has been limited for the original local populations of the region, with livestock still regarded mainly as a subsistence, insurance and capital asset (to be traded only at times of family crisis such as illness or ritual expenses). The buying and selling of livestock has, until recently, mainly involved incoming herds from Afghanistan, moving through the region (especially of course Chitral) on their way down-country, supervised by migrant or transient herdsmen and shepherds (*Gujars*). These movements have offered limited employment opportunities for locals, though they have expanded the availability of meat and dairy products in the local bazaars.

Commodification of Public Goods: The Electricity Example

A further dimension of market development has been the private or common property management of new public goods such as electricity, via micro-hydels. The management of old, traditional public goods such as irrigation water remain outside market relations with sharing of labour input and water distribution arrangements. They are embedded in longstanding socio-cultural institutions and are not easily commodified. However, uninstitutionalised resources like electricity from micro-hydels, where there is a significant material investment cost beyond labour and local materials as well as significant ongoing operations and maintenance costs, have developed internal market arrangements of charging though prices are regulated under common property arrangements (Lawson-MacDowall 2000). Electricity, as a partially commodified service, can have a crucially positive impact upon livelihoods and gender relations, improving the quality of life and sense of well-being. It also crucially contributes to the longer term development of human capital by enabling extended studying time and eventually accessing electronic communications (television and information technology). Its significance for livelihoods thus reminds us of the corresponding significance for those who are excluded, becoming a new dimension in our understanding of relative poverty in the region.

Access: Differential Needs of Non-Idiosyncratic and Idiosyncratically Poor

Finally in this overview of the last two decades in the NAC, coinciding with AKRSP's presence, there are several access dimensions, which determine livelihoods and potentially either reduce poverty or maintain people in poverty. For this discussion, we need to distinguish between two essential forms of poverty: non-idiosyncratic (or structural) and idiosyncratic. We refer again to these categories below, but the distinction basically refers to poverty which is experienced across a significant number of people for structural reasons (such as weak class position and a consequent lack of education and skills) and 'case' poverty which applies to particular families (there may be many of them) for specific reasons (such as reasons of old age without support of children, infirmity, illness, and other personal disasters). Thus, a general lack of access to infrastructural or social sector services such as education, skills training, curative health facilities, favourable public health conditions such as clean drinking water and sanitation negatively affects a whole 'class' of the population and accounts for non-idiosyncratic poverty, alongside other factors. For the idiosyncratically poor, however, in addition to these general access problems, they have access needs to safety nets and long-term forms of social protection (philanthropy, charity, *zakat* and so on). Returning, therefore, to the diversity across the NAC in terms of communications and participation in enhanced and new livelihoods opportunities, there is systemic differentiation between locations in terms of access to generic infrastructural and social sector services. This differentiation partially reflects geographical remoteness, but also, as noted above, cultural affinity with the providers of these services, especially infrastructural and other support interventions from AKRSP and social sector services from the Aga Khan Development Network (AKDN) such as AKES, Aga Khan Health Services (AKHS) and WASEP. To the extent that some communities, not geographically remote, exclude themselves culturally from the AKDN services, so they become more dependent either upon provincial or local government, or upon other non-government providers such as the Sarhad Rural Support Programme (SRSP) in lower Chitral (after the departure of the CADP in the late '90s). Thus, we have two types of poverty pockets with reference to these access variables: those without access to generic services for geographical or cultural reasons (non-idiosyncratic); and those specifically excluded (in the sense of being unable to take advantage of generic provision) when surrounding neighbours are included, and at the same time in need of access to more specific safety net and social protection services due respectively to vulnerability and chronic poverty.

AKRSP AND POVERTY REDUCTION

To recap, AKRSP has always had a poverty focus to its work. The whole of the Northern Areas and Chitral could easily be described as a poor area in the early '80s when its work started, with only a small minority of families having a secure and higher standard of living. With AKRSP and AKDN's efforts having an overall positive impact on the region, together with other initiatives from government and socio-economic trends more generally, the analysis and identification of poverty has become more complex. It is clear that while subsistence has been secured for many, vulnerability, insecurity and poverty remain widespread given the fragile natural resource environment and the generic weaknesses of the Pakistan economy which restricts the value of the down-country, out-migration strategies pursued by many families. Indeed, when looking at Pakistan as a whole, the incidence of poverty during the 1990s has actually increased to an overall level of about 30 per cent at the $1 a day poverty line and an alarming 84 per cent at the $2 a day figure (ADB Report on Pakistan Economy 2001).

The two main categories of poverty remaining in NAC are: geographically remoter areas at higher altitudes and/or at a greater distance from main highways and communications; and households within otherwise coping or improving communities, reflecting the rising social differentiation and inequalities of the region. There are also ever present economic, environmental and human resource threats which keep a further category in a constant state of high vulnerability to even minor crises. The story does not stop here as we have a significant proportion of the population living just above the poverty line and that segment can be termed as highly vulnerable. The following graph and table show the sensitivity of the head count index to the changes in income levels of households and where the poverty line is established.

Figure 2.5. Sensitivity of head count index to changes in incomes

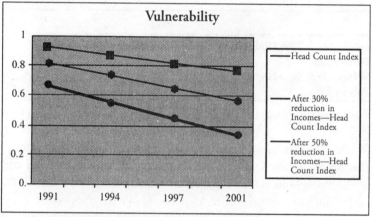

Source: Data from Household Income & Expenditure Survey Series, AKRSP.

Although not shown here, we know that the poverty figure may jump to 40 per cent from 34 per cent if per capita incomes of a household fall by 10 per cent. From the graph above, a drop of 30 per cent in income increases the incidence of poverty to 56 per cent, and this figure may go as high as 76 per cent if per capita incomes fall by 50 per cent. This shows that many households are, in fact, barely coping and live just above the poverty line. Further, the widening gap between sensitivity lines in the graph shows that the proportion of people living just above the poverty line has increased over time.

Another way of looking at vulnerability is to trace the sensitivity of poverty incidence to adjustments in the poverty line. If we take a slightly higher poverty line than the current one, we notice a sharp increase in the incidence of poverty. The table below shows that an additional 16 per cent of households fall into the poverty bracket if we raise the current poverty line by 25 per cent, and this figure jumps to 27 per cent (meaning a total of 34 per cent + 27 per cent = 61 per cent) if the current poverty line is raised by 50 per cent.

Table 2.7. Sensitivity of poverty to changes in the poverty line (%)

	1991	1994	1997	2001
Vulnerable at 25% Higher Poverty Line	11	13	12	16
Vulnerable at 50% Higher Poverty Line	17	22	23	27

Source: Data from Household Income & Expenditure Survey Series, AKRSP.

While three broad categories of poverty can now be identified,[12] the detail is much more complicated. Overall, with about one million people in NAC, 340,000 are estimated as poor with 90,000 to 100,000 of those classified as 'poorest'. Within the poorest, some are judged as having a capacity to work with appropriate support and others without such capacity, thus reflecting chronic poverty status. Above the 340,000 figure is another category of coping but highly vulnerable. If we use the 25 per cent higher poverty line, then we find that about 50 per cent of the population of NAC remains in a precarious condition of poverty or near poverty, justifying focused and targeted interventions, calibrated to particular circumstances and distinguishing between transitory and permanent conditions. While the explanations of near-poor, poor and some extreme poor might be understood as 'structural, non-idiosyncratic and exposed to co-variant risk', the remaining poorest experience idiosyncratic poverty with micro variations in their circumstances.[13] Thus, non-idiosyncratic poverty and some near-poor vulnerability has been addressed through AKRSP's mainstream programme intervention (infrastructure, NRM support, social sector services, social mobilisation and microfinance) plus safety nets. Idiosyncratic poverty and other vulnerable categories on the other hand require more calibrated safety nets and sustained welfare transfers, or social protection. This can be translated programmatically into a contrast between **social development** which relies heavily upon social mobilisation for mainstream activities as well as communities taking on responsibilities for self-development including accessing rights, resources and services from other agencies, and **social policy** via forms of welfare service comprising safety nets and social protection.

These classifications of poverty and corresponding interventions contain some further issues relevant to programme thinking under the heading of counterpart social action. Thus, in addition to the above classifications of poverty, a further distinction between categories of the poor should be made, based on whether structural conditions and/or personal competences support or detract from a capacity for effective agency. Various factors affect this capacity: temporary and transitory periods of high dependency; high discounting of the future and induced short term priorities; and permanent and chronic poverty. All three conditions contribute to adverse incorporation and dependent client status, which is reinforced by decreasing options to exit from local income arrangements due to weakness of the political economy elsewhere. If we distinguish between three current trajectories of livelihood (improving, coping, declining) perhaps only the improving category reflects a capacity for strong social action and agency. A capacity for counterpart agency is also impaired by other forms of social exclusion beyond those noted above, such as gender (especially if a female-headed or managed household), clan/kin positions in the local hierarchy, minority sect locally, low status occupations, loss of farm holding (due to fragmentation, debt, absence of compensating remittances, and expensive family crises).

Whether poor people have a capacity for social action or not is fundamental to understanding the continuum of strategic options from social development to social policy. It is fundamental to realistic participation expectations. It is fundamental to whether priority is given to development/productivist or safety net/welfare transfer options. It is fundamental to whether a poor person is struggling successfully for formalised, predictable rights or reliant upon discretionary, though possibly predictable, informal rights. Social agency as the embodiment of social development might be social (as in forming and joining collective organisations for the pursuit of common interests, including the expansion of formal, secure rights) or economic (as in being entrepreneurial, risk taking, responsive to investment via micro-credit and other financial products).

AKRSP's Mainstream Approaches

If we return to Figure 2.1 in the introduction to this chapter, and additionally recognise that minor changes in poverty line and income assumptions revolve the poverty trends more pessimistically on the central axis downwards on the right side of the diagram, then category A expands along with B, and C reduces. This revised picture has important implications for the mix of poverty reduction strategies within the region. Under conditions of undifferentiated poverty as indicated schematically for Period I in Figure 2.2, AKRSP could validate its mainstream approach of general support to productivity enhancing infrastructure. As a precursor to the late '90s 'discovery' of rural sustainable livelihoods by DFID and others, AKRSP has always had a conception of the interrelation between various forms of capital at the household and community levels: physical, human, financial and social capital. Given the significance of agency and socio-economic action noted above, and given an analysis of institutional vacuum (not completely valid[14]), AKRSP used grant-supported physical capital (Productive Physical Infrastructure (PPI), infrastructure, public goods projects) as the incentive to stimulate formation of social capital via VOs, WOs, Cluster Organisations and so on. This was an agenda of stimulating counterpart social action as the platform for autonomous collective behaviour and participation on a range of local common interests.[15] These incentives extended beyond PPIs into a range of other subsidised and cost recovery 'packages' related to the productive elements of local livelihoods (e.g. farm and off-farm NRM, skills training, small and medium enterprise support via various micro-credit products). Throughout these initiatives, AKRSP promoted a series of principles: participation; inclusiveness (rather than socio-economic targeting); equity principles of access and resource allocation; transparency; use of objective criteria in assessment of household level needs; and group liability as a partial collateral (along with savings) for borrowing (thereby reinforcing collective behaviour). While these aspirations can be tested against a set of realities, they nevertheless represented an ambitious agenda of both socio-economic modernisation and a formalisation of rights, claims and entitlements in a traditional, authority based, deferential society. The realities which challenged these aspirations have been: clan and kin hierarchies reproduced within the 'democratic' VOs; the existence of various significant indigenous institutions, embodying these hierarchies, performing common property management and welfare transfer/safety net functions;[16] screening out of the poorest from microcredit as a threat to group liability; a loyalty and subservience to local elites and their external sponsors among the national and international community.

Relevance of Mainstream Approach to Current Forms of Poverty

By understanding poverty in these two main senses of geographical concentration and pockets within otherwise coping areas, and given the socio-economic changes outlined above and schematically represented in Figure 2.2 Period II, we have to ask how far the classic, mainstream AKRSP approach connects to contemporary poverty as represented by the expanded categories A and B from the modified Figure 2.1 (i.e. rightward swivel arising from shifting poverty line or income assumptions thus expanding the proportions of the poor and near-poor). The main answer is: partially relevant, especially in the geographical areas of concentrated poverty; but also some need for additional approaches whether from within or outside of AKRSP. Thus, while NRM has remained a central feature of the programme, it is not necessarily the central feature of livelihoods for many poor families as well as others who rely significantly upon off-farm activity, including wage labour elsewhere in NAC or down-country.[17] It remains true that, given the fragmentation of holdings and reduced farm size per family, the needs for land development and increases in land productivity persist, alongside off-farm initiatives. Some of these initiatives can be NRM (forest, fruit, home gardens, livestock) but other enterprises and skill training for non-agricultural wage labour are also obviously necessary. For targeted poor households in otherwise coping areas, the case for non-farm, non-NRM interventions is even higher given that the poverty observed is already evidence of people having lost farming and NRM opportunities sufficient for subsistence. And again, distinctions have to be made between those poor who are capable of paid work and those who are not; and those who are included socially, and those who are not. We can be even more specific by going below the household to its members, arguing that adults, especially women, may have no realistic prospect of gaining relevant human or social competences, but the youth within those families might. The challenge for AKRSP and AKDN is to ensure that they are connecting positively to these categories. The particular challenge is between an explanation of poverty in a household derived from general structural conditions (non-idiosyncratic), which could be altered by general programme interventions, and particular, idiosyncratic poverty which requires more specific, differentiated responses of a social policy rather than a social development kind. Expanded category A from Figure 2.1, as well as some households within category B embrace both types of need and response. As the poverty reduction agenda therefore moves further into this terrain, so the relationships of poor and vulnerable households[18] to indigenous, social protection institutions as well as those potentially offered by AKDN become more important.

The Development/Welfare Relationship

In these debates, welfare transfers are often regarded as a competition to development, a drag on productive investment. However the relationship needs to be seen more positively than this. We have to accept that in any society the chronic poor (often referred to as 'case poverty') are always present, as a result of old age, random chance producing crises, and the dislocations to livelihoods caused by rapid economic change. Responding to such poverty is a charge on any society. A further category of families may experience temporary crisis as a result of genuine shocks (in contrast to predictable life cycle events) and can be easily rehabilitated to coping and improving trajectories through short-term safety net support, thus restoring their role in overall development. Failure to enact safety nets at this juncture could result in longer term crisis and dependency and thus create unnecessary longer term charges on investment. A further category may experience a similar transitory problem due to economic change, in which erstwhile employed members become redundant in a declining sector of the economy and require safety net support which includes re-training and perhaps deliberate re-connection to the labour market or new enterprise opportunities. Therefore some short-term poverty is recoverable, with safety nets and insurance making a contribution to rehabilitation and graduation. The basic wider argument here is that an unregulated, market economy produces poverty outcomes which are ultimately destructive for the society unless there is regulation and compensatory formal state, or predictable charitable, behaviour—in other words a political economy which embodies rights in some form for those in need. Thus working exclusively upon economic growth/productivity increases is only a partial response to the inherent processes of any economy and society.

This conclusion leads to a central question for poverty reduction agencies: the relationship between productivist strategies (as reflected in the mainstream approaches of AKRSP to date) and social protection. To what extent are livelihoods to be addressed through the stimulation of economic activity at the grass roots level, or to what extent are broader, social sector interventions (including social protection and particular infrastructure elements, such as drinking water and sanitation) an essential rather than optional feature for sustained livelihoods support? Clearly it is important for sustainable livelihoods in NAC that AKRSP continues its support for enhanced economic productivity, although significantly this needs to be off-farm though within the agricultural service sector as well as outside agriculture and NR altogether. This continues to be achieved directly through NR sector packages (including skills training as well as start-up inputs), supported as appropriate by micro-credit; but also indirectly through infrastructural investment in irrigation, roads and bridges, and more recently micro-hydels. However this continuation of a productivist oriented strategy[19] is based upon one key social assumption: that rural clients have a capacity (structural or personal) for counterpart agency in the form of social action as well as economic entrepreneurialism. However, as now explained above, and also understood widely among AKRSP staff, this productivist approach does not easily or obviously connect to all current forms of poverty partly because the prospects for dynamic economic growth in the region remain severely constrained, and partly because a trickle down concept from category C in Figure 2.1 to categories B and A is unlikely to be sufficient to alleviate their poverty and vulnerability. This introduces the social protection agenda both for below-subsistence families in declining trajectories, as well as vulnerable, near-poor coping families.

The idea of social protection embraces both safety nets and sustained welfare transfers. Safety nets can be partly understood as mitigating both personalised (i.e. idiosyncratic) and structurally (i.e. non-idiosyncratic) induced, short-term misfortune. This might occur in a variety of ways, outlined further below. However there is an important distinction between various types of insurance, which prepare for a predictable range of life-cycle and economic cycle problems on the one hand; and mobilisation of contingency funds, on the other hand, to offset genuine shocks whose effects can be finite and temporary (e.g. flash floods or a sudden drop in tourism induced by distant world events). By contrast to both these forms of safety nets, sustained welfare transfers are directed at long-term, chronic poverty where the realistic option is poverty alleviation rather than reduction. Such transfers derive either from state re-distribution of taxation revenues according to targeting criteria; from other charitable institutional sources outside the family of the recipient,[20] where the standardisation of criteria for charitable allocation may be present or absent; and from other family members, within nuclear or joint, extended arrangements. In societies like Pakistan with a weak tax base, widespread misuse of public funds, patronage and preferentialism, the sustainability and certainty of funds from state sources is likely to be more fragile and precarious than from the charitable or family sources. Under such conditions, formal rights are likely to be of less value than informal ones, although the latter are conditional upon loyalty to the values and interests of the donor, whether institutional or individual.[21]

Mainstream Productivist Packages and Poverty-Targeted Fund Options

What then are the implications of the above analysis for AKRSP's poverty policy? Over and above its mainstream approaches, over the last two years AKRSP has been experimenting with the creation of Poverty-Targeted (earmarked) Funds to offer additional emphasis to both the mainstream and social protection wings of its evolving programme. This represents a significant innovation: incremental for the mainstream wing; new for a social protection initiative. Thus the PF had three main purposes:

- additional support for mainstream activity in geographically targeted areas both as a funding top-up to general allocation (e.g. for infrastructure, or generalised NRM packages) and as specific funds earmarked for identified, poorest households within generally poor areas (e.g. support for hotel training of targeted recipients in Gupis Gammais community, Ghizer District);

- support for targeted productivist activity in areas with poor households in otherwise coping areas (e.g. support for mason

and carpenter training for targeted individuals of poor families
in the growth pole of Gakuch Town, Ghizer District);
- and support to existing institutionalised charitable safety net and
welfare transfers (such as in Sikanderabad, Nagar with the Akbar
Development Fund).

This pilot, plural, threefold strategy signals to those in category B
of Figure 2.1 (i.e. above the formal poverty line but nevertheless
vulnerable to some degree) that their legitimate interests are not
being excluded, since the mainstream, inclusive programmes
(especially with respect to development of public goods) embrace
their interests, while offering access to safety net support in the
event of family crisis (predictable/life cycle or unpredictable
shock).

Social Protection and Safety Nets: Supporting Development

Let us therefore examine the mutual reinforcing connection
between safety nets, the reduction of poverty and vulnerability, and
development. Safety nets can themselves be seen as productive:
partly by enabling re-entry into productive activity for the
transitory poor; and as a corollary by preventing the long-term
decline of families who would then be dependent upon sustained
welfare transfers. Safety nets can thus perform a structurally
significant function by undermining unequal economic and
political power relationships in the local political economy, since
family crisis (predictable or unpredictable) usually leads to increased
dependency upon patrons, employers, and moneylenders in which
rates of exploitation of the weaker party are subsequently intensified.
This reproduces weakness and vulnerability for the future, as
options for exit from such relationships are foreclosed.

Having accepted the analysis deriving from Figure 2.1 (and its
modified version when poverty line assumptions are raised and
income sensitivity is recognised), the key issue for AKRSP then
becomes whether safety nets are embedded into generalised policy

and programme design on a sustained basis using both market based instruments as well as collective action, or whether they are seen as special funds, mobilised by either the state or philanthropic institutions external to the recipients and allocated in response to crisis. The latter option might be favoured by AKRSP in a policy regime, which emphasises economic entrepreneurialism above all else. However, the former is more likely to offer the poor and vulnerable more long-term security, enabling positive time-preference behaviour via higher savings, risk taking and a willingness to incur debt for investment. In well developed economies, this embeddedness is usually attached to the labour market in various forms of social insurance, regulated by the state: obligatory pension schemes; company and/or state allocation of funds to support sickness benefits (usually for a limited period); severance pay and other packages on redundancy; access to skill upgrading and re-training where a sector shift in qualified labour is being induced. In countries with large-scale formal sector employment (typically the OECD countries and some Latin American and South-East Asian ones[22]), such forms of embedded social insurance will cover and 'insure' the livelihoods of a large proportion of the population. However in countries like Pakistan, formal sector employment applies to a small percentage of the population, so that other ways have to be found to achieve this embeddedness. This is the challenge for AKRSP or AKDN more generally across the NAC.

Thus embedded safety nets can be referred to as social insurance, in contrast to non-embedded safety nets, which are better understood as emergency funds earmarked for emergency support. So the goal is social insurance under informal sector conditions (farming, off-farm, outside agriculture, trade, manufacturing and services, and self or paid employment), which are typically accompanied by various family, kin and religio-community institutional arrangements. Given a policy requirement of cost recovery principles under conditions of weak public taxation at the national and even provincial levels, what sustainable instruments are potentially available in pursuit of this goal? Do they have to be market based financial products, or is there scope for mutual insurance through micro-level collective action? Before considering that question, we should return to chronic poverty and the case for differentiated welfare transfers.

Social Protection and Welfare Transfers: Distributing the Gains of Development

By distinguishing above between chronic poverty (category A of Figure 2.1) and vulnerability (category B of Figure 2.1), we are effectively distinguishing in intervention support terms between sustained welfare transfers and safety nets respectively. Within chronic poverty, however, different types should trigger different types of welfare transfer. With such 'case' poverty (in contrast to generic, structural, mass poverty addressed by general interventions), there is programmatic complexity requiring more like a UK social worker function than a social organiser function. While not suggesting that AKRSP, or other parts of AKDN, have the resources to offer such intensity, it will be worth thinking about how AK field staff can develop the capacity of their client activists to broker the link between case poverty and matching intervention support. It might be interesting to speculate, in AKDN terms, how far a generic cadre of social workers could be developed across AKDN, linking families to appropriately specific services offered by one agency or another. The purpose of this section in this chapter is to outline some of the variations in types of chronic poverty in order to understand further the demand side of the social protection landscape as a prelude to a discussion of the supply side.

Thus, the chronic poor can comprise: orphans; widows and divorcees; female-headed households; a woman having no male representatives in local institutions; an unmarried woman; the long-term injured (from a work accident or other event); the disabled (from birth or other reason); mentally handicapped or mentally ill; the elderly without proximate sons or daughters in sympathetic in-law households; resource poor at the wrong time in the life cycle (e.g. losing land when too old to work in the labour market); families enduring extraordinary expenses (e.g. medicine) and obliged to sell productive assets like land and livestock foreclosing recovery (in the absence of safety nets); families with male heads unable to inherit significant property (either due to poor fathers, or a large number of inheriting brothers); families with low education among all members (partly due to induced high discount rates of the future from other reasons); outcasted families due to the pollution associations of their ancestral occupations; 'bankruptcy' from a failed enterprise venture (possibly induced by micro-credit, directly or indirectly, as market distortions encourage easy entry into saturated local markets under low productivity and demand conditions); denial of local credit (and even the liability exposure of, for example, shopkeepers obliged to trade via offering credit); and families experiencing the natural loss of key livestock at a time in their fortunes which prevents recovery.

Let us now consider the internationalised institutional responsibility matrix as a 'framework' starting point for examining the supply side institutions in a social protection landscape.[23] Combining safety net and welfare transfer functions (for the moment), we are basically considering a 'social protection mix' of provision. This charts areas of institutional provision and responsibility, according to the dominant values and rules they embody.

It is increasingly commonplace when analysing Less-Developed Countries (LDCs), first, to extend Esping-Andersen's (1999) social protection triangle of state–market–family to include 'community'. This refers to the multitude of sub-societal organisational forms, including NGOs, and the related notion of civil society. The result is the 'institutional responsibility square' (IRS) operative at micro, meso and macro levels in the domestic society. This distinction between levels is especially important in the NAC regions of Pakistan, where local livelihoods maintenance interacts strongly both with growth poles in the region and down-country labour and product markets. But, second, a variety of international components loom larger in most LDCs. These include supra-national equivalents of the four domestic components: global markets; donors and other international governmental organisations; international NGOs and other 'voice' organisations; and the 'internationalised household'— migration, remittances, and global risk aversion through international welfare and finance institutions. Figure 2.6 exhibits all eight components of the resulting institutional responsibility matrix (IRM).

Figure 2.6. Components of the institutional responsibility matrix

	Domestic	Supra-national
State	Domestic governance	International organisations, national donors
Market	Domestic markets	Global markets, MNCs
Community	Civil society, NGOs	International NGOs
Household	Households	International household strategies

Now, to what extent can we realistically find, within this institutional framework, social insurance (i.e. embedded safety nets) and sustained welfare transfers of relevance to NAC? The intention here is not just to repeat the list of safety net/welfare transfer sources within Islamic philanthropy (e.g. *Zakat, Baitul Mal*) which can be mostly located (though not entirely) at the community level, but to offer additional, strategic possibilities which increase socio-economic, cultural and political embeddedness.[24]

State: perhaps a proportion of local government taxation earmarked for social protection purposes rather than recurrent maintenance of infrastructure and investment projects; perhaps geo-politically motivated endowment funds from both the national state as well as international donors eager to maintain stability in the region; perhaps some examination of army family support services; an extension of pension entitlements to short-term, casual as well as long-term, permanent government and local government employees.

Market: formalisation of informal labour market conditions and development of formal contracts (e.g. with local contractors to the army, employing local wage labour); limited security of employment for short-term sickness and family crises (recognising that non-army employers under NAC conditions can themselves be vulnerable and cannot realistically be over-exposed to such risk); use of collective bargaining over prices (e.g. with potato companies or marble traders, as well as international tourist companies) and wages; micro-financial services (linked to international banking services and markets to avoid locally co-variant risk as well as productivity depressors[25]) to stimulate savings and dividend earning deposits with varying access conditions matching differential fund growth rates (i.e. longer, higher); specially targeted micro-financial services to army pensioners to offer protection to service accumulated equity funds; social insurance tax on national and international tourist profits; shopkeepers' credit to consumers.

Community: aggregated religious-based funds across single sect areas reinforced by a formal hierarchy of mosques and councils (i.e. not confined to small locations), to avoid the burden only falling upon the immediate community as with many present funds, where poverty is more likely concentrated;[26] supported by internationally generated single sect funds (e.g. the global Ismaili diaspora represented locally through AKDN, Kuwait Shia as in the Murfi Foundation, and various Sunni based funds from Saudi Arabia); using local social capital to develop Rotating Savings and Credit Association (ROSCA) and Accumulated Savings and Credit Association (ASCA) versions of micro-financial services.

Household/Family: (NB 'family' needs to be added to household in this context in order to capture various kinds of intra-kin and intra-clan social protection mechanisms) deliberate re-forming of joint/extended families especially under conditions of male out-migration; deployment of remittances beyond the nuclear family claimants in exchange for joint family support; inefficient offers of employment to kin, thus embodying an element of relief; performance of common property maintenance functions for the incapacitated (infirm, elderly, widowed, female headed or managed households); full-board support for short or long periods for diagonally related, junior relatives pursuing education; even support for fees as well; management of poor relatives' land for nominal product shares; managing the livestock of poorer relatives especially during high pasture seasons; sharing in kind at festivals; assistance with house maintenance; full or partial board support for diagonally and horizontally related kin and relatives down-country (perhaps in return for domestic services); financial transfers for medical expenses.

The Strengths and Weaknesses of Informal Rights in NAC

The strategic problem, as discussed in AKRSP's poverty workshops during 2001–2, is whether the greater reliance upon informal rights and entitlements in societies like Pakistan, where the state is weak, offers adequate security and predictability for the poor to enable them to reduce their future discount rate and commit to longer range preparation and investment across their resource profile. We can identify a list of problems associated with informal rights and these will be discussed presently. However, there is a less familiar argument about the significance and utility of these informal rights. Returning to the institutional responsibility matrix, the different landscape elements (boxes) have normative and actual characteristics, which vary with reference to historical and social conditions. Whereas we might imagine the state in the UK acting in compensatory fashion (via formal rights and entitlements, enshrined in effective law) over the unpredictability and chaos of markets and informal relations at community and family levels, it is much harder to make such a claim for the state in Pakistan and other societies like it (Wood 2004).

Under such conditions, the status of informal entitlements in the other boxes becomes relatively more attractive as a source of social protection (in both safety net and welfare transfer senses). To the extent that a strong morally based dimension of responsibility for social protection can be found within community, family and even market relations, so these institutions represent more security and stability for the poor and vulnerable. Although we might argue a general thesis of shrinking moral responsibility and individualisation as in the shift within extended families from diagonal to vertical transfers (whether human capital investment, safety nets or welfare transfers), there remains substantial evidence of caring at the community and family levels as revealed through mosque and non-religious funds, transfers within extended families (kind or cash), labour sharing, covering for common property labour obligations, shop credit, low or free tariff for micro-hydel electricity, and so on. The chronic poor and those in short-term need can, to a considerable extent, rely upon some help from these sources. It is a matter of shame and dishonour for an extended family or larger kin group (even a clan) to allow members to become destitute or so desperate that they must seek charity further afield. Since poverty is often confined to particular clans and families, the caring potential among the coping in those clans and families is understood to be limited. Under such conditions, can wider, community level sources be mobilised without the recipient incurring shame and dishonour? In this sense fortune or the random luck of inequality (due to demographic and idiosyncratic reasons) is not morally attacked, and re-distribution for the sake of honour, moral cohesion, multi-period games of mutual interdependence over time is understood as a combined moral and pragmatic imperative.

In such a moral climate, claims can be quite secure as long as the claimant is perceived as deserving, or worthy in some way. Not to contribute under such circumstances incurs the risk of exclusion and ostracism and a consequent loss of key social, cultural and common property resources, which might be needed in other spheres at other times. This culture of perceptions and obligation re-defines, to an extent, the meaning of 'informal' when describing this category of rights and entitlement claims. They are informal in the sense of not being formally guaranteed in law and upheld by the state through legislation, action and redress, but they are not informal in the sense of being completely unpredictable and arbitrary. Thus, in terms of assessing the value to poor people of informal rights and entitlements to social protection (safety nets or sustained welfare transfers), this element of social predictability can be recognised and built upon as a strategy for AKRSP and AKDN.

However, we can also acknowledge a series of weaknesses associated with informal social protection, which reduce predictability and security of claim. These can be understood as problems of: access; transparency; accountability; and discretion or preferentialism. Thus the practical agenda of trying to reinforce the certainty of local level social protection involves overcoming these constraints. So let us briefly consider each of these problems in turn.

Firstly, **access** difficulties arise under conditions of: imperfect information about resources potentially on offer; when control over such resources is confined to particular leaders or families who are unrepresentative of the needy families and individuals or members of conflicting factions; if the distribution of resources is made conditional upon other forms of compliant behaviour (e.g. free labour, loyalty in disputes, surrendering other legitimate claims); if the act of seeking access requires a public presentation of need and associated humiliation; if the resources are not actually readily available with the 'donor', with 'in principle' commitments from the local 'donor' community having to be converted into hard cash; where no low cost systems exist for regular transfers (i.e. each transaction has to be freshly negotiated and agreed, or the recipient has to be accompanied each time to the bank or shop where the funds might be stored, or where the transaction comprises repeat letters of credit); and where difficult travel is involved (up or along).

Secondly, some of the access difficulties are associated with lack of **transparency** such as imperfect information, but as a result the transparency problem prevents accountability and weakens rights. Although we are all wary of undue bureaucracy, some formal recording of the resources mobilised and publicly announced criteria of allocation and entitlement develop a trust on both donor and recipient sides that practices are fair. This stimulates the mobilisation of funds (informal taxation in effect), reduces avoidance of obligations, enables cases to be ranked and ordered, establishes the criteria of eligibility for entitlements, allows orderly queues to form (queues may be implicit rather than explicit in the sense of actually standing in line) with clients having the security that their 'turn' will come (this happens in well-functioning ROSCAs) when they are in need. Transparency of practices also acts as a constraint upon the misappropriation of funds, with managers of funds more liable to discovery and sanction.

Thirdly, of course, transparency is an essential prerequisite for **accountability**, with managers of funds subject to scrutiny of either some other governing body, or by potential clients themselves. Enabling accountability also acts as reassurance that funds will be used as intended, thus ensuring that the moral or other commitments behind the generation of those funds are maintained.

And fourthly, by having clear rules of access based upon transparent rules of eligibility with regular monitoring by stakeholders, the likelihood is reduced that generally mobilised funds will be used in **discretionary and preferential** ways to sustain particular patron-client networks, or to favour close family members over other worthy claimants.

In other words, the value of informal rights can be improved by elements of community level formalisation of process without seeking to bring in the full weight of state legislation, management and regulation under conditions where the state's competence, probity and legitimacy is under serious question. AKRSP has considerable experience of this in the formation of VOs and its insistence that PPI grants were conditional upon transparent and participatory management practices among VO members. Of course, it is an empirical question whether such practices have been sustained once the grant incentive has disappeared. In many cases, the answer is 'yes' in terms of other packages and savings/credit behaviour; and in some cases, where VOs have collapsed or bifurcated or simply become defunct, the explanation may derive from 'excessive informality' of practice and consequent mounting distrust of each other. But there is also positive evidence of other associational forms appearing and performing collective welfare functions.[27] From this we might conclude that an element of formalisation of process itself contributes to the formation and maintenance of social capital in the sense of maintaining functional levels of trust in the local society. It would seem, therefore, in the whole AKRSP/AKDN policy agenda of social and poverty funds, that a sub-state strategy of strengthening informal safety net and welfare systems is both possible and builds upon experience and existing relationships between AKRSP and local communities.

However, staying with the IRM logic when considering the room for manoeuvre for intervention or support, we must distinguish between public and private institutions. Much of the discussion above is focused upon a public, 'community' set of institutions in which funds are mobilised beyond the family for use beyond the family. While it may be easier to introduce an element of formalisation in the management of such funds for public, collective institutions where the maintenance of mutual trust between families is essential, it is much more difficult to intervene to strengthen informal rights within families and extended kin groups. Indeed, many might argue that this is a 'no-go' area for policy and intervention. But 'Western' social policy is full of examples of intervention at this level, under the general heading of 'de-familialisation'.[28]

Basically there is a western argument that the family is an increasingly unreliable institution through which social protection for all its members can be enacted, but that policy can be devised to maintain intra-household obligations where the moral basis for it is disappearing. Ironically, it has been precisely the strength and pervasive penetration of the state into private lives, which has been partially responsible for this shrinking moral base. Policies and interventions to shore up family level social protection functions have been: tax incentives for families with children or elderly to care for; means testing as a basis for public entitlements whether in terms of pensions or education grants; conversion of fixed assets to annuity schemes to enable the elderly to spend capital on care; tax incentives for long-term saving; varying the rules of inheritance tax; compulsion on divorced fathers to support ex-wives and children (assuming males as the superior earner); enacting standard tariffs for dividing assets on divorce. Most of these options and some of the social and moral premises on which they are based have no relevance for family conditions in Northern Pakistan. However the discussion does prompt the question about how families might be supported to increase the value of intra-family transfers, and particularly inter-generational ones. For example, this might take the form of advice to families on how to protect the long-term value of army pensions, or how best to use remittances, or how to create education funds or medical insurance together with correspondingly innovative financial products through the new 'First Microfinance Bank'.

CONCLUSION: SUPPORTING LIVELIHOODS AND OVERCOMING INSECURITY

This chapter has shown that over the lifetime of AKRSP's participation in the development efforts of the Northern Areas and Chitral District of NWFP in Northern Pakistan, there have been important successes in the reduction of poverty as measured by national standards. But even by these parsimonious standards, a third of the population remains below the poverty line (category A of Figure 2.1) and the 20 per cent plus of the population immediately above the poverty line (category B of Figure 2.1) remain highly vulnerable and economically insecure in their livelihoods. If the standards are set more generously, then a much higher proportion continue to be poor and/or vulnerable. Likewise, if incomes fall even marginally, a high proportion re-enter poverty, reflecting that vulnerability to minor changes in circumstances and shocks. We have also distinguished between forms of poverty which can be understood as structural and generic (i.e. the outcomes of geography, absence of relevant public goods such as physical infrastructure, weakness of market opportunities including migration/remittance options, and low levels of human capital), and forms of poverty which are more personally derived from the random outcomes of household circumstances including dependency ratio, gender composition and point in the family domestic cycle. Borrowing from other literature,[29] these categories of poverty have been referred to respectively as non-idiosyncratic and idiosyncratic. We have also recognised that poverty for some is not a permanent condition, but may be transitory or churning thus potentially responsive to safety net support for a finite period. For others, especially but not only the idiosyncratically poor, poverty may be chronic requiring continuous welfare transfers. Such people, as part of their condition of chronic poverty, also have little if any capacity for counterpart social action or agency: i.e. they can do little for themselves, or in conjunction with others. Their prospects for participation in programmes orchestrated by external agencies is limited, and their effective participation in community level collective action is similarly constrained.

More specifically for the NAC in Northern Pakistan, we have further identified two main forms of poverty in the region. One of these forms derives from geographical remoteness (i.e. poor access combined with single, often precarious cropping and a weak economic base from which to invest in human capital). The other form has been described as poverty pockets of non-idiosyncratically or idiosyncratically poor households in communities where other households have partially or completely graduated from poverty.

Over the lifetime of AKRSP's presence in the region, we have also schematically concluded (Figure 2.2) that the society has changed from a more homogeneous, undifferentiated social structure in which most people were poor in some way (e.g. all were suffering from the poverty of public goods such as roads and bridges, or higher capacity irrigation channels) towards a more differentiated and unequal society, in which a proportion (category C in Figure 2.1) has successfully graduated out of poverty and to some extent vulnerability. The extent of that proportion depends upon the assumptions made about poverty lines, reasonable living standards and quality of life. We have observed that if we divide the last 30 years into two periods, indicating the shift from an undifferentiated to differentiated social structure, the relevance of AKRSP's mainstream rural support approaches for all members of the rural population were higher in the first period than the second. In other words, how far do AKRSP's mainstream approaches address the poverty reduction needs of category A in Figure 2.1? The question is important if AKRSP is to play its part (albeit modestly in terms of absolute numbers) in reaching the Millenium Development Goals.

This leads into an important policy debate for AKRSP,[30] essentially between two positions: promotion of overall economic development via market expansion, with welfare outcomes achieved through trickle down assumptions; and a programme of targeting poor households through a combination of capacity building in order to be market successful and social protection (including safety nets) as both a support for development (see argument above) as well as distributing the welfare gains from development to those who cannot directly participate (i.e. the idiosyncratically and/or chronically poor). It could reasonably be argued that AKRSP's comparative advantage lies in the former position with a focus upon resource development and personal as well as institutional capacity building in order to support sustainable development through an expanded market economy. The danger with just adopting this position is that AKRSP continues to serve category C and parts of category B in Figure 2.1, and effectively by-passes the interests of category A. If AKRSP were convinced that other agencies were better placed to pick up the poverty targeting agenda to address the needs of category A, then it could stay with its comparative advantage. Its current new direction implies this, though a place for a commercially constructed micro-insurance product is also contemplated. But what if other potential agencies are not up to the task? Government offers law and order (just) which is important for socio-economic security, and some infrastructure but no poverty targeting. Other agencies of AKDN offer support for social sectors (including vitally water and sanitation) but not targeted in the main. Other agencies like IUCN and WWF have a conservation and environmental entry point into the principle of sustainable development but not poverty targeting beyond an interest in geographical remoteness (though their documentation includes some poverty rhetoric). Do these conclusions place an additional responsibility upon AKRSP to adopt the second position above as well as the first? In other words to see its concept of 'rural support' as embracing poverty targeting and acting as a catalyst to establish a welfare regime[31] for the region.

This conclusion would imply a 'focused' programme of poverty alleviation and poverty reduction alongside ongoing investment and technical services support for non-targeted economic development in the region. Targeted programmes nevertheless contribute additionality to overall economic development via both 'market' (productivist) and social protection windows. Let us consider a productivist/market example: Gakuch in Ghizer. Due to its strategic position at the convergence of the main Ghizer river coming from the west and Ishkomen coming from the North, the hitherto remote Gakuch has become the location of local decentralisation and therefore a growth pole with expanded government construction for offices and staff houses. The demand for masons, carpenters, electricians and so on has thus become stronger. Therefore it makes sense for AKRSP to use Poverty Funds[32] to concentrate some additional activity in this location supporting poorer households to develop these skills. In other words, a targeted but mainstream project, familiar to AKRSP but specifically supported by a Poverty Fund in this case to enable affirmative action on location criteria. This contrasts with a social protection example in Sikanderabad, which lies on the KKH in Nagar and is not regarded as geographical poverty, but has poor households within it. The Poverty Fund here is being used to support and strengthen an existing 'charitable' fund for social protection purposes.

By developing this poverty targeted element to its 'rural support' approach, AKRSP enables a focus on poverty alleviation and reduction while not threatening its mainstream approach which continues to address the structural conditions (environmental, ecological and economic) which affect the development and livelihoods of people as a whole in the region, and where widespread vulnerability persists. It thus engages with the wider conceptions of poverty and vulnerability identified for the region in this study. The value-added case for adding targeting to its mainstream approach can therefore be seen in five different ways:

- Specific contribution to improving socio-economic security: productivity and social protection;
- Using earmarked funds to strengthen mainstream connections to poverty reduction;
- Incentives for improvement in quality of indigenous practices for welfare transfers;
- Direct and indirect contributions to graduation;
- Realisation of welfare responsibilities as part of defining successful development.

Let us comment on each of these in turn. Given the overall condition of vulnerability in the NAC region, socio-economic security is the primary need for the entire population. For some, this can be achieved via productivist investment at community and individual levels requiring either collective management and/or private risk taking. For others, productivist interventions simply do not fit to community or more likely household level conditions and capacities. For this part of the population, social protection is required in the form of safety net interventions or sustained welfare transfers. The safety net contribution to socio-economic security is crucial, and it may be temporary if the conditions being addressed are themselves finite and specific.

The poverty reduction value of mainstream productivist interventions can be enormously strengthened via affirmative action or positive discrimination, supported from earmarked funds, which permit a specific and targeted response to poverty conditions. Small enterprise productivist interventions are more likely to be household and individual-focused rather than area-focused, whereas public goods infrastructure productivist interventions are more likely to be area-focused. Earmarked funds enable a flexibility of response outside of the main criteria for allocation of budgets across programme districts, and also permit innovation and action-research without disturbing other expectations among other non-targeted parts of the population.

This could be crucial, tactically, to maintain the support of the non-poor and therefore to be able to continue to mobilise entire community efforts behind projects requiring collective management and financial or labour inputs such as micro-hydels. Continuing the tradition of using PPI grants as a lever to improve social capital in the management of joint local productivist activity, earmarked funds represent a lever to improve the social capital of joint local social protection activity, thereby giving AKRSP an entry into a discussion about equity, transparency, access and governance. Without such a fund, there is little incentive for improvement in the quality of informal rights to safety net support or in the security of regular entitlements to welfare transfers. Impacting positively in this way upon indigenous practices is likely to be the most sustainable social protection option for some time to come until more formal, state level provision is either affordable or accepted as statutory responsibility.

Thus in both a productivist and social protection/safety net sense, targeted funds contribute to the graduation of poor families and individuals, enabling poverty clearing outcomes. However, we should also be realistic and accept that such graduation via generic or targeted productivist forms of support is unlikely for the poorest families and individuals, experiencing idiosyncratic, chronic poverty. The evidence worldwide is that the poorest find it difficult to benefit from a general improvement in market conditions achieved by upgraded infrastructure, or from small-scale enterprise microfinance investment, or from social insurance provision connected to employment, or from short term support for liquidity management and consumption smoothing (although the latter can be significant to those with uneven annual income flows and/or those contending with shocks).

Thus finally, when assessing the cost of sustained welfare transfers to the poor and the source of such transfers in money or kind, it is important to find ways of reducing the dependency of the chronically poor upon other categories of the poor in the immediately local community, even though this is where the most intense sense of moral obligation might lie.[33] Typically the chronically poor will be found in households, kin groups, clans, *mohallahs* or geographical locations which are also poor or otherwise highly vulnerable, experiencing non-idiosyncratic co-variant risk. The prospects of coping, graduating into coping status, or insuring against hazard as part of gaining socio-economic security become remoter if these same poor and vulnerable are the sole or primary supporters of the chronically poor in their midst. In other words, the 'development' of the non-chronically poor and vulnerable is more likely when they are relieved of sustained local welfare burdens. To the extent that this is achieved in other, richer societies, some version of a welfare regime is enacted with sustained transfers orchestrated by the state via taxation sources. The legitimacy and therefore sustainability of such transfers is maintained either by universal provision and taxation of all income (e.g. state 'old-age' pensions in the UK will be taxed if part of a broader income, but everyone over a certain age is entitled to receive such a pension) or by means testing and identifying 'deserving' cases within the prevailing moral responsibility framework of the particular society. The challenge is how to achieve this in Pakistan generally and the NAC in particular. The arrangement which gets nearest to universalist principles is *Zakat*. But its operation falls a long way short of secure, universalist rights for the poor to receive *Zakat*, and of the widespread compliance to pay which would make it resemble a tax-based redistributive element of a welfare regime.

NOTES

1. This region, as described in Chapter 1, is defined as the Northern Areas (administered through special institutions as a reflection of the ongoing, unresolved, Kashmir issue) and Chitral (the northernmost district of the North West Frontier province [NWFP] of federal Pakistan). Together these areas are referred to as 'NAC' (Northern Areas and Chitral).

2. This vulnerability can be reinforced by the underlying randomness of family demography in which dependency ratios, inheritance, marriage expenses, family labour and income risk spreading can all become adverse.

3. Four bands of incomes were formed with: Upper Income Group > Rs 3820 (i.e. 30% or more above the mean of Rs 2939); Upper Middle Income Rs 2939 to Rs 3819 (i.e. within a range of 30% above the mean); Lower Middle Income Rs 2057 to Rs 2938 (i.e. within a range of 30% below the mean); and Lower Income less than Rs 2057 (i.e. more than 30% below the mean).

4. See Room (2000) for his Snakes and Ladders Livelihoods model, with passports for improvement and buffers against disaster.

5. See Wood (2003) for a theoretical discussion of these time trade-offs.

6. See Wood (2004).

7. At the University of Bath, we use the notion of a resources profile (for individuals, households and communities) embracing material, human, social, cultural, common property rights and political dimensions, in preference to the terms 'capital' or 'assets'. The term 'resources' entails continuous attention to their maintenance and value, rather than seeing them as fixed items simply to be deployed. Thus for us, the term 'resources' is a social rather than taxonomy concept. Indeed Wood would go further and assert a distinction between social resources as private, personal networks and social capital as public goods institutions.

8. Some of these institutional challenges are explored in Chapter 8 of this volume: Collective Action: the Threatened Imperative.

9. See the various works of Blaikie, Seddon, Cameron *et al.* from the School of Development Studies at the University of East Anglia on road development in Nepal from the late 1970s onwards.

10. See Bryceson, Kay and Mooij (2000).

11. In the 1970s, Wood had a published debate with the US anthropologist Peter Bertocci on his thesis of cyclical kulakism, derived from the analysis of family farms in Comilla, Bangladesh. Bertocci argued the case for demographic differentiation, whereas Wood countered that rising land productivity enabled off-farm diversification, enabling stronger farming families to retain their class position.

12. i.e. geographical, pockets, and near-poor but highly vulnerable.

13. See the World Bank World Development Report 2000/1 'Attacking Poverty' for a use of this terminology, and Wood (2004) for a critique of some of the Bank's conclusions.

14. See Chapter 8.

15. It remains a question whether the development of local responsibility (or acceptance of liability) for the vulnerable and poor in the midst of these 're-created' communities was part of the intended objectives of such intervention.

16. Thus undermining the 'institutional vacuum' point of departure.

17. See Box 2.1 earlier in the chapter for evidence of such diversification in the Gilgit region.

18. And individuals where the heads of households are behaving non-altruistically to particular members, especially women.

19. A strategy very much enshrined in its vision and strategy for the post 2003 phase.

20. That is, various forms of Islamic philanthropy.

21. See Wood (2004) for an analysis of an informal security regime, as a welfare regime variant.

22. See Gough and Wood *et al.* (2004) for a comparison of welfare regime types across these and other regions of the world.
23. *Ibid.*
24. In addition to the work of the Pakistan Philanthropy Centre and studies by the Social Policy and Development Centre in Karachi, it is also interesting to note the current Asian Development Bank (ADB) commitment to examining insurance and social protection possibilities across Pakistan.
25. See Sharif and Wood (2001) for a discussion of these potential international dimensions of local micro-financial services.
26. This is a risk pooling issue, where a wider 'meso' pooling reduces the risk of co-variance, associated with particular localities.
27. See Chapter 8.
28. See Esping-Andersen (1999).
29. Including the WDR 2001 'Attacking Poverty'.
30. And by implication other external catalyst agencies faced with similar socio-economic changes over their programme lifetime. There are many parallels with large NGOs in Bangladesh facing the consequences of limited, but partial success in which distinctions between graduated and non-graduated groups become more significant.
31. Again see Gough and Wood *et al.* (2004) for a detailed comparative discussion of welfare regimes in different development and societal contexts.
32. These have been 'earmarked' funds created over the last three years for pilot, targeted initiatives.
33. Narrow risk pools may maximise social capital but also increase the problem of co-variance; larger risk pools have the opposite problem.

3

Gender and AKRSP—Mainstreamed or Sidelined?

Aalya Gloekler and Janet Seeley

INTRODUCTION

This chapter is about the place of gender in the Aga Khan Rural Support Programme (AKRSP). One cannot understand the gender discourse within an organisation without taking into account the institutional, political and socio-cultural context, and indeed the constraints under which a women's or gender programme has developed. Why decisions are taken to start or stop a particular programme or initiative at a particular time is dependent upon prevailing circumstances as well as the individuals both inside the organisation and outside (such as political and religious leaders, donors, academics and practitioners).

Much has been written about 'women' and 'gender' in AKRSP. Among this documentation is a film produced in celebration of the International Year of the Mountains in 2002 about the women of Northern Pakistan called 'Taller than the Mountains'. In this film women recalled the harsh and restricted nature of their past life in the villages of Northern Areas and Chitral (NAC), comparing the old times with the relative freedom and opportunities many women in the region now enjoy. But as mentioned in the AKRSP Annual Report for 1999, 'women's development in Northern Pakistan, as elsewhere, continues to pose formidable challenges', which require a holistic response from the multiple stakeholders involved in the process of development, such as the government and civil society organisations. Furthermore, these challenges need to be set in the context of the changes that have occurred. This chapter reflects on the history of the 'women' and more recently 'gender' programme in AKRSP in order to distil lessons for policy makers. This reflection is primarily about the women's programme, mirroring the way the concept of gender has been viewed and consequently exercised within the organisation. It is interesting to note that much of this chapter is about 'women' because there has been very little research on the way changes in gender roles and responsibilities have affected the lives of men in the NAC and elsewhere in Pakistan. We believe this to be an important area that deserves attention if equitable gendered development, which takes account of gender relationships as well as roles, is to be promoted in and by AKRSP.

The material presented in this chapter was collected from both primary and secondary sources. There was a wealth of secondary literature available: women's programme studies in AKRSP, annual reviews, monitoring mission reports, other evaluation reports, major strategy papers in AKRSP, gender policy papers of various donors/partners, census data from NAC (where available), and results of various base line surveys conducted in AKRSP. For the purpose of triangulation, interviews were conducted with past and present staff members of AKRSP, members of the AKRSP Board, national and international experts on women's development programmes and gender issues and people working with the Government of Pakistan on the development of gender policy. We also had the opportunity to speak to some members of Women's Organisations (WO) and Village Organisations (VO) groups, as well as local activists, in Gilgit, Baltistan and Chitral.[1]

Box 3.1. WID and GAD

In this study two terms are frequently used: Women in Development (WID) and Gender and Development (GAD). These terms can be defined in the following way:

The WID approach usually seeks to integrate women into development by making resources more available to women, in an effort to increase women's efficiency in their existing roles.

The GAD approach seeks to base interventions on the analysis of men and women's roles and needs in an effort to empower women to improve their position relative to men in ways which will benefit and transform society as a whole (Williams et al. 1994: 7).

'Women in Development' emerged in international development discourse in the late 1970s and early 1980s in response to the growing awareness that women had an influential part to play in development activities and if their energy and, it was assumed, contribution could be harnessed, development efficiency would increase. WID focused on women and their roles in isolation from men. Recognition that the gender relations of women and men often had an impact on women's development activities encouraged, in the 1990s, the emergence of 'Gender and Development' which has various interpretations but generally means ensuring that gender relations, roles and responsibilities are taken into account (and possibly transformed) in development (see Rathgeber (1990), Razavi and Miller (1995a) and Tinker (1990) for the background on WID/GAD). The shift from WID to GAD is often portrayed as a neat historical progression, but it was not so. Individuals as well as the actual place and context of development interventions have been influential in prescribing one approach rather than another, or both at the same time: which means providing a component that focuses specifically on women within a broader initiative which takes into account the complex gender relations between women and men.

In 1982 as AKRSP began, 'women in development' was being institutionalised in donor programmes and emerging as a subject of academic study. This context is important because it helps us to understand some of the changes that have occurred in AKRSP's approach to women and gender, as the organisation experimented with and responded to new ideas on 'how to do gender'. One of the questions we explore in this paper is to what extent AKRSP has moved from WID to GAD by shifting the focus of the gender programme from programmes for women to interventions that transform gender relations. We look at the background to the international discourse in more detail below, but first we focus on the socio-economic context of the programme area.

AKRSP has always prided itself on its flexible, evolving approach, responding to the needs and sensitivities of the time. This philosophy is nowhere more apparent than in the way the organisation sought to address the needs of the rural women of NAC where, given the conservative nature of the area, AKRSP's approach has been cautious. But too much flexibility can also lead to a lack of long term vision and clarity of direction, which many (ex)staff maintain was absent from the women's programme from the start.[2] At the same time, despite being flexible and 'culturally sensitive', AKRSP became vulnerable to pressure from the outside regarding women's activities, particularly from the religious leaders. One result of this could be seen in the late nineties when the women's programme came to an almost complete halt in Baltistan and later in Chitral. In the case of Baltistan, a mullah arriving from Karachi criticised AKRSP's credit programme and the women's programme. In the case of Chitral, a personal feud in which a member of the Sunni sect was killed by a member of the Ismaili sect escalated into a crisis situation in central Chitral, as a result of which AKRSP activities came under scrutiny.[3] In both cases the trust built with the communities over years took very little time to dissipate.

The positive side of having a flexible approach to the women's/ gender programme has been AKRSP's open response to the changing nature of economic/social needs of the women. This was done by, for example, initiating the formation of separate Women's Organisations (WOs); moving from subsistence to productive and economic interventions; experimenting between the individual and collective approaches; taking steps to address some social sector needs; and providing exposure visits for local women where there was demand and acceptability (Shakil and Usman 1997). It is precisely because of such challenges that, while exploring the lessons from AKRSP's approach to gender for other programmes in similar geographic and socio-economic surroundings, it has been necessary in this chapter to take a broader look at the contributions that AKRSP has made to improving women's lives over the last two decades.

More specifically, this chapter looks at the way gender roles have evolved within the NAC in private and public spheres, examining AKRSP's contribution to this process. It is also important to look at the way the organisation evolved internally in dealing with women's issues, the influence that the international gender discourse has had on AKRSP, particularly through its donors and the extent to which national policy on women's development has assisted this process. Furthermore, the chapter seeks to analyse the contribution AKRSP's struggle for women's empowerment makes to our understanding nationally and internationally of approaches to gender and development.

Socio-economic background

The lives of the men and women of the NAC have historically been shaped by the harsh nature of high altitude agrarian life. Only forty years ago, the absence of infrastructure such as roads, electricity, water supply, health and education meant that the people remained isolated, relying primarily on their own available resources. People in NAC developed elaborate systems of sharing work in which young and old, men and women, all played their part in order to survive the extreme climatic and geographic conditions of the high mountains.

In such a remote place as Northern Pakistan twenty years ago when AKRSP started work, education and health care were a privilege enjoyed by a very small segment of society. A result of this can be seen in the 1981 census, where average literacy rates for the Northern Areas and Chitral were 25 per cent for males and five per cent for females. Seventeen years later in 1998, an AKRSP Baseline Survey revealed that although literacy rates for the NAC have increased to 53 per cent for males and 23 per cent for females, these huge differences in male/female literacy rates continue to be a major obstacle to development of the region.

The labour intensive subsistence farming system required that the responsibilities be shared by women and men and further divided according to age. Women had to do a significant amount of the farm activities as well as household tasks and childcare. Women almost exclusively did the collecting of fuelwood and the fetching of water. Within their villages and up to the mountain pastures, women were relatively free in terms of their mobility, as *purdah* was not a traditional practice among all the communities of the North (Streefland *et al.* 1995: 16). But women's lack of mobility outside their villages meant that they had little access to basic social services. Hence women dying in childbirth due to the unavailability of timely medical help was a common feature of Northern Pakistan life.

Men, while sharing the farm responsibilities, were involved in the public sector including jobs in the army, but long-term male out-migration in general was quite rare. As education was not common for children, boys were the ones primarily responsible for livestock grazing and girls helped carry out the household chores.[4]

The simple technologies of the past meant that farm and household chores required much more time and labour for both men and women. For example, men used draft animals as well as wooden tools for ploughing. Threshing was also done using draft animals and both men and women carried out the cleaning of grains. Women used sheep hides and wooden pots to churn butter, which was a very labour intensive activity.[5] Most of the travelling was done either on ponies or by foot. A large part of women's time was spent, especially in winter, on spinning wool to make woollen clothes. Men, through hunting and slaughtering domestic animals, acquired meat. The meals, which were very labour/time intensive to prepare, consisted of traditionally prepared food using apricots (fruit, kernels, oils) or walnuts, wheat, buckwheat or barley, and a few varieties of fruit and vegetables.[6]

Given the geographical and cultural variation in the NAC, it would be difficult to claim that in the last two decades, the lives of men and women throughout Northern Pakistan have changed in the same way or that the change that has occurred is only due to the presence of AKRSP. Many factors have brought about socio-economic change over the last 20 years; the most important of which in the context of the Northern Areas is the completion of the Karakoram Highway in the late seventies. This road brought new social and economic opportunities to the area including tourism, cash crop-based commercialisation, improved health and education services, and telecommunication facilities, as well as increasing out-migration (particularly male) for education and employment. How important such an all-weather road can be in the development of an area can be seen by looking at Chitral, which does not have such a road, where the closure of the Shandur and Lowari passes during the winter months leads to serious shortages in supplies of all kinds.

Over the years, government-led development, coupled with new opportunities in the form of private sector and other development organisations such as Aga Khan Education Services, Aga Khan Health Services, International Union for the Conservation of Nature, WWF, as well as the Aga Khan Rural Support Programme have brought changes in the social, political and economic environment of Northern Pakistan. This in turn has affected the life style of, and division of labour between men and women, not all of which could be termed progressive, thus reflecting the unpredictable nature of the process of development itself.[7] It is important to note that although change has come, the pace of that change has not been the same in different regions. For example, due to the presence and more active historical role of other Aga Khan Development Network (AKDN) organisations in the Ismaili areas, these areas have become the leaders in the development process. Furthermore, relatively more government investment in the Northern Areas as compared to Chitral (because of the latter being a small part of the large North West Frontier Province (NWFP)) has also resulted in diverging trends of progress between the two areas.[8]

When the AKRSP was initiated, it was a major achievement to find properly qualified men, let alone women. Now there is an impressive pool of female masters' degree holders.[9] At the village level, women have also been the ones engaged in the last remnants of the subsistence/barter economy to be brought into the cash economy. However, with increasing moves of the farm economy towards cash cropping and commercialisation, women are also discovering that their new found economic freedom is being taken away from them, as men tend to control any activity which moves beyond the boundaries of the village and into the market place.[10] Dried apricot marketing is one example of this shift in the Gilgit region. Although traditionally women were the ones responsible for apricot drying, now more and more men are taking charge of this activity, due to the large scale profits involved.[11]

Mechanisation in the farm sector has also changed the nature of the workload for both men and women, making it generally less gruelling, but more time consuming for both men and women.[12] For example, the use of thresher machines means more responsibility for men but also a greater workload for women because it has become more tedious to clean the wheat after harvest.[13]

The opening of the area to religious influences from other parts of Pakistan, especially from the Shia/Sunni sects has led to a re-definition of religio-cultural values. This has on the one hand placed more restrictions on the mobility of women by further emphasising the importance of *purdah*, and on the other, has also brought home the importance of education for Shia women as a result of the Iranian influence.[14]

In-migration (for example, the Pathans in South Chitral) and tourism have, as a reactionary side effect, also resulted in the promotion of *purdah* (Streefland *et al.* 1995: 16). Men feel that they must protect their women from outsiders.[15] This also explains why women in the urban centres of Northern Pakistan feel more restricted in their movements even if they are educated. It is the presence of migrant workers in the urban centres, outsiders, which means women keep or are kept away. But, while mobility may be restricted in the urban areas women there do have better access to social services. Women in remote areas might be able to move more freely (at least up to a certain area beyond their own villages) but they have poor access to social services and economic opportunities.

The out-migration of males (temporary or permanent) to other parts of Pakistan has given some men the exposure to influences which place a high value on the importance of education, and outside exposure has also made some more aware of the value of hygiene and cleanliness in general for their women and children.[16] Male out-migration has also re-defined the gender division of labour at the household level, leaving women to deal with the domestic and farm-related demands, especially in small nuclear families. This has encouraged a more active decision-making role for women. But it should be noted that the degree of decision-making varies from place to place and from situation to situation and does not always result in a change in a woman's position in relation to men in the household.

We should not, therefore, assume that the change in gender roles that is occurring in NAC is resulting in changes in gender relations. Because, as we have indicated in this section, relationships between men and women are affected by age, class, household size, commercialisation trends, technologies available, education, cultural differences, access to information (for example, the media) as well as by migration and gender.

Changing gender roles at the household level

In Northern Pakistan culture has been one of the main determinants of the gender division of labour. Women's mobility constraints, for example, have meant that most of them are still involved in subsistence level work at the household level, leaving the outside responsibilities of the cash economy to men. It is generally believed that this limits women's decision-making role in the larger society. This view however ignores the fact that women do retain decision-making rights in household matters, most of which are beyond the male authority.[17]

Within the household and especially in the case of the joint family, limits placed upon women's decision-making are subject to the female hierarchy that exists in the household, which is based upon the status and age of different women in a family. Something that is a constraint for one woman in the household could be termed an opportunity for another. Within the household therefore, older women still retain control over the most important tasks such as food management, consumption and marriage decisions.[18] With the mother-in-law in charge, with the son or sons' welfare at heart, the preferential treatment of men, for example in the practice of saving larger and best portions of food for them, still continues (Van Vugt 1991: 28). The younger women are involved in child rearing as well as carrying out household chores. In a joint family, the youngest daughter-in-law as well as young unmarried women tend livestock, while the elder women are responsible for overseeing feeding, milking and grazing (Hemani & Warrington 1996: 58).

Some women, especially educated ones who earn an income, do eventually manage to attain a higher status and greater respect from their husbands (Varley 1998: 14). They are also often excused from farm labour, which shifts the burden to older women. However, women usually control only the income that they earn, which means that the younger income-earning women might not influence the overall decision-making in a joint household.[19] Similarly young men are increasingly turning to off-farm work, leaving the older men behind to help the women in farming tasks (Hemani & Warrington 1996: 12). Men's absence from home over long periods also affects their decision-making power within the household, whether joint or nuclear. In the case of a nuclear family women are gradually being pushed into the role of major decision-makers, even if they wait for token approval from the husband.[20]

The media has played a part in influencing change in NAC, as radio and television have entered people's homes. This has caused concern to some over the exposure of women and children to liberal views, while others value the opportunities the radio and television have given women and children to learn about life outside NAC.[21]

Over the years, women have emerged as an economic force to provide if not full then at least partial support to male earners in their families. As pointed out by one WO member from Nagar, '[P]reviously one person was overburdened financially in a family, when there was no cash income opportunity in the area. Now we have learnt to contribute financially through small activities like poultry keeping, fruit marketing and mainly our savings.'[22] Such small-scale income generating activities as those introduced by AKRSP have definitely been important for women, as they have opened up a whole new world to them by adding financial value to their unpaid traditional tasks.

Women's role as income earners has also resulted in partial changes in the household division of labour. Due to the high rate of male unemployment (because of the lack of opportunities in NAC), many women have become the sole supporters of the family. Furthermore, many women have also 'forced' their husbands to help them with childcare and other household tasks. The male attendants-cum-babysitters that have accompanied many women from the WOs for various AKRSP training courses illustrate the changing support patterns, which have evolved out of economic necessity. However, it must be recognised that it is often other female household members (mothers, daughters, sisters, daughters-in-law etc.) who provide the support to women who work, because in many places it is still the case that such work is not considered suitable for men.[23] There are also examples of mothers-in-law who have taken up the major burden of farm work, releasing their daughters-in-law to earn income from off-farm sources for their families, particularly the children, something that would have been unheard of a decade ago.[24] But change is slow in such a strongly patriarchal society and the different pace of women's development in the various parts of the AKRSP area also makes it difficult to generalise that women's decision-making power has increased everywhere.

In certain parts of NAC, gender roles are being reinforced by religious interpretations which extol the virtues of women's place in the home: 'to be beautiful for and attentive to the needs of the husband'[25] and frown upon women's mobility. Nevertheless, household livelihood strategies are a process of negotiation and compromise which, while taking into account cultural and religious norms, have to cope with the economic reality of making ends meet. Many of the younger educated women such as Nida, daughter of a WO member in Skardu, are of the view that:

> Education and the ability to earn money have brought new respect for women in their society. However, the negative side of this 'empowerment' for younger women is that often the parents delay the marriages of their income earning daughters to maximise financial support from her, or conditions are set at the time of marriage that the income of the daughter would still come to the parents!

Education, while being one of the most important factors for women's empowerment, does not always mean progress and peace of mind for men as well as women. Both sides want better-educated spouses or better jobs and the lack of either can lead to depression. This has been the case with young girls in parts of the Ghizer and Gilgit district. Many assume that such pressure is leading to the increasing suicide trend among young women.[26] Educated women compared to men suffer more due to unemployment. Men might move to other parts of Pakistan in search of jobs whereas women do not have that opportunity (Streefland *et al.* 1995: 8). A woman's mobility outside of her house or village is still very much dependent upon the male relatives. This is especially true if the woman happens to be young and unmarried.

Young educated men and women are also showing less interest in carrying out farm work. While currently the situation is not critical, there is concern that this could eventually place a greater burden upon the older generation, leading to an 'ageing' of the agriculture sector. On the other hand, it could also encourage the move towards innovative and less labour intensive farming strategies and greater livelihood diversification.

Another negative aspect of the process of development is the erosion of culture and tradition, particularly among the educated youth. Many young men and women, for example, in their quest for independence and because of their knowledge of the outside world, pay less attention to their elders. This view was expressed quite strongly in Hunza, which happens to have the most advanced rate of education, particularly for girls, within the Northern Areas. So far none of the NGOs or other religious institutions have systematically addressed this social issue.

The increase in education for both males and females has still not changed the situation as far as domestic violence against women is concerned. Despite all the gains that women might have made in towns and villages of the NAC, they still lack recourse to government institutions or other forms of civil society support to protect them from different forms of domestic violence: from husbands, in-laws, fathers, brothers or other relatives.[27]

Changing gender roles at the community level

Just as the VO has played an important role in building men's confidence and belief in collective action to solve collective problems, so has the WO become a major source of awareness and confidence building and hence an important forum for many women of the NAC. While in places such as Southern Chitral, the existence and development of WO forums has taken time, and is still considered difficult, women in the Northern Areas have begun to take a role in larger community forums at the village or supra village level. Admittedly, this role is still very minor and they are often passive participants. Many such forums are registered as NGOs and claim to be representative of VO and WO interests. The inclusion of a women's wing in some NGOs (even if it is mostly for cosmetic purposes) is recognition of the importance of addressing women's needs specifically within the broader framework. Much more work, however, needs to be done to give women the confidence and knowledge to be equal partners with men in these public forums.

At the same time, a very gradual increase of female-managed NGOs can also be seen in the NAC.[28] This trend in the formation of separate NGOs for women is in line with the historical formation of the first WO, which was begun because women's needs were not being properly represented in the VOs. It is also a development encouraged by donors who have viewed the formation of independent local civil society organisations as a 'key component of AKRSP's exit strategy'.[29]

A few examples of such women-managed NGOs/community based organisations are:

- Mountain Women Development Organisation, which has been operating Gilgit's first Crisis Centre for Women. Many of AKRSP Gilgit's senior female staff are supporting this NGO.
- Northern Areas Women's Development Organisation, which is being managed by a WO activist. The NGO has organised a few activities such as a women's conference with government funding, a management training course through AKRSP as well

as a vocational centre with the support of AKRSP, UNICEF and the Planning and Development Department of the government.
- Sahara Welfare Organisation, which includes about ten WOs from the Basin area of Gilgit, but has yet to do any major work because of lack of funds.
- In Chitral town a few years ago, an interest group of influential women came together in Chitral, to carry out some activities together for their own interest and for the benefit of the poorer women.
- In Rehankot, Chitral, a group of educated young women (who are strictly observing *purdah*) are working together to improve the environmental sanitation in the area around their homes with support from their brothers.
- All Baltistan Women's Association, which has been actively linking up with various donors to do relief work for women of the remote areas as well as provide vocational centre materials and training to different women's groups.
- Small community based organisations run by female councillors and some of AKRSP's female staff in Baltistan, working on women's welfare.

The formation of women's organisations in many communities has had an effect on gender roles at the community level by demonstrating women's leadership potential. The experience of collective action has provided a platform for some women leaders to move into public life as, for example, Union Councillors.[30]

As noted above, at the start of the AKRSP activities it was difficult enough to find women, let alone educated women to champion the cause of women in the political arena. The situation has changed considerably since then. Women are not only getting more educated, they are also gradually beginning to play a major role in different spheres of life, as teachers, lawyers, social scientists, doctors, and engineers. The majority of the women however are still confined to the traditionally acceptable professional fields of health and education,[31] where they do not challenge the status quo.

Politics is an area that has always been considered a male domain in NAC (and elsewhere), as it required interaction at the wider community level and therefore was beyond women's domestic/ private sphere. As is generally observed, 'participation in public sphere requires some personal autonomy along with a certain degree of independent control of resources. An element particularly difficult for women in Pakistan' (Siddiqui, 1995: 6).

Women's role in politics, in NAC (like the rest of the country) has been largely limited to just a few individuals, mostly from influential families, who had the political and financial clout to face resistance in order to work on women's issues. The establishment of the first Crisis Centre for women in Gilgit town, for example, was the result of the personal commitment and motivation of an ex-female councillor.

In the last few years, women have suddenly been given the opportunity to take an active role in the political field by the government, under the Local Ordinance 2001, which allowed for 33 per cent of seats for women at all levels from the district to the union council. This has already brought a large number of WO activists to the fore as councillors in Chitral, giving AKRSP an excellent opportunity to build the capacity of these women and assist them in influencing public policy.[32] In the Northern Areas, many women have come forward as members of the Village Councils or as District Councillors. Recently, two female advisors have been added to the Northern Areas Legislative Council. Currently, one female each from Baltistan and Gilgit hold these positions. This is to be followed by the establishment of the Women's Directorate in the Northern Areas as well as a Human Rights Committee with male and female members.[33]

As mentioned above, women's entry into the public sphere is still dominated by the educated and elite class of the NAC. At the same time, although the government is creating new venues for women's political participation, they still need to gain enough confidence to be treated on equal terms by men. In addition, the government needs to work on its own structure to bring gender related attitudinal reforms in its departments, by working on men to provide women the space and co-operation that they need to move forward.[34]

At the national level in Pakistan a number of developments have taken place which have influenced women's status; this background has a bearing on development for women in Northern Pakistan, so it is to this national background that we now turn.

Women's Development and Activism at the national level

Various commentators observe that 'women in NAC are better off' than many other women in Pakistan. Afzal Ali Shigri, an AKRSP Board member, reminded us of the plight of many women in Sindh, where he had served, when we met him in June 2003. He cautioned us not to forget that women in the hills and mountains are often in a better position than women in other parts of Pakistan.[35] Even so, if it is true that many women's 'condition' is better in NAC, their 'position' may not be better, which makes it very difficult to draw comparisons based on poverty levels. The focus on practical needs rather than strategic interests in AKRSP has meant that by taking a measured and cautious approach to women's empowerment, less attention has been given to advocacy and raising the voice of women, and thus substantially changing their position in society.[36]

The women's movement in Pakistan needs to be seen in historical and social context where women's lives and their status in Pakistani society have generally been seen as an embodiment of an undefined Islamic identity, which was quite often manipulated by the state, not to mention the class system behind the state apparatus. The limitations placed on women's mobility as well as their rights can generally be evidenced by the way the government has historically employed women in Pakistan. Although the government is the largest employer of the women, they have generally been directed into traditional, non-threatening areas such as the social welfare departments or the Women's Division, the latter being a product of General Zia's time which never really challenged women's subordinate role (Siddiqui 1995: 35).

There has been considerable change (not always positive) in the national policy context over the time that AKRSP has developed. In 1982, when AKRSP began, General Zia's government had proposed the 'Law of Evidence' (passed in 1984) which curtailed the weight of women's testimony, building on the changes brought in by the Hudood Ordinances of 1979, which replaced the existing Pakistan Penal Code for the crimes of adultery, rape, prostitution, theft, drinking alcohol and bearing false testimony. Khan (1998: 11) suggests that the 'oppressive political environment may be a major reason why the Women's Division [in government] took up its social sector development role with the greatest enthusiasm. The purpose of funding projects to provide special facilities for women was to fill in gaps left by other development programmes'. As such, the approach of government and NGOs in Pakistan at the time was in line with the 'Women in Development' approach being promoted by donors in many parts of the world (see above). In the ten years from 1979, 107 NGO projects for women-focused initiatives had been funded by the Women's Division (Khan 1998: 13). This WID approach provided specific support and funding for initiatives to integrate women into development, by making resources more available to them, in an effort to increase women's efficiency in their existing roles.

Meanwhile, in 1982, the women's activists and organisations in Pakistan demonstrated against the Law of Evidence, a protest that ended with some well-known women publicly being beaten by the police which attracted attention to the event. 'The day was to be celebrated as the birth of the women's movement in Pakistan' (Khan 1998: 11). In the years that followed, after the death of General Zia in 1988, the governments of Benazir Bhutto and Nawaz Sharif were challenged by the women's movement to cancel the amendments put in place by Zia. But powerful groups who supported the form of Islamisation promoted in Zia's time opposed such changes. Nevertheless, the women's movement has continued to push for the greater political participation of women in Pakistan. The government's 'Ministry of Women's Development', (MOWD) in its various forms, found support from a range of donors' representatives actively pressing the WID agenda, such as the

United States Agency for International Development (USAID) (until 1992, when USAID left Pakistan), UNDP and the World Bank.

The 1995 World Conference on Women was a landmark event, which helped Pakistan's main actors in the women's development process (government, civil society and donors) to move forward. The MOWD was responsible for co-ordinating Pakistan's contribution for the conference and the preparation of a National Report on the status of women. The Pakistan government encouraged participation, with the Prime Minister (Benazir Bhutto) leading a 21-member delegation at the conference. The partnerships between donors, government and civil society initiated for this event in support of the MOWD preparation of the Report and, after the conference in setting up 'Beijing Follow-up Units' in MOWD and Women's Development Departments, were important in drawing key organisations together around a common agenda. However, as Khan (1998: 42) points out, the 'post-Beijing scenario was much more difficult for donors and NGOs to co-ordinate. First, the government changed in November 1996, delaying implementation [...] Second, the MFU [Multi-donor Facilitation Unit] phased out in June 1996 and UNICEF assumed responsibility on its own for Beijing follow-up activities in Pakistan.' However, before the change of government that year Pakistan acceded to the UN Convention on the Elimination of All Forms of Discrimination against Women (CEDAW), under which it assumed the obligation to protect women from sexual and other forms of gender-based violence perpetrated by state agents and private actors alike.[37]

The present government, as noted above, has increased the opportunities for women's political participation, which has provided the space for a number of NGOs and donors to engage in activities to support collective political action by women as well as providing practical skills to enable women to operate in the public sphere (such as legal literacy). Many of these activities openly challenge existing hierarchies and human rights abuses.[38] A National Commission on the Status of Women was established in 2000 for a three-year period to, among other things:

[E]xamine the policy, programmes and other measures taken by the Government for women's development and gender equality [...] review all laws, rules and regulations affecting the status and rights of women and suggest repeal, amendment or new legislation essential to eliminate discrimination, safeguard and promote the interest of women and achieve gender equality in accordance with the Constitution and obligations under international covenants and commitments.[39]

The Commission set up a special committee to review the Hudood and other Ordinances. The Committee has reported back to the Commission.[40] The government in March 2002 published a 'National Policy for Development and Empowerment of Women', setting out the approach to be taken by the present government to addressing gender equality at the policy level. These are all positive steps which move the country towards what the founder of the nation, Quaid-i-Azam Muhammad Ali Jinnah, stressed in March 1944: 'I wish to impress on you that no nation can rise to the heights of glory unless your women are side by side with you.'[41] It remains to be seen how sincere the government really is in its commitment to women's social, economic and political empowerment, because 'working to change the attitude of bureaucracy in itself is the most difficult task.'[42]

The Dilemmas and Successes of the Women's Programme in AKRSP

There was initially no well thought out plan for women in AKRSP, as is evident from early project documents such as Annual Reviews. This information was reinforced during interviews with some of the (ex)staff.[43] In the initial years it is apparent that the management was undecided whether to work with separate WOs or with women through VOs. This indecision was a result of the focus on the *household* as the unit for development. Women within the household were not seen as separate individuals, for focused development. Women had very little decision-making power due to lack of property rights, so it could be assumed that any activities for them should be channelled through men (AKRSP 1984:17).

This focus was common in development at that time; few projects made an effort to look inside the household.[44] The main emphasis at the time concerning women was to make their traditional work, i.e. agriculture, easier by focusing on the reduction of their workload, and an up-gradation of their agricultural and household skills (AKRSP 1985b). It is no wonder then that the women/gender discourse and awareness related work in AKRSP is silent on one of the core issues hindering women's greater decision-making role, i.e. women's lack of access to property rights.

Women's development: getting the right mix

Although it is still a matter of debate as to whether the separate women's programme was a donor driven agenda or not, the fact remains that some of the first women's organisations, such as in Sherquilla in 1983, followed by Hyderabad, Hunza and Oshikandass, in Gilgit, were formed as a result of the demands from the women themselves. The women felt that men were not able to represent their needs properly.[45] It needs to be mentioned that this demand came initially from the Ismaili areas where the programme generally received a better reception due to its affiliation with the present Imam of the Ismaili sect. But this affiliation has also made AKRSP an easy target for criticism from the religious leaders of other sects. Such criticism has consequently had a profound influence on the approach taken to 'women's development', which has been non-confrontational and cautious throughout the two decades. At the same time, as the history of the struggle faced by the more politically active NGOs in Pakistan such as Aurat Foundation, Sungi, Shirkat Gah shows, the NGOs have never had an easy time working on women's rights issues.[46] Religious and other vested interests have often focused on 'women's issues' by targeting the women's work of, and in, NGOs.

So it is hardly surprising that AKRSP, as one of the earliest NGOs of its kind in Pakistan, adopted the same careful, traditional service delivery route pursued by other organisations in Pakistan. This was particularly critical given the need to strike a delicate balance between the three sectarian communities of NAC. At the same time, although these political and cultural constraints were there, they do not explain why AKRSP throughout its two decades never felt comfortable enough with its communities to move beyond its cautious approach. Part of the explanation could be that its parent organisation, the Aga Khan Foundation (AKF), itself has been even more conservative than AKRSP concerning gender issues. Hence no particular urgency was ever expressed by AKF to push the women's programme more aggressively.

The evolution of the women's programme in the early years of AKRSP (between 1983 and 1985) very aptly reflects such caution and the development related dilemmas as a lot of time was spent looking for a viable approach to development that could best meet the needs of the women of the area without being too confrontational. These years therefore showed two parallel models of women's development, one of separate WOs that accumulated savings among a recognised membership and the other of an integrated approach, which included some representation of elderly women in male-dominated VOs. However, 'the basic principles of the AKRSP approach were never tried in the women's programme with as much vigour as they deserved' (AKRSP 1986: 16). For example, 'Productive Physical Infrastructure' (PPI) as an investment in social organisation was used to bring the men together, but such a concept was never systematically and strategically pursued for women.[47]

During this period, although there was no separate WID section, the women's programme activities were developed which included the introduction of appropriate technology items, agricultural development, credit for essential inputs and training. By 1985, these activities were formalised into 'WO packages'.

In 1985, a female Senior Social Organiser was hired to push (among other things) the process of WO formation. The establishment of a separate WID section with a WID co-ordinator followed this first in the Gilgit region, where the regional office operated at that time out of the Core Office, followed by Chitral and Baltistan. This finally legitimised the formation of separate WOs, although the process of formation and reactions across the programme area were different. In the Ismaili areas, both in Gilgit and Chitral, group gatherings (for men and women) were common. Hence the idea of WOs was readily accepted. In Sunni areas like Jaglote in Gilgit, or South Chitral larger women's forums were never encouraged as they aroused suspicion and resentment. In Shia areas such as Nagar and Baltistan in the Northern Areas, discussion had to take place in 'Imambargahs' with 'Sheikhs' (Muslim clergy), to convince them of the legitimacy and value of the women's programme. Interestingly enough, in areas such as Baltistan, the idea of a separate WO formation met with resistance from the male Social Organisers, who considered it an unacceptable approach and maintained that it was 'pushed' by the donors.[48]

Although the patterns of introducing the women's programme showed regional differences, caution continued to be the common theme. In later years, such a cautious approach kept the women's programme behind in terms of the acceptance and adoption of the idea of gender mainstreaming[49] at the organisational level. It also created gaps in the programmatic approach, where only women's practical needs were addressed but those also in traditionally accepted areas, and there was no clear strategy to take them any further, particularly in economic and socio-political empowerment.

At the same time, questions were being asked about how proactive a role AKRSP should play in meeting social sector needs. In fact, the role of AKRSP in social sector versus the productive sector linked to the role and function of WOs became one of the 'strategic worries' for the organisation (AKRSP 1992b: 32). Perhaps it was partly as a result of this debate that AKRSP initiated in the mid-nineties Small Infrastructure Projects (SIPs) for women in the form of water supply schemes in Astore; adult female literacy projects in Chitral, Baltistan and on a small scale in Gilgit, as well as Traditional Birth Attendant (TBA) training in Baltistan.

Women's public role

Women's activities were added on to the programme as new issues unfolded and needs arose rather than being part of a long-term strategic plan with a specific vision. Not surprisingly, the focus was on meeting women's immediate practical needs. Having said that, it must be remembered that the decision to go for WO formation was in itself a strategic one as it provided women with the first ever such forum to come together to voice their concerns and to derive strength from numbers. Taking men into confidence for WO formation has however always been important as key male supporters often proved invaluable in cases where the institution of the WO has been threatened by other vested interests within a community.[50]

While the WO forum in itself was a place in which the confidence of women was built, many staff and outside opinion makers have recently argued that had AKRSP put more financial investment in the WOs through appropriate schemes such as the ones for the VOs, then much of the resistance that the women's programme faced in the last two decades would not have materialised. Be that as it may, one of the most important contributions of the process of WO development has been the encouragement that it gave women to come forward as leaders within their small semi-public and public spaces. This trend became more apparent with an increase in the availability of educated women and as women realised that women themselves were better at representing their needs.[51]

As noted above in the discussion of women's move into local politics, it is through the WO forum that many women acquired skills, knowledge and exposure, which consequently gave them confidence. However, as the recent Operations Evaluation Department (OED) evaluation report states, the WOs have perhaps been '...too relevant. They have responded to women's practical needs but not to their aspirations or potential as public citizens.'[52] Although the wider role of WO forums, beyond confidence building within women's private domains, has not been aggressively pushed by AKRSP, it is not to deny that the women have not learned anything on the public front. The political representation of women in Chitral's local body elections, many of whom happen to be WO members,[53] or women members of *dehi* councils in the Northern Areas are proof of that.

Box 3.2. Women who make a difference (1)

Fatima lives in a small village Jafferabad of Nagar valley in the Gilgit region. She is the mother of eight children: five daughters and three sons, aged between one and fifteen. Fatima's husband works as a peon in a government school.

Fatima is one of the pioneers in establishing the WO in the village. When AKRSP staff came for the first time and asked about their village problems and introduced the concept of village and women's organisations, there was speculation and disagreement about these ideas. She however decided to lead the effort to form a WO. It was very difficult for her to convince women, as they needed permission from the men for any activity. However, she motivated some, who eventually got permission and together they started weekly meetings and saving.

The religious leaders in the village were not happy with her participation and preached in the mosque against working with AKRSP. They declared the WO activities un-Islamic and anti-cultural and even formed a committee to stop the women's group activities, which took by force the WO documents from the WO manager as well as saving cards from the members. This action made the WO defunct for months.

After months of being inactive, Fatima finally motivated some of her female friends and relatives to reorganise the WO. This time the women resisted against the religious leaders by refusing to give up their savings cards or to stop WO meetings. The religious leaders responded by stopping Fatima's family from attending the mosque and banned their attendance in other religious/collective activities.

This decision by the religious leaders and other rigid members of the community made it difficult for Fatima and her husband to socialise in the village and attend the ritual practices. Furthermore her decision to send her daughter to a nearby village school as there was no school in her own village, also brought criticism from her community. Fatima however held her ground and sacrificed her personal freedom for the sake of the development of her village and for her WO, a freedom that she eventually won.

One of the major achievements of the WO activities was the raised awareness about the importance of education. 'If our people would have started to work on education earlier, our children and perhaps we ourselves would have got respected jobs and could be on good positions,' she says with sorrow and further adds, 'However, personally I saw the world, and learned how to talk to people and run my household properly, which I would not have known, had I been confined to my home and not joined the WO.'

Many of the 'new women in politics' are untrained for their role and the majority are also unducated (Gloekler 2002: 7); nevertheless they are struggling in their own right to fight for the cause of women, something which many of them openly attribute to their role in the WO forum. Fighting for the cause of women however is not an easy task as they are out numbered by men, meet constant resistance and are bogged down by the cultural/religious constraints.[54]

Box 3.3. Women who make a difference (2)

Shama Chirag

Shama is the mother of eight children. She lives in Jagir Basin, a village in Gilgit town. Her husband died a few years ago, which has put all the domestic and external responsibilities on her shoulders.

In 1998, AKRSP staff came to her village and discussed the process of WO formation with her. Although she was a bit hesitant initially, she followed the suggestions and motivated about fifteen women to form the WO for the first time in her village. The number soon became thirty as the women began to realise the value of the WO forum as a way to get together and share their problems.

Under her leadership, the WO increased its saving and started the credit programme with Rs. 20,000. Each interested member was given Rs. 3000, which was invested in poultry keeping, fodder production and garment making. All reported a net profit. As Shama says, 'Paisa bolta hai' (money talks). When other women heard of the benefits incurred by WO members, it inspired them also to join, with the result that the WO currently has 90 members!

Shama was very keen on the development of her village and it is through her persuasion that two years after the WO formation, the men also formed a VO. She was the force behind the launching of a vocational centre for uneducated girls and women. Twenty five of the fifty 'graduates' of the centre are still engaged with it, making school uniforms and wedding dresses.

In 2001, she motivated the WO members to establish a primary school for boys and girls who for some reason were left out of the regular school system. There are now a total of seventy students in this first ever co-education school in her village. She was also able to establish a literacy centre in the village with the help of AKRSP.

She has recently also established a NGO comprising of 15 WOs and is also a member of the Village Council (VC). Initially men opposed her nomination and removed her name from the list. She however fought for her position by suing the authorised government official and took a stay order to stop the activities of her male counterparts. The matter was resolved only when the male members gave her status in the VC a public recognition and also gave her a written apology. After a few months, the chairperson of the VC resigned for personal reasons. The other members came to offer her the vacant position and she is currently the chairperson of the VC.

It was not all such smooth sailing for her. When she started her social work, people from her village used to spy on her. She was accused of going to hotels and keeping late hours. Her married daughters stopped visiting her and for a while she was also ostracised by her neighbours and other family members. Her confidence and belief in her work however were able to eventually change people's attitude towards her. This is evident from the way she received the support of the community on the numerous projects that she helped initiate in the village to bring development to their doorsteps.

Yasmeen, the District councillor from Gilgit, is an example of such women who had to fight an uphill battle. She used to go secretly to various WO meetings with the Woman Social Organiser in Nagar, because in the initial years of the AKRSP the WO forum was looked down upon by men. Similarly, during a discussion with two women councillors (who are WO members) in Koghuzi, Chitral, the women commented that there is a big difference in their lives. Now they can sit together with a male councillor and argue over the council budget; something that would have been impossible only a few years before.[55] Not surprisingly, it is active women like these who are also behind the budding female-managed NGOs of today. An important question here is whether AKRSP supported this capacity building or were the people selected in their political roles 'natural' leaders anyway? It also calls into question whether the donors have been justified in criticising AKRSP for its lack of emphasis on policy and advocacy.[56] Perhaps an important lesson here is that even if AKRSP helped to create a pool of activists engaged in WO activities, to come to the frontline, it has never really disseminated the lessons from political activism.

Just as the NAC exhibit wide social, cultural and political differences, so does the role that women take in (semi) public spheres. In south Chitral, bringing women onto the WO forum in itself was an achievement, whereas in other areas such as Gilgit or Baltistan, women are slowly appearing as members in the supra VO/WO forums registered as NGOs.

The potential of women in such forums has not been fully realised so far. For example, women's development in the form of education, health and vocational training forms a major part of the work of almost all local NGOs. However working *for* women does not mean that all women members develop leadership qualities in the *public sphere* to plan and manage their lives without the help of the intermediary NGO. That is an area where AKRSP certainly needs to support women in moving forward as the organisation has never really developed a proper strategy to build the skills of local female leaders beyond giving the WO manager training or a few WO management workshops. As a member of a local NGO in Gilgit, Hatoon Development Organisation pointed out, 'It is the larger NGOs like AKRSP which themselves never give our women members the opportunity to come forward on public forums. They always designate our male members.'[57] Unfortunately, women's appearance in public forums is hampered by their mobility and other cultural constraints, such as being restricted from travelling alone, which means women have to be accompanied by a male relative.

An important lesson drawn here is that if we have a multi-sectarian, culturally conservative, mountain society like AKRSP's programme area, then it should be assumed that the public role of women in general may not be replicable even across valleys. However, this does not mean that programmes should not recognise this diversity and come up with specific strategies to take account of different cultural scenarios or emerging needs of the time. Furthermore, programmes need to be aware that such strategies should still feed into the realisation of a common vision of development, something that gender programmes often shy away from, using diversity as an excuse to block women's development.

From women to 'gender'

In 1992 AKRSP initiated the Accelerated Professional Development Programme (APDP) for women of the NAC, through which many women acquired degrees in Natural Resource Management subjects.

AKRSP and other organisations later hired many of the women, who benefited from the APDP. This programme alone set a powerful precedent for women of the Northern Areas to move forward educationally and professionally and could well be considered one of the first capacity building programmes of its kind in the NAC.

Within the same year, 1992, the decision was taken to integrate WID technical staff into sections for better communication and co-ordination between VO and WO activities. It was also the first time that the word 'gender' was incorporated into AKRSP's planning framework, followed by the first 'gender awareness workshop', which included undertaking the gender analysis of the apricot marketing package (AKRSP 1992b). As would be seen in subsequent years, this set the AKRSP organisational pattern in place to focus the bulk of the 'gender' activity on sensitisation workshops (Moffat 2001).

By 1993 female technical staff were incorporated into the technical sections and by 1994, with the establishment of the Field Management Units (FMU), female social organisers along with the female technical staff began to be integrated into the FMUs, as also happened with the male staff. The WID section was abolished along with the post of the WID co-ordinator, to be replaced by the post of the Gender Co-ordinator.[58] At the core office WID concerns were merged within the post of the Programme Manager Policy and Research, thus abolishing the post of the Programme Manager WID. Although the role of other programme managers in the core office was also becoming irrelevant for the regions, this move seems to have affected the WID programme much more than the other sections.[59]

From then onwards it was assumed that gender concerns would be 'mainstreamed' across the organisational and programme levels. Unfortunately, as has been the case in many other programmes 'mainstreaming' meant the 'evaporation of gender' as it lost the structure that sustained the focus on women and gender in the programme. At the same time, a vacuum of leadership was felt to have appeared as regards the women's programme across the regions. The Gender and Development co-ordinator's post was merged into another section such as MER or later Social Development (Gilgit/Baltistan) or was given specific responsibilities such as literacy projects in Chitral.[60]

The attempts at 'mainstreaming' also marked a time of divergence in approach among the regions as each went its own way as regards the handling of the women's/gender issues at the programme and organisational level, depending on how it was seen to fit in the cultural context.[61] Some examples of these regional variations are: developing a separate regional code of conduct (Baltistan), pushing for women's health and education needs (Chitral and Baltistan), forming groups smaller than WOs around a common interest (Chitral), initiating water supply schemes for WOs (Gilgit and later in the other two regions), reviewing terms of partnerships of all WO packages to make them more gender sensitive (Gilgit) and using vocational centres as entry points for WO formation (Chitral).

Given this variation, it is no wonder that a common gender strategy could not be developed. It took until late 2000 for work to begin on the formulation of the first ever gender policy within AKRSP, which was to be incorporated into the personnel policies. Along with it the need was once again felt for a gender focal point at the core office to bring a sense of unified direction to the women's/gender programme.[62] The efforts to formulate a programme level gender strategy continue to date. However, it should be noted that the position of the Programme Manager Gender and Development has been incorporated into the senior management.[63]

A little in-depth analysis of the WID to GAD progression within AKRSP reveals some important lessons for development practitioners in similar environments and situations. The AKRSP example shows that the strength of a development project in the field is very dependent on the type of people who are implementing it and the kind of support (policy/logistical) that is available to them. The top leadership for the women's programme always came from outside of the NAC because it was quite difficult to find local women who were qualified beyond Field Assistant (12th grade). Furthermore, probably as a consequence of being dependent on 'outsiders', the leadership has changed frequently.[64] The ownership of the programme as a result has always been weak, and no one has felt it more than the female staff themselves.[65] A lesson derived here is that a strategic capacity building programme should be in place for all top-level posts from an early stage in the project. This might initially require outside expertise but management positions, particularly for women, should at least have local counterparts (trainees) from the start so that local people receive mentoring on performing the role.

The isolation of the WID programme (ironically due to the existence of its independent budget for all women-related activities, in agriculture, poultry, appropriate technology, training etc.), coupled with the fact that the female staff were less 'qualified' than their male colleagues, further discouraged their participation in larger forums.[66] The female staff's lack of qualifications did present a major constraint to the women's programme's strategic development. Nowhere was it more obvious than at the time of gender integration. While GAD was a new concept for male and female staff, the women themselves generally assumed that because they were women they knew what it was all about. Looking back, many now realise that the gender approach was never properly understood or utilised even by the women themselves.[67] The lesson learned here is that those promoting gender approaches have too often assumed that women, because they are often less privileged than men, are therefore naturally able to understand the link between the conceptual and the practical applications of gender. This link is not as obvious as is often assumed by the women themselves or those promoting the approach.

'Gender' is actually a donor driven agenda' is a comment that has quite often been heard within AKRSP (Seeley 2000: 2). A major component of promoting gender equity is changing the power relations, something that the staff in AKRSP (given the organisation's generally conservative approach) were not used to dealing with, which raised suspicions in the Programme that this was something being pushed by outsiders.[68] AKRSP staff, particularly the men in what continues to be a male-dominated organisation, are not unusual in reacting defensively to the pressure from staff responsible for the Gender Programme, as well as donors on 'gender'. The problem with WID/gender policies is, unlike many other issues, that they intrude into what is considered to be the private sphere of relations between men and women, challenging the existing distribution of resources and power at work and in the home. Religion mixed with cultural perceptions has been used as a defensive strategy against what was widely perceived to be a package of alien values.

A new concept remains alien until it is properly internalised within the organisation. Beyond a few workshops in each region which involved staff sensitisation and some gender analysis of the women's programme activities, policy and procedures to institutionalise the gender approach were missing. While the workshops gave staff the opportunity to become familiar with some of the 'gender vocabulary', there was no sustained attempt to transform gender-relations. Indeed, well founded fears over cultural and religious sensitivities constrained the programme. Thus gender concerns were not taken seriously and were seen as something that was for the women only. Consequently, this is how the gender approach moved forward. It was WID disguised in a new wrapper. In addition, while 'gender mainstreaming' was being talked about, no proper on-going comparative analyses of men and women's changing needs took place which could then be translated into concrete projects. Indeed, the discussion taking place in many parts of the world on the importance of involving men in 'gender and development' and the importance of understanding how concepts of masculinity influence gender relations seems to have largely passed AKRSP by.

Hence while gender rhetoric continued at the organisational level, its translation into practical strategies remained largely unexplored. Having said that, finding a way to bridge the gap between the attitudinal and the programmatic aspects of the gender training and gendered programmes remains a challenge in development in Pakistan and elsewhere.[69] Managing to balance advocacy and activism with service delivery at the same time and with the same measure of commitment and energy has so far not been possible for any NGO in Pakistan. There are so many organisations like AKRSP which are faced with a strategic choice.[70]

'Gender' brought along another controversial understanding about the role of women in development. Going through various awareness workshops, many staff began to understand gender to signify simply the culturally ascribed roles given to men and women. This implied that if women's roles are subordinate then that is the way it should be and projects just need to take that into account. The underlying implications of this trend were that resources for women were merged into the mainstream activities with the justification that it benefits all. In this context, female social organisers in Gilgit (where the GAD approach was the most 'forward') ended up carrying the workload of their male colleagues by looking after the VO issues also (in the name of 'gender integration').[71] It follows that a gender approach, if not properly understood and followed through, can mean that women lose out if women-targeted interventions that are needed are stopped in the name of 'gender-integration'. In addition, if gender is to be truly viewed as involving men and women then the stress needs to come from the donors/policy makers themselves first, who so far have focused on women, thus confusing the real message behind 'gender mainstreaming'. A better way to introduce a new concept such as gender would have been to graft it upon local cultural values including religion through a series of acculturation seminars involving intelligentsia such as (religious) scholars, activists and philanthropists.

In the post-gender integration phase of AKRSP, due to organisational need and as a result of recommendations by the Joint Appraisal Mission to AKDN (1996) and the Joint Monitoring Mission to AKRSP (1996b), a policy of positive discrimination was used to recruit more female staff on a lower minimum requirement compared to that required for male staff, due to the difficulties encountered in finding qualified women. In addition, a 10 per cent higher salary was given to equally qualified women compared to men (Shakeel and Usman 1997). A childcare facility was also provided to women in the field hostels.

The number of female staff compared to male staff is shown in the following table. This table shows that the percentage of female staff has remained quite low and relatively constant (although there was a dip in 2000) over the last nine years up to March 2003. Seventeen per cent of staff were women by August 2003 following restructuring which resulted in a reduction in overall staff numbers.[72]

Table 3.1. Number of male and female staff by grade in 1996, 2000 and on 31 March 2003

Grade	1996 Male	1996 Female	2000 Male	2000 Female	2003 Male	2003 Female
9	5	0	3	0	2	1
8	6	0	7	0	6	0
7	4	2	12	0	10	1
6	15	1	30	3	37	4
5	32	6	37	4	47	10
4	97	31	86	20	43	19
3	19	15	15	7	7	5
2	94	0	99	0	81	0
1	27	0	28	0	27	0
Total	299	55	317	34	260	40
	85%	15%	90%	10%	87%	13%

Source: AKRSP records

In the case of Baltistan, additional steps were taken in the late nineties to assign separate vehicles to the female staff in the field and they were also able to spend one week per month in the Skardu office to write reports, learn to use the computer or to just get the opportunity to share information with other colleagues. This experiment had mixed results. There were fewer complaints from the female staff because they had been assigned special resources and they felt more confident but it did not lead to an overall increase in the quality of work that was expected because of the female staff's own capacity and skill limitations.[73]

As the above example shows, despite the introduction of a few positive steps, the results were not uniform across the programme area. One reason for that has been the performance of the female staff, many of whom retained the same position (as social organiser) that they had during the WID phase, with no apparent understanding of the shift in direction or sustained on-the-job-support in order to make the change.[74] Another important reason has been AKRSP's consistent failure to develop and institutionalise a proper gender sensitive appraisal system which could match job requirement with capability. Hence over the years many female staff were getting the benefits of AKRSP's affirmative action but they either did not manage to utilise their skills or were not given the guidance and training to develop their skills to do their jobs effectively. Gender mainstreaming in AKRSP suffered because it was very dependent upon positive support from male staff and the approach taken overestimated female staff capacity.[75]

At the other end of the spectrum, various staff discussions revealed another side-effect of the positive discrimination towards women. When qualified women were put into their respective positions, it was often assumed that they were there to fill numbers due to donor pressure and not because they were the best qualified individuals available for the post. The absence of a proper gender sensitive appraisal system over the years that could provide a means of judging people's performance by their assigned tasks and level of responsibility has also not helped to lessen this perception. The lesson derived is that positive discrimination policy is a commendable step for any organisation which is trying to take steps to be gender sensitive. However, professionalism also demands that there should be clear job descriptions and a gender sensitive appraisal system in place to ensure that those who reap the 'extra benefits' also have the skills to deliver.

Women and economic empowerment

During the last two decades the bulk of activities for women of the NAC have been in the socially acceptable traditional on- and off-farm areas which include poultry, livestock, vegetable/fruit production and processing, stitching and embroidery (AKRSP 2001: 11). This trend follows the original thinking within AKRSP, that given the constraints on women's mobility and decision-making, it is easier to start assisting them by first improving upon the tasks that they already perform (AKRSP 1984: 22). Hence labour saving devices were introduced as well as skills to increase the productivity of the work performed by women. With the increase in productivity, the idea of earning cash income through small-scale sales of the additional produce was also a novel approach introduced by AKRSP.

Over the years, women's productive skills and their incomes have increased. In addition, being able to hold a personal bank account through the WO has given them the 'legitimacy to keep their earnings' (AKRSP 1994a: 25). In many cases, women do gain economic bargaining power with their small scale earnings which also has a value in improving their status in the eyes of male members of the household, by showing them that women can manage finances (Varley 1998: 13; Muzaffar 2002: 12). One could also argue that women's control over their own earnings exists because the gains in most cases are quite small and most of the money earned is used on children's health and education.

Although AKRSP's work on small-scale income generating projects has been very important for women, the development of women-owned and women-run enterprises has not been an easy process and it continues to pose a challenge for AKRSP (see Chapter 6). For example, poultry management has been a popular package among women because of their familiarity with poultry rearing, but the introduction of new poultry breeds from other parts of Pakistan meant high mortality, irregular supply of chicks and high feed costs (Ali 1991; Van Vugt 1991: 37). Furthermore, except in a few cases, commercialisation has meant that men have taken over control of the enterprise.

The proliferation of vocational centres/training across the programme area, over the past few years is also a cause for concern. Such centres may not be able to provide training on crucial areas such as product quality and marketability, which are two of the main problems that often arise. The training of 132 women in Hatoon in an AKRSP-sponsored vocational centre is a good example.[76] The women got the training but are unable to build upon it because no marketing channel is available to them and no one has provided business training to any of them. The lack of a market was also lamented by the young women in the vocational centre in Mogh, Chitral, who were busy knitting and sewing children's clothes which they are unable to sell. The Chitral NGO Network (with 151 member NGOs) leaders also commented that the lack of a market for the products from their organisations' vocational centres is a continuing problem. In Baltistan, AKRSP has so far provided 919 women with vocational training. Many are earning an income by further training other women or through tailoring but mostly in villages that are 'relatively affluent' (Muzaffar 2002: 13). For the majority of women, lack of marketing channels due to their mobility constraints or mediocre quality in a competitive business dominated by men means they only get a marginal income.

Vocational training courses have therefore produced very few real entrepreneurs and raise serious questions about the way projects are launched on a mass scale without properly studying the market. It also raises the issue of donors pouring in a lot of money behind 'ill-organised development-based businesses.'[77] On the other hand, given the constraints that women in most of the NAC face, one could argue that the promotion of development-based small scale businesses is the only way for some time to come to provide women the support that they need in a cash/resource strapped economy. An important lesson here is that in its enterprise development efforts, AKRSP must recognise the important role of other players, for example banks, large businesses, even multi-nationals to invest or to demonstrate how businesses work. In addition, enterprise development should be tackled through linkages with practising professionals, for both male and female managed businesses with real solutions to real problems.

Development could be termed a double-edged sword as the dilemma of increasing incomes and some gains in decision-making is matched by an increasing workload of women. Reduction in women's workload was one of the initial aims of the women's programme and to that end various labour saving devices were introduced along with improved skills to increase production per unit. The track record of most of the labour saving devices introduced has not been very good as most of them posed management and maintenance problems (Ali 1991). It is unfortunate that further work in this area was discontinued by AKRSP instead of investing more resources to develop easy to use and women-friendly technologies.

Over the years donors such as DFID have cautioned AKRSP about the increasing workload of women, not only as a result of male out-migration but also due to the income earning activities. Although the overall workload of women and that of men might have increased in the sense that they are perhaps working longer hours, the gains (financial and others) are much more than before. The nature of work has also changed over the years, becoming less physically intense but more activity-intense. Nevertheless, there is no single answer to the question of workload. It varies according to the nature of a household (extended or nuclear), cropping area (single or double), geographical situation of the area (centre or periphery), status of the family (with or without an out-migrated male) among other things. AKRSP's weakness here has been that this issue has not been properly researched and documented to address such criticism (see for example Miers 1996: 20).

Box 3.4. Women who make a difference (3)

Sifat Jamal is the president of WO Benazir Sonoghor in Chitral. The WO was formed ten years ago. Sifat Jamal is the mother of eight children, all of whom are married by now. Her only son is in Chitral scouts. Her husband is deaf and dumb and he cannot work properly in the fields.

Sifat has a good amount of land. After joining the WO she got training in poultry farming and vegetable production. Unlike many other trained women, she made full use of her skills. For the last few years she is running her own poultry farm and commercial vegetable plots. She is in effect the head of the household and manages her household expenditures. Although her son also provides some money, she considers it insufficient for her household expenditure. Therefore she utilises her own skills to help her son run the household. Her WO savings at the moment are Rs. 10,000.

She is also managing a forest nursery for which she is not dependent on AKRSP. She sells the saplings within the village. Whenever she is in need of some advice etc. she travels to the AKRSP office 35 kms away from her village on her own.

She suffers from asthma, and gets treatment from her own expenses. She was the role model for other villagers to form WOs in the area.

Improvements in women's decision-making in terms of control over the household budget and farm-related decisions have been recorded as a result of their own income earning capacity or due to their husband's out-migration (Moffat 1999: 9; Varley 1998: 8-9; Makeen 1999: 27). Women's decision-making power, however, is largely restricted to the domestic sphere and within the home depends upon a particular woman's status within the household (Moffat 1999: 11; Hemani and Warrington 1996: 12).

AKRSP has aimed to reduce poverty from the NAC by raising people's income and by giving them the skills of empowered communities to plan and manage their development independently. Although the general poverty levels have been significantly reduced and now stand at 32 per cent for the programme area,[78] the issue of targeting the poorest needs further attention and strategic planning.[79] Within the category of the poorest, women, due to their limited mobility, can suffer the most. Their health suffers due to lack of access to health services and the female children more than the boys are deprived of education due to domestic responsibilities as well as proper nutrition. They may lose out financially because they cannot market produce themselves. Often the poorest women are also the ones to lose out first wherever there is erosion of traditional charity giving practices.

Targeting and working with the poorest requires careful planning to ensure that women are not further marginalised from the benefits, and that incentives are not given just to meet a Programme (or donor) requirement that development initiatives should involve the poorest women, an issue that AKRSP is still grappling with. Two examples below illustrate the problems as well as benefits of poverty targeting initiatives by AKRSP in a village in Khaplu, Baltistan.

Hamida has all the farm responsibility because her husband has a problem with his leg. She was given 19 chicks as part of the poverty initiative. Her husband is currently taking care of the 12 remaining hens. The rest died due to disease, as there was no vaccination provision in the 'package'. The commercial feed for the hens is quite expensive and the husband claimed that he sometimes has to borrow money to buy the feed, which costs Rs. 700 per bag! On top of that the hens are laying eggs quite infrequently. The family makes Rs. 1000 over 2-3 months. The project is good only to meet short-term small needs. The sad part of this story is that the oldest girl who was attaining first position in her class (grade 5) has been removed from school to take care of domestic tasks.

Zahra has been given a sewing machine by AKRSP because she has some knowledge of tailoring. She earns about Rs. 500 a month although she has kept no record. No training has been given to her either in tailoring or in financial management. She uses the money to buy more material for making clothes and also contributes to paying her children's fees. Her husband goes to Lahore during winter months to work as a cook but is in the village during the agricultural season.

It can be deduced therefore that economic empowerment alone does not always guarantee social empowerment. Although addressing economic needs does bring about, in the long term, changes in the gender division of labour and roles, development projects must be sensitive to the various factors affecting female decision-making. Consequently there is a need to have an awareness-building element in their activities to provide such information to women, which helps them to plan and take decisions. There is also a need to support men in understanding, and where necessary accepting, the changing roles so as to encourage a change in gender relations. Most importantly, the process of awareness-building should also include giving women and men the knowledge of what their rights are and how they can gain confidence in their own abilities, something that affects the poorest the most.

Women and social sector needs

As an organisation that believed in the by now famous motto of 'learning by doing', AKRSP has often moved forward without preconceived ideas. The programme was known for its 'method of experimentation, adaptation and trial and error innovation.'[80] The debate over whether the women's programme should have gone in the direction of social sector services provision as opposed to adopting the production model for the women's programme to this day remains unresolved. Suffice it to say that the initial objectives of AKRSP, given the extreme poverty of the area, were to raise the living standards of the people of the NAC by doubling their per capita income. It therefore followed that the first place to start was with the agrarian economy of the area in which both men and women played an important role. Social empowerment (collective forums giving strength to deprived communities) was being matched by economic empowerment (an ability to earn extra income and raise confidence).

Initially, as the Aga Khan Education Services (AKES) and Aga Khan Health Services (AKHS) were traditionally involved in the education and health sectors respectively, it was considered best by AKRSP to pursue those needs at the community level through these existing services. One could argue that by doing so, AKRSP perhaps expected more of the two organisations than they were able or willing to deliver, given that this entailed reaching out equally to the 'non-traditional' (non-Ismaili) areas. In addition, it was also assumed that WOs would independently form links for health and education with these organisations and therefore 'join up' the approaches of the various Programmes (Ali 1991). Over the years, it could be debated whether WOs in general were able to live up to that expectation independently of AKRSP.

Some donors, however, have had their reservations about AKRSP venturing in a big way into the social sector.[81] CIDA for example, although not against paying attention to social sector needs, has expressed concern over the heavy focus (in Baltistan) on the social sectors, arguing that emphasis on income generation is also needed because without access to income, people cannot fully benefit from the social sector services.[82] Others such as the World Bank, have called literacy centres and water supply schemes 'modestly effective,' but questioned whether the strategic framework that AKRSP has for such projects fits into the overall 'village and regional (and not just women's) development' (World Bank 2002: 22).

The success of AKRSP's venture into social sector services will be briefly examined below, through the example of the literacy centres. Literacy centres were originally meant to be the focal points around which the WO could build its collective strength while providing a modest solution to the problem of low adult female illiteracy rates which limited women's role within and outside the household. Different approaches for these centres were developed and adopted in Chitral and Baltistan.

Chitral developed a highly sophisticated adult literacy curriculum which required careful planning and selection of the target group. By default it meant that such a facility could be provided to the best WOs, which left out the use of these centres as an entry point in areas where AKRSP did not work.

In Baltistan, due to the lack of proper government investment in education, many of the adult women as well as young girls have missed out on formal education. The objective of taking literacy centres to scale in Baltistan[83] is to provide basic education and schooling facilities to adult female learners and to create awareness about the importance of literacy within the region (Hussain 2002). The original idea of using literacy centres as an entry point or as a way to further develop WO activities has been given only marginal attention. In addition, many of the 'adults' in the centres are girls between the ages of eleven and fifteen.[84] Literacy centres therefore cannot be said to have really linked WO members in a collective manner to strategic aspects.[85] The critical question therefore remains: where would social sector interventions such as literacy centres, the training of traditional birth attendants, and continued education programmes lead AKRSP in terms of the strategic direction of the programme?

As AKRSP tries to keep up with the community demands by directly getting into the provision of social sector services, the pursuit of social sector goals by out-sourcing them to smaller/local NGOs is a formula being tried by other Rural Support Programmes (RSPs).[86] In the context of the NAC, it is still questionable whether small NGOs such as Al-Nusrat Welfare Organisation or Yugo

Welfare Trust in Baltistan, which are taking up the cause of female education in their villages, could take up this responsibility on a larger scale, but it is certainly worth trying. On the other hand, slightly larger local NGOs such as Naunihal Development Organisation in Nagar, which was initially assisted by AKRSP, have played a major role in the spread of female education in the area. In Chitral many NGOs are also working on raising the awareness of parents about the importance of girls going to school.

There are a few lessons to be learned from AKRSP's activities in the social sector. To begin with, lack of potable water, basic health services or functional literacy remain crucial needs as long as the macro infrastructure supported by the government is not put in place to meet them. Given the great importance of these needs, many development projects might be 'pushed' into the role of becoming providers of social sector services, particularly because they affect women much more than men as a result of the cultural constraints and gender roles which prevent them from more strategic intervention.

However a careful analysis of an organisation's own strengths and weaknesses is necessary so that the best possible ways could be explored to meet those basic needs, which could also involve other actors in the area and lead to changes in strategic needs too. Collaboration not only builds trust but also the capacity of other partners, particularly local level institutions, to carry the extra responsibilities and bring about change. At the same time, creating the right interface and balance between the responsibilities of the government and civil society organisations is subject to the nature and urgency of local needs and the partners' capacity.

Wider Gender Scene in South Asia and Pakistan

The NAC has often, as noted above, been viewed as a particularly difficult place in which to encourage gender equitable development. But are relations between men and women so particularly different in NAC compared to parts of India where women's mobility is restricted and patriarchal norms place men firmly in control of decision-making? Or in Bangladesh where there is considerable discussion on Islam and women's development, as a result of which many NGOs' support for women's empowerment is questioned because of concern that such interventions are destabilising family and society and going against Islamic teaching?

Bangladesh and India

The 2001 World Bank OED evaluation team observed that the issues that AKRSP faces in the gender and women in development programme 'are common to most well-established development agencies in South Asia that started with separate programs for men and women but have since developed coherent and integrated objectives and structures' (World Bank 2002: 44).

In this section we focus on the experience of the transition from WID/GAD of some organisations/programmes in South Asia, working in a similar field to AKRSP. It is difficult to draw direct comparisons; indeed one of the reasons AKRSP has often stressed the need to 'learn by doing' has been the view that the NAC social context is so different that lessons from elsewhere are difficult to apply. While each context is indeed unique, particularly because of religious and cultural differences, there are some common threads. We look first, and in the most detail, at BRAC[87] because this is an organisation that has made considerable progress in the development of a 'gendered approach' within an Islamic context.

BRAC is a large rural development NGO/private sector development organisation in Bangladesh which has been working to alleviate poverty and empower the poor, particularly women, for the last 25 years.[88] BRAC has, since the mid-1970s, had projects for women, particularly credit programmes, so those women could be less dependent on male members of their families.[89] During the 1980s a range of programmes began on rural development, education and social safety net initiatives which were targeted at women. A women's health development programme began in 1991 (a child survival programme had been started in 1986). In the late 1980s BRAC began to actively recruit women staff but found it difficult to retain them, so in 1993 a 'Women's Advisory Committee' was set up in the Training Division which looked into the reasons for the drop-outs. A module on behavioural aspects of gender awareness was developed for both men and women staff, which was developed further into a gender awareness and analysis course.

In 1995 the 'Gender Quality Action Learning' (GQAL) programme began to strengthen the staff's capacity to: 'i) plan, deliver and monitor gender equitable programmes and ii) work with managers and staff to strengthen organisational systems, policies and procedures in support of BRAC's gender goals' (Murshed 1998: 5). In the same year the Gender Resource Centre (GRC) was established to disseminate gender-related information throughout all levels of the organisation. The GRC team had the remit to 'improve gender equality both within BRAC and in the provision of services to poor rural women in Bangladesh' (Rao and Kelleher 2002: 16) thus keeping 'gender on the agenda of BRAC' (Murshed 1998: 5).

Rao and Kelleher (*op. cit.*) stress that the process of getting 'gender on the agenda' was not simply a question of providing special programmes for village women and training on gender; it involved field-based learning while working closely with senior management in order to look critically at ways of working, and to change organisational norms, systems and professional relationships among staff. Rao and Kelleher comment that the GQAL programme 'enjoyed the support of the Executive Director who encouraged the Gender Team to 'say it like it is' and take risks' (1998: 183). This illustrates the importance of working in an organisation with men and women staff *at all levels* while promoting gender equitable development in the field programme, which addresses women's strategic interests. 'BRAC realised that many of their women members were suffering from illegal divorces and inheritance disputes. They therefore initiated a para-legal training program that taught women to understand their rights and to claim them' (Rao and Kelleher 2002: 24).

Challenges remain: not all programme managers have been equally supportive of the 'gender agenda' which has affected implementation. In addition socio-political change as well as natural disasters, such as floods, have necessarily slowed down the GQAL programme. In 1998, Rao and Kelleher wrote of the challenge of 'reinstating a focus on women's empowerment [in BRAC's programme] while not jeopardising the credit programme imperatives', which meant changing programme targets to reflect changes in empowerment (rather than looking at amounts loaned or enterprises established) and working for social change. They go on to say '[H]ow much BRAC can and wants to get into this area is still open to question' (1998: 183-4). In Rao and Kelleher's 2002 paper they indicate that BRAC has increasingly embraced a rights-based approach, but given the political and religious context of Bangladesh the organisation needed to address social change cautiously, ensuring that men and women at all levels are supportive of the changes.[90]

A similar pattern of a shift from women-focused interventions to initiatives working with women and men together to encourage gender equitable development in 'the field' and in the organisations themselves, is found in the history of AKRSP (India) (AKRSP(I)), the Navinchandra Mafatlal Sadguru Water and Development Foundation (Sadguru) and the West India Rainfed Farming Project (WIRFP).[91] The focus of their work is on natural resource management for rural development (soil and water conservation, agriculture etc.) unlike BRAC which began as a relief organisation moving into more general development and micro-credit, which provided the basis for its large 'women-focused programme.[92] These organisations in India have been working, like BRAC and AKRSP in Pakistan, in a patriarchal society in which men dominate the public sphere. Writing of AKRSP(I) in the 1980s, Shah (1998: 244) says 'Meetings of VIs (village institutions) remained largely a male preserve. In Bharuch District, [Gujarat] it is not socially acceptable for women to share a common platform with men of their village, nor are women expected to speak in a public gathering where men are present'.

Sadguru's response to the difficulties of working with women as well as with men was to support supplementary off-farm earning opportunities for tribal women, which was part of an effort to prevent widespread distress migration. This initiative grew into SAHAJ, an independent entity which is promoting and marketing art and craft-based income-generating products.[93] AKRSP(I) and WIRFP also developed separate self-help groups and credit and savings initiatives for women and also provided 'gender sensitisation training' for staff and for men and women in the villages where the projects worked. As the language and approaches changed internationally, so these projects adapted too with AKRSP(I) developing a 'gender strategy document outlining all the steps to be taken to increase the institutionalisation of gender equity at all levels of the organisation, and in VIs [Village Institutions] and in different programmes' in 1997/8.[94] AKRSP(I) developed 'Equity Policy Guidelines' in 1998 which embraced the principles of gender equity. The WIRFP also developed a Gender Strategy in the late 1990s. An end of Phase 1 (1993–1998) report observed that 'implementation of the gender strategy has depended very much on the presence of key senior staff. There is little inbuilt incentive to pursue gender objectives—in fact the reverse, since concern with gender equity significantly slows implementation progress' (Mosse 1999: 39). This frank observation strengthened the resolve of staff and donor (DFID) to press for the implementation of the gender strategy in phase 2 (from 1998) 'taking account of the weaknesses of Phase 1'.[95] This is being done by encouraging an increase in numbers of women involved in the project (staff and village-level activities) and trying to ensure that gender-sensitive approaches are nurtured.[96] The pursuit of an agenda which ensures 'equal rights and opportunities for women' in all project activities is certainly being helped by the presence of a woman manager, with skills in encouraging gendered development, as a State Co-ordinator.

Project review documents and consultancy reports for AKRSP(I), WIRFP and Sadguru in the late 1990s document lessons on gender equity, recognising that all changes in the projects and programmes have had 'a potential impact on women in that they shift patterns of responsibilities (with implications for control and workloads). Many of these changes involve areas of strategic importance for women.' (Mosse 1999: 38). All acknowledge that addressing gender and equity issues at all levels in the programme has been and remains a challenge and men and women need to be involved in the process.

Four clear lessons emerge from these Programmes and the BRAC example outlined in more detail above:

1. Space to innovate and funding earmarked for 'WID/GAD initiatives' have given opportunities for programmes to adopt innovative approaches towards gender and development.
2. The existence of individuals (women and men) within the programmes with the responsibility for and interest in accelerating gender equality have been crucial in building a wider constituency for gender mainstreaming.
3. Strong collaboration between programme staff, consultants and (sometimes) particular advisers from donor organisations with a commitment to women's empowerment and gender equality, has contributed to the development of gender equity within the organisations themselves as well as in the programme approach.
4. Evolving and implementing effective gender approaches requires commitment and leadership from senior management.

While battling with some of the same gender related issues at the organisation and programme level, AKRSP (in Pakistan) has increasingly recognised that the Programme can gain from the experience of other projects in South Asia. To this end, through participation in South Asian Network of Gender Activists and Trainers (SANGAT), AKRSP aims to build the capacity of its own staff by sharing experience with other organisations in the region.[97]

Pakistan

Moving to the national context within Pakistan, there is no doubt that AKRSP has been one of the pioneers in developing a unique service delivery approach to women's development, by focusing on building the collective strength and capacity of women. The programme, compared to other RSPs that followed its example, can still be considered one of the more 'women' and 'gender' aware if one takes into account the amount of work that has been done with women as compared to men.[98] For the RSPs as a whole, however, the political aspects of gender and rights-based equality have been missing from their approach to social mobilisation, much as they have been missing from their parent organisation, AKRSP.

Although it is now being realised within AKRSP that strong networking with other RSPs is needed to pursue gender equality objectives, this has been missing in the past. Part of the blame could be placed on AKRSP's own isolationist approach in assuming that it had nothing to learn from others given its special social, political and physical environment. Part of the fault also lies with other RSPs where gender was often not really an issue to be discussed or pursued in detail.

Most of the RSPs have operated as service delivery organisations through the extension of micro credit to men and women for various activities or by linking the men's and women's groups up with various government line departments to access various services including the social sector. Gender concerns therefore as mentioned above have not been so well formulated in most of the RSPs except the Sarhad Rural Support Programme, which is facilitating (along with the International Union for Conservation of Nature [IUCN]) a network called Gender Voices, of which AKRSP is also a member.[99]

It is only rather recently that the RSPs have started working closely with the government and hence getting a chance to get more intensively involved with the devolution process through their work in the areas of policy and advocacy as regards 'gender'. For example, a Memorandum of Understanding has been signed between the National Rural Support Programme (NRSP) and the government to work on social mobilisation.[100]

The capacity-building efforts of NRSP are going to focus on working with female representatives. This is an area where collaboration has slowly begun to develop between AKRSP and the rest of the RSPs with particular reference to Chitral. In addition, the networking wing of the RSPs, RSPN, also now feels the need to work towards influencing women's policy. Efforts are being made, for example, to create a network of women representatives in the Parliament. The RSPN management anticipates that a similar strategy of networking and partnership could be developed between the Women's Department and WOs in various sectors in the Northern Areas.[101]

In its current gender efforts, the RSPN has also focused on gender advocacy with some Islamic scholars. In addition, a gender monitor has been housed in the RSPN, on behalf of ICIMOD (International Centre for Integrated Mountain Development), to monitor the gender related progress of all IFAD funded projects in Pakistan.

The response of the RSPs to work in gender equality on the political front is a sign that major changes are also taking place within the government structure, especially since the formulation of the National Policy for Development and Empowerment of Women. To this end, the Ministry of Women's Development (MOWD) is now working on increasing gender awareness in all the Ministries by creating gender focal points within each Ministry. Some positive effects so far have been the increasing awareness within the government of empowerment and rights. There is now recognition of violence against women and there is an opening up in terms of attitudes within the government to work with NGOs on women's issues and not just with the international donors.[102] MOWD is also considering organising training of the Parliamentarians on gender, human rights, advocacy and development.[103] There is, however, recognition that changing attitudes to gender equality is a slow and exhausting process.

Another recent initiative is the setting up of a 'Gender Support Programme' (GSP) between the Government of Pakistan and UNDP to work towards the eradication of poverty in Pakistan 'through gender-responsive governance and a rights-based approach to sustainable human development.'[104] At the policy level, AKRSP has been asked to participate in the programme steering committee of GSP, thus giving the organisation an excellent opportunity to disseminate its experience and approach to development in conservative and remote areas. In the process AKRSP is also gaining credibility to assist the government to work on gender advocacy and rights issues.[105]

Establishing 'Tawana Pakistan' as a partner NGO to the Aga Khan University with MOWD also offers AKRSP an opportunity for partnership with the government. Through this programme, AKRSP is to assist the government in reducing inequities in traditional feeding practices between boys and girls and thus enhancing primary school enrolment of girls especially in the Northern Areas (Ghanche and Ghizer).

What the above examples tell us is that as an initial step it is necessary to work with women to strengthen their collective action. However, projects should have a long term vision with the realisation that eventually a change in public policy or legislation is required to bring about a change in women's position. The devolution plan has brought home this realisation to AKRSP and has also provided it (and other RSPs) with an excellent opportunity to venture into the culturally and politically sensitive area of women's rights (including issues of domestic violence) for which networking on regional and national levels can be an important support. In this regard, access to political representatives provides an excellent opportunity for NGOs such as AKRSP to use them as a channel to push awareness on women's rights issues.

When reflecting on women's development, in the context of the NAC, although the Aga Khan Education Services (AKES) and the Aga Khan Health Services (AKHS) predate AKRSP,[106] '[...] AKRSP's success in working with mixed and non-Ismaili communities helped to bring about the broadened mandates of other AKDN institutions' (World Bank 2002: 14). In addition, 'AKRSP is exemplary among the AKDN institutions in giving the institutional priority that it does to women's development and gender principles' (AKRSP 1996b: 78). These two AKDN organisations as well as the later Water and Sanitation Extension Programme (WASEP) have relied heavily on the structure of WOs to expand their programmes into areas such as Nagar, Astore and Baltistan in recent years.[107] A similar experience can be seen in Chitral. At the same time, literacy centres and other schools in

Baltistan have benefited from the teacher training courses organised by AKESP.[108]

The language of 'gender equality' is relatively new within the rest of AKDN. This could partially be explained by the fact that the Aga Khan Foundation (AKF) itself has been measured in its approach to gender issues until recently when it brought out its first ever Gender Equity Strategy. Gender mainstreaming however is still being approached with caution in AKF.[109] This 'slowness' to bring about gender equality is also reflected within the management structures of AKES and AKHS, where the presence of women at the management level is still limited.[110]

From a strategic perspective, it must also be remembered that it is organisations like AKES which have in part built the female education force of the NAC; producing educated women who are now making their presence known as the new workforce in the market. On the basis of regional parity however, this means that the best-educated women who have access to the best jobs are from the Ismaili areas.

The work of AKHS has also contributed to improving the health facilities of the NAC, eventually increasing women's health and hygiene standards and also reducing in particular infant mortality rates in the area. AKRSP's economic and social development contributions to women's lives in the NAC have to be understood alongside the contributions of the other AKDN organisations.

There is, however, much more room for institutionalised collaboration at the AKDN level, not only to manage resources more efficiently but also to deal with emerging social issues that are largely a product of the increasing education but lack of employment opportunities. The situation is further aggravated by the absence of a comprehensive skills development programme for those who do not make it into the labour market, and a changing division of labour with ever increasing workload for both men and women. There is therefore need to develop an AKDN 'image' along the lines of that which has been developed in Tajikistan.[111]

It should be noted that in terms of regional networking, AKRSP has also been on the steering committees of Mountain Area Conservancy Project, (in the NAC) and Northern Areas

Conservation Strategy, two projects under the overall administration of the IUCN. In both cases, the WO as well as VO forums have provided a sound base for the above projects to initiate their own work and to bring conservation-related awareness to the communities.

An important lesson learned here is that the isolated nature of the mountain societies and the harsh and restricted lives particularly of women make it essential for projects to collaborate and pool their resources and knowledge rather than each working separately in a vacuum.

Key Lessons

Above we have highlighted a number of specific lessons for policy from AKRSP's experience. While each lesson is important in its own right and particular circumstance, the experience of AKRSP and other organisations in Pakistan and the region at a more macro level draws attention to some overall lessons for policy makers.

To begin with, while training is an integral part of a gendered approach, it is also its most difficult aspect: attitudes take a long time to change. Thus, providing training on 'gender awareness' and 'gender sensitivity' has little value unless men and women can see something practical and, of course, beneficial that will come out of changed behaviour and approach. This does not imply that sensitisation is not important but rather stresses the aspect of carefully assessed training with a long term perspective. In addition, it should be a part of a broader approach supporting change in working practice and programme approach, which addresses equity issues in all areas of activity.

Any development programme working with gender aspects in conservative societies inevitably faces a backlash at some point because of the challenge and threat it presents to the status quo. Policy makers need to realise that religion and culture are important and should not be ignored by those promoting a gender equitable approach to development, so organisations should explicitly engage with religious and cultural opinion leaders. This does not mean that gender and women's programmes in societies which face resistance from the religious and conservative forces should always follow a policy of 'compliance'; a common tendency. Such a response is not necessarily healthy for development organisations or for the women who need their support to voice their concerns and find confidence in themselves. Dialogue by its very nature requires interaction on an equal basis with mutual respect of views rather than that based on a superior-inferior relationship.

At the programme level, gender policies and strategies must take greater account of the practical experience in the field and take note of that knowledge in order to build ownership and increase the chances of devising policies that work. Donors (and external commentators) have often failed to acknowledge the local evolution of concepts and approaches, which provide lessons on what works and what does not work, as well as pointers for how to ensure that 'gender' is embraced as a local issue, not viewed as a foreign concept. In this regard, it is also important that the language of policy is simple and the concepts clearly spelt out so that all men and women involved, at all levels, understand what gender awareness and gender sensitivity means practically for their lives and work and their professional development in their religious and social context. Gender must be understood within a broader framework of working for equity and justice. There must also be a clear understanding of why 'gender' means men as well as women!

Gender 'mainstreaming' as an approach and concept is very much in vogue, but it is not well understood. 'Mainstreaming' does not mean that a programme no longer requires the existence of individuals (women and men) within the programmes with responsibility for and interest in accelerating gender equality. While 'gender' has to be everyone's concern, unless there are well-trained men and women (NOT just women) who have the responsibility for promoting and supporting a gendered approach to development, 'the buck stops nowhere'.

In addition to firm organisational support, strong collaboration between staff, consultants and other organisations with a commitment to women's empowerment and gender equality, contributes to the development of gender equity within the organisations themselves as well as in the programmes, feeding in new ideas and sharing successes and problems (and solutions). Helping to build and sustain networks on gender nationally and regionally is a valuable contribution that AKRSP can make.

And finally and importantly:

Without senior management commitment to putting into practice what is written in gender policy documents, nothing will really change in terms of the status of women and the lives of women and men in the programme area and among the staff. If senior management, men and women (at all levels whether local Project, Programme, Board or Donor), are not actively engaged in gender mainstreaming, if they are not judged by their superiors and staff who report to them on their success in promoting a gender just and equitable organisation and development programme, 'gender' will be, at best, a concept that interests just a few women.

The Role of the Donors

'The women's programme lacks vision, direction, and core leadership' (World Bank 2002: 43). This observation contained in the most recent OED review report is one of the more critical comments from donors on the women's programme and AKRSP's approach to gender. Donor representatives have often over the years expressed concern that the pace of the gender programme has been too slow and cautious, and too focused at the practical rather than the strategic level of women's needs.[112] There has also been criticism that, as in other areas of work, 'learning by doing' has meant that AKRSP has failed to learn from the experience of other organisations within Pakistan and more broadly in Asia or engage with the development of gender policy at the national level.[113] Various studies have noted that the gender issues facing the programme in NAC are dynamic and are not so different from those faced in many other places, both within Islamic cultures and elsewhere.[114] It is perhaps because society is so obviously segregated by sex in

NAC that one is given the impression of uniqueness, a fact that has often been stressed to outsiders.

In the early days, as noted above, because AKRSP's role was seen to be service delivery to communities, there was no hint of any particular attention being paid to a 'women's programme'. It must be remembered that at this time in the early 1980s, and throughout the last two decades donor policy was also evolving, with different donors evolving their approaches at different speeds and with different modes of delivery and emphasis. These differences, in addition to the very nature of the donors' concern for gender issues, have posed a challenge to AKRSP.

DFID, for example, has never had an institutionalised WID presence.[115] From the 1970s attempts were made to integrate first 'women in development' and then gender into the whole programme, which has been a slow process. There has never been a separate gender unit.[116] With the publication of a 'Target Strategy Paper' *Poverty Elimination and the Empowerment of Women* in 2000, DFID pledged to ensure that women's empowerment and gender equality were to be actively pursued in all development activities. The Target Strategy Paper is built around the International Development Target framework, and by extension the Millennium Development Goals, which are themselves built on the 1979 Convention on the Elimination of all Forms of Discrimination Against Women (CEDAW). CEDAW provides the basis for realising equality between women and men through ensuring women's equal access to, and equal opportunities in, political and public life through measures to end discrimination in all its forms. In the late 1990s, DFID adopted a so-called 'twin-track' approach by trying to address inequalities between women and men in all strategic areas of work, while supporting specific activities to enhance women's empowerment (Derbyshire 2002: 9).

CIDA has, since the early 1970s, been among a group of donor organisations[117] that have most actively pressed the WID/gender agenda and have 'gender managers' and 'gender monitors'.[118] CIDA's policy on gender equity has undergone several updates (1976, 1984, 1991, 1995, and 1999). Meanwhile, ideas on 'women in development' have progressed into 'gender and development' and CIDA has built on its own experience and that of partners. CIDA's updated policy, from 1999, focuses on equality between women and men as a key objective of its development co-operation programme. This policy has served as a model for the development of AKF's own *Gender Equity Strategy 2002-2006*.[119]

This background is valuable, because it serves to remind us that the donors' approaches were developing as their own organisations gained experience and this helps to explain why and when particular concerns surfaced in donor reviews of AKRSP. But the increasing focus in recent years on monitoring the 'women's programme' and 'gender strategy' raises questions about the degree of 'ownership' that AKRSP (and other partners) has over the WID/gender agenda. As certain donors have given more prominence to 'gender' this has fuelled views that this is actually a 'feminist' and 'western' agenda being imposed on the NAC.[120] For the donor representatives, supporting a more active stance on gender policy in AKRSP, the lack of ownership by staff in AKRSP, as well as, until very recently, within their own donor organisations, has been a source of frustration, while the more experienced among them recognise that change takes time.[121]

The history is also important in order to understand the confusion that has arisen in AKRSP over whether a 'WID' or a 'GAD' approach should be followed, with donors and newly trained AKRSP staff becoming enthusiastic for GAD while in NAC encouraging a WID approach had scarcely made headway.[122] New ideas continue to surface because time has not stood still in the international discourse following the advent of GAD. But for many organisations like AKRSP, the challenge of addressing gender inequalities and the inequities that exist in gender relations, the central agenda of GAD, is so great that new ideas and terms have not begun to take hold in AKRSP. So, while some academics and gender activists have shifted their policy discourse to discussion of 'masculinities', 'rights' and 'intersectionality' (which acknowledges the multiple identities of each woman and man that affect gender relations), implementers (including donors) are involved in a development struggle to draw men into the gender debate and move the gender agenda beyond a focus on women alone.[123]

Conclusion

While the international gender discourse broadens to acknowledge the importance of the multiple identities of women and men in the causes of vulnerability and discrimination, linked to rights-based approaches to development, we may wonder what these new concepts might mean for AKRSP which has, as we describe above, struggled to establish even a women's programme let alone mainstream a gendered approach in development in NAC. Undoubtedly, the multiple identities of women and men are important in NAC: a new woman councillor may, for example, find her new authority compromised by kinship relations with certain men in her community. But for AKRSP in the programme area and in the offices in Gilgit, Balistan, Chitral and Islamabad, men are still sitting on the edge of the gender programme often untouched by an approach that is perceived by some to undermine their authority in the patriarchal societies of Northern Pakistan.

We began this chapter by recalling the film 'Taller than the Mountains' made for the International Year of the Mountain in 2002, which tells stories of the lives of women in the Northern Areas and Chitral over the time of AKRSP. We conclude with an image from that film which sums up, for us, a very clear message for policy that comes out of the two decades of work on the women's programme and gender programme in AKRSP.

In the film the husband of an AKRSP staff member recalls how his wife worked to support him through university and how, because of this, he realised that he should support her in what she wanted to do too. Their relationship, their support for each other, has resulted in both fulfilling their ambitions. Their experience illustrates the difference that a man and woman's respect for each other, their belief in what each other can achieve and the value of a supportive environment at home, can make to the family, as well as at work and in society.

In this chapter we have recalled how AKRSP, like many other organisations, has sometimes struggled to broaden from a 'women's programme' to a 'gender programme' and how, very often 'gender' is still reduced to just meaning interventions for women. Unless men as well as women on the staff and in the villages believe in the benefits that will come from equitable development and a 'gender-just' society, the 'gender programme' will continue to be seen as a separate initiative and the preserve of a few dedicated (women) specialists, easily sidelined by mainstream development.

Appendix: Chronology of National, Donor and AKRSP Development on Policy in Women over the last 25 years

Year	National Developments on Women and Policy[124]	Donor Developments on WID and Gender Activities/Policy	AKRSP Development of WID and Gender Activities and Policy
1979	General Zia promulgates the Hudood Ordinances overriding existing Pakistan Penal Code in various areas including cases of rape, adultery, and sex outside of marriage. Maximum punishments include stoning to death, for which a woman's evidence is not admitted. General Zia establishes a Women's Division within the Cabinet Secretariat. Women's Development Cells established within the Planning and Development Departments in the provinces in order to create a link to the Women's Division.		
1982	General Zia promulgates the Qanoon-e-Shahadat (Law of Evidence) Ordinance which said that in financial matters the testimony of one male witness will be equivalent to that of two female witnesses. Women's Action Forum, a group of urban women's rights groups and activities, demonstrates in Lahore against the Law of Evidence. Police break up the demonstration and a number of women were subject to police violence. This day in February has become a milestone in the history of the women's movement in Pakistan.		AKRSP starts.

1983	Planning Commission includes a chapter on women's development in the Sixth Five-Year Plan (1983-1988), for which an expert working group is constituted. The Ansari Commission is appointed to submit proposals for Islamising the state of Pakistan. General Zia establishes the Pakistan Commission on the Status of Women to identify women's needs in a wide range of sectors.		First Women's Organisation formed in Punyal, Gilgit. Others formed in Hyderabad, Hunza and Oshikandass. Khalida Nasir appointed as Senior Social Organiser to assist process of WO formation in Gilgit
1984	The Commission on the Status of Women submits its report, but it is suppressed. Parliament doubles the number of reserved seats for women from ten to twenty. Parliament enacts the Law of Evidence as an Act. It still reduces the evidence of a woman in some cases to half that of a man.	A few women professionals now working on WID issues within USAID, UNICEF and ILO in Pakistan. CIDA updates WID/gender policy (first produced in 1976).	Women's Programme developed in Gilgit with 35 WOs in the area.
1985			Separate WID section established in Gilgit.

1986	AKRSP Baltistan office established. Kulsoon Farman appointed to work with women in Baltistan.
	AKRSP Chitral office established.
	Two sisters from Dera Ismail Khan (Southern NWFP) recruited to work in AKRSP Chitral (no women from down-country willing to come because of remoteness of Chitral and they are unable to recruit women locally).

1987			WID Programme Manager appointed for Core Office (in Gilgit). 18 WOs formed in Chitral by end of year.
1988	Planning Commission includes another chapter on women's development for the Seventh Five-Year Plan (1988-1993) and has a working group to submit recommendations. Pakistan holds its first post-martial law elections after the death of General Zia. Benazir Bhutto's People's Party wins. The Constitutional provision for women's reserved seats lapses.	UNDP encourages donor agencies to form INWID (Information-sharing for Women in Development) group. Gender training becomes compulsory for all ODA (DFID) staff.	Female technical staff begin to be hired in AKRSP.

1989	Prime minister Benazir Bhutto upgrades the Women's Division to a full-fledged Ministry for Women's Development. Bhutto publishes and disseminates the 1985 Commission Report on the Status of Women. The First Women's Bank (FWB) is created to provide improved credit facilities to women and increased employment opportunities for women in the banking sector. Monitoring and Evaluation Cells are established at the centre and provinces to replace the Women's Development Cells within the Planning Commission and its provincial Departments. Minimum five percent quota for employment of women in government services is established through Cabinet decision. However, no mechanism is put in place to ensure its implementation.	WO involvement in TBA training in Nagar through AKHS. Also linkages made for health between WOs and AKHS in Jaglote. Orchard Development Package introduced as a PPI for WOs in Gilgit. Total of 65 WOs now formed in Chitral, supported by two WID staff.
1990	Women's Ministry holds National Conference on Policy Recommendations for Women's Development. Draft policy prepared but not finalised. President dissolves the PPP government and new elections bring in the Muslim League and its coalition partners into power. Parliament amends the constitution through the Shariat Act to ensure that all legislation is in accordance with Islam. The Qisas and Diyat Ordinance is re-promulgated, which equates a women's value to half that of a man for the purposes of compensation in the case of murder.	Marked increase in numbers of WOs in Gilgit and Chitral.

1992	INWID granted permission by Planning Commission to review 8th Five Year Plan and provide suggestions to improve the gender-sensitivity of the language. INWID persuades UNDP to include a mention of WID issues in opening address to 1992 Pakistan Consortium meeting in Paris. USAID, which had been actively pushing WID approaches, leaves Pakistan. 'Enhancing the status of women' became one of DFID's seven priority objectives.	Accelerated Professional Development Programme (APDP) for women initiated. Decision taken to integrate WID technical staff into sections. First time the word 'gender' is incorporated into AKRSP's planning framework. First 'gender awareness workshop' held in Gilgit.
1993		Female technical staff integrated into technical sections.

1994	Muslim League Government dissolved by President, and new elections bring the PPP back to power.	Donors have begun to use Gender and Development (GAD) terminology.
	National Inquiry Commission on the Status of Women is established, headed by a Supreme Court judge and including political representatives and experts.	
	Women's Police Stations are set up on an experimental basis at nine locations nationwide to facilitate women's access to the police without fear of violence at the hands of male officers.	
	Women appointed to the superior judiciary for the first time. There is an increase in the number of women in senior official positions (not sustained by the next government).	
	Legal Aid Centres established within Dar ul-Amans (government-run homes for destitute women).	
	National consultative committee set up to recommend legal reform and measures to increase women's political representation. It does not complete its work.	
	Pakistan actively participates in the UN International Conference on Population and Development held in Cairo.	
	Women's Development Cells in the provinces disbanded and fully-fledged Women's Development Departments established to facilitate de-centralised ownership.	

1995	Punjab government passes an ordinance reserving one-third of all local council seats for women. UN World Conference for Women takes place in Beijing with a large contingent from Pakistan present, led by the Prime Minister.	CIDA updates Gender Policy.	Female social organisers integrated into the newly established Field Management Units, together with technical staff. WID incorporated into the position of PM Policy and Research.
1996	Govt. of Pakistan acceded to CEDAW with one reservation (Article 29, paragraph 1). Later in the year, a process of Beijing follow-up is launched by donors and government, which includes the formation of National and Provincial Core Groups to monitor the government's implementation of the Beijing Platform for Action. Gender training becomes voluntary for ODA (DFID) staff.	A series of cross-regional gender training courses initiated.	
1997	The PPP government is dismissed and the Muslim League wins elections.		

Prime	Labour government comes to power in Britain. British Government publishes White Paper on Development, which has 'gender equality' is a central issue. A DAC gender equality marker introduced which replaced DAC-WID classifications and DFID's own Project Identification Marker system is revised in order to more effectively monitor the gender impact of aid policies and programmes.	Regional efforts begin to formulate gender strategies with Gilgit leading the exercise.	
1998	In the wake of international sanctions imposed on Pakistan after it conducts nuclear tests, a state of emergency is declared. The constitution is suspended.		
1999	October 1999 Army General Pervaiz Musharaf takes control of government. State of Emergency proclaimed on 14 October 1999.	CIDA updates Gender Policy.	Gender Strategy drafted for Gilgit and Chitral. Women in AKRSP begin to travel overseas for Masters level courses and diplomas (on AKRSP sponsored scholarships, Chevening awards, etc.).

2000	President Musharraf promulgates an Ordinance establishing the National Commission on the Status of Women. According to the Devolution of Power Plan (local government plan), 33 percent of local legislative seats are reserved for women in legislative councils at the union, *tehsil* (municipality) and district levels. Except for the union councils, the members of the *tehsil* and district councils are indirectly elected by the elected councillors at the union level.	British Government's second White Paper on Development places a stronger emphasis on women's empowerment and human rights. DFID publishes Target Strategy Paper on 'Poverty Eradication and the Empowerment of Women'.	WID Policy drafted in Baltistan. Work begins on formulating a gender policy for AKRSP. Gender focal point post created in core office.
2001	National Consultation by the Ministry of Women and Development requests a 30 percent reservation in National Assembly. Government issues Local Government Ordinance which allows for 33% women seats at all levels from the district to the union council.		Gender Strategy drafted for whole of AKRSP, which feeds into the development of a draft strategy for the whole of AKRSP.

2002	Legal Framework Order issued on 24th August 2002 announcing Provincial Assembly elections to be held in October 2002, and Senate elections in November 2002. The LFO revives the 1973 Constitution. Cabinet announces that 60 of the 332 seats in the National assembly be allocated for women (17%). For the six provinces, the same 17% quota is applied for women (this is a 7% increase on the 10% allowed in the Pakistan Constitution of 1973). Ministry of Women's Development publishes 'National Policy for Development and Empowerment of Women'.	AKF publishes 'Gender Equity Strategy 2002-2006'.	79% of WOs in Gilgit have women managers. 40% of all infrastructure schemes in Gilgit initiated 2000-2 have female representation on the management committees. 99 different WO incentive packages initiated in Chitral 200-2 which are planned, implemented and managed by WOs.
2003	National Commission on the Status of Women forwards its report on the Hudood and other Ordinances.	'Gender Support Unit' is set up by the Govt. of Pakistan and UNDP collaboration to work towards the eradication of poverty in Pakistan through gender-responsive governance and a rights-based approach to sustainable human development.	'Programme Manager Gender' becomes a senior management post.

NOTES

1. Material for this chapter has been provided by a number of different people to whom we are very grateful. We acknowledge the help of Fareeha Ummar Malik in providing information, moral support and for setting up and then accompanying us to many of the meetings. We are grateful for all the support and comments we have received from Mujtaba Piracha (RSPN), AKRSP staff, Steve Rasmussen, Steve Jones (DFID), Jim Green (HTS) and the CIDA monitors in the finalising of this chapter. We also thank our children for their forbearance during the fieldwork and the preparation of this draft.

2. Regional Management Teams: Gilgit/Baltistan, Female staff meeting AKRSP Gilgit and Chitral, Shandana Khan, CEO Rural Support Programme Network (RSPN).

3. Women's empowerment programmes, if perceived to be disrupting social relations by people in authority (religious or political leaders, for example), have been threatened with closure in other parts of the world, for example in Bangladesh where the women's programmes in several NGOs have been criticised by religious leaders for being contrary to the teachings in the Holy Quran.

4. For a more detailed account of the livelihood strategies of the Northern Areas and Chitral, see Chapter 2.

5 The milk was put inside a cleaned sheep hide, which had been sewn up so that it did not leak, and then the sheep hide was shaken to churn the milk.

6. See Streefland, et al. (1995: 138-9), and discussion with GAD/MER managers AKRSP Gilgit.

7. See Chapter 2 for a more in-depth discussion on how development has positively and negatively affected livelihoods in the Northern Pakistan.

8. See Chapter 2 for further details of these regional differences.

9. Focus group discussions, Female staff, AKRSP Gilgit and AKRSP Chitral.

10. See Varley 1998:10.

11. Discussion with Managers GAD & MER, AKRSP Gilgit.

12. Workloads have also increased for women as increasingly children have joined school and are no longer at home during the day to help their mothers (Joekes 1995: 69).

13. Azam Ali 1991.

14. This is particularly the case in Baltistan (interview with Nazir Ahmed, September 2003).

15. This concern was repeatedly voiced by male members of NGOs interviewed in Punyal and Hunza and religious leaders we spoke to in Chitral, who were all worried about the way the 'moral values' of the young people, especially girls, were getting too relaxed. In places like Hunza, the resurgence of conservatism in Shia areas such as Nagar and other Sunni parts of Gilgit was

also a factor that was pressurising the Ismaili community to be stricter in their view of women's mobility.

16. Opinion of male members of the Regional Management Team, AKRSP Gilgit.

17. As explained by some members of the Regional Management Team, AKRSP Gilgit, women and men have divided responsibility in different areas and they cannot intervene in each others' decisions in those areas.

18. Streefland *et al.* (1995: 20) and Van Vugt (1991: 28); It should be noted that even with the increasing rate of education most marriage decisions are not taken by the youth but by the parents. Hence both, young men and women lack the decision-making power in this matter.

19. Discussion with women workers from Threadnet Hunza.

20. In the case of the joint family the father or mother's decisions dominate, or even those of grandparents, even if the son is the earner. In a nuclear family, where the man has out-migrated over a long period, his decision-making authority might often be only symbolic. This however varies from situation to situation.

21. Discussions with leaders in Chitral (June 2003) and Sultana Bibi (who undertook a study of the role of the media while undergoing training in social research with AKRSP). It is interesting to note that in some parts of the Federally Administered Tribal Areas women are being stopped from watching television because they are told by religious leaders it is not allowed according to the Holy Quran (discussion with Rashida Syed, International Fund for Agricultural Development (IFAD)/RSPN). See Schech and Haggis (2000) who provide a useful introduction to the influence of the media on culture, gender and development.

22. Fatima Mumtaz, WO member Shel-e-Har, Nagar.

23. Discussion with members of a WO, Booni, Chitral.

24. Focus group discussion with female workers of Threadnet Hunza.

25. Discussion with a religious leader in Chitral, June 2003.

26. This trend was indicated by members of Hatoon Development Organisation, Punyal; Civic Management Society, Hunza and also mentioned by Afsal Shigri, AKRSP Board Member and Mrs Rizvi, Chairperson of the National Commission on the Status of Women (NCSW).

27. Many staff of AKRSP are of the view that this is a very important area but are not sure how AKRSP could address this issue without inviting criticism from the local stakeholders such as politicians, religious leaders and other notables, many of whom normally do not like to talk about this. Domestic violence is not only between men and women, older women may persecute younger women in the privacy of the home or aid and abet the violence to daughter-in-laws, for example, perpetrated by men.

28. See Qureshi (2002: 4), for discussion on this process in Baltistan.

29. DFID's Project Memorandum for AKRSP-Gilgit (1997: 61) which goes on to state 'In the next phase, it is expected that AKRSP will continue to make

a very positive contribution to improving social and economic conditions for communities in the project area [...] and improving women's status and as a resource and training base for other NGOs' (p. 62).

30. Thirty three percent of seats are reserved for women in Pakistan's 7000 Union Councils, the lowest tier of Government, in the Devolution Plan of the Government of Pakistan.

31. Discussion with Regional Management Team, AKRSP Baltistan.

32. Socorro Reyes of UNDP stressed that this is a key part of AKRSP's future role (interview in June 2003).

33. Kaneez Zahra, Advisor Northern Areas Legislative Council (interview in July 2003).

34. The Government's continuing gender blind procedures and structures despite the inclusion of women in politics, for example, was lamented by all female councillors interviewed.

35. This is an observation often made on women's position in the hills and mountains compared to the plains of India and Nepal (see Dreze and Sen (1995), for example).

36. An approach that has long come under scrutiny from critics of 'women in development', see Buvinic (1986) for example. During meetings in June 2003, Sabira Qureshi, Yasir Dildar of ROZAN and Socorro Reyes of the United Nations Development Programme (UNDP) all mentioned that while AKRSP had been successful at working with women at the practical level, and was recognised for this, AKRSP was not known for mobilising around rights issues. The work of the Aurat Foundation, Shirkat Gah and ROZAN itself were given as examples of NGOs working at this strategic and policy level which AKRSP might be encouraged to network with more.

37. As a party to CEDAW, Pakistan is obliged 'to pursue by all appropriate means and without delay a policy of eliminating discrimination against women' including 'any distinction, exclusion or restriction made on the basis of sex which has the purpose of impairing or nullifying the recognition, enjoyment or exercise by Women.' Pakistan did, however, declare one reservation to Article 29, paragraph 1 which refers to accountability to an international court of justice.

38. For example, ROZAN is actively engaged in working with men to counter gender-based violence. See Rashid (2003).

39. National Commission on the Status of Women (n.d.) p. 5.

40. Interview with Mrs Majida Rizvi, Chairperson of National Commission on the Status of Women, 10 June 2003. The newspaper *Dawn* reported on 31 August 2003 that the Commission had recommended to the government that the Hudood Ordinances be repealed. The newspaper reported that Mrs Rizvi said 'The NCSW has the mandate to make recommendations only on certain issues, what happens next is none of the Commission's business.' The same newspaper carried a story later in the week about a rally of women

calling for the NCSW recommendation to be disregarded as 'anti-Islam' and for the Hudood Ordinances to be upheld.

41. Address at the Muslim University Aligarh, 10 March 1944.
42. Amina Qadir, Ministry of Women Development, interview Febraury 2003.
43. Discussions with: Shandana Khan, CEO RSPN; Regional Management Team AKRSP Gilgit/Baltistan.
44. AKRSP was not unusual in this focus on the household as a unit, rather than differences among the individuals within it. See Harris (1981), Guyer and Peters (1987), Hart (1995), Hart (1997) and Guyer (1997).
45. Discussion with female staff, AKRSP Gilgit.
46. The same is true in other parts of the world, for example in Bangladesh where the NGOs like Njeri Kori, which actively campaign with local women and men for land and other rights have faced opposition from local elite groups, including politicians.
47. AKRSP did for a brief time introduce an Orchard Development package for WOs as a PPI in 1989. While this package was for many women the first lesson in collective (economic) management and subsequently confidence building, it was discontinued eventually due to various operational issues such as the limited time frame of the land lease agreement. The land was eventually returned to the owner who then reaped the benefits of the fruit trees. Here was a chance missed by AKRSP to build further upon women's collective strength as a result of short-sighted planning.
48. AKRSP Women's Programme Meeting Minutes, 1999.
49. By 'gender mainstreaming' we mean that there is a commitment to ensure that women's as well as men's concerns and experience are integral to the design, implementation and monitoring of all policies, processes and programmes, so that women and men benefit equally, rather than treating 'gender' as a separate issue or an 'add on' to development.
50. See Varley 1998:19.
51. Jeevunjee 1996.
52. World Bank 2002:20.
53. Gloekler 2002:8.
54. There are only two female district councillors in Gilgit and one each in Khaplu and Skardu in the Northern Areas. Following the Devolution Plan, Chitral District Assembly has six female councillors out of 22. All of the women however complain of difficulties in working with men, who always try to put women down, especially when it comes to accessing funds.
55. Interview in June 2003.
56. See for example the DFID 1999 Annual Review report, p.12.
57. This is a view echoed in the World Bank (2002) report, where the team complained that during their visit 'not a single women's group planned a presentation; no woman got to her feet to make even the shortest speech' p. 20.

58. In Chitral the WID section was abolished in 1996, rather later than in Gilgit and Baltistan (Miers 1996: 6).
59. Stephen Rasmussen, ex-General Manager AKRSP.
60. This was in line with donor recommendations, for example, the integration of the Gender Unit into the Social Development Unit at RPO level was recommended in the DFID Annual Review of 1998 (p. 5).
61. Women's programme meeting minutes, 1999.
62. See Seeley (2000: 2) and Shakil and Khan (2001).
63. A move strongly recommended by the OED Evaluation Team in 2001.
64. Information from meetings with RMT (AKRSP Baltistan) and female staff (AKRSP Gilgit). We were told that in Chitral it was impossible to find local women at all initially so in 1986 two sisters were recruited from a remote part of southern NWFP. It was not only impossible to recruit women locally but women from Peshawar were not willing to go to Chitral because it was so remote (conversation with Masood Ul Mulk).
65. Female staff, AKRSP Gilgit and Chitral and discussions with ex-staff.
66. Female staff, AKRSP Gilgit.
67. Female staff, AKRSP Gilgit.
68. Stephen Rasmussen, former General Manager, AKRSP.
69. Discussion with Sabira Qureshi in June 2003 (gender consultant, Canadian International Development Agency (CIDA)).
70. Discussion with ROZAN staff June 2003.
71. Female staff meeting, AKRSP Gilgit.
72. In August 2003 there were 176 male staff and 36 female staff, following the restructuring. The grading system was changed, which makes comparison difficult. One woman, the GAD Programme Manager, has been appointed to senior management, for the first time in AKRSP.
73. Fareeha Ummar, GAD Programme Manager AKRSP.
74. Gloekler, personal observation as staff of AKRSP (1994-2000).
75. Stephen Rasmussen, ex-General Manager AKRSP.
76. Interview with Hatoon Development Organisation.
77. Stephen Rasmussen, ex General Manager AKRSP.
78. AKRSP Baseline Survey 1998.
79. A point stressed in the DFID MTR report, 2001: 13.
80. Comments from the First World Bank Evaluation in Annual Review 1986: xi.
81. As a female staff member explained, AKRSP Baltistan has greatly expanded the literacy programme. There are however problems of follow-up and of continuity beyond the funding period, although some literacy centres have linked up with other institutions such as Allama Iqbal Open University for higher education. Chitral literacy programme on the other hand has been very carefully designed to meet the needs of the women, but it is more expensive and therefore is being more slowly expanded, due to follow up issues. TBA training is being provided mainly in Baltistan with the help of

the Family Planning Association of Pakistan. Even here follow-up remains a problem.

82. Anne Woodbridge, CIDA. Also, the DFID Project Memorandum for Chitral (1998) emphasises 'the need for AKRSP to adopt a more proactive role in encouraging women into income generating activities' (p. 76).

83. There are currently 220 adult literacy centres in Baltistan.

84. Discussion with Ghulam Hussain, Area Manager Skardu, AKRSP Baltistan.

85. This is based on the staff's own perception (interviews with staff July and August 2003).

86. Shandana Khan, CEO Rural Support Programme Network.

87. BRAC was formerly known by the full name, 'Bangladesh Rural Advancement Committee', but changed its name to the diminutive 'BRAC' when its remit broadened.

88. This information is taken from Murshed (1998), Rao and Kelleher (1998) and (2002) and the BRAC website www.brac.net.

89. The micro-credit programme began in 1974 and Jamalpur Women's Project began in 1975.

90. Some commentators on socio-political developments in Bangladesh have recently been expressing concern about the spread of a more conservative approach to Islam and the impact this may have on women's development initiatives.

91. All three are working in the same part of India: Gujarat, Madhya Pradesh and Rajasthan.

92. Sadguru began in 1974 (Sahaj Sadguru Handicrafts, an income-generating arm of Sadguru was established in 1989 with the aim of empowering women by improving their economic status), AKRSP (I) in 1984, and WIRFP in 1993.

93. A brief description of the growth of SAHAJ and their activities is given on their website www.sahajindia.org.

94. AKRSP (India) MTR Recommendations Action Plan (1998).

95. 'Project Memorandum, Western India Rainfed Farming Project—Phase 2' 1998, Annex 5, page 11.

96. Personal communication with Meera Shahi, State Co-ordinator, Gramin Vikas Trust (WIRFP), Jhabua, Madhya Pradesh, India, September 2003.

97. Fareeha Ummar, Programme Manager GAD AKRSP.

98. It must be cautioned here however, that as pioneering as AKRSP is on the service delivery aspect regarding women, the investment that has been made in the VOs is still much larger than what has actually been invested in the WOs by AKRSP.

99. Fareeha Ummar, Programme Manager GAD AKRSP.

100. Shandana Khan, CEO Rural Support Programme Network.

101. Shandana Khan, CEO Rural Support Programme Network.

102. Aamina Qadir Adham, Gender Policy Specialist UNFPA/MOWD.

103. Aamina Qadir Adhan, Gender Policy Specialist UNFPA/MOWD.

104. DAWN newspaper, 23/08/03:17.

105. Fareeha Ummar, PM GAD AKRSP.

106. In the Northern Areas, AKES started its first Diamond Jubilee School in 1946; AKHS started its first Mother Child Health programme in 1974.

107. Hurmat Khan, AKES; Dr. Mohammad Nazir, AKHS.

108. Hurmat Khan, AKES.

109. Aliya Sethi, Aga Khan Foundation.

110. Through its recent gender policy, AKES has only now created the post of a gender co-ordinator and aims to eventually bring the level of females in the management to 35%. In the AKHS efforts are being made to bring women into higher positions beyond the level of Lady Health Visitors, such as co-ordinators and female health officers.

111. Dr. Mohammad Nazir, AKHS.

112. Charlotte Heath, DFID-London (personal communication with Janet Seeley).

113. Discussions with DFID in 2000 and 2002, CIDA February 2003, AKF 2003 and UNDP June 2003.

114. Streefland et al. (1995) and World Bank (2002) for example.

115. See MacDonald (2003: 19ff.) for discussion on institutionalising gender in DFID.

116. Although 'gender' was, and still is to some extent (with responsibility being gradually shared more widely), seen as one of the responsibilities of social development advisers.

117. According to Razavi and Miller (1995b) these were 'the Nordics, The Netherlands and Canada'.

118. Qureshi (2002: 10) commented that 'the only donor pushing the gender agenda within AKRSP is CIDA'.

119. Interview with Aliya Sethi, AKF February 2003.

120. The 'feminist' label often being reinforced by the fact that the donor staff responsible for 'gender' have been women. Interestingly, during a recent visit to Iran staff from AKRSP-Baltistan were surprised by the relative freedom of the women compared to Baltistan, and what they had thought was 'western behaviour' with men and women working together did exist in Iran (interview with Nazir Ahmed, RPM Baltistan 2/9/03).

121. Anne Woodbridge, February 2003.

122. See Miers 1996: 6 for a discussion of this issue in AKRSP Chitral.

123. For an explanation of emerging terminology in gender equity discourse see Shaukat (2002).

124. Adapted from Gender Unit, KHAN (1998: 49 ff.) and Ummar (2000: 28 ff.).

4

Community Infrastructure

Abdul Malik, Ali Effendi, and Muhammad Darjat

INTRODUCTION

Mountain regions often carry a connotation of remoteness and inaccessibility due to their peculiar geographic characteristics. This inaccessibility can be viewed as an outcome as well as a source of under developed physical infrastructure in such regions. The Northern Areas and Chitral (NAC) region presents one such example of difficult mountainous terrain that has remained isolated from the rest of the world for centuries, until recently when the construction of the Karakoram Highway (KKH) and the opening up of a seasonal road link through the Lowari Pass in Chitral has partially broken the spatial trap faced by the people of northern Pakistan.

AKRSP got involved in the business of community infrastructure development not because it was a part of some preconceived package but because communities were prioritising physical infrastructure as their top development agenda. During the initial dialogues, the communities were quick to recognise the limitations posed by a general lack of physical infrastructure. The communities saw the absence of small-scale infrastructure, such as link roads, as the key constraint that was barring them from internalising the potential benefits created by large-scale projects such as the KKH. Mindful of these genuine needs and opportunities, AKRSP launched a community infrastructure development programme that was aimed at harnessing local resources for economic and social development.

Community infrastructure development at AKRSP was not about just creating roads, bridges or irrigation channels, but about creating these resources in a different way. For instance, the practice of involving communities at all stages of the Project Cycle and entrusting to them the maintenance function was a complete departure from the traditional systems followed by government. Similarly, at AKRSP, physical infrastructure development was not viewed as an economic investment only, but its value was also assessed against the criterion of its ability to promote collective action. In other words, AKRSP looked at the interaction between community infrastructure development and social organisation as a 'symbiotic relationship' where the two processes reinforced each other.

Today, the infrastructure development programme of AKRSP is twenty years old and its dividends are flowing to the communities in ample amounts. Apart from creating direct impacts such as increasing incomes and improving communication, infrastructure projects such as roads and bridges have also triggered a multiplier effect. New opportunities in the business, health, and education sector have arisen due to increased connectedness and increased wellbeing of the communities. This better access to health, education, and off-farm employment is not only fetching better development outcomes today but also serves as an input to future development.

This chapter is an attempt at presenting the story of AKRSP's community infrastructure programme with a particular focus on some specific insights about impacts and process innovations. In the first few sections, a brief history of infrastructure development has been presented with an aim of introducing the reader to the overall context so that the need for interventions by a development agency like AKRSP can be fully understood. In the latter half, the chapter delves into the details of specific insights and concludes with the highlights of new challenges in the management of community infrastructure development.

The Traditional Infrastructure Development System

For centuries, the physical infrastructure in the NAC region was developed by the princely states. The main components of infrastructure were irrigation channels, pony tracks, seasonal roads, and bridges. These different types of infrastructure were financed by the princely states and constructed and maintained by the local communities. Over time, the workers in the community became skilled in masonry, stone cutting, and the use of dry stones in construction. They also learnt engineering concepts of stabilising the slopes, managing run-offs, and sealing the road surface to limit damage from snowmelts and rainfall. These indigenous skills were put to maximum use by the local rulers to develop traditional infrastructure, particularly irrigation channels.

According to tradition, the princely states would provide consumable stores to the local workers to construct physical infrastructure, irrigation channels in particular, and then would demand a payment (*maalia*) from the users of the newly developed infrastructure in the form of livestock and/or agricultural produce. In other instances it was the local leader who provided the support and assistance for construction. This traditional system of infrastructure development started to weaken in the early twentieth century and became completely inoperative when the princely states were abolished during the late 1960s and early '70s. This was when the repair and maintenance of existing channels became completely dependent on the meagre resources of the local communities.

The local communities lacked the resources as well as the institutions to undertake new initiatives and there was an urgent need to develop an alternative institutional mechanism that could address the needs of the communities at the grass roots level. The government was lagging behind in developing and strengthening relevant institutions that could have supported infrastructure development at different levels. There were no signs of any significant initiatives until the mid-1960s when the government of Pakistan decided to establish a land link with neighbouring China through the construction of the KKH.

Government Institutions and Initiatives

In the mid 1960s, Pakistan and China agreed to start one of the most ambitious road projects in the history of infrastructure development in Pakistan. The plan was to develop the old Indus valley road by linking Gilgit to Kashgar in Xingjian through the Khunjerab Pass on the Sino–Pakistan border. This project was completed in late 1978 when the Government of Pakistan, with technical and financial assistance from China, finished the construction of what is considered to be one of the engineering marvels of the world—the Karakoram Highway (KKH). Although this marvellous project was constructed out of geopolitical reasons, it brought about profound changes in the lives of the people of the Northern Areas.

Once all-weather access to the Northern Areas was ensured, the federal government took the initiative to establish specific organisations and line departments to construct and maintain the physical infrastructure within the Federally Administered Northern Areas (FANA) comprising Gilgit and Baltistan.[1] These newly established institutions included the Frontier Works Organisation (FWO) and the Northern Area Public Works Department (NAPWD).[2] The FWO was initially held responsible for the maintenance of the KKH. Later on, the FWO was given the additional responsibility of constructing high cost mega projects, especially roads and other communication schemes. The NAPWD was made responsible for all medium-level projects as well as inter and intra valley infrastructure initiatives. These initiatives included construction and renovation of valley roads, bridges, hydel power stations, water supply and sanitation schemes.

In the 1970s, a new institutional arrangement was established in the form of the Local Bodies and Rural Development (LB&RD) Department. The LB&RD was a successor to the Village Aid/Basic Democracy Programme[3] which was started in the early 1960s to establish co-operative shops and to provide agricultural extensions programmes (Government of Pakistan n.d.). In its new role, the LB&RD started financing a limited number of small infrastructure schemes in some villages in and around Gilgit. The outreach of this programme was limited due to financial and staff constraints. In the 1980s, the thrust of LB&RD infrastructure activities shifted towards UNICEF-funded water supply and sanitation projects. The outreach of this programme was also limited as it was being implemented in selected villages.

Despite all the efforts and initiatives taken by the government in the form of large-scale projects such as the KKH and new institutional arrangements, there continued to remain an unmet demand for village level infrastructure. It was realised that the construction of large- and medium-scale projects was not sufficient to address the village level needs. A network of small infrastructure was required at the village level to make the most of the opportunities created by the large-scale projects. The efforts of LB&RD were, to some extent, addressing this later concern but its outreach was very limited due to resource constraints. Furthermore, there were some inherent shortcomings in the process followed by the LB&RD.[4]

Community Infrastructure: Complementing the Government

Amidst all the challenges mentioned above, AKRSP initiated its activities in the Northern Areas in 1983. It initiated an extensive dialogue process with the communities to assess the ground situation so that a package of productive activities could be conceived. It came out loudly that there was a genuine need to develop a portfolio of productive infrastructure at the village level so that people could utilise their existing resources in an efficient manner.[5] For instance, it was noticed that the potential benefits of large-scale projects such as the KKH and valley roads could only be internalised through constructing link roads at village level.

Mindful of the genuine need for basic physical infrastructure at the village level, AKRSP decided to develop a community infrastructure strategy that could be seamlessly integrated into its participatory approach to development. Both national and international experiences showed that the effectiveness and sustainability of infrastructure programmes could only be enhanced through fostering institutional mechanisms at the grass roots level. Therefore, AKRSP decided to use the infrastructure projects as 'entry points' to start and promote partnership with the local communities.

From the very beginning, AKRSP looked at infrastructure projects as investment in social organisation. This assumption was based on the premise that there existed a symbiotic relationship between social organisation and community infrastructure development. In other words, the two objectives—social organisation and infrastructure development—were mutually reinforcing. At the first stage, communities were encouraged to form village organisations and follow procedures such as the holding of weekly meetings, accumulation of savings, and enhancement of the technical and managerial skills of their members. Once these pre-conditions of social organisation were met, only then were the communities given the opportunity to implement an infrastructure project in partnership with AKRSP.

AKRSP's infrastructure development approach was different from the conventional approach followed by the government and other centralised organisations. Unlike the government's top-down approach, AKRSP decided to involve the communities at all stages of the project cycle. A well thought-out process of dialogue was designed to elicit the communities' involvement in a manner that promoted the twin objectives of social mobilisation and productive infrastructure development. This process was called the Diagnostic Survey[6] and it entailed a series of interactive dialogues with the communities at the stages of project identification, preparation, and appraisal.

Portfolio of Community Infrastructure

Today, the twenty year long partnership between the communities and AKRSP has resulted in a sizeable portfolio of community infrastructure projects in the NAC. The statistics for infrastructure projects show that a total of 2,113 projects were completed by the end of 2002, impacting a total beneficiary base of 207, 177 households (see Table 4.1 below).

Table 4.1. Productive physical infrastructure projects by region (as of December 2002)

	Gilgit	Chitral	Baltistan	Total
Projects initiated	748	873	923	2544
Cost of projects initiated (million rupees)	327.71	397.33	310.30	1,035.34
Beneficiary households	86,282	57,569	63,326	207,177
Projects completed	588	730	795	2,113

Source: AKRSP Core Office, Islamabad

The distribution of the infrastructure projects shows that about half of all these projects were irrigation-related, followed by communication schemes which accounted for 456 projects. The rest were miscellaneous in nature, comprising protective works, energy generation units, and water delivery schemes (see Table 4.2 below).

Table 4.2. Infrastructure portfolio by sector and region (as of December 2002)

	Gilgit	Chitral	Baltistan	Total
Irrigation	345	300	412	1,057
Communication	115	200	141	456
Micro Hydel	7	153	11	171
Others	121	77	231	429
Total	588	730	795	2,113

Over time, the portfolio of community infrastructure has evolved in response to the changing needs of the communities (Tetlay and Raza 1998). The composition of community infrastructure projects has changed in three distinct ways. The first variation is in the type and sophistication of the projects undertaken by the communities. During the initial years of AKRSP, most of the Productive Physical

Infrastructure projects (PPIs) were traditional in nature, such as gravity fed irrigation schemes, link roads, pony tracks and bridges. However, over time, new types of projects such as lift irrigation schemes and micro hydels[7] also became popular.

The shift from traditional to non-traditional projects was very visible in the Chitral region, where communities expressed their huge demand for micro hydels. Initially, AKRSP was hesitant to introduce such schemes as the response of the communities to similar pilot projects was found less promising in the Gilgit region. However, due to the growing insistence of the communities from Chitral, AKRSP decided to start micro hydels in the early 1990s. These projects were well received by the communities, and today Chitral has the highest concentration of micro hydel projects in the world (World Bank 2002).

The second shift in the portfolio was in terms of project size and focus. During the 1997–2001 phase, there was a growing realisation that AKRSP's policy of granting one PPI per Village Organisation (VO) was not sufficient to address the socio-economic needs of the communities. Therefore, it was proposed that AKRSP should scale-up the size of projects from *mohallah* to village level and supra-village level. Further, these relatively large-scale projects were not strictly viewed as investments in social organisation only. Rather, the new focus was on broadening the economic base in the region.

The third evolution in the portfolio of infrastructure was with regard to the purpose and beneficiary group of the projects. During the initial phases, AKRSP treated households as the beneficiary units of the infrastructure projects and all the efforts were focused on increasing the assets of a household as a whole. As a result, most of the projects initiated by AKRSP such as link roads and bridges were relatively gender-neutral in nature. However, growing concerns about some of the genuine practical needs of women and urges to involve women at the village level decision-making process resulted in the initiation of projects that directly targeted women. Due to this strategic shift, many Women's Organisations (WOs) initiated small-scale infrastructure projects, particularly water delivery schemes, that were directly geared towards reducing the workloads of women[8] (See Table 4.3).

Table 4.3. Summary of WO infrastructure projects (as of December 2002)

	Initiated	Completed
Water Supply/Delivery	109	71
Link roads and Pony tracks	11	7
Community Centres	16	11
Sanitation projects	17	13
Others	16	15

Self-Help: How has AKRSP Defined It?

Conventional concepts of self-help consider contributions of land, labour or material for a project as the appropriate measure of community contribution. This is particularly true for developing countries where rural development projects are often financed through such arrangements. The tradition in Pakistan is very much similar to what is called the conventional concept of self-help, where community contribution is shown as a certain percentage of the total project cost (AKRSP 1983). In such arrangements, the communities' involvement is reduced to a one-off input, also in the form of material or labour.

At AKRSP, the concept of self-help and community contribution goes beyond this conventional thinking. The concept of self-help is not merely reduced to a one-off contribution in the form of land or labour, but it involves a whole set of roles and responsibilities taken by the communities. This is an important distinction between AKRSP's approach and the more conventional approaches followed by government and other development agencies (AKRSP 1987b). AKRSP requires the following contributions from the communities:

- The communities *should* organise themselves into an institution called the VO that represents the majority of village households. They *should* strictly adhere to the rules and regulations of a VO which include holding VO meetings regularly, accumulating savings, building the technical and managerial skills of its members.
- The VO members *should* constitute a Survey Committee at the stage of project preparation and the committee *should* take the responsibility of making the alignments of infrastructure projects. The Survey Committee *should* also contribute to the project design by giving information on the history of the project site, hazards, and conflicts related to the project.
- The communities *must* resolve conflicts related to the projects and not look to AKRSP for this purpose.
- The communities *should* regularly maintain their records and keep their financial matters clean.
- The VO members *should* save part of the project grant so that it can be used for the maintenance of the project and other productive purposes.
- The communities *should* contribute land required by the project, and they *must* take the responsibility of compensating for any losses induced by the project.
- The communities *should* agree to assume the responsibility of maintaining the project after its completion.

The concept of self-help proposed by AKRSP is not just a fulfilment of some procedures but it is the internalisation of a value system which requires the communities to take responsibility for their own development. This distinct feature of self-help forms the basis of partnership between AKRSP and the communities, and it is very important from the perspective of creating ownership of the whole development process.

An Overall Assessment by the World Bank

As mentioned above, AKRSP's infrastructure programme was initiated with two objectives in mind: to catalyse the process of social organisation, and to develop productive infrastructure that could bring immediate economic returns. While assessing the performance against the said objectives, the recent Operations Evaluation Department (OED) evaluation reveals that the gains from the infrastructure component have been substantial and largely sustainable. The performance of AKRSP's infrastructure programme was gauged against the criteria of relevance, efficiency, efficacy, and sustainability. The evaluation team reports that the community infrastructure projects have been relevant and efficient; their efficacy has been substantial; and their sustainability is likely with few exceptions (World Bank 2002). The question arises as to what factors have been responsible for this highly satisfactory performance of the infrastructure programme. The following paragraphs attempt to address this question and explore some of the key operational insights, which are relevant to the debate.

SPECIFIC INSIGHTS

Innovations in the Process of Infrastructure Development

Generally, development initiatives in Pakistan are organised and managed under one of three distinct approaches. The first approach is called the managerial approach, and it is usually followed by the government and other centralised institutions. In this approach, which is top-down in orientation, managers are responsible for taking decisions and they follow fixed rules and procedures. The second approach is called the representative approach, in which committees or elected or nominated representatives take decisions mainly driven by influence or political considerations. The orientation of decision-making in this case is often divisive. The third approach—the participatory approach—works in contrast to the two aforementioned approaches. In this approach, community institutions are the decision-making units, which take decisions keeping in view local needs and resources, and the principles of consensus, compromise, and reciprocity are followed (Husain 1990).

AKRSP's infrastructure development process mirrors the participatory approach in its true essence. It starts with the Diagnostic Survey,[9] which is a series of interactive dialogues between the communities and AKRSP. In the first dialogue, AKRSP's senior management visits a village where community members are briefed on the objectives and methodology of AKRSP. Once the community members agree to form a VO and accept the preconditions,[10] only then are they invited to identify and prioritise an income-generating activity that would benefit the majority of households.

The experience suggests that AKRSP made two important procedural innovations at the Identification stage, which were distinct from the managerial approach followed by the government. First, the communities were given the opportunity to identify and prioritise their need in a consensual manner. For example, in a typical project, the majority of the households in a village gathered at a place to debate their priorities and selected a project of common interest. This was contrary to the managerial approach, in which line departments in a distant place would decide what was good for the communities. As a result of this shift from the managerial approach, the identification of infrastructure projects became demand-driven instead of becoming supply-led, thus the relevance and success of such projects increased.

The second procedural innovation was the incorporation of additional Feasibility concerns that were not found in the conventional concepts of economic and technical feasibility. The communities were provided with clear criteria[11] for the identification and prioritisation of a project. Various elements of the criteria, such as the capacity of communities, acceptance by the majority and equity concerns were available to increase the desirability and sustainability of a project. These criteria were also used at the Appraisal stage to check the feasibility of a project. Contrary to this approach where the concept of feasibility was taken a step forward, the managerial and representative approaches gave primacy to political considerations and tended to overlook even the basic economic and technical considerations.

Once a project is identified following the procedures mentioned above, the second stage of the Diagnostic Survey starts, which is called the second dialogue. The second dialogue is about the preparation of a project and involves a survey to prepare the project design and cost estimates. The second dialogue starts with a feasibility survey undertaken jointly by AKRSP engineers and a team of villagers. The information gathered during the survey is used to prepare the project design and cost estimates. The formation of a Survey Committee comprising of knowledgeable villagers was an important process innovation at this stage. Experience from the field suggests that the joint Survey Committee was responsible for taking the lead in the project survey by suggesting the alignments of infrastructure projects. AKRSP engineers were encouraged to listen actively to the views and suggestions of the local villagers regarding various aspects of the project design. This arrangement of combining technical expertise with indigenous knowledge was very useful in gathering important information on various aspects like water rights, land disputes, project site history, and hazard zones. There were instances where lack of attention to the value of local knowledge, both by the communities and AKRSP, proved very expensive.[12]

Contrary to this approach, in the government implemented projects, the project survey was the sole domain of the engineer. At best, some representatives or influential people from the benefiting communities were included in the survey process who, in some cases, worked to the disadvantage of the general masses. There are various examples where local influentials and representatives influenced the project authorities to change the alignments and actual layouts of the project to get undue advantage.[13]

Once the project survey is completed and feasibility prepared, the third dialogue takes place. This dialogue is usually done in an open area with the majority of households to ensure maximum possible participation and transparency. The purpose of this dialogue is to share with the community information on all aspects of the projects. The details of how the PPI will be implemented and what will be the Terms of Partnership (ToP) between AKRSP and the community are discussed at this stage. Once a consensus is arrived at, a written agreement is prepared and signed by both sides. After the agreement has been signed, the first part of AKRSP's grant is handed over to the communities to initiate the infrastructure project.

In the third dialogue (the Appraisal stage), open sharing of all the information with the majority of villagers was an important procedural innovation. Unlike the typical government approach, in which appraisal was a desk exercise and done behind closed doors by some representatives and technical staff, AKRSP made this process a public exercise and enhanced its transparency. All the aspects of a project including specifications of the project design, cost estimates and ToP were presented before the communities and openly debated. This open debate on every financial and technical aspect of the project was aimed at promoting transparency and participation.

In other words, the communities were empowered with information on various aspects of the project so that they could hold different players accountable for their actions. The process of appraisal followed by AKRSP had important implications for the implementation and maintenance of the project. Since the communities were informed on all the aspects of the project, such as the time span, project cost break-down and project specifications, they were in a better position to evaluate progress at the implementation stage. Similarly, the clarity of roles and responsibilities regarding the maintenance of the project was important for its sustainability.

It is important note that lack of information sharing at the Appraisal stage in government implemented projects meant the elimination of communities' effective involvement at subsequent stages of the project cycle. Because communities knew little about the project details, they were not in a position to hold the implementers accountable for their actions. Similarly, due to non-clarity of roles at the early stages of the project, there were occasions when disputes between communities and the implementing agencies arose at the operations stage.

At the implementation stage, the direct involvement of the communities in the implementation of projects was a major innovation as other agencies were hiring contractors to implement the infrastructure projects.[14] As a direct result of this new arrangement, all the procedures followed at the implementation stage were significantly different from the conventional approaches followed by the government and other agencies. For instance, the formulation of a project work plan according to the availability of local labour was an important step in the VO-implemented projects; in contractor-implemented projects this was not a major concern.

An important innovation at the implementation stage was related to the supervision and performance monitoring of community infrastructure projects. AKRSP decided to pay the project grant in four instalments and tied the disbursement of each instalment to the physical progress on the project as well as the performance of a VO on other institutional indicators. The communities were required to pass a VO resolution confirming the progress of the VO and that of the project to qualify for the next instalment of the grant. This performance-based reward mechanism was useful in many ways. It encouraged the communities to actively take part in the affairs of the project. As the VO members were required to pass the resolution, they actively sought the information on the expenditures and physical progress of the project and, as a result, a downward accountability mechanism evolved in the VOs.

In contrast to this full involvement of the communities at the implementation stage, in a contractor-implemented project the major stakeholders—the communities—were reduced to mere spectators. They were not given a proper institutional mechanism to register their concerns regarding various aspects of project design and implementation. As a result, progress on the project often remained very slow and huge amounts of money was wasted due to the poor quality of work and losses in the system.

Once a project was physically completed, the community took over the responsibility of its operation and management in accordance with the agreed ToP. At this stage, a considerable amount of flexibility was granted to the communities to decide on how to operate and maintain the project. It was due to this flexibility that a diverse but effective set of maintenance mechanisms were put in place by the communities.[15] All these mechanisms worked because the communities took the responsibility of maintenance right at the start of the project. The evidence from the field suggests that some of the infrastructure projects developed by the government became inoperative because clarity regarding who would maintain the project was missing right from the start of the project.

Over time, the institutional mechanisms for the implementation and maintenance of infrastructure projects have evolved, but the essence of what has been described above remains intact. The current practice is to form three committees, namely, the Management Committee, Audit Committee and Maintenance Committee, to look after project progress, finances and maintenance, respectively. These committees are selected by the VO/WO members and are required to present their progress reports to the General Body. These new institutional mechanisms have evolved in response to the programmatic shift towards relatively larger projects, which involve a greater number of beneficiaries.

While the procedural innovations made at each stage of the project cycle are discussed in detail, there were some important lessons in the overall Project Cycle as well. The whole project cycle was designed in a manner that promoted the principles of participation, partnership and reciprocity. At each stage of the project cycle the communities were fully involved in the decision-making process, and AKRSP encouraged this by placing pre-conditions such as the presence of the majority of villagers at the time of project identification and appraisal.

Similarly, the overall infrastructure development process was geared towards inculcating the values of partnership among the communities. The participation of senior management in the first and third dialogues symbolised AKRSP's commitment to enhancing the well-being of the communities. Further, the senior management always emphasised that the nature of relationship between AKRSP and the communities was that of partners. As opposed to this partnership approach, the conventional approaches promoted a culture in which the relationship between the service provider and the local communities was seen as a benefactor-beneficiary relationship.

Technical and Financial Innovations

There is a general consensus among the practitioners of development that infrastructure projects implemented through community institutions are more relevant, cost-effective, and more sustainable. These good attributes of a project can only be achieved when things are done differently. From the very start of its infrastructure programme, AKRSP encouraged innovations in the financial and technical matters of the projects. As a result, new financial and technical arrangements evolved which were very different from the conventional arrangements made by government and other agencies.

One of the important innovations in the implementation of infrastructure projects was the elimination of the contractor. This was not just a new arrangement for the construction of infrastructure projects but a whole paradigm shift that endorsed the communities' ability to plan, implement and manage infrastructure projects.[16] A direct benefit of this arrangement came from the elimination of the contractor's overhead costs. Similarly, the direct involvement of the communities in the implementation of the project proved very effective in reducing system losses. Above all, due to this arrangement, community institutions received recognition as the most cost-effective conduit for infrastructure development.[17]

Changing the techniques of project cost estimation was an important innovation, which contributed to the efficiency of projects. Initially, AKRSP followed the costing methods that were generally used by the government departments. The government departments used to adjust an outdated schedule of rates with some inflation factor. This method of costing often resulted in over estimation of project costs. In order to avoid these distortions, AKRSP decided to use market rates of materials and labour as the basis for cost estimation. Further, in the government's costing method, project costs were grossed up to accommodate the profit margin of the contractors which was no more relevant for community implemented projects.

Another important step in changing the costing method was the decomposition of cost estimates into different components such as skilled and unskilled labour, and local and other material.[18] These decomposed cost estimates were now simple to understand. This simplicity in costing was introduced to enhance transparency in the financial matters of the project. This again was an improvement over the conventional costing procedures, in which cost estimates were given in terms which, because of the non-segregation of various cost items, were difficult if not impossible for the communities to understand and monitor.

The decomposition of cost estimates enabled AKRSP to negotiate labour rates with the communities. Through negotiations, AKRSP encouraged the local communities to work with wage rates that were below the prevailing market rates.[19] For instance, on average, during the mide-1980s, the VOs paid Rs 15 per day against the prevailing market rate of Rs 20 for un-skilled labour, and Rs 35 per day instead of Rs 55 for skilled labour (AKRSP 1987b). Such arrangements were helpful in reducing project costs and, at the same time, for increasing the community contribution in ways that were acceptable to and affordable by the communities.

A direct reduction in project costs came from the elimination of the compensation for major cost items such as land under project structure. The communities were not compensated by AKRSP for the land that was utilised in the construction of link roads, channels and other projects. Similarly, it was made clear at the very outset that AKRSP would not compensate for any losses induced by a project, such as damages to crops or fields. In such cases, the VO was made responsible for making appropriate compensation arrangements if necessary.

Some financial arrangements were specifically designed to attain the objective of sustainability. These financial arrangements included the community's responsibility to maintain the project through labour or cash contributions, and save a quarter of their wages for a maintenance fund. The full involvement of communities at the maintenance stage was an important arrangement that enhanced the true community contribution manifold. Even a conservative estimate of Rs 10,000 per project shows that the communities contribute more than Rs 20 million every year for the maintenance of the entire community infrastructure portfolio.[20]

While the gains from the various financial arrangements mentioned above can be treated as measures of efficiency from one angle, one can also argue that these are not the true economic gains as the communities are paying for the costs in one way or other. However, we believe that the importance of these gains should be looked at from the perspectives of community contribution and ownership. There are two important implications of these arrangements: first, these financial arrangements are indicative of how communities internalise project costs and demonstrate ownership; and second, such financial arrangements have helped initiate important projects with very low capital cost. In the absence of such cost-effective financial arrangements, many useful projects might never have been undertaken.

On the technical front, three particular innovations are worth mentioning. These include initiation of small-scale projects, development of context specific standards, and the integration of indigenous knowledge into modern techniques of infrastructure development. Before AKRSP, the majority of government-funded projects, particularly for roads and energy generation, were of a larger scale. As a result, projects suited to the needs of a particular village received very little attention. Through the initiation of village and even *mohallah* level infrastructure projects, AKRSP redefined the scale of infrastructure projects. This redefinition helped AKRSP customise its projects according to the needs of smaller groups.

The redefinition of project scale was very important because it enabled many small communities to build the much-needed infrastructure in their villages. Previously, this was not possible because the government used to grant projects on the basis of population. As a result, small communities living in isolated villages often received very little attention. In such situations, AKRSP's small infrastructure development approach proved very helpful to the communities.

The second technical innovation was in the form of integration of indigenous knowledge into the modern techniques of engineering (World Bank 1987). AKRSP encouraged the use of modern technology only when there was true value addition. Otherwise, the indigenous techniques and skills were applied at the stage of project design and construction. For instance, traditional dry stone masonry and slope stabilisation techniques were followed in irrigation projects. This proved very useful as the cost of construction and maintenance went down. However, modern instruments were used to improve the gradient of irrigation channel instead of relying on traditional techniques. This reliance on modern technology paid dividends in the form of reduced losses of command area, which was the major problem with irrigation channels constructed with traditional methods.

The third technical innovation was the development of context-specific specifications and measurements as opposed to textbook solutions. AKRSP engineers revisited the textbook estimates and measures for various engineering elements, and redefined them according to the local conditions. For instance, local workday standards were developed by the engineers to replace the outdated schedule rates. Similarly, in view of the local irrigation systems and soil properties, the textbook standards for irrigation were changed from one cusec per 60 acres to one cusec per 100 acres of command area for the NAC.

The role of the communities, as it emerged through the community infrastructure programme, and the innovations introduced by AKRSP, as described above, led to the recognition that other agencies too could usefully employ parts of the AKRSP approach. This recognition is reflected in a decision made by the government that its Khushal Pakistan Programme (KPP) would be implemented through the communities in the Northern Areas, rather than through contractors, which has been the norm in Pakistan. As a result of this decision, AKRSP and LB&RD staff have been co-operating in the KPP, and the process through which village-level schemes are identified and implemented under the KPP seems to represent an improvement over the process employed earlier by LB&RD. This can be seen in the following description of the KPP project cycle, as noted by AKRSP:

• A first dialogue is held for scheme identification and the scheme lists are passed on through the Union Council to the District Advisory Board (DAB). The DAB consists of 10-15 members, including the Deputy Commissioner (who also chairs the DAB), representatives of NGOs including AKRSP, members of the Northern Areas Council, Chairman of the Municipal Committee and Chairman of the District Council.
• DAB prioritises the identified schemes according to its formula for the allocation of funds, in which neglected areas are given more weight than in a population-based allocation.
• The list is finally approved by a Steering Committee consisting of the Chief Secretary, other Northern Areas Secretaries and representatives of the army.
• Then the engineers initiate their field surveys and costing. This is followed by a dialogue among the engineers (from AKRSP and LB&RD) and the members of the Dehi (Village) Council to arrive at negotiated rates for the final costing.
• The first instalment is released by LB&RD to the Dehi Council at a public meeting. The community then starts the work, and no contractors are involved.
• The second instalment is released to the Dehi Council on a resolution passed by the council regarding the status of work. Random checks are made by LB&RD and army officials.
• The remaining 20-25 per cent of the total project cost is released after a completion inspection of the scheme.

Evidence from the field suggests that the KPP approach has been highly appreciated by the communities for its visible impact on the lives of the local communities (Government of Pakistan 2003).

Impact of Community Infrastructure

The construction of large-scale projects is a necessary but not a sufficient condition for broad based development. The potential of large-scale projects can only be exploited when a network of small and medium infrastructure creates the link between the large projects and the ultimate beneficiaries. The Northern Areas faced a similar situation where the construction of the KKH had opened up a plethora of options but a vast majority of the local communities was not fully benefiting from this opportunity due to the absence of secondary and tertiary roads. It was on these grounds that AKRSP started its infrastructure programme to complement the government's efforts, through developing various kinds of infrastructure at the village level so that communities could make the most of the large-scale infrastructure developments.

The OED evaluation shows that the benefits from the overall infrastructure programme have been substantial. The Internal Rate of Return (IRR) of the overall infrastructure programme is estimated at 19 per cent, which is well above the returns of most other infrastructure projects.[21] The net IRR for land development is estimated at 22 per cent, followed by communication and energy projects each generating an IRR of 19 per cent (World Bank 2002). Other evidence from the field also suggests that the communities have greatly benefited from the infrastructure development programmes, particularly irrigation channels, link roads, and water supply schemes. The greatest impact of infrastructure projects, particularly irrigation channels, has been on the poor, whose asset base has increased due to new land development initiatives (Government of Pakistan 2003).

A number of internal evaluations were conducted to assess the impacts of major infrastructure initiatives including irrigation channels, communication projects, and power generation projects.

The findings show that the overall impact of all the major projects has been generally very positive. Major impacts of irrigation channels include increased food, fodder, and fuel security. A very immediate effect of the irrigation channels was increase in the monetary value of land. The magnitude of change varied across the regions depending on the relative availability of land. For instance, the per *kanal* value of land in village *Baltarang* in Baltistan increased from Rs 5,000 to Rs 25,000 while in *Krui Jinali*, a village of Chitral, the per *kanal* value of land increased from Rs 5,000 to Rs 50,000 (AKRSP 2000a).

The impact of communication projects was visible in the form of reduced expenses on travelling, increase in the sale of farm produce, and reduced prices of inputs. Similarly, there was an increase in the business and tourism activities within those villages that were connected through newly constructed bridges and roads. The evidence from the field suggested that there were significant increases in the value of real estate as a result of improved connectivity. For instance, the value of land in *Parsan* Chitral increased from Rs 3,000 to Rs 12,500 per *kanal*. Similarly, the value of land jumped from Rs 90,000 to Rs 600,000 per *kanal* after the construction of the Al-Barakat link road in Hunza (AKRSP 2000d).

The greatest impact of power generation projects was noticed in the form of reduced expenditure on kerosene oil and batteries. Apart from these direct effects, reduction in the workloads of women, increase in the study time for children, and increase in productive activities like embroidery work during the nights were among other visible changes. The reports from the selected villages showed that the average savings on kerosene oil were in the range of Rs 58,000 to Rs 210,000 per village per annum. Similarly, the savings on batteries were reported in the range of Rs 19, 000 to Rs 80,000 per village per annum (AKRSP 2000e).

While most of the infrastructure projects have been very successful, there are some examples where things did not work according to the plans. For instance, although one can find many success stories on what happens once an irrigation channel is completed,[22] there are cases where very little has happened after the completion of the project. This concern has also been raised by the OED team in the fourth evaluation of AKRSP. There are examples where land is yet to be fully developed although irrigation channels have been completed quite a few years ago. One such example comes from Aliabad, Hunza where most of the new land is still barren although the irrigation channel was completed more than ten years ago. It emerges from the study of such cases that, apart from disputes on the rights and division of land, other factors such as increased availability of off-farm opportunities reduce the incentive for land development.

A very important but less orchestrated impact of the infrastructure projects is on the vulnerability of the poor. For instance, the irrigation schemes reduce the vulnerability of local communities in many ways. They reduce the chances of crop failures by improving the availability of irrigation water. Similarly, the development of new land and subsequent increase in farm production improves food and fodder security. Like the irrigation schemes, communication projects are also very effective in reducing people's vulnerability. Due to the construction of hundreds of roads and bridges, many previously isolated and inaccessible villages have been connected to markets and health facilities available in major towns of the NAC. As a result of this increased connectivity, communities are in a better position to purchase food items during slack times and access health facilities during emergencies.

The additional value of infrastructure projects can be seen in the 'options' that such projects create over time. For example, a link road directly benefits a community by saving travel time, and facilitating the transportation of agriculture produce from farms to market. At the same time, it also creates 'options' to initiate a multitude of other activities as well. The impact study of the *Gapstrung* link road reported that it was only after the construction of the link road that the Aga Khan Health Services started conducting regular health check-ups of women and children. One can find examples of similar options in the case of irrigation channels as well. Once an irrigation channel is completed, people exercise the option of settling at the newly developed lands and make new houses.

Operations and Maintenance of Infrastructure Projects

The nationwide experience shows that hundred of projects have ceased to operate due to ineffective mechanisms for their operations and maintenance. AKRSP has a different story to tell where, with few variations, most of the projects are effectively managed by the communities. The OED evaluation reported that nearly 92 per cent of all projects are effectively maintained by communities. Similarly, a study recently conducted in Chitral reported that 90 per cent of all irrigation channels were being properly maintained. The maintenance rate for link roads was at a high of 100 per cent while the corresponding figure for micro hydels was only 80 per cent.

Figure 4.1 shows the relationship between the state of maintenance and various explanatory factors. The list of explanatory factors presented in the figure is by no means exhaustive.

Figure 4.1. Infrastructure maintenance matrix

Type of Project	Maintenance Status	Major Input	Institutional Mechanism	Beneficiary Base	Alternative Provision
Irrigation Channels	Good	Labour	Old system	High percentage	None
Link Roads	Good	Labour	Old system existed but not fully developed	Maybe: Average	LB& RD
Micro Hydels	Less than satisfactory	Capital plus skilled labour	No old system	High percentage	Yes: Govt
Protective Bund	Variable	Capital plus labour	Systems less evolved	Low Percentage	Maybe: Govt

From the figure presented above, various relationships can be explored between the state of maintenance and the nature of major input required for the maintenance of a given project. The first relationship can tentatively be established between the state of maintenance and the type of major input required for the maintenance. Evidence from the field suggests that the maintenance status of irrigation channels and link roads is better compared to energy and other projects. This is mainly because a major input required by the former two types of projects (irrigation channels and roads) is unskilled labour that is readily available in most cases. In most cases, villagers provide unskilled labour for the maintenance work and in a few cases villagers contribute in the form of cash or in kind. Therefore, we can tentatively conclude that projects demanding more capital and skilled labour, such as bridges and micro hydels, are likely to suffer in those places where people have low cash incomes to purchase non-local material and labour.

The second important indicative relationship is between the institutional mechanism and state of project maintenance. It seems that some infrastructure projects which have been traditionally managed by the communities are likely to be maintained properly. In most of the places in the NAC, traditional systems for the maintenance of irrigation channels existed even before the arrival of AKRSP. As a result, it becomes easier for the communities to rely on these systems for the maintenance of new irrigation projects. On the contrary, micro hydel projects are likely to require new arrangements for maintenance, and these new institutional mechanisms may or may not work due to their novelty.

The third relationship is between the state of maintenance and the beneficiary base of a project. The infrastructure projects which are designed to benefit the majority of villagers are likely to draw more resources for maintenance compared to those which serve a small beneficiary base. This is also important from the perspective of activating the traditional system for maintenance work. For instance, an irrigation channel that serves the whole village is likely to activate the traditional institution of *rajaki* (a traditional system where every household in a village contributes labour for collective work) compared to a small protective bund that benefits a small beneficiary base within a particular village.

The fourth relationship can be established between the state of maintenance and the availability of less costly alternative service delivery mechanisms. Evidence from the field suggests that a particular type of project, for example public utility, suffers when an alternative player, particularly governments, starts providing that service. This is the case with some of the micro hydels in Chitral and Gilgit, where the supply of electricity from government sources has reduced the incentive for the communities to participate in the maintenance of their village micro hydel projects.

Conclusion

The amount of benefits accruable to community infrastructure projects and the kind of momentum these projects are able to generate among the communities leave little doubt about their efficacy as powerful levers of social mobilisation and economic development. The twenty year long history of AKRSP is witness to the profound economic and social impacts created by community infrastructure in the NAC. The key operational insights suggest that not only are the impacts of community infrastructure very visible, but a whole range of process innovations have taken place that provide a sound basis for the continuation and replication of this approach.

However, the model of community infrastructure development followed by AKRSP is not insulated from the effects of the fast changing socio-economic context of the NAC. One key challenge that has recently gained primacy is the whole issue of ensuring continued collective action in the implementation and maintenance of infrastructure projects. Due to increasing non-farm engagements and economic migration, the previously readily available labour for maintenance is increasingly becoming scarce particularly in the growth poles of the NAC. Communities are coping with these challenges by developing alternative institutional mechanisms, such as hiring permanent labour for the implementation and maintenance of infrastructure projects. However, such institutional mechanisms sometimes reduce if not fully threaten the entire notion of collective action and community participation in the whole affair of infrastructure development.

The second but interlinked challenge is emerging in the form of difficulty in adhering to some of the principles and processes that were elicited during the initial phases of AKRSP. For instance, increase in the coverage and scale of operations of AKRSP has limited the physical participation of the top management in each first dialogue; this was one of the important features during the initial phases of AKRSP. Another example of deviation from the initial principles is the relaxation of the condition of holding weekly VO/WO meetings in view of the increases in the economic and social engagements of community members.

NOTES

1. Chitral is the exception as it has been formally integrated in the North West Frontier Province.
2. In Chitral, the District Works and Services Department is responsible for similar activities. The NAPWD comes under the jurisdiction of the Northern Areas Government.
3. From an interview with Muhammad Anwar Khan, who was one of the pioneering staff of Village Aid and later retired as Assistant Director of the LB&RD Department.
4. Different approaches to project organisation and management have been discussed under the specific insights later in this chapter.
5. It was indicative of this genuine need that in the first quarter of 1983, about 168 projects were identified in Gilgit district. About 56 per cent of these identified projects were related to irrigation (AKRSP 1983).
6. The process of Diagnostic Survey is discussed in a later section.
7. Micro hydels are small scale electricity generation units that run on the energy of falling water. Hussain Wali Khan, the first Senior Programme Engineer of AKRSP, pioneered the introduction of these units in the Northern Areas. Masood ul Mulk, the then Regional Programme Manager in Chitral, was the key person who advocated the construction of micro hydels in Chitral.

8. Fetching water from distant sources during the winter is a major role performed by women in the NAC. On occasion, this activity leads to serious injuries to women who carry huge loads of water.

9. Tariq Husain, the first Programme Economist of AKRSP, articulated the Diagnostic Survey by comparing it with the standard Project Cycle. He observed Shoaib Sultan Khan's process of dialogue with the communities and realised that each step of the diagnostic survey corresponded to a distinct stage of a project cycle. More specifically, AKRSP's first, second and third dialogues corresponded, respectively, to the identification, preparation and appraisal stages of a Project Cycle. This perspective on the Diagnostic Survey helped to standardise it, which proved very helpful in communicating AKRSP's planning and implementation approach to the communities as well as to external audiences.

10. The preconditions have been discussed earlier; they include holding meetings, accumulation of savings, book keeping, and technical and management skill building.

11. The criteria included the following elements: (a) the project should reflect a priority economic need; (b) the majority of the villagers should benefit from the identified project; (c) There should be no disputes on land or any project consideration; (d) the community should be willing and able to implement and maintain the project; (e) the implementation time and community share should be within certain acceptable limits; (f) the community should be willing and able to compensate villagers for any loss induced by the project; (g) the benefits of the project should be distributed among the community members in an equitable manner.

12. The Jutal Channel in Gilgit was one such case where incorrect information on the availability of water from the source resulted in the failure of the irrigation channel.

12. The Hatoon channel was one such example where the project was designed to benefit an influential group. At the time of handing over disputes erupted, especially when the whole community was held responsible for project maintenance.

13. This major shift is discussed in the financial innovations described in the next insight.

14. The arrangements vary from hiring permanent *chowkidars* (watchmen) to provision of labour from each household on a rotation basis. There are composite systems as well, where communities have hired *chowkidars* but the community works collectively at the time of heavy maintenance jobs.

15. Some may compare this arrangement to the Local Contractor Society concept where some members of the communities organise themselves to replace a contractor. However, the fundamental difference here is the full involvement of communities in executing the project as opposed to selecting some key technical people from the community to perform the contractor-like job.

The objective in the latter case is to ensure that the money goes back to some community members instead of a contractor.

16. This is reflected, for example, in the government's decision to implement a large-scale programme of infrastructure development through the communities, and through a process that reflects elements of the AKRSP methodology. A brief description of the government's approach to this programme, called the Khushal Pakistan Programme, is given at the end of this insight.

17. Many of the NGOs engaged in infrastructure development follow this practice, but government departments do not.

18. The stated rationale for this practice was that villagers were getting employment at their door-step, and in the off-peak season.

19. During 1987, one community in Gilgit incurred an expense of Rs 722,440 to repair a channel damaged by heavy snowfall (AKRSP 1987b).

20. It is estimated that large-scale projects generate returns in the range of 12 to 15 per cent.

21. See Chapter 5.

5

Natural Resource Management

Marc Aljoscha Gloekler

INTRODUCTION AND OVERVIEW

The State of Natural Resource Management (NRM) when AKRSP Started

When AKRSP began its activities in the Northern Areas and Chitral (NAC), the area was one of the poorest and most inaccessible in all of Pakistan. Except for those who served in the army or the government, villagers were almost completely dependent on small-scale subsistence agriculture. Per capita income was approximately 36 per cent of the average for Pakistan (FHIES 1991) and most rural areas were still dominated by a barter-subsistence economy. With villages situated between 1,300m and 3,000m above sea level, irrigated agriculture and pastoral transhumance are the most important components of the prevailing mixed farming system. Farms were, and still are very small, with average landholdings below 1 ha in 1987, approximately half of which is cultivated land.[1]

Annual precipitation varies greatly depending on altitude; whereby elevations beyond the upper limits of plant life may receive up to 2,000mm (Miehe and Miehe 1998), and natural forests between 3,000 and 5,000m still receive adequate water, mostly in the shape of melted snow (IUCN 1987). Below 3,000m, forestry and agriculture are not possible without irrigation, with annual precipitation varying between 500mm in the dry temperate ecosystem of Astore Valley and Southern Chitral and below 200mm in the cold mountain desert ecosystem of the rest of Northern Areas and Northern Chitral (Miehe and Miehe 1998; IUCN 1987).

The main crops were wheat (double cropping zone, up to 2,000m), wheat/barley (single cropping), millet, maize, and at higher altitudes buckwheat and a variety of local catch crops of high food-security value. Only seven varieties of vegetables were grown (Hussain 1993), and staple crops were supplemented with various wild fruits, roots and weeds. Dried apricots and dairy products represented the most important nutritional supplements. Livestock breeds, including local cattle as well sheep and goats, were unproductive, and emphasis was put on large herd sizes[2] for food security and as a mobile bank. Livestock mortality was high, estimated between 10 and 15 per cent per annum.[3] Dependency on common wild resources, including pastures and natural forests was crucial for survival, and those villages at higher altitudes commanding access to these resources still considered themselves better off than those at the valley bottom near the recently built Karakoram Highway (KKH).

The time when AKRSP began its work was also marked by rapid and drastic socio-economic change, largely due to better communications through the opening of new roads and passes coupled with the inherent problem of small and increasingly fragmented landholdings. The combination gave rise to an increasing trend towards seasonal male migration to the cities and *down-country* as well as an increase in education, all of which resulted in labour shortages. As a result of this women had to get involved in farming activities to a greater extent and the pasture culture declined.[4] This brought about demand for better livestock breeds that would be easier to manage, i.e. that could be stall fed around the year (AKRSP 1987a). In the context of all this, a greater demand for fodder and perennial crops (forestry) developed (IUCN 1987). For a schematic picture of the NRM system of NAC, see Figure 5.1.

Figure 5.1. The livelihood system in Northern Pakistan in transition

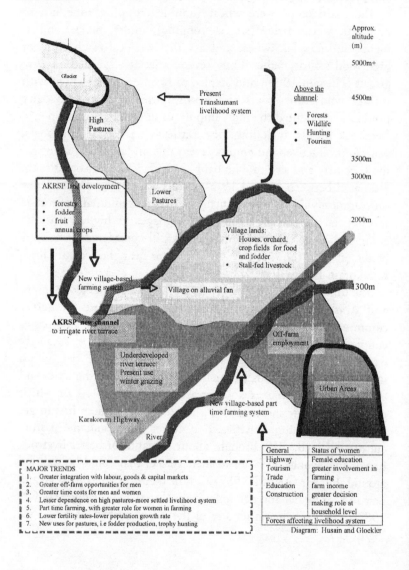

Approx. altitude (m)

5000m+

Glacier

Present Transhumant livelihood system

Above the channel:
- Forests
- Wildlife
- Hunting
- Tourism

4500m

High Pastures

3500m
3000m

AKRSP land development
- forestry
- fodder
- fruit
- annual crops

Lower Pastures

2000m

Village lands:
- Houses, orchard, crop fields for food and fodder
- Stall-fed livestock

New village-based farming system

Village on alluvial fan

300m

AKRSP new channel to irrigate river terrace

Off-farm employment

Underdeveloped river terrace: Present use winter grazing

Urban Areas

Karakorum Highway

New village-based part time farming system

River

MAJOR TRENDS
1. Greater integration with labour, goods & capital markets
2. Greater off-farm opportunities for men
3. Greater time costs for men and women
4. Lesser dependence on high pastures-more settled livelihood system
5. Part time farming, with greater role for women in farming
6. Lower fertility rates-lower population growth rate
7. New uses for pastures, i.e fodder production, trophy hunting

General	Status of women
Highway	Female education
Tourism	greater involvement in
Trade	farming
Education	farm income
Construction	greater decision making role at household level
Forces affecting livelihood system	

Diagram: Husain and Gloekler

The Initial Years

Initially, AKRSP, through its agriculture programme concentrated on developing new agricultural lands, training villagers and organising a reliable system of input supplies with emphasis on fertiliser loans and the introduction of new crop varieties. Acting as an intermediary, AKRSP initially supplied a wide range of inputs, including fertiliser, insecticides, seeds, and threshers directly to the Village Organisations (VOs), village specialists and farmers, some of these free, some subsidised, and others backed by a credit programme (AKRSP 1983).

A good example of AKRSP's input system is exemplified by the fertiliser credit system (see Husain 1986b). AKRSP would obtain a revolving fund from financial institutions and procure fertiliser in bulk at Gilgit. Then, loans to VOs were disbursed in terms of fertiliser. A VO representative transported the fertiliser to his village and got reimbursed for this task from the VO. The farmers took fertiliser to their fields and, at the end of the season, paid back the VO, who in turn reimbursed AKRSP. During the late 1980s, this system was changed into a cash loan and eventually abandoned altogether. The system was replicated at the VO level and the agricultural input loan in kind is now being practised by VOs internally. Khunjerab Village Organisation (KVO), a cluster of seven VOs and seven Women's Organisations (WOs) in spring 2003 purchased fertiliser and wheat seed worth Rs 1 million for 300 kanals of land and distributed it among its VO members. At the end of the season the members paid the money back into the Agricultural Development Fund of KVO with 5 per cent interest.

The initial approach to training and extension of AKRSP was based on the model piloted in the Comilla and Daudzai projects in the 1970s. In these projects training was provided at the highly decentralised *Thana* (police station) level at Training and Development Centres (TDCs). Thus, AKRSP initially conducted their training through fortnightly sessions at four extension training centres which were supposed to be scaled up to nine centres, covering all valleys or *tehsils* of Gilgit District. AKRSP staff listened to villagers' problems and gave advice on agricultural and engineering issues (AKRSP 1983).

Realising that this model would unrealistically stretch AKRSP's human and other resources,[5] a regular training hostel[6] was established in Gilgit and curricula developed for agriculture and livestock training based on a village survey. Training candidates were selected by their respective VOs, and the trained specialists were remunerated for their services by the VO members at cost of medicines/inputs and their time. Specialists received kits with the implements of their trade (spray pumps, syringes) and were also taught the basics of bookkeeping and organisational management.[7] During the early years, half of the training was provided by government specialists who received honoraria from AKRSP (World Bank 1987). This had a double advantage of building relations as well as over-coming staff shortages. 'A major conclusion drawn after a first review of the preliminary extension training sessions was that an NGO...cannot replace the government machinery in the field or imitate it but has to supplement its efforts' (AKRSP 1983).

1985–1990: The Formative Period

Zoning for small farmer development was introduced during 1985–1990 under AKRSP's Agriculture & Resource Management programme. Agro-ecosystems analysis (AA) was introduced with input from Imperial College, University of London.[8] The concept of cropping zones, which has remained an important operational aspect in NRM up to this day, was introduced. In the context of forestry research, rapid rural appraisal methods were used in six pilot villages in upper Hunza, some of which were covered by the AA approach already.[9] In the context of wheat research, a farming systems approach was employed.[10] Significant realisations and far reaching strategies were formulated during these formative *learning by doing* and *research* years. A major realisation was the inter-relatedness of agriculture, livestock and forestry, as well as the need to address new socio-economic trends and needs. Another realisation was that perennial crops (trees) have a distinctly comparative advantage over annual crops by optimising the short growing season and addressing more effectively the acute shortage of biomass in the NAC (IUCN 1987). AKRSP's forestry programme evolved from this realisation.

A wide range of new varieties of crops was brought in for trials and testing at different altitudes. The main emphasis of this adaptive research was on wheat and maize, featuring crop-cut surveys and variety trials[11]. Furthermore, orchard and fruit development packages were introduced, initially on a co-operative (VO/WO-owned) basis. In terms of Women in Development work, research into the feasibility of women's involvement in forestry activities and potential for pasture interventions was looked into in the context of the World Conservation Union (IUCN) supported forestry pilot project (1987–1990). In terms of pasture development, the role of women was found to be dependent on cultural traditions, i.e. graziers being women (Gojal area) or men (most other areas of NAC) and type of livestock, i.e. dairy cows being most labour intensive for women in the villages and sheep and goats being dependent on pasturing (Abidi 1987).

The collective *WO Fruit Orchard* experience launched in 1988 laid the foundation for collective action by women. In this package, a WO would lease a plot of land collectively for a period of 15 years. Payment was recovered from WO members or was sometimes made in kind from the profits of the sale of vegetables, which were inter-cropped between the fruit trees. Vegetables were sold collectively, often involving a Village Marketing Specialist trained by AKRSP. Collective production gradually gave way to private management, by which the women would grow and market the produce individually.

By 1993, the last fruit orchard either turned private or was closed down. The lessons drawn from this experiment were a) fruit trees took longer to bear fruit than originally expected,[12] and b) although the package contributed to the economic empowerment of women,[13] collective action by women could not be sustained in the long run through this intervention. Through the Heifer Breed Improvement Project, AKRSP learned that whereas farmers were able to appreciate improved breeds, they cannot manage livestock as VO-owned property. The bulls, cows, heifers, and offspring of the project therefore were divided among the households of the nine VOs participating in this project, in some of which the project has led to a complete transition from seasonal pastoralism to round-the-year stall-feeding of cattle.[14] The important lesson learned from this project was the operational concept of prioritising disease control and feed improvement prior to the introduction of improved breeds. Along with the Friesian cows came a whole line of interventions including silage making and straw urea treatment as well as manger construction. Most importantly, the breeds were only given to villages where Livestock Specialists were effectively providing medical treatment and vaccinations to the whole villages.

Thus, during the end of the 1980s, AKRSP shifted its interventions away from a VO/WO-owned and managed- towards a private ownership approach. The rationale was that collective management, albeit a very important aspect of reciprocal labour exchange and common property management, does not readily translate into collective ownership of property. Lessons learned from collective management directly fed into the design of other packages, for example the *Fruit Nursery* package, launched in 1995 under the WID programme was an individually managed activity based on the *Fruit Orchard* experience.[15]

By now the poultry package was augmented by large-scale research on brooding centres and cluster hatcheries. Not being able to reach economies of scale, these were abandoned after a few years, albeit poultry (*home-based* and *semi-commercial* packages) have remained the most popular activities taken up by women besides vegetable packages. Poultry Specialists, a total of 3,634 of which have been trained between 1984 and 2001, were almost exclusively female. Poultry packages have significantly contributed to the economic empowerment of women through the sale of eggs, birds and provision of technical services at the village level.

1991: The Forestry Section Formally Joins In

Realising right from the start by way of the enthusiasm with which VOs planted trees on new land that there is a great need to boost forestry activities, AKRSP requested IUCN–The World Conservation Union to initiate a three year pilot project in 1987, to investigate the possibility of organising tree plantations on scientific lines (AKRSP 1991b). The overall goal of the programme was: '...a strategy for optimal long term use of natural resources at a high level of productivity' (IUCN 1987). This pilot project led to the development of the first 5-year sustainable forestry development plan and the establishment of AKRSP's forestry section in 1991. Working closely with the VOs and WOs, Forestry Section staff trained Village Forestry Specialists and later on Valley Foresters (Master Trainers). That VOs played an important part in forestry can be seen by the fact that VOs have planted 310 per cent more trees than Non-VOs (FHIES 1991). Since then, about 40 million trees were raised with ca 70 per cent survival and 1,500 private nurseries were established (World Bank 2002).

An important contribution to forestry was also made by WO members through the micro nursery package, whereby women would plant tree cuttings near their homes. These plants would then be purchased by AKRSP. Even though the system never graduated to the commercial level, the activity has contributed significantly to afforestation efforts and capacity building in forestry.

The forestry section also joined the AKRSP mainstream activities, implementing its own technical training, extension and research components. One of the important foresights regarding NRM that came out of the forestry section was the idea of a super-VO level 'apex institution to help planning at valley and watershed levels, sharing experiences, running seminars...' (IUCN 1987: 41). This strategic vision was realised later in the context of cluster VOs representing all VOs at the valley or watershed level. The Forestry Section played an integrating role and contributed towards collective action and institution building at the community level. Free grazing control and collective bans on poaching and illegal forest cutting were the major achievements in this regard.

Another major achievement was in linkages. Not only did forest and range land research lead to very fruitful linkages with WWF and IUCN at the valley and watershed level (see also section below), but the Forestry Section also implemented the Social Forestry Project of the Government of Pakistan.

1990–1995: The Sectoral (Agriculture, Livestock, Forestry) Packages

With the NRM sub-sectors of agriculture, livestock and forestry (ALF) complete, AKRSP consolidated its sectoral NRM programme during the period 1990–1995 by elaborating and re-designing its packages. Work on cash crops such as wheat and potato as well as new maize varieties continued, and the breed improvement programme through improved breed cows and bulls was continued on a private entrepreneur basis.[16] A co-operative agreement was formalised with the National Agricultural Research Council (NARC) for crossing local varieties with suitable varieties from Pakistan. In 1999, AKRSP finally made the transition from variety trials to Participatory Varietal Selection (PVS) and Participatory Plant Breeding (PPB).[17] During the early 1990s, farmers' associations were formed to market potatoes and linked with markets to break the dependence on one buyer and enhance farmer incomes by a large proportion. In Women In Development, the vegetable packages became the most popular activity.

In training, criteria for specialists' performance[18] and the concept of *Master Trainers* was developed to ensure sustainability. Master Trainers, besides training others and representing a middle-level cadre of experts, would also become entrepreneurs in the input supply sector. Criteria (education level, past performance village specialist and potential entrepreneurial skills) were developed to identify the best specialists to be trained for this (AKRSP 1995c). In terms of input supply, the private sector, including a significant involvement of Master Trainers, caters to a high proportion (some say 70–80 per cent[19]) of the needs of the local farmers.

By expanding the scope of sectoral (ALF) activities, the sub-sectors now began competing for 'turf' and resources at the VO and valley level. In part, this competition was exacerbated by some separate donor funding for different ALF programme components, such as the NORAD (Norwegian) funding of the forestry component in Baltistan. Annual planning of ALF activities was done in segregation, by each sector on its own, which increased isolated strategic vision and led to a sense of inter-sectoral competition. At the village level also, it was seldom that the ALF staff went together as a team to plan interventions.

1995 Onward: NRM 'Above' and 'Below' the Water Channel

The period after 1995 saw the gradual integration of NRM sub-sectors. In addition, during the mid '90s, the interplay of 'below' and 'above' the water channel was re-discovered. The NRM (ALF) sections now began to accommodate one another formally through integrated planning at the watershed and valley level. NRM and MER/WID[20] staff conducted Participatory Resource Appraisal (PRA) exercises to assess resource needs and the scope of potential interventions. These appraisals were compiled as action plans,[21] usually by MER staff on behalf of NRM sections. This approach provided an interesting learning experience for both AKRSP and the VO/WO members involved.

Integrated NRM planning and the NRM pilot project experience also led to the realisation that common property management and wild natural resources play an important role in small farmers' livelihood strategies and require advocacy. VO-led initiatives in common property management began to spread and snowball once villagers realised that this would give them greater control over their wild resources. This immediate need for empowerment resulted in numerous successful community based projects, most notably the Bar Valley Project with assistance from WWF, the Khunjerab Buffer Zone (funded by UNDP/GEF), Chalt-Chaprote (see section on Common Property Management, below) and the numerous valleys participating in the IUCN implemented project called *Maintaining Biodiversity in Pakistan with Rural Community Development*. The lesson distilled from this has been that 'broad-based village institutions and support organisations can create an enabling environment for evolving simple and complex strategies for the conservation and sustainable use of their natural resources' (Ahmed 1998a).

Interventions now began to increasingly aim at understanding and supporting small farmers' risk-spreading strategies through mixed farm approaches and local knowledge. With livestock as the link between agriculture and forestry, a shift away from goat towards sheep farming and an increasing trend of fodder production to support stall-feeding as opposed to free grazing were some of the new emphases of the NRM strategy. In 1999, the improved-breed based poultry package was finally re-defined in favour of local variety poultry centres of 50-100 local hens each for breeding and extension purposes. This had the advantage of much lower mortalities due to transportation, as well as many of the input-intensive practices associated with improved chick production (Ali 2002a).

While gender issues (previously *Women In Development*) were not a new concept, a concerted effort was made at gender sensitisation of professional staff as well as analysing the gender division of labour within the NAC farming systems in order to address NRM issues more effectively.[22]

Impact of AKRSP's NRM Component

The World Bank evaluation report (2002) has confirmed the relevancy, efficacy and efficiency of NRM activities. Their economic analysis of NRM component reflects an economic rate of return (ERR) of 25 per cent. The report further adds that the improved wheat and maize varieties and other inputs delivered by the NRM activities have significantly increased cereal production. Cropping intensity between 1991–97 (FHIES) has increased by 15 per cent. Growth in fruits, vegetables, livestock, potato seeds and fodder production have increased farm incomes. Per-capita incomes in real terms increased by 2.7 times from Rs 2,647 in 1991 to Rs 7,046 in 1997.

Farm Income

One aim of AKRSP's mandate has been to increase the income of the people of NAC. The programme has achieved this quite successfully. According to the Farm Household Income Expenditure Surveys (FHIES) conducted since 1991, per household farm incomes in the programme area have increased almost by 10 fold. With farm income still constituting 60 per cent of total income (World Bank 2002), this increase is quite significant. Much of this increase can be attributed to the AKRSP. Table 5.1 illustrates this trend.

Table 5.1. Per household farm incomes: programme area and the regions 1991–2001 (Rupees)

Year	Programme Area	Gilgit	Chitral	Astore	Baltistan
1991	6,414	9,237	4,992	3,235	7,310
1994	28,499	33,714	32,659	22,419	21,310
1997	48,771	61,278	38,530	38,186	51,844
2001	61,246	65,731	57,787	41,882	63,928

Source: Provisional Results of FHIES in NAC 2001, Policy & Research Section AKRSP Core office.

The table indicates that per household farm incomes have constantly increased between 1991–2001 in the programme area and all the regions. The greatest increase has been recorded for Gilgit (Rs 65,731), followed by Baltistan (Rs 63,928), Chitral and Astore. In Gilgit region incomes have increased by more than seven-fold. In Chitral and Astore more than twelve-fold and in Baltistan almost nine-fold during 1991–2001. The share of household farm incomes in the total household incomes is presented in the following table:

Table 5.2. Percentage share of per household farm income: programme area and the regions, 1991–2001

Year	Programme Area	Gilgit	Chitral	Astore	Baltistan
1991	24	29	17	12	39
1994	56	52	59	60	61
1997	55	56	50	53	58
2001	42	38	49	37	46

Source: Provisional Results of FHIES in NAC 2001. Policy & Research Section AKRSP Core office.

The table shows that share of farm incomes in the total household income have first increased up to 1994 in the programme area and the regions except Gilgit and then have started declining in 1997 and 2001. For Gilgit region the household farm income share has increased up to 1997 and then sharply declined to 38 per cent in 2001. These results point to the important fact that the share of non-farm income is now contributing increasingly to the total household incomes.

Issues Illustrated in Specific Insights

One recurring issue in NRM since the very early days has been the importance of land-development in the context of VO formation around an infrastructure project, particularly water channels and the subsequent land development interventions. The case of Khyber village gives an interesting picture of a collective vision of NRM in a time of changing socio-economic realities. Another issue looked into is the case of the para-veterinarian. This highly successful AKRSP trained specialist has played a key role in the organisations' learning by doing history. A look at the wheat story, tries to shed light on the different lessons learned in trying to improve yields through *Participatory Plant Breeding* (PPB), *Participatory Varietal Selection* (PVS), local seed production, and other important interventions in the mountain wheat culture. Finally, common property management, which plays such an important part in mountain areas will be explored by looking at the case of Chalt-Chaprote and Khunjerab Village Organisation (KVO), two different types of community based experiences with sustainable resource management.

SPECIFIC INSIGHTS

The Interplay Between Infrastructure and Land Development

Land development schemes in Pakistan traditionally have been implemented through what may be called a managerial approach to development (Husain 1992). Such projects are typically identified, designed and implemented by technical experts and managers according to pre-determined blue prints out of a centralised government agency. Beneficiaries and the community do not have any control over the project.

The participatory approach on the other hand is very different. Communities have greater control of their development agenda. They identify, prioritise and implement projects addressing their needs and forge the necessary linkages for technical and financial assistance (Husain 1992). Support organisations do not meddle in the internal affairs of the community organisation and the ultimate decision making power rests with the beneficiaries who can reject any project design which does not suit their needs.

AKRSP applied the participatory approach not only to community infrastructure (see Chapter 4) but also to the land development process that followed infrastructure development. This is the reason why infrastructure schemes implemented through the participatory approach have led to high impacts and rates of return. According to the World Bank, AKRSP infrastructure schemes and subsequent land development have led to high impacts and rates of return (World Bank 2002). An AKRSP survey of 13 land development projects has shown that the internal rates of return range from 13 per cent to 56 per cent (AKRSP 2000a). Only three projects have internal rates of returns below 20 per cent while the rest have rates of return above

20 per cent. The benefit-cost ratio ranges from 1.23 to 3.44. Khyber represents an excellent example of this.

At Khyber village, situated in upper Hunza, the people were faced with development challenges not unlike those faced by people in similar environments and other parts of rural Pakistan. The socio-economic trends over the past 20 years towards better education, seasonal out-migration and off-farm labour, resulted in a shortage of labour, increased involvement of women in NRM and a trend towards less dependency on common wild resources. These trends can all be clearly observed at Khyber. But instead of opting away from farming, the people of Khyber have successfully diversified their farming system to suit their new socio-economic requirements. Thus, a shift away from traditional rotational cropping[23] with emphasis on cereals in favour of new cash crops like potato (table and seed potato) and fodder crops has been the major agricultural change over the past 20 years.

Khyber village with its two VOs and two WOs and a total population of 800 people is an excellent example of how land development through gravity irrigation channels can have a major impact on the whole farming and livelihood system. With a total of nine water channels, the villagers of Khyber have constructed three channels during the past twenty years. Table 5.3 below gives an overview of the various gravity irrigation channels at Khyber:

Table 5.3. Water channels at Khyber village

Infrastructure Project	Date of completion	Length RFT (Running Feet)	Command Area (acrtes)	Community Contribution (Pak Rs)	Total Cost (Pak Rs)
VO Khyber PPI*	Dec. 1984	7,800	100	12,000	105,000
IUCN Channel	1997	7,800	100	176,000	500,000
Government	2002	16,100	500	500,000	2,656,000

*Productive Physical Infrastructure (for more detail, see Chapter 4)
**Extension and broadening of IUCN Channel
Source: AKRSP records, Revised PC1 (government project proposal and IUCN records).

One of AKRSP's intentions associated with physical infrastructure has been to reduce pressure on the natural forests and pastures above the water channel, which constitute a vital common resource base to the village. It is this strategy that the people of Khyber have internalised and promoted as *their* model of natural resource conservation. The first channel was completed in 1984. Since then, motivated by this entry point, other land development projects have followed. The land development strategy of Khyber aims at substituting wild natural resources with biomass grown on new land.

Representing one of the first VOs and WOs of the programme, Khyber village has become a model for a wide range of NRM activities, ranging from afforestation and livestock development to conservation through sustainable use of wild resources. Through AKRSP's forestry extension, the villagers have planted over 100,000 trees on the new land, inter-cropped with leguminous and soil-binding fodder varieties. Increased fodder production supported livestock breed improvement. The village has taken part in AKRSP's Heifer breed improvement project,[24] introducing Friesian cows and associated feed improvement, disease control and other cattle management interventions. Once the advantages of stall-fed improved breed milch cows was realised, demand for fodder increased.

The project was replicated by the majority of village households resulting in a marketable dairy product surplus, significantly contributing to per household farm income. More than Rs 1 million from the sale of F1 and F2 (first and second generation) cattle offspring has been another benefit of this intervention. Most important of all, total livestock numbers have been drastically reduced. Apart from a very small flock tended by two old shepherds on a rotational basis on wastelands near the village, all animals are stall-fed around the year, ensuring almost 100 per cent free grazing control and zero pressure on the high pastures. Thirty per cent of villagers do not keep any livestock anymore. Whereas stall-fed dairy cows have presented an increase in labour for women and children, the economic benefits of this activity have been significant.

This in turn has opened opportunities for wild resource conservation through sustainable use of wild resources. In 1990, the villagers were motivated by AKRSP staff and conservationists of the area to put a ban on local hunting of ibex. As a result of this self-enforced ban, the ibex population increased exponentially.[25] AKRSP linked Khyber community with the *Biodiversity Conservation Project*[26] promoting a sustainable use oriented community conservation paradigm. Since then, Khyber has been successfully hosting 13 trophy hunts of Himalayan ibex (*Capra sibirica*). From the 75 per cent share of the trophy hunting fees issued by the government, the community earned a total of over Rs 1 million. Sport hunting has become a lucrative income generating activity, and contributed to the villagers motivation to ban a whole side valley from livestock grazing and fuel wood collection, dedicating it exclusively to wildlife. After hosting a number of visitors who came to learn about the Khyber model of development, the community is now constructing a Village Guest House to host hunters, visitors and other small NGO staff on exchange visits.

How typical is Khyber?

The trend observed at Khyber is no isolated case. The land development impact study (AKRSP 2000a) has shown that increases in livestock (particularly improved cattle breeds) in conjunction with fodder production increases are commonly found throughout the programme area. In Aishi Paen, there has been a 250 per cent increase in the number of livestock per household. The Chalt and Ghulapan assessment reported doubling fodder production since before the project. The fodder security contributed to an increase in the number of livestock, which in turn increased the consumption of livestock by-products by the households. The village Bombagh assessment reported that livestock numbers have increased by almost 90 per cent. In village Tiston consumption of dairy products had increased from 146 kg per month in 1991 to 392 kg per month in 1999.

The impact studies under review demonstrate that the land development projects had a direct and significant impact on timber and fuel wood production as well. Like in Khyber large areas of new land have been allocated to agro-forestry in the beneficiary villages with the result that the rate of afforestation has increased. Communities also grow forest trees on the new land to improve the soil's structure and fertility. The assessment of village Kroy Jinali's irrigation channel reported that the community planted 102,375 forest trees on 29 per cent of the new land. The impact studies on Ghulapan and Baltaring showed a substantial increase of average tree holdings per household.

Making the Para-Veterinarian Effective

Livestock plays a central role in mixed farming systems. More than others, small farmers are more heavily dependent on livestock for dairy products, meat, manure, draft power, wool and hides.

The government system is not accessible to small farmers in general, particularly in remote areas. This has been the main reason for high livestock mortality due to epidemics and disease. Small farmers therefore spread their risk by keeping large herds as a mobile bank. Another reason for preferring a large number of inferior breeds is the frequent need for sacrificial animals for social occasions (weddings, funerals, religious festivals, etc.). All these factors pose constraints on breed improvement and reduction of herd sizes.

Livestock also plays a central role in the livelihood systems of NAC. Both agriculture and forestry are directly linked to livestock through fodder production, which by now, at 30-40 per cent, represents the largest land use.[27] Being estimated at 2.8 million heads (including 24 per cent poultry) in 1986,[28] livestock figures since then have increased for cattle and decreased for goats and sheep.[29] For cattle, this increase in number as well as quality would not have been possible without an effective loss reduction programme, including medical treatment and a massive vaccination campaign.

The very success of the AKRSP livestock development programme lies in the fact that the reduction of losses component was introduced before feed improvement and breed improvement. Other projects in Pakistan have made the mistake to first go for the improved bull, which more often than not has led to the bull turning into kebab.[30] AKRSP's experience has shown that the essence of a successful livestock programme lies in the correct chronological sequence of interventions: 1) reduction of losses; 2) feed improvement; and 3) breed improvement.

Loss reduction through village extensionists dates back to the early 1970s when the Government of Pakistan launched their programme. Villagers nominated their specialists, who were trained by experts and were supposed to provide services free of charge. This system collapsed as soon as the government withdrew its support.

UNDP/FAO (Food and Agriculture Organisation) followed up on this issue by training entrepreneur-veterinarians. This scheme collapsed, because the 'vetrepreneurs' expected remuneration that was too high for the average villager.

Box 5.1. Livestock trends in the programme area

Livestock, being the programmatic link between forestry and agriculture, plays a pivotal role in NRM. The number and type of livestock kept by farmers also says a lot about the whole farming system. According to the 1986 Pakistan Livestock Census cited in the AKRSP Ninth Annual Review 1991, there were 2.8 million livestock in the Programme Area in 1986. Out of this, cattle constituted 16 per cent, sheep 24 per cent, goats 36 per cent and poultry 24 per cent. In absolute numbers, this would mean:

Table 5.4. Number of livestock in the programme region (excluding Astore) by type in 1986

Type	Number
Cattle	448,000
Sheep	672,000
Goat	1,008,000
Poultry	67,200
Total	2,800,000

Source: AKRSP 1991b

FHIES 1991 and 1997 has also provided livestock population figures by household averages:

Table 5.5. Average livestock holdings per household in the programme region (excluding Astore) in 1997

	Gilgit	Baltistan	Chitral
Cattle	4	5	4
Goat/Sheep	11	10	12

Source: FHIES (1997)

The number of rural households as per the 1998 census has been:

Table 5.6. Number of rural households in the 1998 Census

Gilgit	44,229
Baltistan	35,770
Chitral	36,185
Total	116,184

Multiplying these household figures with the per household livestock holdings given in Table 5.6, and comparing with the figures in Table 5.5, the following trend emerges:

Table 5.7. Livestock holdings and growth rate between 1986 and 1997 in the programme region (excluding Astore)

	1986	1997	Growth between 1986 and 1997 (%)	Growth per annum (%)
Cattle	448,000	468,034	4.5	0.4
Sheep	1,680,000	1,189,141	-29,2	-2.7

Source: FHIES (1997), AKRSP 1991b, Census 1998

From the above table it becomes evident that whereas cattle holdings have increased marginally, sheep and goat holdings have decreased by almost 30 per cent. This trend confirms the socio-economic trend over the past 20 years, whereby labour shortages due to education and off-farm opportunities determine preferences for less labour intensive livestock breeds.

AKRSP's innovation in 1983 was the concept of letting the villagers fix the price for vaccinations. The response to this concept was very positive. In the third quarter of 1983, 30 VOs sent their nominees, and within a year (by June 1984), 68 VO representatives treated 1,888 animals, including 904 vaccinations and medicine distribution worth Rs 1,116. In comparison, sales of medicines and vaccines distributed privately in the year 2000 valued Rs 457,330 and Rs 299,714, respectively. By 2000, 2,368 specialists were trained in 140 courses and livestock mortality was reduced by an assumed 50 per cent through medication and 4 and 2 per cent respectively for cattle and sheep through vaccinations (World Bank 1995b).

Important lessons learned during the first decade were to ensure that medicines were kept at a cool place in the Specialist's home. Another problem, the time-consuming door-to-door vaccination campaign, was overcome by treatment and vaccination at the village centre on fixed days. Causing only a few problems due to vicious animals and crop damages, this practice turned out to be very effective.[31]

Box 5.2. Poultry specialist and businesswoman Shahida Numa of Princeabad Women's Organisation, Gilgit

Shahida has received training from AKRSP in poultry management and disease control. She is one of the few poultry specialists who has developed an enterprise by selling eggs. Shahida tells us of how her skills enabled her to start her own enterprise.

Q: What difference has the training made to your skills?
A: I used to keep chickens before but I used to treat them through traditional methods by feeding them garlic. Now, I know how disease spreads and how to prevent it effectively.
Q: How much do you earn from your business and how has that affected your life?
A: Before training, I used to keep a maximum of ten birds and rarely sold eggs as they were kept for guests. My monthly earnings then were Rs. 300-400. Now, I have one hundred and thirty five chicken, and I earn about Rs 2,000 per month. Earlier, I used to wait for my husband to bring his salary home. Now, I am earning money every day, and my earnings are running the household, whereas my husband's are being saved to build a new house. My family is eating more eggs and so am I—after all, it is my hard work that has gone into the business.
Q: Do you not feel that this business has increased your workload?
A: Earlier, I used to work more in the fields, now I pay attention to my poultry enterprise, as this involves less work and my children also help me. The work is less, the income higher.

(adapted from Box 2.2, AKRSP 1992b: 29)

Whereas Village Livestock Specialists were mainly male, Poultry Specialists were almost 100 per cent female and played a crucial role in women's empowerment in terms of confidence building, mobility and economic contribution to household income. This in turn has had an impact on financial decision making within households.

A major boost to the livestock specialist component happened during the early 1990s, when trained Livestock Specialists neared the 1,500 mark. In order to make this service delivery more efficient and sustainable, AKRSP began training Livestock Master Trainers (MTs), who, besides training others and representing a middle-level cadre of experts, would also become entrepreneurs in the input supply sector. Criteria (education level, past performance as Village Livestock Specialist and potential entrepreneurial skills) were developed to identify the best specialists to be trained for this. By 1995, MTs backed up by NRM and Enterprise Development Section staff were profitably running input supply stores in Gilgit and Skardu. A particularly successful input supply enterprise, Renmushey Stores, was run by 14 MTs in Skardu (main depot) and all major valleys of Baltistan (branches). Net profit of Renmushey Stores was above Rs 3 million in 1995 (AKRSP 1995c). MTs and private input stores have finally established a functioning cost-recovery mechanism pointing the road to sustainability.

The Story of New Wheat Varieties

Wheat is the main staple cereal in Pakistan, and this is also true for the Northern Areas and Chitral (NAC). For small farmers, wheat is also extremely important for *thinnings* as fodder for the livestock kept in the villages during the summer months and as straw during times of critical shortage, particularly during the winter months when no green forage is available. The region has been importing between 25 and 30 per cent of its wheat consumption (Streefland *et al.* 1995). Low productivity has been the main constraint faced by farmers. The underlying causes were old varieties that have lost their vigour and disease susceptibility (Husain 1986a).

Before being overtaken by fodder production and until the mid 1990s, wheat, with a share in annual cropping of above 50 per cent, represented the major crop of the whole programme area. Until recently, wheat represented 40 per cent of all farm income (Streefland *et al.* 1995). Historically, wheat varieties have been locally tested and improved for hundreds of years, and farmers have adopted new varieties from far-off places. Varieties introduced during the 1960s, which are by now considered 'local' include *Dirk* (locally *Kuruto* = 'small ears'), Vulfin (Japanese), C-591 and C-278 (Husain 1986a). The new dimension of this story is the fact that until AKRSP got involved there was no functioning system, whereas AKRSP has achieved in 20 years of farmer based research 'the most advanced Participatory Plant Breeding (PPB) programme in wheat that is being undertaken anywhere in the world' (DFID 2003).

After some discussions between AKRSP management and CIMMYT at the very beginning of the programme, AKRSP started off its cereal programme by conducting research based on crop cut surveys (Husain 1986a). In 1985, AKRSP began introducing Pak-81 in the area around Gilgit town, which falls into the double cropping zone. By 1988/89 Pak 81 was planted on 24 per cent of the farm area by 26 per cent of the farmers, and Suneen, another new variety, was planted on nearly 15 per cent of the area (Ahmad and Longmire 1990). A minor area was planted with other new varieties, including Shegaste, which was later to become a big success in the single cropping zone.[32] An important observation made during those early trials was that small farmers in NAC, much like small farmers in the rest of the country, only plant one variety at a time due to small landholdings and therefore are not easily persuaded to risk their livelihood on a new un-tested variety (Ahmad and Longmire 1990). Another important early lesson learned was that new varieties need to fit into the farmers planting and harvesting timeframe, which must be considered a 'given', in order to allow for critical amounts of farmyard manure to accumulate during spring and allow for early harvesting, so that the second crop, usually maize, can ripen (Husain 1986a).

AKRSP then helped to establish a seed production system in the villages. The seed production system was based on a dialogue process, in which AKRSP would, as a first step, identify suitable seed production villages, from among which seed producers would be nominated by the VOs. Then, project staff would explain the need for sound production and post harvest seed treatment to the villagers and transfer technical skills. Finally, it would be agreed between the producers and AKRSP that seed would be sold at a premium above wheat.

AKRSP then conducted adoption surveys for a number of years showing very encouraging adoption rates. Dr Majid, head of AKRSP Agriculture Programme 1991–94, estimates that an average of 60 per cent of farmers used Pak 81 on a regular basis, and Pak 81 became by far the most successful and popular variety. Adoption rates depended on three main factors: taste, grain-straw ratio, and length of ripening season.

Taste as well as colour are very important adoption factors, and otherwise highly successful new varieties have been rejected because of local culinary trends and because they were not white, the colour of preference. As yield is in many ways inversely related to quality (particularly taste),[33] farmers initially consider their local varieties superior despite significant inferiority in the other criteria. Straw ratio plays an important role in food security in relation to livestock management. Whereas a higher grain yield is a desirable aspect, straw is as important as fodder. This importance has been noted in rain-fed as well as mountainous areas and among small farmers all over Pakistan.[34]

Altitude plays a factor as well, because the higher cropping zones are more suitable for pastoralism and therefore are dominated by livestock and fodder production. In this context, the wheat programme gained additional importance: whereas subsidised wheat has been cheaply available, fodder cannot easily be imported from elsewhere due to its bulk. Duration of the crop has been another important adoption criteria due to the harsh and unpredictable mountain climate of NAC. The margin of farmers' tolerance for difference in duration is a few days, depending on the cropping cycle of the different zones (Husain 1986a).

AKRSP subsequently also introduced other varieties, but by far the most successful one remained Pak 81, until 1994–95 when Pak-81 was hit by *stripe* or *yellow rust*. By then, AKRSP had entered into a partnership with the National Agricultural Research Council (NARC) through which local varieties were taken to the national research station for crossing with improved Pakistani varieties for higher grain yield, early ripening qualities and disease and lodging[35] resistance traits.

Through this collaboration and through funding and technical support from the UK Department for International Development (DFID), a start was made in 1999 on the PPB programme in wheat. F1 seed of 8 crosses was produced in 1999 based on local germplasm collected during the 1970s in Northern Areas (AKRSP 2000g). The significant aspect of PPB is that whereas the desirable traits of local cultivars like colour, taste, straw yield can be retained in the new cross, improved traits like early maturity, disease resistance and higher grain yield can be incorporated as well.[36] Simultaneously, ten lines from CIMMYT and NARC without names plus two local varieties as a control group were put on the Initial Evaluation Trial. This trial would be conducted on a 10 kanal plot rented by AKRSP. The planting and crop management would be supervised by an AKRSP trained Agriculture Valley Specialist or Master Trainer. Once the crop ripened, AKRSP would invite all farmers of the village for a Field Day extension campaign, where the participants would evaluate the lines through ranking for each different trait: colour, early maturity (relative to local), grain yield, plant height and seed weight (Ali 2002b).

The five top lines would go to the next trial, the Introductory Varietal Trial during the following year. Again, ranking by all villagers would determine the three best performing 2-3 varieties and every farmer would get 1kg of the new cultivars free of cost as a mini-kit for the final *Advanced Varietal Trial* evaluation. At the end of year three, the farmers would pass a demand resolution through their Agriculture Valley Specialist to AKRSP for the amount of seed of the type of variety they plan to plant. AKRSP would request release of wheat seed from NARC and distribute to the farmers at 100 per cent cost. Farmers would get from AKRSP a 20 per cent production premium. The currently best performing lines are NR 152 (double cropping zone) and Chakwal 86 (single cropping).[37]

Common Property Management: The Different Experiences of Chalt-Chaprote and Khunjerab Village Organisations (KVO)

In Pakistan, like in many other places, common wild resources, rangelands, natural forests and wildlife are under severe pressure from over-exploitation and mismanagement. Experiences with Forest Co-operatives[38] and other representative institutions since the 1970s have proven that unless a truly participatory community approach is promoted in earnest, wild resource management will continue to fall victim to the timber mafia, poachers and other corrupt elements in society (Husain 1992). It has only been for a decade or so that forest policies that work for people have begun to be taken seriously by government institutions and have gained momentum.[39]

The formation of VO-based institutions facilitated by AKRSP enabled villagers to increase their control over the common lands. In the mid-1980s, this attracted the attention of academics, journalists, conservationists and donors. Local influentials, including prominent religious leaders,[40] began spreading conservation messages up and down the Karakorum Highway to the communities, and villagers began imposing bans on cutting down natural forests and hunting wildlife on their own. The case of Chalt-Chaprote has been a prominent example, whereby the VO forum played an important role to legitimise popular opinion against forest exploitation (Hunzai 1987).

The interesting twist in this story is that whereas the Forest Department initially supported the community of Chalt-Chaprote to jointly manage the forest through a so-called *Reform* (*Islahi*) *Committee*, the Department went back on its commitment during 1988 and as a reaction of civil disobedience, the community 'banned' all Forest Department staff to interfere in its area and 'their' forest (Gohar 2002). While this form of self-empowerment worked well for some time, the market forces driving the timber mafia finally got the better of Chaprote and Chalt communities, creating rifts and finally breaking up the well-formulated community system. Finally, after a particular severe bout of pasture user rights conflict mixed with local politics,[41] in summer 2000, the Deputy Commissioner Gilgit took 38 village notables from the different villages into police custody as a signal to re-possess the forest (Gohar 2002). Eventually, a new agreement for joint forest management was drawn up between the Forest Department and the two parties in June 2001 (date of signatures on the agreement).

According to Reform Committee representatives of Chalt, Chaprote and the block officer concerned, the joint management system has been working well since then as far as controlling the transport of timber out of the area. Each party is vigilantly observing the other parties, which provides an ideal system of checks and balances. In terms of sustainable management of forest resources at the local level however, traditional silvicultural practices, i.e. girdling, lopping and outright cutting down of green trees, are rampant and unchecked.[42] To add to the concern, AKRSP has given a pasture link road to the VOs of Chaprote to make their life easier in terms of transport to and from the cultivated pasture settlements. The road, which is only half finished, passes right through the forest, including the few dense patches still remaining!

The experience of the villagers from the seven villages around Sust has been very different to that of Chalt-Chaprote. Whereas in the latter case, the VOs have approached the Forest Department for help, in the former case, the Forest Department took the first initiative, by declaring the area around Khunjerab pass bordering China to the North as Khunjerab National Park (KNP)[43] in 1975. One year later, the newly designated park staff rounded up all grazing cattle and herders in the village pastures that fell into KNP's core zone and locked them up inside the police station at Sust, registering a police case against the villagers. This event traumatised the whole area, and created negative awareness about the concept of a national park.

It also did not help much that WWF stepped in during the early 1980s and designed a management plan for KNP which clearly outlined the areas where community use rights would continue to be valid and those areas where grazing and other use activities would be banned. If nothing else, the management plan increased the sense of urgency among the communities around KNP to secure greater control and legal status for using what has been theirs for generations.

The opportunity for empowerment materialised when Shoaib Sultan Khan, then General Manager of AKRSP, urged the villagers to conserve their wildlife and come up with a strategy to make better use of this resource during the early 1990s.[44] This idea fell on fertile ground and VO activists formed the Khunjerab Village Organisation (KVO), a cluster of all seven VOs and seven WOs of the seven villages in the area.

After several years of successful implementation of a community ban on poaching, KVO was facilitated by AKRSP in proposal formulation to obtain a Global Environment Facility (GEF) small grant worth Rs 431,000.[45] This proposal was for a three-year project (1996–1999) piloting a community managed watch and ward system for wildlife, particularly Himalayan ibex (*Capra sibirica*) and blue sheep (*Pseudois nayaur*) in the *Khunjerab Buffer Zone*.[46] WWF assisted by building local capacity for wildlife survey techniques and the Wildlife Department provided legal cover to a community check post, notified the area as *Community Controlled Hunting Area* and notified *Honorary Wildlife Officers* from among the community.[47] The project was highly successful. The ibex population increased significantly,[48] and the community approached the government for the issuing of trophy hunting licenses for Himalayan ibex. KVO earned Rs 586,000 from the community share of 75 per cent from the trophy hunting licences during the period of the project.[49] Apart from creating awareness about the potential added value of wild resources, the community successfully asserted their rights in the *Khunjerab Buffer Zone*.

Part of the money earned from trophy hunting was re-invested into conservation activities and into a *Valley Conservation Fund*,[50] which was established in 2001 with assistance from the Mountain Areas Conservancy Project (MACP). The interesting aspect of this fund is that the women's share is 10 per cent, which represents a proportionate (10 per cent) stake in the profits from trophy hunting by the women of KVO. They feared that otherwise all the profit would be controlled by the men.

Besides the annual income from trophy hunting (24 hunts up to date[51]), the government finally began paying the community share of park entry fees to the community of KVO. This share has been Rs 3.1 million up to date, the initial Rs 1.7 million of which was distributed among the households of KVO, the rest of which went into various revolving funds. Out of these revolving funds, in 2003, Rs 1 million went into purchasing agricultural inputs for 300 kanals (15 ha) of village lands as an internal loan in kind,[52] and Rs 4.86 million went towards purchasing land for the *KVO Biodiversity Centre.*[53]

The Chalt-Chaprote and KVO experiences point to the importance of collective action in common property management. Facilitating the formation of participatory grass roots institutions and creating effective linkages with relevant partners in development has therefore always been the most crucial operational process in the common property management sector. This example also illustrates that different categories of resources require different types of institutions for their effective management. As a rule of thumb, the more widely shared a resource is, the higher the institution to manage it. The figure below tries to illustrate this point:

Figure 5.2. Resource management by institution

RESOURCE TYPE	Household	Village	Valley/ Watershed	Government
Agriculture	/////////			
Livestock	/////////	/////////		
Forest Plantation	/////////	/////////		
Natural Forest	Clan/lineage	/////////	/////////	/////////
Pastures		/////////	/////////	
Wildlife			/////////	/////////

NOTES

1. One hectare equals 20 kanals of land. Whereas average landholdings were given for Baltistan, Chitral and Gilgit as 0.73 ha, 0.9 ha and 1.08 ha. in 1987 (AKRSP 1987c), now landholdings for Baltistan, Gilgit, Astore and Chitral were given as 34, 34, 39, and 54 *kanals* respectively (FHIES 2001). Based on survey samples, these figures are open to debate.

2. For an analysis of per household livestock trends see Box 5.1.

3. Dr Akhtar Ali and Dr Mastan, AKRSP, personal communication. Besides epidemics, other contributing factors were crowding, bad hygiene and insufficient nutrition due to seasonal fodder shortages. Typically, livestock mortality therefore has been highest during early spring.

4. For more information on this debate, see Oehmke and Husain (1987); Kreutzmann (1985, 1993); Gloekler, Raza and Iqbal *et al.* (1995).

5. This point was made during a visit to Gilgit by Dr Akhter Hameed Khan, who maintained that the population of Northern Pakistan is too thinly spread to replicate the Comilla/Daudzai experience (Tariq Husain, personal communication).

6. Trainees would now receive travel and daily allowances for the trip to Gilgit for training.

7. During the first five years, AKRSP trained some 207 Livestock Specialists (para-veterinarians) who vaccinated 137,000 livestock and 152-plant protection specialists (World Bank 1987). Perhaps the most effective type of all AKRSP specialists has been the para-veterinarian, a total of 2,368 of which have been trained to date (see section on 'Making the Para-Veterinarian Effective').

8. For more information on AA, see Conway *et. al.* (1987).

9. For more information, see IUCN 1987.

10. For more information on the wheat research debate, see Byerlee and Husain (1993).

11. See 'The Story of New Wheat Varieties', below.

12. Bearing age turned out to be 10-12 years instead of 7-8 years, and therefore the orchards would not bear profits (other than from the sale of vegetables) before almost the end of the lease period of the land. The WO Fruit Orchard at Nomal village for example was repossessed by the landowner just when the trees began to bear fruit (AKRSP agriculture and forestry staff, personal communication).

13. Through its fruit orchard, WO Gulmit raised the major part of its Rs 1.5 million savings (Sosan, Forester, AKRSP, personal communication).

14. For more detail on the *Heifer Project*, see Ali and Tetlay (1991).

15. AKRSP forestry and agriculture staff, personal communication.

16. By now, there is an F1 (first generation) Jersey population of 7,000 head in Baltistan, where this programme has been most successful (World Bank 2002).

17. For more detail on the wheat programme, see 'The Story of New Wheat Varieties', below.

18. One issue affecting performance has been the problem of village elites hijacking the role of the specialist, often in several fields of expertise. For more detail see Gloekler and Hussain (1995).

19. Dr Farman Ali, Regional Programme Manager, AKRSP Gilgit, personal communication.

20. Monitoring, Evaluation and Research and Women in Development Sections.

21. For an example of such plans see Raza *et al.* (1996); or Gloekler *et al.* (1996).

22. See Malik and Ahmed (1994); Warrington and Hemani (1996).

23. The traditional cropping patterns at Khyber were wheat, barley and black beans in annual rotation.

24. The *Heifer Project* was funded and technically assisted by *Heifer International, USA*. For some details about this project see section on 'The Formative Period', above.

25. From a few remaining animals during the early 1990s, the ibex population increased to 43 in 1995, 150 in 1997, 272 in 2000 and 577 in 2002 (MACP/IUCN joint survey results).

26. For more information on this four year IUCN implemented pilot project see Gloekler (1999).

27. Gilgit 45 per cent, Chitral 23 per cent, Baltistan 34 per cent (FHIES 1997); average fodder produced among 13 villages studied was 33 per cent (AKRSP 2000a).

28. Pakistan Livestock Census for Northern Areas and Chitral, cited in the 9th Annual Review, (AKRSP 1991b).

29. For a trend analysis of per household livestock holdings see Box 5.1.

30. *Kebab* (Urdu) means barbecue. A lesson stressed upon AKRSP staff in the early days by Akhtar Hameed Khan (personal communication Tariq Husain).

31. Dr Akhter, Co-ordinator Livestock, AKRSP Gilgit, personal communication.

32. In 1991, 12 VOs from Shigar Valley, Baltistan earned Rs 33,400 by producing 5,400 kg of 80 per cent pure Shegaste seed for export to Chitral to meet local demand there (AKRSP 1991b).

33. Dr Majid, personal communication

34. Dr Majid, personal communication.

35. *Lodging* is the bending of wheat plants when they cannot support their own weight any longer.

36. Salman Ali, Coordinator Agriculture, AKRSP Gilgit, personal communication.

37. For more information on this process, contact Salman Ali, Coordinator Agriculture, AKRSP Gilgit.

38. Forest Co-operative Societies were established by the Forest Department between 1980 and 1993 in the Hazara District as an attempt to hand over management responsibilities to the communities.

39. For more information on this debate see Ahmed 1998b.

40. Some prominent leaders were Syed Yahya Shah of Nagar, ex-Divisional Forest Officer (DFO) Ghulam Rasool and Master Sirat from Khyber.

41. According to Mr Khudadad, Chairman Dehi Council Chaprote Bala (personal communication), herders from Chalt grazed their livestock inside the cultivated area of Chaprote pasture. In this conflict, local political party representatives also took part and the whole issue became highly politicised.

42. Personal observation during a visit to the forest in June 2003.

43. The underlying reason for the establishment of the KNP has been the declining population of charismatic wildlife species found in the area such as the snow leopard (*Uncia uncia*) and Marco Polo sheep (*Ovis amon*). KNP was managed on outdated premises based on the assumption that local people are the main cause for resource depletion (Mock 1990). The populations of Marco Polo sheep have kept declining however, the main reason being uncontrolled hunting. Today, only a few animals remain.

44. This story is partly based on verbal information obtained from Mr Mohabat Karim, Office Secretary of KVO.

45. UNDP/GEF proposal INT/02-G31.

46. The concept of a *community use zone* adjacent to a national park has been a completely novel concept to the Wildlife Department, but eventually contributed significantly to create awareness among government staff about the effectiveness of community based approaches of wildlife management.

47. See government notifications F.4(5)/90-NA-IV/I and F&A-101(F)/98, respectively.

48. From 78 ibex in 1996 to 152 in 1998 (GEF Small Grant Flyer). A joint wildlife survey in Nov. 2002 found a total population of 385 ibex, including 31 trophy size males (MACP/IUCN wildlife survey data).
49. GEF Small Grants Flyer on KVO: *Community Management of Wildlife Resources.*
50. Invested into a Term Deposit Account, the annual profit of this revolving fund is meant to meet the recurrent costs of conservation, i.e. watch and ward activities, wildlife surveys and official expenses. For more information see Gloekler (1999).
51. KVO office figures.
52. For more detail on AKRSP's fertiliser loan system of the early days see section on 'The Initial Years', above.
53. Contact: Khunjerab Village Organisation, Dreamland Hotel, P.O. Sust, Village Gircha, Gilgit District, Northern Areas.

6

Enterprise Development

Fatimah Afzal

Universally, creating new business is a risky task. The odds are stacked against one attempting it, even within thriving and robust commercial milieus. The example of the United States of America, the bastion of capitalism and described as the land of opportunity, best substantiates this view. '...It is a cold hard fact that more than half of the 800,000 businesses started [in 2003 in the USA] will not be around five years from now. Some will fail, some will be sold to people who think they can beat the odds and some will be closed by their founders because they are just not worth the time or the effort. Only 20 per cent of the businesses started this year will be around in ten years. Half of the survivors will be producing only a marginal profit' (Harper 2002).

INTRODUCTION

Over its twenty-year history, AKRSP has experimented with almost all private business development interventions available at given times. It has provided business support services directly on a one-to-one basis, established its own businesses, serviced larger groups through strengthening indigenous associations and of late it is trying to adopt a more facilitative role in strengthening local markets for business development services (BDS). All successive programmatic shifts emanated directly out of AKRSP's own experiences, and placed it each time in step with the given international contemporary trends in small business promotion. Nevertheless, business promotion, with its inherent message of competition for scarce resources, and survival of the most market-savvy is conceptually at odds with AKRSP's core philosophy and practice of collectivist rural development governed by social and economic equity concerns. In this respect, the birth and growth of AKRSP's enterprise development programme has been tumultuous and has often been considered external to its mainstream development agenda. The intensity of AKRSP's business promotion experience, in addition, make it strikingly different from other social development organisations in Pakistan, most of which continue to focus on interventions traditionally associated with NGOs, for example, health, education, community infrastructure schemes, and women's development.

AKRSP's non-conformist trajectory raises a fundamental issue: should a rural development organisation even as successful and innovative as AKRSP be in the business of servicing business, in the first place? The record reviewed in this chapter attempts to answer this question. It is, however, equally pertinent to question if anyone can or would even be inclined to attempt to promote the development of the commercial sector, in areas well acknowledged as some of the most formidable mountainous terrain in the world.

While the peculiar realities of northern Pakistan provided an excellent ground for applying the tried and tested community based rural development models for the physical and social development of the region, in contrast, they provided an equally subversive environment for business promotion. The characteristics of the northern regions place a ceiling on its economic and commercial growth, limiting the nature, scale and scope of indigenous businesses. The only marginal exceptions to this fact are the few urban administrative centres in the north, such as Gilgit, Skardu and Chitral. Commercial activity remains nestled within an infant industry, comprising micro and small businesses catering to the functional and basic needs of the local communities. People have low purchasing power. Seasonal and small cash in-flows of the vast majority of the potential consumers engaged in small scale agricultural activities leave sellers with negligible leverage vis-à-vis customers. Such a buyers' market, thus, provides limited space and commercial impetus for traders to compete among themselves, expand their businesses, or even establish new ones.

Despite the challenges and issues associated with the programme and its areas of operation, AKRSP singularly stands out as the only organisation in Pakistan—in both the private and the public sectors— unmatched in the depth and breadth of its experimental support services offered in the way of spurring commercial activity and growth. At the time that AKRSP initiated its activities, the commercial sector players had no stake or interest in the weak markets of the north. Therefore, AKRSP was bereft of the advantage of seeking the counsel of business experts regarding best business practices, or an appraisal of its own interventions from the perspective of business people, or mechanisms for devolving the business support functions to commercial sector stakeholders who, after all, know business best. This is why AKRSP's remarkable overtures to the commercial stakeholders were made in the spirit of building *equal* partnerships for collectively assisting the private commercial sector in the Northern Areas and Chitral (NAC). In time, through the demonstration effect of its business programmes and its active lobbying efforts, AKRSP did, however, ignite the imagination and interests of other commercial sector stakeholders in the northern hinterlands of Pakistan.

Today, at the national policy level, attention has begun to shift towards creating a more small business-friendly environment in Pakistan as an important mechanism for reducing poverty and boosting the national economy. Development practitioners and policy makers are increasingly valuing AKRSP's business experience, to draw out lessons not only for marginal and remote areas, but to inform the national policies and frameworks governing the micro, medium and small enterprise (MSME) sector in Pakistan. These achievements are indeed commendable—even more so given their inexpensive price tag. Through the last twenty years, AKRSP's enterprise development budget has not exceeded more than 2 per cent of the total organisational budget.[1] This study explores the seemingly enigmatic experiences of AKRSP in the business field.

The Contextual Background

In 1982, AKRSP commenced operations in a subsistence-based agricultural economy, lacking even basic commercial markets. There was no manufacturing industry and the service industry was confined to a few hotels and public telephone services.[2] The monetised economy was limited and restricted to urban areas. Villagers met most of their consumption needs through barter, by exchanging dried fruits and grains with items such as soap, matchsticks, and paper.

Surplus food requirements and household consumption items were imported from down-country at prices controlled by the district government through issuance of Price Lists.[3] In fact, exports from Chitral were prohibited (AKRSP 1985a) due to the vulnerable food security of the region and subsistence-based agricultural production. The regions were, however, rich in natural resources, such as mineral and gem deposits. Favourable climatic conditions offered a wide variety of fresh and dried fruits, and vegetables. The mountain ranges attracted international tourists, and offered scope for scaling up tourism in the regions.

According to the 1980 Agriculture Census for the Northern Areas (NAs), inequality in land ownership—the principal productive asset at the time—was only moderately skewed. This implies that significant socio-economic class distinctions did not exist and communities were largely homogenous. Equally, it also meant absence of engagement in more non-traditional areas, such as private business. Though a substantial portion of the incomes was generated through off-farm employment (Table 6.1)—open only to men—these mainly comprised of military, the government, and unskilled jobs such as porters and migration down-country for seasonal wage labour. Although women contributed more than half the workload on-farm (AKRSP 1999a), their contributions went unacknowledged and public commercial roles for them were unheard of.

Table 6.1. Trends in average annual household farm and off-farm incomes in the programme area (Rupees, 1991–2001)

Year	Farm	Off-farm	Off-farm as a Percentage of Total	Total	Per Capita
1991	6,414	20,434	76%	26,848	2,939
1994	28,499	22,050	44%	50,549	3,976
1997	48,771	40,649	45%	89,420	4,851
2001	61,246	83,699	58%	144,945	6,257

Source: AKRSP Core Office, Islamabad

According to a market survey conducted by AKRSP in 1982 (AKRSP 1983) there were 90–100 fruit and vegetable retailers in Gilgit but no wholesale markets of any kind. Surplus fruit and vegetables perished in the absence of appropriate storage, high costs of transportation, and lack of transport at appropriate times. Farmers had no negotiating leverage with buyers. Faced with the prospects of having to carry their perishable produce from shop to shop, they were compelled to sell it on buyers' terms. Farmers had little awareness and lacked resources to consider mechanisms for addressing these trade issues or exploring new commercial arenas. The prohibitive transportation costs of servicing a small market made NAC unattractive to traders in the south. Traders from down-country capitalized on these handicaps and the local taboos associated with selling fruit and vegetables, to purchase at cheap rates and sell at high profits in the down-country markets. Although this meant good income earning opportunities for the traders, the low value received by farmers for their produce limited their social and economic uplift, and reduced the incentives for producing improved varieties (Roomi *et al.* 2000).

According to the Contextual Study of the Northern Areas and Chitral (Streefland *et al.* 1995), until the feudal system was abolished in 1972 farmers had had no experience of decision-making in organising agriculture. Accustomed to working as tenants and labourers for the large landowners, farmers were incapable of making independent decisions regarding the optimal use of their land. The information and lack of exposure created by years of isolation, within a susceptible environment wary of external influences, had nurtured a socio-economic culture devoid of entrepreneurial ethos and capacity. Given the vulnerable environment and the inherent risks laden in private ventures, understandably there was a cultural distaste for private business. Professional, military or government careers were considered far more secure and prestigious than setting up shop.

AKRSP's Tool Kit: The Interventions

AKRSP's underlying objectives of job creation and income generation have been served by a combination of interventions, which have varied over the years with AKRSP's programmatic focus and approach. Broadly, interventions can be categorised into skill and enterprise management related training, exposure visits, chamber-of-commerce type functions, and credit.

During the early to mid 1980s, the priority was development of farm-related skills such as post-harvest management (fruit picking, grading, and packing) fruit drying and fruit processing. These skills were complemented with dissemination of technology, inputs and training for improved farm productivity. During the late 1980s the trend began to change, and by the mid to late 1990s attention shifted to creating a range of off-farm vocational capacities such as: hotel management, carpet weaving, school uniform stitching, quilt making, carpentry, plumbing, hair cutting, pottery making, motor rewinding, mine blasting, gem-stone cutting and polishing, candle making, and fabric dying.

In step with the focus on off-farm related enterprises, starting in the 1990s, the scope of enterprise management training also expanded considerably. It included: accounting and bookkeeping, costing/pricing, preparation of financial statements, understanding cash-flows and trade channels, marketing, product promotion, and short-term training programmes in business management/enterprise development.

Since the early 1980s, sponsoring exposure visits for the business people of the north has been an integral part of AKRSP's capacity-building initiatives. Starting from visits to commercial and wholesale markets down-country in the 1980s, exposure visits became more diverse with visits to private businesses, and commercial and trade forums down-country and abroad.[4]

In the absence of business service providers in the north, AKRSP's role also evolved to provide chamber-of-commerce type facilities. When AKRSP began its work information dissemination and business counselling services for walk-in clients were more predominant. Very soon, however, AKRSP also engaged in establishing linkages with private and public sector financial and non-financial stakeholders (for example, the Export Promotion Bureau, and Chambers of Commerce and Industries) including private businesses[5] down-country for expanding value-added commercial opportunities for small businesses in the NAC.

In the 1980s, AKRSP offered short-term credit to support marketing of farm produce, purchase of inputs and other seasonal activities. An 8 per cent service charge was introduced in 1988, following the government abandoning an interest-free policy. In its efforts to decentralise and simplify credit procedures, since 1989 the short-term credit facility has been devolved to the Village Organisation (VO)/Women's Organisation (WO). Between the early and late 1990s, AKRSP also offered credit facilities for small businesses in its efforts to ameliorate their access to relatively large financing requirements.

AKRSP's Enterprise Development Experience: An Overview

The diverse spectrum of AKRSP's business support activities can be categorised into the following three broad phases, with one leading to and merging into the next:[6]

- VO-Based Cooperative Marketing (1982–1991)
- Alternative Approaches to Enterprise Development (1992–2002)
- From 'provider' to 'facilitator' to developing BDS markets (2003–2007)

The journey began very conventionally in the footsteps of first generation rural development programmes. The central preoccupation was with increasing production. Nevertheless, increased production did not translate into increased incomes, which is why during the 1980s rural development programmes began to explore marketing. AKRSP adopted the collective marketing model. The experience,[7] however, clearly indicated the significance of the individual entrepreneur as a prerequisite for any successful venture.

Nevertheless, like all NGOs the staff who joined AKRSP were economists, technocrats, administrators and social scientists and mainly devotees of the traditional rural development thinking, which was still under the influence of the cooperatives. AKRSP decided to continue with the cooperative experiment, though with modifications, in light of the collectivist experience. Though this experience was disappointing, subsequently the range of diverse businesses, which emerged as a result of supporting individual entrepreneurs, was very encouraging. In sub-sectors with commercial potential but no private investor, AKRSP went as far as to establish its own businesses. Subsequently, improved opportunities also emerged for devolving some of AKRSP's functions in the private sector. This augured well for developing a more sustainable approach towards servicing the small farmers and businesses in the long run. Examples of such opportunities included the creation of farmers' associations, which functioned as intermediaries between AKRSP and the large and widely dispersed clientele of farmers, and the privatisation of AKRSP's agricultural and livestock input supply functions.

These developments improved prospects for building capacities in the private sector to service micro, small and medium enterprises (MSMEs) on a commercial basis instead of directly providing BDS to the MSMEs by AKRSP.[8] The BDS direction is equally endorsed by international best practices, and it will govern the future course (2003–2007) of AKRSP's Market Development Programme,[9] under which AKRSP will focus more on adopting a facilitative role for developing the commercial markets, rather than directly servicing the individual businesses.

The diverse business legacy of AKRSP raises questions. How did AKRSP, a rural development programme, become a notable provider of BDS for MSMEs? How has AKRSP, an organisation steeped in social development traditions, fared as an entrepreneur in the business field? The following analysis attempts to address these questions.

Of all the tests, perhaps the one most difficult and for which AKRSP was most ill prepared was the complex business of promoting business itself. An organisational culture, expertise, and most of all a playing field required for developing the commercial sector were quite different and in many respects conflicting with what was required for the equitable collectivist social development agenda of AKRSP to flourish. AKRSP dared to take the lead in trying to promote business activities among the isolated mountain communities, compelled by the opportunities for addressing the pressing economic poverty of the region and the vacuum for business support services. In this endeavour, AKRSP had negligible experience and already several intertwined strikes against it.

The northern regions served as a haven for development practitioners and social scientists and fuelled the imagination and engagement of some of the best available expertise in rural development. However, they did exactly the opposite for private sector business professionals, potential investors, and small entrepreneurs. Due to this innate setback, over the years AKRSP's ability to lure seasoned business professionals from the private sector remained very difficult, and the efforts to build a strong and experienced business team to see the programme through over a long term period were erratic and brief. This very fundamental constraint had major implications for how the programme evolved and the many limitations that beset it over the years. The Report of the Joint Monitoring Mission at AKRSP raised this issue in

1994, 'The business section had traditionally been a small section, absorbing two per cent of the AKRSP budget with a relatively small number of staff in each region, and often no full time head leading the regional teams. This is an obvious constraint on its impact'. Thus, over the years, efforts have been driven by the ideas and excitement of a few staff—working in isolation—whose lack of business knowledge has been compensated by the organisational philosophy of learning-by-doing, which in turn has allowed experimenting with small budgets.[10]

The absence of a relevant role model business programme to draw upon, and the deficiencies of a national policy environment supportive of small businesses did not help to compensate for the lack of consistent engagement of business professionals at AKRSP. AKRSP was the first initiative of its kind in the northern regions. The programme was conceived and evolved through times when development initiatives nationally and even world wide had limited business experience and insight to offer differing from those of AKRSP. Above all, it is noteworthy that there was no business programme whose environmental context resembled or had relevance to that of AKRSP. Insightful examples of successful business incubation in Bangladesh and elsewhere,[11] limited as they are in their contextual relevance to the NAC in terms of easier access to larger and growing commercial markets and better economic and physical infrastructure facilities, however, do raise the question regarding how business promotion activities may have evolved differently had AKRSP been more attentive to others. With limitations in replicating other NGOs' successes, no role model programme to draw upon, and being the first programme of its kind in the NAC, AKRSP had limited options but to adopt an experimental organisational culture of *learn-as-you-do* rather than adopting a formal strategy to guide its work. According to Mr. Rasmussen, ex-General Manager of AKRSP, 'Course corrections and reinforcements have been dictated not by capitalist orthodoxy or theories but by practical experience which has shaped the evolution. The confidence, sense of ownership and understanding of the issues that comes from hands-on experience is invaluable'.

The absence of a business development strategy and the organisational philosophy of learning-by-doing, allowed the enthusiasm of a few staff to expand programmatic activities in several directions. In 1995, the JMM (AKRSP 1995b) appreciated the dynamism and vigour of the programme but advised balancing the budget and staff time, taking into account the available expertise. Interventions often appeared opportunistic rather than strategic, and a consequence of sensitivity to community pressure rather than a response to community needs. One such example[12] is the initiation during the 1990s of a credit facility to address the relatively larger credit needs of small businesses.

Other than limited access to business expertise, there were issues germane to commercial business activity itself, which conflicted with the blanket collectivist approach of AKRSP, which was working so well for all of its other rural development interventions. The very first major evaluation of AKRSP by the World Bank in 1986 (World Bank 1986) highlighted the need for a well-deliberated production model (improved co-ordination and synergies between infrastructure, production and marketing sections) along the lines of the well-conceived institution development paradigm[13] of AKRSP. The evaluation explained that the production decisions were made at the household level—once transferred from AKRSP's sphere of influence and its interactions with the VO—while marketing decisions fell within the purview of the VO. This made it difficult to co-ordinate production and marketing mechanisms and decisions.

In 1993, soon after AKRSP enhanced its agenda beyond the VOs, an evaluation by the Joint Monitoring Mission[14] (ARKSP 1993a) pointed out the incompatibility of the enterprise development programme with the equity objective, which was central to AKRSP's institutional culture. In 1999, JMM (ARKSP 1999b) raised concerns whether an appropriate business mind-set could be evolved within the aegis of a social development organisation. The separation of the business support activities from AKRSP's mainstream development activities, and housing it within an independent Enterprise Support Company (ESC), under the AKRSP umbrella was advocated as early as in 1993 by the JMM

(Report of the Joint Monitoring Mission AKRSP 1993a), and subsequently endorsed by a series of World Bank evaluations[15] and by AKRSP itself. The JMM (Report of the Joint Monitoring Mission ARKSP 1999b) went on to say, 'If ESC is to have a development and profit agenda, this is muddy water, it will require a more exact definition of inputs to be used and results anticipated. Good planning should ensure that this input/result linkage is right.'

Yet ever since the late 1980s, when AKRSP moved into the unfamiliar and increasingly mainstream commercial territory of individual entrepreneurs, the business promotion activities were characterised by lack of strategic planning and priority-setting and the resultant dearth of monitoring and evaluation indicators. This adhoc approach contrasted sharply with AKRSP's mainstream rural development activities, which were well conceptualised and generated a plethora of valuable statistical information. Despite the JMM reports and the World Bank evaluations raising the concern repetitively, at least until 2001[16] the formulation of a strategy remained pending the creation of an ESC. The creation of the ESC was itself pegged to the creation of a development finance institute (DFI). The DFI did not materialise and there was no funding to establish the ESC (AKRSP 2002a).

Emanating out of a rural development programme, operating within weak markets and without consistent recourse to the required expertise, paradoxical situations have challenged the ingenuity of AKRSP, the business promoter. While AKRSP filled a large vacuum for the provision of business development services (BDS),[17] including for example, advisory/consulting, training, marketing services, information resources, linkages etc. by servicing small businesses, directly on a one-to-one basis, by doing so it created an intense element of dependency of the MSMEs on itself. Moreover, by becoming a market player it was crowding out small indigenous BDS providers and thus distorting markets. In 1995 the JMM (AKRSP 1995b) suggested focusing on sector-neutral capacity building and facilitative interventions[18] given the limits to what AKRSP could do itself. AKRSP's evaluators and its own interventionist experience also endorsed its move towards facilitation rather than getting involved in management and finance of enterprises. The following example is illustrative: AKRSP decided to work with only those entrepreneurs who initiated the business idea themselves, rather than to sell the business idea to them—a decision reinforced when an entrepreneur who was supported in establishing a fruit-processing unit sued AKRSP for financial losses and misguidance: squash bottles had begun to explode due to problems in the squash formula!

The fourth World Bank evaluation also endorses the organisational search for institutionalising programmatic interventions, so that they live beyond AKRSP. This very quest is ushering in the BDS market development approach and defining a more pronounced role for AKRSP in the policy advocacy sphere. Though the BDS terminology is new and will call for a high degree of professionalism, BDS interventions represent a subset of activities of which AKRSP has undertaken more in the late 1990s and in the 2000s than in earlier years. As yet, there is limited evidence of the success of this approach in terms of establishing self-sustaining businesses and targeting the marginalised, particularly in environments such as the NAC. For AKRSP the challenge is further compounded by the business acumen of a social development organisation to lead in the business sector.

The latest evaluation of AKRSP (World Bank 2002), states, 'It is difficult to evaluate the efficiency of such a diverse collection of activities. No separate economic rate of return could be estimated nor efficiency could be evaluated for such diverse activities. Efficiency has probably been modest'. The overall efficacy of the programme has been summed up as '...a tale of many hopeful starts but fewer lasting results that suggests the need for some change in approach'. This criticism holds, especially when comparing the business promotion activities with the other sectoral programmes which have well-calibrated performance indicators. Nevertheless, it is dismissive of the pioneering efforts of AKRSP in the business arena, plus the unfathomable market trends, and the commercial momentum that these efforts have begun despite the major organisational constraints.

In speaking with business people in the northern regions, the poignancy of the multiplier effect of AKRSP's business initiatives and its achievement in raising awareness and interests in commercial activities comes up repetitively in statements referring to the *before* and *after* AKRSP scenarios. 'AKRSP has changed our attitude towards business forever...earlier we considered selling our fruit and vegetable below our dignity but now we plan our plantations according to what will fetch good price', said one marketer of apples based in Gilgit. In particular, news of AKRSP's innovative business activities travelled rapidly within the small markets of the NAC, planting ideas in the minds of people with an entrepreneurial bend, not necessarily engaged directly with AKRSP. Thus, the impact of the business activities spilled far beyond the groups that AKRSP was working with directly. For example, many fruit marketing associations came up drawing inspiration from the few which AKRSP had helped establish. Similar examples are strewn across other sub-sectors, in particular the gems and mining businesses. Additionally, AKRSP's proactive lobbying efforts have helped develop sectoral markets in the NAC and cultivated the interests of the private sector financial institutions in making investments and other stakeholders in promoting commercial activities in the NAC.[19] Above all, lessons emerging out of AKRSP's innovative experimental projects—most notably its wholly owned businesses—are informing and shaping AKRSP's future course and providing valuable insights to enterprise development practitioners both within Pakistan and overseas. Considering that until very recently the enterprise development agenda was a low priority, low budget programme at AKRSP, these activities have indeed paid dividends.

Specific Insights

Presented in the remaining sections of this chapter are specific insights focusing on the following four operational areas. Their order broadly follows the chronological sequence in which they occurred.

- VO-Based Cooperative Marketing
- Alternative Approaches to Enterprise Development
- AKRSP in Business (AKRSP's wholly owned businesses)
- From 'provider' to 'facilitator' to developing BDS markets

VO-Based Cooperative Marketing

There is a strong perception among development practitioners in Pakistan that the interactions between farmers, traders and moneylenders are exploitative of the farmers. Moneylenders have usurious interest charges and traders pay a low price to farmers, pocketing the entire profit themselves! In its early years, like many others in the country, AKRSP broadly subscribed to this way of thinking, influenced as it was by the Raiffeisen[20] and other cooperative models. Cooperative marketing based on the VOs was considered the logical answer, given that equity concerns[21] were a pivotal driving force, and internationally alternative approaches for supporting business activities were then not known.

It was explained to farmers that they could retain their private property, yet pool their resources to overcome their individual constraints of limited production, access to financial resources and down-country markets, while bypassing the middleman. The VO was responsible for purchasing the produce of its members—at the village level—organising transport to and selling in the market, managing the related expenses and distributing the profit/loss to the participating members. AKRSP, on the other hand, focused on strategic inputs such as awareness raising, provision of credit, building the technical and managerial skills of the VO, and market and product research alongside advisory services. Nevertheless, AKRSP frequently directly engaged in packaging and transporting the produce in its efforts to assist the poor farmers.

The interest free credit offered by AKRSP provided farmers with market leverage by freeing up the excess produce for sale, and allowing produce to be stored until market prices were favourable. AKRSP also helped develop the entrepreneurial resource for the VOs—a cadre of village marketing specialists who were chosen by the VO on the basis of their entrepreneurial acumen. In addition to serving as the AKRSP conduits in the field, the marketing specialist performed the following operational work: supervised fruit and vegetable picking, distributed packaging materials, collected farmers produce, branded crates according to quality, arranged transport to the market, sold the produce, distributed the income, and maintained VO records.

High levels of enthusiasm and untested assumptions drove the early collectivist efforts. The initial guiding principle steering the collectivist efforts was not what would sell in the market but what could be grown in the NAC. The Strategy Paper for the Second Phase (AKRSP 1987a) acknowledges that collective marketing proved to be far more complicated than had been envisaged. NAC was believed to have surplus fresh and dried fruits for which lucrative markets were waiting down-country. Farmers' subsistence-based production patterns, however, were ill prepared to meet the commercial market requirements, which demanded economies of scale, product uniformity and quality. According to one research report (AKRSP 1993b) out of 20 varieties of fruits grown in the Northern Areas (NA), only eight had potential markets down-country due to constraints related to marketing infrastructure, such as storage facilities, appropriate packing, and timely transportation.

On the demand side, consumers down-country had taste preferences not necessarily satisfied by fruit varieties grown in the NAs.[22] Fruits from other parts of the country provided stiff competition. There was also the need to identify deficit and surplus areas within the region, in order to avail marketing opportunities for maize and firewood. Moreover, direct selling by VOs to wholesalers in distant markets also proved risky and often unprofitable. AKRSP was caught off guard!

In response, AKRSP developed a relatively more sophisticated approach focusing on a few value-added promising sub-sectors with the objective of making meaningful interventions at all levels, i.e. starting from production to the actual marketing of the produce. This approach led to increased coordination between the agriculture, 'women in development', and enterprise sections. Market niche strategies utilising brief windows of opportunity down-country were successfully tested. For example, farmers from Baltistan were able to earn twelve times more than usual in off-season pea marketing, when supplies from other areas to down-country markets receded. In fact, market and accounting modules became a component of all the sector specialists and lead trainers[23] courses offered by AKRSP (AKRSP 1994c).

Farm-gate prices increased through collective marketing. From marketing a wide range of products, the VOs finally narrowed down to fresh and dried fruits. These products had higher price volatility and market scope, which could be availed better by shielding risk through collectivism. New technologies for value-added products such as processed fruits (jams, pickles, squashes and apricot candies) fruit dehydration and packaging and the sale of dry fruit were also introduced by AKRSP. Enterprise management training was also provided to help VOs manage these specialised functions.

Discussions with participants of collective marketing reveal anecdotal evidence regarding the demonstration effect of collective marketing. Reportedly, after a few rounds of collective marketing the down-country *artis*[24] found their way to the northern villages and began to gain direct access to the villagers/VOs. This reduced dependency on the marketing specialists,[25] demonstrated the efficiencies of integrating with private marketing mechanisms, laid open alternative marketing channels for VOs, and increased VOs' negotiating powers vis-à-vis traders from down-country who competed with each other to get better quality fruit. AKRSP had provided equal opportunities to all VOs but ultimately it was the competitive market forces which determined who survived and flourished in the market.

There were, however, operational issues[26] emanating out of the VOs' limited capacity to understand commercial transactions. For example, short-term credit originally intended for collective marketing was predominantly being used for purchasing fertilisers (World Bank 1990b). Though a commercial orientation had begun to set in, initial rounds of collectivism revealed that all was not well. Strategically, was VO based collectivism the right intervention for spurring commercial activities?

At its peak in 1988, cooperative marketing enrolled no more than 53 per cent of all VOs (Table 6.2). By 1997 only eight per cent of the VOs were engaged in cooperative marketing. These were presumably market-savvy VOs who were earning 38 per cent of their household income through collectivism (see Table 6.2 and Figure 6.1). Moreover, volumes marketed through the VOs had fallen short of the increase in production and sales *outside* of VOs. The solution of cooperative marketing was adopted only by a small percentage of the VOs and addressed a small fraction of the regions' marketing activity. Nevertheless, those who did adopt and learn the ways of cooperative marketing eventually did well for themselves.[27]

Table 6.2. Collective marketing (1983–1997)

	1983	1984	1985	1986	1987	1988	1989	1990	1991
No. of VOs	11	8	45	164	191	215	222	246	244
Total No. of Vos	129	286	312	345	371	409	446	470	494
Output marketed (metric tons)	46	23	176	293	431	973			
Gross sales (Rupees)	324,000	159,000	940,000	2,735,000	3,432,000	6,360,000	10,340,000	9,020,000	11,100,000
Marketing expense (Rupees)	42,120	20,670	122,200	355,550	446,160	826,800	440,000	270,000	490,000
Net income (Rupees)	281,880	138,330	817,800	2,379,450	2,985,840	5,533,200	9,900,000	8,750,000	10,610,000
Beneficiary households	514	251	1,070	4,372	6,581	8,522	7,824	5,636	6,336
Income per household (Rupees)	548	551	764	544	454	649	1,265	1,553	1,675
Average sale price (Rupees)	7,043	6,913	5,341	9,334	7,963	6,536			
Ratios									
% increase in sales		-50.9%	491.2%	191.0%	25.5%	85.3%	62.6%	-12.8%	23.1%
Marketing expense/sales	13.0%	13.0%	13.0%	13.0%	13.0%	13.0%	4.3%	3.0%	4.4%
Income/sales	87.0%	87.0%	87.0%	87.0%	87.0%	87.0%	95.7%	97.0%	95.6%
Increase/decrease beneficiary households		-51.2%	326.3%	308.6%	50.5%	29.5%	-8.2%	-28.0%	12.4%
Inome/household increase/decrease		0.49%	27.89%	-40.43%	-19.96%	30.12%	48.69%	18.50%	7.29%
VO in mark/total VOs	8.53%	2.80%	14.42%	47.54%	51.48%	52.57%	49.78%	52.34%	49.39%

	1992	1993	1994	1995	1996	1997
No. of Vos	162	241	370	221	98	62
Total No. of Vos	501	539	559	676	701	768
Output marketed (metric tons)						
Gross sales (Rupees)	5,290,000	11,130,000	50,190,000	17,030,000	12,230,000	49,820,000
Marketing expense (Rupees)	440,000	280,000	10,480,000	1,070,000	190,000	3,970,000
Net income (Rupees)	4,850,000	10,850,000	39,710,000	15,960,000	12,040,000	45,850,000
Beneficiary households	3,594	4,848	7,601	3,864	2,479	1,346
Income per household (Rupees)	1,349	2,238	5,224	4,130	4,857	34,064
Average sale price (Rupees)						
Ratios						
% increase in sales	-52.3%	110.4%	350.9%	-66.1%	-28.2%	307.4%
Marketing expense/sales	8.3%	2.5%	20.9%	6.3%	1.6%	8.0%
Income/sales	91.7%	97.5%	79.1%	93.7%	98.4%	92.0%
Increase/decrease beneficiary households	-43.3%	34.9%	56.8%	-49.2%	-35.8%	-45.7%
Inome/household increase/ decrease	-24.09%	39.70%	57.16%	-26.48%	14.96%	85.74%
VO in mark/total VOs	32.34%	44.71%	66.19%	32.69%	13.98%	8.07%

Source: AKRSP Core Office, Islamabad.

Figure 6.1. Collective marketing (1983-1997)

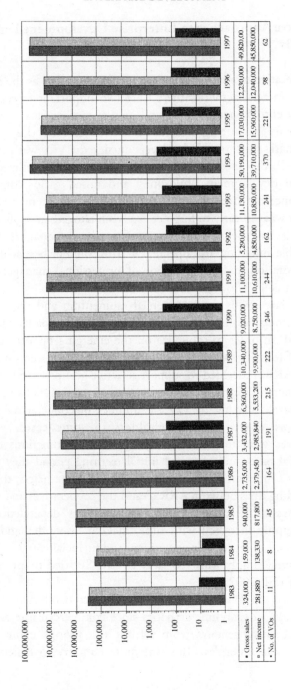

	1983	1984	1985	1986	1987	1988	1989	1990	1991	1992	1993	1994	1995	1996	1997
Gross sales	324,000	159,000	940,000	2,735,000	3,432,000	6,360,000	10,340,000	9,020,000	11,100,000	5,290,000	11,130,000	50,190,000	17,030,000	12,230,000	49,820,00
Net income	281,880	138,330	817,800	2,379,450	2,985,840	5,533,200	9,000,000	8,750,000	10,610,000	4,850,000	10,850,000	39,710,000	15,960,000	12,040,000	45,850,000
No. of VOs	11	8	45	164	191	215	222	246	244	162	241	370	221	98	62

Alternative Approaches to Enterprise Development During the 1990s

The cooperative marketing experience had taught that at the heart of all commercial activities there were two important forces: the individual entrepreneurial drive and market mechanisms. Despite the evidence favouring individual entrepreneurs, the actual programmatic shift to include players outside the VOs was painful for ARKSP, the social developer. The change contradicted its traditional development philosophy and raised socio-economic equity concerns. Even for the enterprise development staff of ARKSP, it was too early to forgo collectivism altogether. 'Collective marketing had been most successful when managers with considerable autonomy had operated it. This could be best achieved in incorporation and appointment of professional management' (World Bank 1990b).

By the late 1980s the commercial momentum and the socio-economic metamorphosis of the region required a broader agenda for AKRSP in order to capitalize on the emerging opportunities. Instead of focusing on the all-inclusive VOs as had been done in the past, AKRSP decided to support selective groups of individual entrepreneurs to form formal cooperatives at the regional and sub-regional level. Starting in 1992, a number of cooperatives were formed, with over 300 shareholders in some cases.[28] The cooperatives were to deliver many of AKRSP's functions on a commercial basis, and after the initial teething period they were expected to function independent of AKRSP. Nonetheless, due to hazy dividing lines between AKRSP and the cooperatives and their weak professional management, the cooperatives' dependence on AKRSP simply increased with time, making heavy demands on AKRSP's staff to settle their operational and financial issues.[29] '[The Cooperatives] simply withered away as AKRSP tried to 'privatise' them' (AKRSP 2002a).

A lesson from collective marketing resurfaced. Collectivism had mixed results in economic activities since commercial interests of individual entrepreneurs from within the groups came into confrontational interplay. This was quite contrary to collectivist experience in the creation and maintenance of public properties sponsored by AKRSP. Business-minded people are driven by the ambition to increase their net-worth. The business milieu is itself defined by competition, which is more divisive than cohesive, particularly where struggling entrepreneurs have access to a scarce pool of resources intensified under mountain conditions of low effective demand.

Moreover, the significance of creating sustainable job opportunities had become critical. The fragmented small and scattered land holdings could not support the increasing population.[30] Meanwhile, the private and public sectors were not growing fast enough to provide job opportunities to the growing numbers of educated youth who faced immense competition for limited jobs down-country (AKRSP 1999c). Thus, mid-1990s onwards, AKRSP's attention came to reside more concertedly on entrepreneurial individuals for bolstering commercial activity through specialised functions, in order to create job and income-earning opportunities through diversification of the economy, selective import substitution, and introduction of new technologies.

With rejuvenated vigour by the mid-1990s, AKRSP began to research and support commercial opportunities in the off-farm sector and value-added products in the on-farm domain. In the continued absence of any BDS provider in the region, AKRSP was providing comprehensive and generous business development services.[31] Assistance took the shape of: specialised business management training, a range of vocational training programmes, fully covered exposure trips, investments in machines and equipment, market intelligence, counselling services, and an acutely intense 'hand-holding' approach which had by now become the hallmark of AKRSP assistance.

During the 1990s, frustrated by the absence of small business lending facilities in the NAC, AKRSP decided to initiate a credit programme for small businesses that were too large to be financed through the microcredit programme and too small to be of interest to the formal banks. A credit pool not exceeding Rs 1.5 million was established and average loans varied in the range of Rs 300,000.

AKRSP had limited knowledge of how to design such a credit programme. Experience revealed that even if loan recovery was satisfactory, the credit could potentially hurt the businesses, which it did in many cases due to the mismatch between the cash-inflows of the business and the repayment schedules. Moreover, contrary to the much articulated need for credit by the businesses, close scrutiny revealed that credit was not necessarily the most binding constraint for them. In view of the feedback from JMM and World Bank evaluations this credit window was discontinued as it was depriving the non-financial mandate of resources and exposing the enterprise development programme to high risks. Instead, AKRSP decided to bridge the gap between the formal financial sector and the small businesses by improving their understanding of each other. Subsequently, due to the direct efforts of AKRSP, one private sector leasing company initiated lending operations in the NAC. Refer to Box 6.3 for more details.

As a result of the growing entrepreneurial capacities among individuals and its concern to disengage from direct involvement with MSMEs, AKRSP privatised its agriculture and livestock input supply functions. New businesses also emerged in the areas of: gem mining and exploration, soap manufacturing, tourism, village guest houses/hotels, carpet weaving, motor rewinding, pottery making, honey bee keeping, vehicle repair, key making, and fruit processing. The emerging small businesses were providing investment and job opportunities, and improving cash inflows to the region. Within the small markets of the NAC, the novelty and impact of this approach had high visibility and inspirational value, as did AKRSP's role in sponsoring it and generating further demand and *dependency* on itself.

It appeared that finally AKRSP had identified the appropriate vehicles—the individuals and small groups of them (the informal and formal farmers' associations) with similar interests—for creating potentially sustainable enterprises. Nevertheless, concerns arise regarding the nature of inputs provided to individual entrepreneurs, and the *values* that are passed on by a social development programme servicing businesspeople. The impact of the widely dispersed set of training and inputs has not been assessed through any comprehensive study, but some striking insights emerge from interviews[32] of a broad group of individual entrepreneurs in Gilgit.

It appears that sustainability and growth remain confined to those businesses that draw upon the comparative advantages of the region in terms of existing vocational skills and resources, and target *realistic* markets that are within the reach of the entrepreneurs. Illustrative examples are, a honey bee keeping business, which now sells branded honey and a *shu* manufacturing and retail business. Both are catering to the local market. Where AKRSP has tried to introduce completely new skills, and compete in the international or mainstream commercial markets down-country, businessmen have suffered. The following example effectively encapsulates the range of issues that typically emanate out of AKRSP's interventions for individual businesspeople.

AKRSP supported a Hunza-based retailer of handicrafts[33] and carpets to establish a carpet weaving and handicrafts production unit in Hunza. 'I wanted to do something for the poor in my region', said the businessman. AKRSP supported the business attracted by new skills and job opportunities that would be created. 'Since there is no tradition of carpet weaving here, considerable resources were spent in teaching this skill, even then it is difficult to retain trained labour[34].... my labour costs are more than twice those of weavers down-country who employ either children or people who have been in this business since generations. Down-country weavers work on looms in their homes, while I rented two houses for the weavers to work in and served them free lunch! I wanted to compete in the export market but at these costs I can't sell even in the down-country markets', said the businessman despondently.

He further added, 'NGOs distort the market for small businesses when they try to establish income-earning projects backed by huge donor funds. How can we [small businesses] compete with them? NGOs can afford to learn through mistakes but mistakes of a businessman like myself can wipe us out...because AKRSP was supporting me, other people also followed my example, without proper market research, but due to high costs of production carpet weaving business can not compete with that down-country.' When questioned regarding his future plans, the entrepreneur replied, 'I'm going to start thinking like a businessman not a social worker.'

The enterprise development programme staff argue, 'Our intention was never to ensure the profitability of the business itself but to develop products and markets [let competition determine who survives in the market]....our role was demonstration...just show the light but it was our enthusiasm which led us to get far more involved with the businesspeople.' Aside from the implication of this approach on the businesses, it also reflects what happens when interventions pick up momentum and begin to guide the programme in the absence of a well-delineated strategy. For example, in some cases AKRSP's subsidies and level of interventions artificially enabled businesses to reach thresholds that could not be self-sustained by the business once AKRSP withdrew.[35]

The owner of a (now struggling) fruit-processing unit in Gilgit, a food technologist, described his situation as follows:[36] 'AKRSP was so actively involved in marketing my products down-country and I was doing so well. Then AKRSP decided that it had shown me the way and I could do it on my own. I don't have the resources that AKRSP was providing! Why doesn't AKRSP invest in local entrepreneurs like myself instead of setting up its own businesses such as the Dry Fruit Project [DFP]?[37] Had AKRSP ploughed the same amount of money in my project as it has in DFP I would have been equally successful.'

En masse vocational training was also provided to women in response to demand for non-traditional commercial activities.[38] This training was invaluable in terms of enabling women to save household expenses by producing items at home, and improve their self-esteem, by providing women a mentally stimulating and enjoyable outlet to collectively meet often, learn new skills and improve their self-confidence. The training did little, however, in the way of producing women entrepreneurs in proportion to those who received training.[39] Nevertheless, a cadre of women entrepreneurs did emerge who served as inspirational models to expand women's mobility and the choices available to them while remaining within the socially prescribed sphere. A notable example is the establishment of the 'ladies' shops' within the precincts of the home. Women manage these shops, including maintaining accounts and making trips down-country to purchase stocks—though accompanied by a male family member. Most importantly, these shops have provided women—for the first time—an opportunity to go shopping for themselves instead of the men shopping for them.

AKRSP's overall interactive approach of working with small businesses raised a critical question: Were the interventions pushing the right levers or were they simply substituting for long-term sustainable marketing mechanisms? The large numbers of people trained and businesses set up were the barometers of AKRSP's success (Table 6.3). Behind the numbers simmered serious concerns regarding a highly resource-intensive approach which restricted outreach given the subsidies involved, the limited staff, and the widely dispersed clientele. If AKRSP were to withdraw from the NAC, it would leave behind a large vacuum for the provision of BDS for MSMEs.

Table 6.3. Cumulative achievements in enterprise development: programme area and the three regions (as of December 2002)

| Serial Number | Indicators | Cumulative Achievements | | | |
		Programme Area	Gilgit	Chitral	Baltistan
1	No. of viable enterprises supported	626	350	264	12
2	No. of entrepreneurs trained (males)	2,309	548	1,087	674
3	No. of entrepreneurs trained (females)	2,409	1,000	841	568
4	No. of enterprises adopting micro-tech./ new skills	316	49	8	259
5	No. of male entrepreneurs provided loans	11,473	4,405	2,977	4,091
6	Amount of loans disbursed (Rupees in millions)	297.17	135.07	74.06	88.04
7	No. of female entrepreneurs provided loans	1,357	249	745	363
8	Amount of loans disbursed (Rupees in millions)	25.58	5.86	12.08	7.64

Source: AKRSP Core Office, Islamabad.

AKRSP in Business!

In the early 1990s, in its effort to make the transition from its subsidy-oriented direct service delivery approach AKRSP assisted the formation of local intermediaries to whom it could devolve some of its direct service delivery function, and thus address problems associated with cost inefficiencies, limited outreach and, hence, unsustainability of interventions. As a result a plethora of cooperatives emerged in areas such as fresh and dried fruit and vegetable trading, and retailing of household consumption items. The cooperatives, however, did not take off due to their excessive dependence on AKRSP for their daily operation, capacity gaps, and poor management systems.[40]

From its experience of the cooperatives, AKRSP learned three lessons which shaped its approach to establishing its wholly owned businesses. First, AKRSP needed to establish its businesses with well-researched profitability prospects. Second, there was a need to establish businesses as entities with financial management, and accounting systems distinctly separate from AKRSP. And third, that the job of managing a large business was complex and too specialised a task to be left to the largely illiterate poor farmers whose commercial exposure was confined to the narrow economic environment of the NA. Subsequently, in conjunction with the Aga Khan Foundation and the Shorebank, AKRSP developed the following criteria for establishing its self-owned businesses. The objective in doing so was *not* to open the doors to private sector investments but rather to make AKRSP more fastidious in its choice of investments.

AKRSP was to invest in sectors:
- of which AKRSP had acquired technical knowledge, and practical experience of engaging the communities;
- where the business was expected to have a marked layered development outreach impact in terms of creating employment and income-earning opportunities;
- where barriers to entry were so high that AKRSP would not be retarding the market for private sector initiatives and distorting the market; and,
- where a business plan indicated prospects of succeeding.

Many business ideas came up at AKRSP that were rejected when judged against the criteria mentioned above. In fact, AKRSP rejected many more ideas than it accepted as result of this tight screening. The AKRSP business projects discussed in further detail below passed these criteria and offered prospects in terms of high outreach, enhancement of livelihood opportunities from within agriculture/farm sources—areas where farmers enjoyed familiarity and comfort—that were no match to what could be accomplished by supporting indigenous small businesses or businesses in any other areas. Drawing from the experience of the cooperatives—with the single exception of Shubinak—rigorous feasibility studies were prepared, and business plans with exit strategies were developed. The projects were provided with professional management that was to operate their respective projects as private businesses of AKRSP *completely removed* from AKRSP's mainstream work—though under the management and Board of AKRSP.

It can be questioned that given its unsuccessful experience of formal cooperatives and despite being cautioned by a series of JMM and World Bank Interim Evaluations against establishing AKRSP-dependent businesses, why is it that AKRSP still went ahead with the experiment, though with modifications? Collectively AKRSP business projects have consumed Rs 103 million until year-end 2002, also raising the issue regarding whether this amount has been utilised as prudently as a private investor would. In answering these questions, it is important to keep perspective of the underlying objectives that motivated the creation of AKRSP-owned businesses in the first place, and the peculiar circumstances of the NAC which inherently made the areas unattractive grounds for potential investments.

Had AKRSP's guiding objective been profits *per se* or the highest available monetary returns on investments, then—like any other private investor—AKRSP would have established these businesses in growing and lucrative sectors set in promising commercial markets external to NAC. Nevertheless, the fundamental motivation for these businesses lay in AKRSP's socio-economic objective of expanding livelihood opportunities for a vast majority of the poor at the grass roots level who otherwise had limited livelihood alternatives available to them. Therefore, AKRSP's business ideas were based on capitalizing, on a large scale, the given resources and skills of the region. These were high-risk ventures with promising prospects of influencing the local markets much more effectively than any outcomes that could be expected from supporting micro and small businesses. In the long run AKRSP was to disengage itself from these projects by turning them first into profitable businesses and then privatising them.

No development finance institution or serious private investor[41]—from outside NAC—would have invested capital in any of the business projects due to their multifaceted high-risk profile, the high opportunity costs of capital, and the absence of any other comparable professionally operated business in the NAC. The locals lacked the resources and the expertise to manage heavy investments. AKRSP, however, took advantage of its exceptional position to try the experiment with cost free donor funds, which were forthcoming due to what these unique and daring projects promised and the process of the experiment itself. Driven by its knowledge of the local dynamics and mixed business experience, AKRSP, a rural development programme, therefore took the lead drawing from its earlier experience of the cooperatives.

There is an inherent element of subsidy in the very concept of setting up these businesses in the NAC due to their high opportunity costs. AKRSP had to make do with only the few business ideas with potential profitability—all farm or agriculture related—available to it within the defined geographic area of its operations. Conceptually there is a parallel between AKRSP's actions and the ongoing stance of the less developed countries lobbying for concessionary terms and conditions of trade with mounting pressures of globalisation. Since markets do not provide a level playing field, space and allowances are needed for the less developed to catch up with the more privileged. It is arguable that AKRSP had neither the mandate nor the capacity to undertake businesses of the scale that it did in the NAC. The jury is still out on the wisdom of having done so, since it is still quite recent that the businesses were established. Nevertheless, at least two of the businesses have had a tremendous impact on their respective underdeveloped and weak sub-markets within the NAC. Equally, these businesses also provide insightful lessons for small business development programmes internationally, and particularly in the remote mountain areas, vindicating to some extent the risks that AKRSP took in taking these initiatives.

Table 6.4. People benefiting from the projects/year (as of year end 2002)

	Dry Fruit Project	Shubinak	North South Seeds
Number of People Benefiting from the Project	Over 500 families	Over 4,500 people	Over 500 farmers[42] (close to 50% of whom are women)
Project Costs (Pak Rs millions)	4.0	37.9	60.0

Discussed below are the insights into the individual experiences of these projects.

The Dry Fruit Project (DFP): Preparation Meets Luck
DFP is the most successful example of an AKRSP-owned business. Established in 2000 with an initial investment of Rs 4 million, DFP operationally broke even within 18 months and it has already paid back part of AKRSP investment. Interconnected reasons account for this success. DFP benefits from many years of AKRSP's research into community-friendly fruit drying technologies and the investments that have been made since the early 1980s in building communities' skills to manage and operate them. One of the most crucial reasons for DFP's success, however, is the leadership of an entrepreneurial food technologist who took the risk of resigning from his permanent job with AKRSP in order to bring it all together.

Preparation met opportunity when a consultant visiting from the UK, impressed with the budding efforts of the project, gave the reference of a potential buyer in the UK. DFP was lucky to find a fair trade buyer, Tropical Whole Foods (TWF), which currently purchases the entire production of DFP. The DFP brand is not, however, competing directly in the consumer markets of the UK.

Various established UK-based food brands use DFP apricots as inputs into products. This simplifies business for DFP, insulating it against vicissitudes of consumer market trends, and in the process saving it heavy marketing machinery and investments. Thus, DFP is able to maintain a business threshold within its capacity and resources. Of late, in order to reduce its vulnerability to a single client and the volatility of the export market DFP, is making efforts to diversify its market and cultivate markets in southern Pakistan where the DFP apricots will sell under the DFP brand name. Moreover, test production and trial marketing of dried apples, mulberries and tomatoes, among other fruits and vegetables, is also underway.

DFP has changed the local market for good quality dried apricots forever. It has done so by working through a large network of enterprising farmers who have been appointed as its *Commission Agent* (CA). The CAs serve as DFP's conduits at the village level, helping to train additional farming families in new fruit drying skills, disseminate new technologies, purchase dried fruits on behalf of DFP, and ensure timely delivery of the stocks to the DFP factory in Gilgit. By setting unrelenting high quality standards and paying a premium over the market price for 'A grade' apricots, DFP has helped increase the local market price of good quality apricots by almost 100%. Farmers are competing to produce better qualities that they can sell as 'DFP quality apricots' in the local market. Over 500 families are engaged with DFP. Given the market potential for dried apricots and the significant demand in other villages for DFP to initiate work with them, much remains undone.

Shubinak: Romance vs. Reality
This project was established with the objective of improving women's income earning opportunities from *shu*.[43] With very few alternative livelihood opportunities available to them, shu had traditionally been an important source of income for women. Nevertheless, the motivation to produce quality shu had been slipping, as cheaper varieties of shu produced in other parts of Pakistan through mechanized processes were undercutting the price of handmade shu. Since spinning was the key determinant of shu

quality and since women were constrained in the quantity of wool that they could spin—given their farm and household responsibilities—AKRSP's marketing strategy came to be driven by this production constraint rather than market research indicating consumer tastes and preferences.

AKRSP's strategy aimed to improve shu quality significantly by making interventions at all stages of its production. The basic premise was that the fine handmade shu would be valued by the fashion conscious segments at home and abroad who would be lured by the appeal of the handmade woollen fabric produced by women in remote mountain valleys. The superior quality shu accompanied by the 'shu story' was expected to fetch a premium price. This fundamental assumption on which the project was based was driven by beliefs regarding the romantic appeal of shu and not by any market research regarding its commercial potential among its target clientele.

Within the weak and limited commercial markets of Chitral, the impact of Shubinak in improving and expanding the local shu market has been phenomenal. The wholesale price of high quality shu has increased by close to 100% and traders make advance booking for the 'Golden' shu varieties even before its production! Prior to Shubinak, there were only a handful of shu retail outlets in Chitral. Currently, their number has swelled to over 25, as many shu traders who were based in the southern city of Peshawar have relocated to Chitral.

Initially, the project purchased[44] the high quality shu at prices higher than the local market in order to raise market value and awareness for superior quality of shu. Shubinak's support price policy was discontinued (within four years) as it outlived its purpose. In competing to buy limited quantities of high class shu the local wholesalers were willing to pay far more than Shubinak was offering! In the process women's incomes increased well over 100%. Women in the advanced clusters are demanding further training in enterprise management and simple book keeping, while those belonging to conservative communities who earlier shunned the project are eager to get involved.

Aspects of Shubinak related with marketing shu among the upper end mainstream commercial consumers down-country have not been disappointing and quite contrary to the impact that the project has made on women's development and the local market for shu. The project had established a shu garments manufacturing unit with an outlet in Chitral. One objective in doing so was to improve the quality and styles of shu garments and to sell to the upper market echelons in Pakistan and abroad. The project learnt the cardinal principle of marketing—*offer people what they want to buy not what you want to sell*—the hard way after investing Rs 26 million, a major part of which was consumed in unrealistically exploring an international market for shu. Shubinak had been focusing on *selling* to an upper market segment and not on trying to understand what its target consumers wanted.

Had Shubinak conducted market research it would have discovered that the demand for high quality shu was very small— even within Pakistan—and lay not among the fashion conscious elite but among the landlords and tribal chiefs of the mountain and tribal areas of Pakistan. Moreover, the mainstream market for shu lay among men in the middle to low-income bracket who were far more conscious about price than quality, which explains the popularity of cheaper varieties. Within this segment the popularity of shu caps far exceeded the demand for shu garments (Afzal 2003b). Other than missing the pulse of the market, the garment manufacturing and marketing unit of Shubinak remained without experienced professional management until very recently. While it was difficult to find experienced professionals from within Chitral, it was even more challenging to attract someone to Chitral. Consequently, there was mismanagement of accounts and inventory, which aggravated losses and delayed course corrections in the marketing strategy.

Shubinak's experience highlights the value of market research particularly when venturing into competitive consumer markets. Experience verifies theory (Kotler 1986) that new business creation should be based on tapping existing opportunities in the market and not on trying to create new markets. Given that there are many existing market opportunities—that is, unmet demands of the consumers—waiting to be discovered and catered for, it is highly resource-intensive to try and create a new market, particularly for a rural development programme which has neither the resources nor the mandate to gain a grasp of complex consumer market trends and behaviours.

The experiences of both DFP and Shubinak illustrate the challenges of balancing business goals with social development objectives, particularly with regard to targeting the poor. Shubinak, for example, is in a consumer market where domination of mechanised production processes have shifted the basis of competition from quality to price. Like other shu wholesalers/retailers in the market, 'officially' Shubinak cannot purchase the cheaper machine-made shu from down-country producers and sell it as the 'Chitrali shu'. Similarly, traders in Chitral buy and sell shu on a credit basis, whereas Shubinak makes cash purchases from the community women but sells on a credit basis, which increases its working capital needs and cycle. Most down-country retailers buying from Shubinak do not fulfil their payment obligations on time and have to be pursued (Afzal 2003a).

Similarly, in the case of DFP the project is challenged in balancing its profit motivations with its choice of villages where it initiates its operations. Initiating operations further afield may assist in bringing the poorer within DFP's folds but it also means higher overhead costs, higher business risks and steeper initial investments in training the communities, particularly since due to their distant location they may have been marginalised even from basic social service provisions, such as those related to health and education.

North South Seeds (NSS): Waiting to Exhale
AKRSP was attracted to the vegetable seed business due to the climatic advantage of NAC for the production of quality disease-free potato and vegetable seed, which was promoted by a number of agencies and specialists, before the establishment of AKRSP. No concerted effort had been made to exploit this potential even though the market potential and profitability were phenomenal: the Pakistan market for vegetable seed in 1999 was estimated to be

over Rs 260 million,[45] increasing at almost 14 per cent[46] per annum. 64 per cent of this demand continues to be met by low quality, black market Indian seed, seed manufactured locally by farmers for their own consumption and seed produced by small-scale local companies. This seed is low priced and affordable for farmers, but quality is poor and unpredictable. Remaining market demand is met by imported seed from Europe which though superior in quality is too expensive for small-scale farmers. In theory there is, therefore, potential for new entrants who could produce quality seed, and where, once established, company profits could be very high. To AKRSP, vegetable seed production appeared to represent one of the few opportunities of an alternative cash crop offering high returns in an environment where there is limited scope for diversifying incomes from both agriculture and non-agriculture sources. The local agricultural sector faces constrained opportunities, and potato cultivation, the main cash crop, faces declining yields, disease and other problems. Alternatives such as vegetable and fruit production face constraints in marketing because of their perishability.

Therefore, in 1999 after some experimental work in vegetable seed production and marketing, AKRSP established NSS as a commercial project which was to produce commercial vegetable seed in northern Pakistan and sell it across the down-country markets. Specialised tasks for commercial production of vegetable seeds such as market research, production, research and development (R&D), processing, and marketing seeds down-country are centralised within NSS. Farmers in the NAC serve as the 'factory' of NSS, producing vegetable seed under a fixed price contract with NSS that assures them guaranteed incomes irrespective of the market price fluctuations of vegetable seed. In order to ensure the availability of quality seed in a timely manner, NSS supplies the farmers with the stock seed/basic seed, builds their capacity and technical knowledge, and farm management skills, and also provides the farmers with other important inputs such as fertilisers and pesticides. This seed is then processed and packed at NSS and sent to its marketing offices down south for onward delivery to the dealers.

In reality none of the apparent advantages that attracted AKRSP to vegetable seed production were as straightforward as thought by AKRSP. Whilst the NAC climate is favourable, local farmers are largely small scale and illiterate, and physical access can be problematic—both factors that are likely to push up costs. The forbiddingly high barriers to entry[47] that attracted AKRSP to the seed business in the first place posed severe challenges to AKRSP itself since it discovered that it had highly underestimated the depth and sophisticated technical know-how and experience required for managing the multifaceted production and marketing cycles, which varied for different seed varieties of a single vegetable. A major challenge remaining is access to specialised resources including staff expertise for developing improved varieties of vegetable seed. Moreover, AKRSP can not afford the high investments in R&D required for the production of hybrid seeds and given its own low technical capacity the chances of producing hybrids under licence from an established seed company are also negligible.

As of the end of 2002, NSS remains unprofitable and the chances of its operationally breaking even, forecast by the end of 2004, remain bleak. Increasingly, the experience of NSS indicates contradictions between the goals of a development organisation and that of a commercial business. For example, in order to keep its production running all year round, NSS contracts larger farmers outside of the NAC for those vegetable seeds that can not be grown in the NAC. In addition, while working on developing its production and marketing operations, NSS has also resorted to trading vegetable seed so as to meet its sales targets. These measures—though creative from a business standpoint—question the underlying rationality for creating NSS, which is to create livelihood opportunities for farmers of the NAC. Thus, even if NSS does become a profitable business it may have little meaning for AKRSP, a social development organisation working for the people of the north.

Though the business side of NSS is controversial, the project has introduced improved farming practices to the local farmers that are assisting them in managing their crops other than vegetable seeds. In addition, one of the most valuable asset's that NSS has acquired over the course of its operations is the extensive market information regarding the vegetable seed business in Pakistan. Such a resource is highly valuable and unique and this accomplishment alone has attracted at least two potential private sector partners and investors. Nonetheless, the Board ruled out these opportunities, revealing an inherent contradiction in NGO-owned businesses—*if a business shows signs of becoming successful privatisation is not desired, and if it isn't successful ways are looked for to enable it to become profitable enough to attract private investors.*

Reshit Coal Project: Opportunity Lost

This is the only case in which at least three private parties were interested in obtaining a mine lease. Against its original intention, AKRSP engaged in coal mining as the locals feared exploitation of their resources at the hands of the 'outsiders'. AKRSP was lured by the prospects of 12,000 tons of annual exploration which would bring in huge cash income, ameliorate the fuel shortage by providing a low cost alternative fuel, build local technological capacities in mining, and above all turn around the economic profile of the Northern Areas forever. (AKRSP 2002b).

The mining operation ended prematurely due to the poor quality of the geological survey and lack of expertise guiding the operations. AKRSP tried convincing its Board to allow further expenditure for ascertaining the location and presence of coal. AKRSP wanted to establish grounds for attracting private investors engagements in mining in future. In view of the Rs 6 million that had already been consumed, the Board[48] vetoed further expenditure and with that sank hopes of any private party pursuing this business proposition in the future.

AKRSP set up its businesses on an experimental basis with performance indicators limited to the business entities. Without doubt, the most outstanding impact of the projects has been in developing their respective local sub-sectoral markets. This windfall accomplishment neither targeted nor planned by AKRSP also provided the most enduring lesson with major implications for AKRSP's future approach to business. It reinforced the value of market forces and the need to assess them beforehand rather than being caught off guard by them or trying to change them.

Overall in availing its comparative advantage, that is, development interventions involving the communities, AKRSP has created outstanding income earning and job creation opportunities, with wide reach (both in terms of access and outreach), for the local people. Moreover, all the projects provide a range of capacity building services which are helping the communities access improved technologies and technical know how in order to improve their traditional skills. These accomplishments, nevertheless, come at a steep price, and have entailed heavy initial investments and subsidies (in the form of incentives, capacity building and technological investments for engaging the communities, research and development etc.), and very long payback periods. Above all, the projects[49] remain dependent on AKRSP for capital investments and finances required to see them through the ebbs and flows of the business cycles. In order to cultivate business-like transaction-based relations, certain sections of the projects charge the communities partially for some of the services, such as training and equipment that they receive. Nonetheless, most of the services offered by the projects are investments in the business operations of the project enabling production of better quality products. The costs of these investments, therefore, should be recovered from the end consumers not the input suppliers or vendors, i.e. the communities.

Complex issues shroud the seemingly well placed long-term goal of privatising AKRSP businesses—assuming that at some stage in the future the projects do become self-sustaining entities. What would be an appropriate price for a private investor to pay for the businesses? Should AKRSP write off some of its investments as the costs of developing the local subsectoral markets and community skills or should it charge a premium for all the groundwork that it has done to make the business a venture worthy of investment in the first place? What would be the price of the goodwill created by the projects, which in turn drew heavily on the goodwill of AKRSP, the integrated rural development programme, over its twenty-year history? Even if a transparent merit-based approach were adopted for selecting the potential buyer(s), how would the relationship between the different stakeholders—that is the communities, the management and the new buyers—play out, and how would that affect the business? Would the communities have any ownership stakes, and if yes, are they capable of making long-term strategic decisions as potential owners? What obligation would a private investor have in safeguarding the interests of the communities, or investing in community training, particularly if it means compromising profits or forsaking them in the short run? Would privatisation on terms and conditions—for safeguarding communities' interests—be acceptable to a potential buyer, given that as it is NAC is a business unfriendly environment, and what guarantee would there be that the private party would abide by those terms? Privatisation will, therefore, open a new set of risks and issues for these projects and place them on their next threshold for survival. Thus, there are important implications for the sustainability of a business in deciding whether a development organisation—even one working in marginalized regions—wants to set up its own business or facilitate its initiation in the private sector from the very start.

From 'Provider' to 'Facilitator' to Developing BDS Markets

Starting in the mid-1990s, an overriding concern in designing suitable enterprise development interventions had come to rest on creating sustainable initiatives with wide outreach and impact. The business projects of AKRSP had been a major effort in this direction. Nonetheless, the intricacies of managing large resource-heavy projects had raised issues regarding their long-term viability, including the scope and potential for their privatisation and their continued dependence on AKRSP for capital injections and investments.[50] It was evident that there remained a need to reach a wide clientele at the grass roots through strengthening *indigenous* mechanisms cost-effectively rather than trying to create new ones. Encouraging episodes within AKRSP's own experience, an international paradigm shift in approaches for supporting small businesses, and a changing donor-funding environment, further paved the way for reaching out to larger number of entrepreneurs and small businesses through redefining a new role for AKRSP, more distant from servicing small businesses directly or becoming a market player itself.

By the late 1990s, it was evident that outreach could be enhanced cost-effectively by creating and working though local institutions, such as the informal and formal interest groups functioning as business and farmers' associations. Secondly, at least within the urban centres, there was scope to develop the capacity of indigenous BDS providers, such as accountants, auditors, vocational and business management trainers who could provide their services to the MSMEs on a commercial basis. AKRSP had privatised its agriculture and livestock input supply functions in recognition of the growing capacity within the private sector to take on such ventures. These occasions enabled AKRSP to concentrate more on a facilitative role for itself, focusing on creating and building indigenous intermediaries to whom AKRSP could devolve several of its direct service delivery functions, and thus move one stage back from working directly with the MSMEs. Equally, it was also becoming evident that AKRSP's efforts had a bearing on the larger macro level environment governing small businesses, where it had focused on policy reforms and advocacy for the MSMEs and tried to cultivate the interests of the other stakeholders in the NAC. 'EDC should develop relationships with broader business community and any other organisations that are involved in SME that will allow it to capitalise on their strengths rather than developing all the capacity in-house' (AKRSP 1999b).

Despite the persuasive experience of facilitation, this function had yet to grasp AKRSP's attention singularly. Programme interventions continued to be flexible and therefore a mix of direct and indirect services combining the role of a direct provider and facilitator respectively. Nevertheless, at the organisational level introspective deliberations had begun towards giving more coherence to AKRSP's identity in the business milieu, compelled by issues emanating out of AKRSP's own experiential context, i.e. cost-effectively increasing outreach and undertaking sustainable initiatives. These developments—without AKRSP's knowledge—were coinciding with events in the international enterprise development arena, which sooner than expected would have major implications for AKRSP's future approach for business promotion.

In April 2000 AKRSP was invited to the Conference of the Committee of Donor Agencies for Small Enterprise Development[51] in Hanoi, where AKRSP 'discovered' the BDS philosophy.

Figure 6.2. BDS market development paradigm

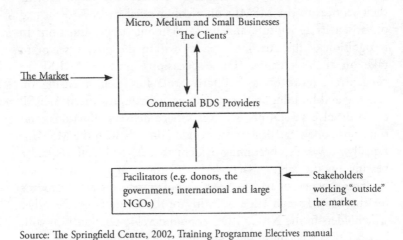

Source: The Springfield Centre, 2002, Training Programme Electives manual

---

Box 6.1. Business development services (BDS)

The BDS Market Development Paradigm: The BDS market development approach aims to develop a robust commercial market for BDS, where the micro, small and medium enterprises (MSMEs) are purchasing BDS and the BDS suppliers are selling the services, and where these transactions are happening on a commercial basis. The new approach strongly discourages the facilitators (large resource organisations) from servicing small businesses directly and thus distorting the market for the commercial sector BDS providers. The BDS market development approach says that an organisation should clearly define what role out of the two—BDS Providers or BDS Facilitators—it wants to adopt. Providers are expected to operate on a commercial basis, charge the MSMEs that they serve a fee and thus make a living out of providing BDS to businesses. On the other hand, the facilitators, i.e. the donors, international and big local NGOs and organisations which have large operational costs that cannot be covered through the fee income from servicing small businesses, should not provide BDS to MSMEs since this will distort the private sector market for BDS and displace private sector BDS providers. The facilitators should therefore focus on identifying the gaps in the supply and demand of BDS in the market, and design interventions that aim to address these market failures. Facilitators' interventions should not directly influence the transactions in the market between the MSMEs and the BDS suppliers, instead their interventions should be in the shape of indirect subsidies that aim to develop the overall market for BDS. Facilitators should, therefore, not favour any one MSME or BDS supplier *per se* but rather develop the market for a given BDS. For example, improving the awareness for a certain BDS through advertisement or promotional support and improving the supply of a given BDS through training for BDS suppliers. This approach is expected to minimise market distortions, and facilitate the emergence of private sector suppliers of BDS who sell their services to discerning MSMEs who buy the BDS of their choice and demand quality for what they have paid.

Business Development Services: Any non-financial service provided to a business on either a formal or informal basis which adds value to the business.

At the international level, work has been initiated in this area only since the late 1990s, instigated by issues and concerns very similar to those of AKRSP's, such as enhancing outreach and access cost-effectively and making sustainable initiatives. Though internationally practitioners continued to be challenged in implementing this approach, particularly among marginalized communities, there was little doubt that the BDS market development approach was not a passing fad and that the enterprise development paradigm had shifted to BDS market development.

The new approach caught AKRSP's attention as AKRSP had been moving in this direction without knowing the BDS terminology. AKRSP's adoption of the BDS market development approach is however steered by evidence out of its own experience and not by any theoretical compulsion to pursue international best practices. It also marks a sharp departure from how AKRSP approached business development earlier. First, at the organisational level, realizing the demands of a market driven competitive approach, AKRSP has formulated its first formal strategy for BDS market development in an effort to mirror the businesslike professional values in commercial transactions that it is trying to promote under the new paradigm. Second, contrary to its isolationism of earlier years, AKRSP is actively linking up with the international BDS expertise[52] in order to enhance its own understanding and methodology for a new and evolving approach. Third, to some extent the BDS strategy also enables the enterprise development programme to reinvent itself and remain attractive to the donors in an increasingly competitive funding environment with shifting funding priorities, particularly of the larger international donors.

Presented below is successful evidence of AKRSP's role as a facilitator reaching out to larger groups of MSMEs through indigenous intermediary institutions, such as the informal and formal farmers and business association and local small-scale consultants, and AKRSP's role in the advocacy and policy sphere:

Formal and Informal Farmers and Business Associations

AKRSP had played an instrumental role in assisting the formation of interest groups of like-minded people with common commercial interests, in both the farm and the off-farm sub-sectors.[53] Some of these interest groups subsequently matured to form formal associations registered under the Partnership Act of 1932. The associations were formed voluntarily on a partnership basis with members' own investments, and profits were shared accordingly. There was a keen awareness within AKRSP to build the institutional capacity of these nascent groups in order to prepare them to serve as effective indigenous institutions through which AKRSP could reach out to a larger clientele at the grass roots. In the long run these groups were expected to play a more strategic role of local partners for advocating and lobbying for an improved regulatory framework governing their respective sectors.

Table 6.5. Number of local intermediaries assisted

Region	On-Farm Interest Groups & Associations	Off-Farm Interest Groups & Associations	Small Scale Consultants
Gilgit	4	3	2
Chitral	16	5	-
Baltistan	3	1	-
Total	23	9	2

AKRSP provided a range of cross-sectoral capacity building services to the association members, such as preparation of business plans and identification of sound financial opportunities, including technical skill development training relevant to the sub-sector of the association's operations. Moreover, AKRSP also sponsored members' exposure trips to down-country markets, and linked the group members with retailers, wholesalers, and research and resource organisations[54] and private and public stakeholder further south. Associations in the farm related sub-sectors were provided a range of technical skills, prominent among which were post harvest management, fruit and vegetable marketing, and new technologies for fruit drying and processing. In addition to marketing these groups were also assisted in other income generation activities such as honey bee keeping and retailing agriculture inputs. Refer to Box 6.2 for illustrative examples of the kind of assistance provided to interest groups in the off-farm sub-sectors.

Box 6.2 Illustrative examples of business associations in the off-farm sectors

Baltistan Gems Association (BGA): AKRSP facilitated BGA in drafting its bylaws and in developing an understanding of the district administration. By training the members in the intricacies of gem identification and recognition and improving the mine blasting techniques, AKRSP enabled the miners to avoid exploitation by gem traders and the gems and mines from being damaged by crude blasting techniques which often render the mines unfit for further excavation. Trainings in gem cutting techniques opened new possibilities of more value-added business to be conducted regionally. The AKRSP-sponsored gemstones exhibition held in summer 2002 in Skardu Baltistan attracted gem traders from all over Pakistan and abroad and, according to some estimates, had a turnover of over Rs 3,000,000 in three days.

Chitral Association for Mountain Area Tourism (CAMAT): CAMAT was established in 1998 as a result of AKRSP's efforts to promote indigenous tourism development initiatives in Chitral. CAMAT provides a common platform to the tourist guides, hoteliers, tour operators, and other stakeholders to pool their intellectual and financial resources towards generating new ideas for promoting tourism in the region. AKRSP assisted CAMAT to develop its strategy and provided assistance in management of finances and reporting requirements for donors. CAMAT is now working independently in collaboration with the United Nations Children's Fund (UNICEF) towards promoting tourism in Chitral.

One of the most significant roles of the farm-related interest groups—aside from engaging in commercial activities for their own benefit—was in servicing non-group member small farmers. This addressed AKRSP's concern for disengaging itself from working directly with widely dispersed farmers and creating indigenous institutions for providing services to them. The farmers' associations in conjunction with AKRSP provided training and other services to interested farmers in the villages, and thus served as extension workers for AKRSP. The groups organised most of the pre-requisites of the on-farm training programme such as delivering invitation messages to trainees, organising their transportation to the training site, arranging food, training venues, and training material for the trainees. The training sessions while informative for the farmers were cost-effective in terms of outreach and actual cost to AKRSP.

Earlier, farmers were paid to attend training sessions, but gradually this practice was reduced culminating in the introduction of nominal fees for training courses to encourage only genuine participants. Even though training to farmers remained subsidized, some of this subsidy came from interest groups (as opposed to AKRSP), as interest groups incurred costs in arranging training that were not fully recovered through fees or reimbursed by AKRSP. By providing such training, the groups established linkages and goodwill with farmers and developed their market in either purchasing farmers' produce, or selling them agriculture inputs available in the group's agriculture supply retail stores. In addition, farmers' interest groups provided neighbouring farmers with a range of services and inputs appropriate to the main activities of the groups in order to improve the quality of the products available in the neighbourhood. These services and inputs were provided on a commercial basis by the groups, and effectively cross-subsidized the costs of the training provided. An interest group stood to benefit if the quality and quantity of produce purchased from neighbouring farmers improved. Thus, the costs incurred by farmers' interest groups in training neighbouring farmers were recovered as farmers' interest groups earned higher margins on better quality products and increased their turnover though increased yields (Roomi *et al.* 2000).

Figure 6.3. Increasing outreach through interest groups

Model	Recipient	Provider	Services	Facilitator
Farmers' Interest Groups **(Model A)***	Farmers' Finerest Groups	AKRS	Packaging Material Development, Linkages Development, Technology Dissemination, Market Information, Exposure Trips/Test Marketing, Post Harvest Management Training, Food Processing Training, Entrepreneurial Training	AKF, DFID, other donors
Farmers' Interest Groups **(Model-b)****	Farmers	AKRSP/ Farmers Interest Groups	Fruit Drying, Fruit Processing, Post-Harvest Management Training, Agricultural Input Supply, Marketing of Produce	AKRSP/ AKF, DFID, other donors

* Model A: AKRSP provides training/services/facilities to the groups
** Model B: Groups provide training/service
Source: Roomi *et al.* (2000).

In addition, benefits accruing to the associations inspired others to follow suit. For example, emulating the example of the Gilgit based cherry marketing association fifteen other cherry marketing groups came up who are lucratively catering to the down-country markets. Competition among these groups has increased the farm-to-gate price of cherries for the farmers. Similarly, after the formation of the apple marketing associations between 1999 and 2000, the value of apples exported down-country increased by 91 per cent while the value of exports increased by 189 per cent. These progressive trends are continuing and over 300 farmers are directly benefiting from this activity.

The Small Scale Business Consultants: Strengthening BDS Providers in the Private Sector

AKRSP's vocational and management related trainings were also subsidised heavily, though the level of subsidy varied inversely with the perceived value of the training. For example, if AKRSP's assessment revealed that a certain business service could add value to MSMEs but that the MSMEs had little or no awareness of it, then AKRSP would offer incentives such as *per diem* and free meals as a tool to get the participants interested. On the other hand, where the training was in demand, the subsidy would be nominal. The following example illustrates how transition from needs assessment-based training to demand-based training creates space for the commercialisation of BDS.

An AKRSP survey revealed that small traders in Gilgit needed training in bookkeeping in order to distinguish between their personal and business accounts. Consequently, AKRSP offered subsidised training through a local small-scale service provider called Eagle Enterprise (EE). The value of the training was amply demonstrated when traders were willing to pay for the follow-up training in order to clarify questions that they had regarding implementing what they had learnt earlier. Instead of subsidizing the training for the participants, AKRSP began to focus on building the capacity of EE to serve as a commercial provider of BDS. EE is currently delivering business management trainings (bookkeeping, marketing, small business management) to local retailers. Further,

NGOs operating in Gilgit hire the services of EE to undertake their administrative support needs when conducting workshops, seminars and conferences in Gilgit.

AKRSP's Role as a Facilitator in the Advocacy Policy Sphere
The impact of working with a variety of stakeholders towards common goals has been amply demonstrated in AKRSP's social development programme. The same principles have been applied in the commercial sector in order to rationalise application of useful resources and efforts, through sharing experience and know-how with stakeholders working towards shared objectives. AKRSP's non-bureaucratic, flexible decision-making mechanisms and proactive approach has enabled it to take advantage of opportunities and make inroads with private sector players. On the other hand, AKRSP's appeal as a credible potential partner lies in the good reputation that it has earned through first-hand experience of directly working with small businesses, which in turn has been rewarded by the popularity of the AKRSP *brand*[55] within NAC. Equally, business activities have benefited from AKRSP's reputation of a model rural development programme with deep ties with the communities.[56] AKRSP's efforts in lobbying for an improved commercial environment and building relationships with organisations such as the Small and Medium Enterprise Development Authority (SMEDA), Chambers of Commerce and Industries, Export Promotion Bureau, the private sector banks[57] and the government have assisted in addressing institutional constraints for MSMEs. More importantly, these collaborations have provided AKRSP with the leverage to influence policy dialogues affecting the MSMEs at the national level, and carved space and rationality for a definite role for AKRSP in this area in the future. AKRSP's commercial sector relationships present a very broad and unusual array of partnerships. The process of partnerships itself has been a learning opportunity for AKRSP indicating what works and where more vigilance and caution is required, for example as in the case of the Graduates Business Promotion Scheme (GBPS)[58] of AKRSP. Illustrative examples of AKRSP

commercial sector relationships including the GBPS are presented in Box 6.3.

Box 6.3. Illustrative examples of AKRSP's partnerships with commercial sector stakeholders

Ameliorating Access to Finance: AKRSP played a critical role in cultivating Orix Leasing Limited's (OLL, a Japanese company with growing interests in Pakistan) interest and expediting its presence in the NAs. Leasing products are particularly advantageous for start-up businesses, as they allow access to long term fixed assets, without tying up large capital (examples include leased vehicles and small machinery). AKRSP conducted a survey to assess the demand for lease products in the NAs. To substantiate the encouraging findings of the survey and give OLL a feel of the local market, AKRSP organised workshops for potential lessees, and OLL staff in Gilgit. These get-togethers provided the opportunity for OLL to meet with potential clients, understand their demands and issues and explain lease products and services. To further improve understanding regarding lease products among MSEs, AKRSP organised an interactive workshop where business-people's issues and concerns regarding lease agreements were addressed.

While AKRSP assisted OLL in finding suitable staff and premises, it shared its own office premises and facilities with OLL in order to hasten its operations in the NAs. The congenial rapport developed between the staff of the two organisations helped in operationalising coordinated strategies for assisting MSMEs. Since 2001, OLL has been successfully building its lease portfolio in Gilgit. Clients referred by AKRSP are given serious consideration as they have already gone through the initial rounds of scrutiny.

Lobbying for Sectoral Support: Despite being well endowed with a variety of natural resources such as gems, pink and white marbles, soapstone and coal, the mining sector in Chitral had been neglected by the Government. This exacerbated an already difficult exploratory and business environment for the mining industry. Due to AKRSP's successful lobbying efforts with the Provincial Director of Industries, Commerce and Mineral Development it was decided that the locals would be given preference in granting mining leases and an Office of the Mineral Development Officer was established to solve the problems of the local mine lessees. The mining policy for the North West Frontier Province (NWFP) was also announced in Chitral. Such events help promote the district, bringing it to the attention of potential investors external to the region.

Trade Forums: Over the last few years AKRSP has been collaborating with the Northern Areas Chamber of Commerce and Industries (NACCI) and *Lok Virsa* (a public organisation established for the preservation and promotion of indigenous arts and crafts) to organise the Silk Route Festival, a four-day trade show which brings together businesses from down-country, Northern regions and overseas and gives them the opportunity to display their products, develop linkages, strengthen marketing networks, and exchange ideas. The presence of foreign traders provides an added opportunity to interact with and explore new international markets. The management of such events by AKRSP and in particular its role in mobilising local businesses to participate, provides AKRSP with additional leverage with public sector organisations engaged in promoting and developing the commercial sector.

Graduates Business Promotion Scheme: In 2001, AKRSP introduced a scheme under which it intended to help educated people with innovative business ideas to establish new businesses. The 'Apna Karobar Scheme' (AKS) was structured very professionally The training and internship programme for the 'Apna Karobar Scheme' (AKS) participants was designed by Lahore University of Management Sciences (LUMS), one of the premier business schools in Pakistan (the training and internship programme was designed by Lahore University of Management Sciences (LUMS), one of the premier business schools in Pakistan), launched with a fanfare and engaged the SME Bank Limited (SME) as a supporting partner. A written Memorandum-of-Understanding was signed with the SME Bank Limited under which AKRSP would help identify potential clients (through AKS) while credit decisions would be made by the bank based on its due diligence. Candidates were selected jointly by AKRSP and SME officials, after a process of written tests and interviews. The brochure advertising the scheme also alluded to AKRSP's support in finding seed capital for establishing new enterprises. The scheme was proceeding as planned until participants approached SME for funding. SME's lead management had changed, and drawbacks of the cumbersome credit procedures began to surface. A focus group discussion with the scheme's participants revealed that they had taken bold risks in order to raise equity in anticipation of *assured* funding from SME. The scheme has not enrolled its second round of candidates due to this experience of the existing participants.

The appeal and rationality of the BDS market development approach, and AKRSP's commitment to draw from international best practices notwithstanding, AKRSP's organisational context, the complexity of the purist BDS approach in mountainous programme environment, and its embryonic stage at the international level will all continue to challenge the ingenuity of AKRSP in the years ahead. At the organisational level, though AKRSP has made heavy investments in building staff capacity to understand, build ownership and develop expertise for BDS market development, much remains to be discovered. Understandably, there are apprehensions among staff in foregoing the known turf of direct provision of services to MSMES—without having to abide by any formal strategy delineating the 'dos and don'ts' of business promotion—in exchange for the more complex domain of developing markets for BDS.

Though the market development approach promises innovative opportunities in the few urban centres in the northern regions, it poses challenges regarding its scope in the rural villages and the more inaccessible far-flung areas where the underprivileged may be further marginalized rather than embraced by it. Even within the more fertile areas, there remains the risk of facilitators focusing on a few BDS providers of a given service rather than strengthening the market for that service. Moreover, there is a risk that skilled people with the potential to serve as commercial BDS providers will be lured by better paying career opportunities outside NAC rather than engaging in the demanding task of cultivating commercial markets for their services within NAC. In addition, due to limited coordination of donors and varying donor strategies, market-based initiatives of one can be undermined by another providing subsidised services directly to small businesses. While the challenging environment of northern Pakistan poses a trying environment for the latest course correction of AKRSP—no different from what emerging BDS market development programmes face elsewhere—it nevertheless holds the promise of equally insightful experiences of managing a market-driven programme in some of the most marginalised regions of the world.

NOTES

1. Excluding the investments made in AKRSP's wholly owned businesses.
2. At the time there was only one public call office in Gilgit town. Nevertheless, on payment people could also use the telephone services of the military bases in the region.
3. A listing of the maximum price that a retailer could charge for the household consumption items sold in the NAC.
4. For example, AKRSP facilitated participation of gem traders from Gilgit in an exhibition in Munich.
5. For example, efforts were made to establish linkages of fruit producers in the north with leading fruit processing companies in Pakistan, such as Shezan and Mitchells.

6. Starting in the late 1990s AKRSP also established three wholly owned businesses, the experience of which cuts across the second and third phases given below.

7. Further details regarding collective marketing are presented as an operational insight further ahead in this paper.

8. The example of indigenous intermediaries.

9. To reflect the changing emphasis of the programme, in 1987 the Marketing Section was renamed the Commercial and Industrial Development Division, in 1992 it was christened the Enterprise Development Programme, and from 2003 onwards it has been called the Market Development Programme.

10. Traditionally, that is at least for the first fifteen years, the enterprise development programme of AKRSP had a budgetary allocation not exceeding two per cent of the organisational budget.

11. Insightful lessons emerge out of the Population and Community Development Association's (PDA) approach to job creation for the poor in Thailand. PDA believes that the NGOs and the villagers do not have much business sense. The project director Mechai Viravaidya internationally recognised as Mr Condom - leveraged PDA's success in birth control and rural development to engage multinationals to adopt a village and develop a sustainable business project involving the villagers. Against the target of engaging a thousand companies in fifteen years, to date 30 multinationals including Upjohn, Singer, Swedish Motors and Mobil Oil have been involved.

12. More details on this are given further ahead in this paper under the operational insight 'Alternative Approaches to Enterprise Development'.

13. The institution development model of AKRSP aimed at social mobilisation and strengthening communities' capacities for building and managing their resources themselves.

14. Joint Monitoring Missions consisting of multilateral and bilateral donors have periodically evaluated AKRSP.

15. Between 1982 and 2001, the Operations Evaluation Department of the World Bank has evaluated AKRSP four times at intervals spanning three to six years.

16. A strategy focusing on market development has been formulated for 2003-2007 after a series of brainstorming sessions between the enterprise development staff and external expertise.

17. 'Business Development Services (BDS) refers to the wide range of services used by entrepreneurs to help them operate efficiently and grow their business with the broader purpose of contributing to economic growth, employment generation and poverty alleviation' (Miehlbradt and McVay 2003).

18. Such as credit, business management and enterprise development related training, and building market linkages.

19. More details regarding such activities are presented in the last operational insight on BDS market development in this paper.

20. Raiffeisen was of the view that in the 1880s there were three giants crushing the farmers: the landlord, the moneylender and the middleman.

21. Equity concerns were emphasised in socio-economic terms whereas gender equity came much later.

22. Northern Areas comprise Gilgit and Baltistan, whereas Chitral is part of the Northwest Frontier Province.

23. Sector specialists were people with technical expertise in agriculture, and natural resources while lead trainers were instructors who trained other community members.

24. Traders and middlemen.

25. In some cases, the VOs were distrustful of the financial dealings of the marketing specialists and viewed him with suspicion. Here the 'neutrality' of the social organiser as opposed to the marketing specialist was more handy in improving the understanding of the VO members regarding business issues.

26. Farmers confused the farm-to-gate price with the market price in Gilgit (not comprehending the additional transportation and commission charges). They also refused to remunerate the marketing specialist for his full time but 'intangible' services. Moreover, AKRSP had proposed a marketing reserve fund as an insurance shield to cover potential losses of a bad season. The VOs never bought the idea (AKRSP 1985a).

27. As can be seen in Table 6.2, during the 1990s net incomes from collective marketing had increased substantially over that in the mid 1980s, going as high as Rs 45.8 million in 1997, the equivalent of Rs 34,000 per household.

28. Notable among these are: Gilgit Apricot Marketing Association (GAMA) and Baltistan Apricot Marketing Association (BAMA), the agricultural marketing associations; Tanzeem Corporation, a supply cooperative dealing in basic commodities such as soap, cement, cooking oil and tea; and Ramoshay Tanzeem, a retailer of livestock inputs.

29. The example of *Idara-e-Kisan* (IK, Organisation of Farmers) based in the Punjab, offers useful insights regarding mechanisms and the organisational structure most suitable for adding value to farmers' production and the incentives for engaging them. IK is incorporated under the 1860 Societies Act as a cooperative. The management attributes the successful expansion of the project—post-donor's departure—to the entrepreneurial vigour of the Chairman and centralisation of all specialised functions such as milk processing, product diversification, packaging, distribution and marketing with IK. There is no undue interference by people (farmers) who lack the potential to undertake advanced specialised tasks. Since GTZ left in 1989, IK has expanded its operations to cover 500 villages, with close to 20,000 farmers who are collectively paid Rs 1,500,000 each day for milk purchased by IK. The operation itself engages close to 200 staff members who are successfully processing milk at four plants, which were leased from the

government as 'sick units'. IK's growth has been financed with retained earnings—without any debt or donor money.

30. See Chapter 2 on poverty and livelihoods for similar observations on farm fragmentation.

31. Over the years AKRSP has been making investments in building staff capacity to counsel micro and small enterprises (MSEs) and provide enterprise management trainings to potential entrepreneurs. In 1993 training was offered in collaboration with the Cranfield School of Management. Subsequent enterprise management related courses have been designed in conjunction with international consultants and the Lahore University of Management Sciences (LUMS).

32. Between June 17 to 19, 2003 a series of interviews of and discussions with recipients of AKRSP's business support services were held in Gilgit by the author of this chapter.

33. Primarily embroidered tapestries, cushions, household accessories and trinkets.

34. Initially women were employed but they either moved away after marriage or could not spare sufficient time from their domestic chores. It takes a long time to master weaving skills and men generally tend to shift to more familiar tasks.

35. Refer to the chapter on micro-finance for similar observations.

36. The author interviewed the businessman at his factory premises.

37. This project is further described in this paper under the Specific Insight 'AKRSP in Business'.

38. Such as candle making, school uniform stitching, bookbinding, fabric dying and production of traditional handicrafts.

39. One indication of this fact is that between 1982 and 2002 out of the total credit extended by AKRSP, only 15 per cent was availed by women.

40. For example, most cooperatives had hundreds of shareholders but there were no reliable official records of shares owned by individuals either with the individual shareholders or the cooperative! This matter raised grave complexities and disputes and consumed much of AKRSP staff time, and financial resources when the cooperatives were finally dissolved.

41. The only exception is the Reshit Coal project where three private parties were interested in obtaining a mining lease.

42. The number of households working with NSS has grown progressively from 184 to 280 in 2002.

43. *Shu*, a pure wool windproof fabric, has been produced for centuries in Chitral. It is made from wool hand spun by women and woven on the traditional hand-looms. Also known as 'patti/pattu'.

44. At any given time in the past, Shubinak never purchased less than 2 per cent of the total shu produced in Chitral. The remaining shu was sold through the existing market channels.

45. Data for the actual market size is elusive but by integrating the government, FAO and market information this appears to be a realistic estimate.
46. This rate includes 5-6% inflation.
47. Due to the complex and expensive nature of R&D required for the business it takes about 7-8 years of capital-intensive research to develop improved seed varieties (particularly hybrid seeds which are indispensable for a successful seed business), and anywhere between 8 to 12 years before the enterprise becomes profitable.
48. AKRSP's unsuccessful experience of trying to tap the export market for Shubinak was very recent and still fresh in the mind of the Board, making it sceptical and weary of large exploratory investments of AKRSP.
49. This includes DFP which is the only project operationally breaking even so far.
50. For example investments to finance research and development, purchase of additional or improved machinery, and exploring international markets.
51 This Committee, comprising a number of multilateral and bilateral development agencies, has done pioneering work in initiating a global dialogue on BDS and developing Donor Guidelines for market development through initiating and strengthening BDS. For more information visit www. sedonors.org.
51. Two senior staff members attended the BDS Training Programme at the Springfield Centre, Glasgow, UK in 2002. Subsequently, every quarter workshop sessions on the BDS approach were arranged for the staff team and expertise from Springfield Centre was directly engaged in order to help operationalise the BDS market development strategy (2003–2007).
52. For example, growing and marketing apples, cherries, and pears; mining; gemstone cutting; tourism.
53. Such as: Fruit and Vegetable Development Board, Agriculture Research Centre, Pakistan Council for Scientific and Industrial Research (PCSIR) and national beverage companies such as Shezan and TOPs
54. The AKRSP name has become a trademark of quality, as indicated by the popularity of 'AKRSP apricots' or 'AKRSP apples' (AKRSP 1992a)
55. Business activities can draw upon the network of over 4,000 VOs/WOs and the expertise of the other sections of the programme such as infrastructure, natural resource management, social development and monitoring and evaluation/policy research.
56. Such as the SME Bank Limited, Soneri Bank Limited, Orix Leasing Limited and Bank of Khyber.
57. Entitled *Apna Karobar* Scheme in Urdu.

7

Micro-Finance

Maliha H. Hussein and Stefan Plateau

INTRODUCTION

AKRSP has been a pioneer in the field of micro-finance and has managed one of the most successful micro-finance programmes in Pakistan. The micro-finance sector is a rapidly growing sector in Pakistan and many of the existing NGOs have emulated the AKRSP model in designing and implementing key aspects of their micro-finance operations. However, the lessons from AKRSP's experience need to be properly assessed, synthesised and fully shared. The purpose of this study is to attempt an analysis of the lessons that can be learnt from AKRSP's rich and pioneering experience. In selecting areas for focus, the research team chose those issues that were of particular value for micro-finance practitioners and posed special challenges in the sector. Some of these issues include aspects such as the rationale and cost of including savings as part of the micro-finance operations, the credit operations and their evolution, impact of micro-finance on poverty reduction, sustainability of micro-finance operations and the lessons that can be learnt from AKRSP's experience in establishing a micro-finance bank. Through a study of AKRSP documentation and recording of the oral history of the programme in interviews with current and past staff members, an attempt has been made to examine the rationale for the specific path that was adopted in the evolution of micro-finance thinking and operations at AKRSP. This particular analysis covers AKRSP's experience from 1982 to 2002.

AKRSP's micro-finance programme was designed for an economy that was basically agrarian in which close to 90 per cent of the population made its living from subsistence farming. AKRSP started its operations in an area with a poor natural resource base, rapid population growth, poor communication facilities, lack of employment opportunities and few banking facilities. Per capita income in 1982 was estimated to be $150 which was less than half the national average. Lack of credit facilities, high cost of transportation and inadequate distribution networks made it difficult for the average farmer to invest in technologies that would increase farm productivity. AKRSP's success lay in properly understanding this environment and designing a savings and credit programme that catered to the needs of its target population. The essential features of the programme were: low transaction costs for the client; catering for low volumes of savings and loans; catering to individual needs of security, liquidity and information about savings; personalised loan products. This entailed the creation of an institutional tier at the village level which would help to reduce transactions costs, convert low volumes to high volumes and enable clients to create social and financial collateral.

Tracing the Roots of AKRSP's Village Organisation (VO) and Micro-Finance Model in Early Co-operative History

The Asian Co-operative Movement was greatly influenced by Co-operative Development in Europe. Since AKRSP also derived inspiration of its VO model from the co-operative movement in Europe, particularly Raiffeisen in Germany, it is relevant to begin with an understanding of this movement (see Appendices). There were considerable similarities in socio-economic situations between Asia and Europe during the Eighteenth and Nineteenth century. The co-operative Movement in Europe was an attempt by the working classes, workers and artisans, supported by many social thinkers and reformers, to fight poverty and exploitation, arising particularly from the deteriorating socio-economic conditions of workers as a result of the industrial revolution (Sharma 1998: 1-29).

In the early years at AKRSP, it was repeatedly emphasised that AKRSP's VOs were patterned on the co-operatives of Raiffeisen in Germany, and its model of rural development drew important lessons from development efforts implemented in Comilla (Bangladesh) and Daudzai (Pakistan). However, the lessons from these models and programmes were never shared at AKRSP and the micro-finance components of these earlier models, if they had any, were never discussed at AKRSP. AKRSP did not come with a micro-finance blueprint and any micro-finance component in these programmes failed to provide AKRSP with any concrete lessons for replication. Thus, in designing its micro-finance component, AKRSP was not emulating a well defined programme which had been implemented elsewhere but was pursuing the simple objective of social organisation that taught that capital formation was essential for rural development. AKRSP's micro-finance experience was one that evolved as the programme progressed and there were few preconceived notions of how this might develop. There was also little examination of how AKRSP could learn from the experience of the early co-operatives or credit unions. AKRSP drew inspiration from these early efforts but never deeply examined how this intellectual heritage could be used to shape its own destiny.

AKRSP has always prided itself on being innovative and not following a blueprint approach. It is true that AKRSP's unbridled energy paid dividends in many areas of its work and allowed it to develop innovative and exciting models of village development. However, in some areas, particularly micro-finance, its refusal to draw lessons from the past stymied its growth, led to ad hocism and steered it in directions which did not contribute to its long term objectives. There was never any discussion at AKRSP about the outcome of Raiffeisen's co-operatives and whether they had a similar micro-finance component and, if so, what could be learnt from their experience. There was also virtually no examination of what was happening in the area of micro-finance in the 1980s elsewhere in the world and what current thinking existed in this field.

What Lessons Can we Learn from AKRSP's Saving's Experience?

Many non-governmental Organisations (NGOs) which have entered the arena of micro-finance in Pakistan have done so primarily with a focus on loans and not on savings. The exception to this norm is generally those NGOs whose micro-finance programmes are patterned on the AKRSP model such as the rural support programmes. The question is, why did AKRSP initiate a savings component as a critical part of its micro-finance and rural development model? In its very initial stage, AKRSP did not have a well established credit component as part of its early conception of what constituted a package of micro-finance services. In fact, when AKRSP first started its operations, loans were not part of its portfolio at all. At this stage, savings was the only component of the AKRSP model due to its basic premise that social capital, human capital development and capital formation constituted key elements for rural development. Its strategy for capital formation was to insist that its members save during their weekly Village Organisation meetings. There was no restriction on how much each member should save and saving was not compulsory in the sense that each member did not have to save each week if they had nothing to deposit. Even as AKRSP insisted upon savings and had put restrictions on what its clients could do with these savings, it did not itself have a clear idea of how they were to be used.

AKRSP stressed savings by Village and Women's Organisations (V/WOs) from the outset as an investment in social organisation and to build the capital base that would enable investments in productive opportunities. The combination of equity capital and loan capital at the village level was expected to contribute significantly to a self-sustained development process. Many NGOs involved with micro-finance today are focusing on loans and have not been able to reorient their programmes in a manner which allows them to effectively utilise members' savings. This is an important issue for organisations wanting to capitalise on the opportunities made available by the Micro-Finance Ordinance in Pakistan today, as members' savings would allow them to build their own capital base and offer them the potential to transform their operations into that of a formal sector bank. AKRSP began with a focus on savings and its principal advantage was that it came with a well-developed strategy for social mobilisation which made this possible. Even though the micro-finance regulation in Pakistan is such that it does not allow an organisation not registered under the banking ordinance to take savings deposits of members, AKRSP found a way around this obstacle by having the savings deposited in commercial banks in a joint account. Security of individual savings was preserved through a two-tier banking system under which individual savings were recorded in individual pass books issued to each member, and the collective savings of the V/WOs were generally invested in commercial banks in high-yielding term deposits. The profits earned on the collective savings were recorded on individual members' pass books on a pro-rata basis according to the savings held by each member. Originally V/WOs were not allowed to withdraw these deposits but in later years V/WOs were allowed to make withdrawals from their savings. However, in practice, commercial banks checked with AKRSP before allowing any organisation access to their savings. Savings were generally invested in high-yielding long-term investments offered by the banks.

The savings programme generated considerable interest among both men and women and, in fact, provided the main motivation for the first women's organisations established in the Northern Areas. Given the past failures of rural organisations to preserve the equity of their members, the level of, and increases in equity per member were regarded as impressive in the first year of operations. At AKRSP, savings were a pre-requisite to the awarding of a Productive Physical Infrastructure [1] (PPI) and this fact accounted for the high savings growth during the PPI work. Many organisations deposited the first PPI grant as part of the collective village savings. However, in most cases savings was considered an individual enterprise and people preferred to save their money in separate individual accounts. Savings continued to register rapid growth between 1983 and 1998 due to several reasons: AKRSP's savings programme entailed low transactions cost, it secured individual savings, and for many, provided the first opportunity to save with the formal sector. Savings also registered a rapid growth due to the fact that the rapid increase in the number of VOs entailed a natural increase in savings due to the requirement of minimum savings to attract productive infrastructure investments, the policy to prevent withdrawals from savings and a favourable financial environment that encouraged savings through high interest rates in the formal banking sector and availability of relatively inexpensive credit through AKRSP. Among many WO members, savings was claimed to be especially earmarked to cover future education expenses. It was generally held that AKRSP's savings programme allowed its clients most of the attractive features of savings such as safety, regularity, convenience and access. AKRSP, after the initial years, also allowed the villagers to withdraw their savings and thus meet the high liquidity preference for households with vulnerable livelihoods.

The Village Organisation was conceived of as a social innovation that enabled access to micro-financial services by its members by taking collective responsibility for the latter. Subsequently extending loans and recovery of loans were also added as an important part of the VO responsibility. Savings was visualised as a 'common equity pool' (AKRSP 1983: 40) which would act as security against which VOs could borrow from outside agencies, as land was considered inadequate as collateral and many people did not have title deeds to land in the Northern Areas. Thus savings was considered as the security which AKRSP used to underwrite loans from commercial banks to VOs. VO savings were placed in accounts to which AKRSP was a co-signatory. The institutional innovation of the VO helped to reduce the transactions costs for farmers and for commercial banks as only one member was required to transact with the banks. The quantum of lending did not diminish as everyone had access to loans. The risk of default was covered by the common equity capital of residents of the same village. Mass default was prevented by making subsequent loans conditional on repayment of earlier ones. Increase in equity capital was motivated by linking VOs' borrowing to their savings according to a pre-specified ratio.

While there was a steadily growing number of formal sector banking institutions in the programme area, the outreach of these was limited to urban areas and households and businesses with the capacity for much larger savings. Commercial banks did not have mobile banking services and most villages were left still outside the reach of the formal banking sector institutions. By 2001, there were 28 branches of commercial banks and 21 branches of the Co-operative Bank in the Gilgit and Ghizer Districts. However, their coverage and outreach was restricted to the main towns. While the commercial banks have also been able to accumulate an impressive amount of deposits[2] these were in large measure generated from corporate and establishment accounts. A household survey undertaken by M. H. Khan in AKRSP's programme area in Gilgit in 1989 showed that only eight per cent of the household savings were invested with the V/WO, while 50 per cent were with banks or post offices, 21 per cent were in cash and 21 per cent were given out as loans to others However, AKRSP's savings programme met the needs of the rural poor households to save small amounts at regular intervals through the mechanism of the village and women's organisations. Thus while the commercial banks were able to attract the relatively larger accounts, AKRSP's savings programme helped attract the small savers

It is generally asserted by empirical studies that the rate of return offered on deposits is not as influential a consideration in the decision to save as other factors listed above (Von Pischke 1998), especially for the savers at the lower end of the spectrum. The fact that the money is earning some nominal return while being stored safely, and is accessible in one form or another, is good enough for the typical saver. However, AKRSP's experience with savings shows that the rate of return on savings does matter and influences the growth and trends in savings. Once the financial environment changed, there was a rapid decline in the rate of growth of savings between 1998 and 1999 and an overall decline in savings between 1999 and 2000. A major challenge to savings mobilisation was the low real and perceived returns being earned on savings under the then prevailing financial conditions in the country. High inflation, constant devaluation, declining deposit rates and economic instability compelled people towards greater present consumption. As commercial banks lowered their rates on variable-rate term deposits, V/WO members argued that their expected returns from savings deposited in banks were decreasing while AKRSP was increasing its Group Loan rates. The use of savings for generating greater returns was more likely to be practised by more mature V/WOs where members were able to calculate their returns and compare them with other market options available. The question that was frequently asked was whether it wouldn't be better for the VO to just use its own savings rather than take a loan from AKRSP. In response, many VOs initiated the practice of internal lending, as a result of the lowering of interest rates offered by banks and the increase in service charges by AKRSP on different loan products. These V/WOs started withdrawing their savings from banks and using them for on-lending purposes. This practice was most widespread in the Gilgit region and in particular in Hunza where trading opportunities with China made off-farm and trade options more attractive. This practice grew rapidly between 1996 and 2000 and it is estimated that a total of Rs 71 million was being used for lending to members internally by the V/WOs. In 1998, these issues presented a real challenge in the management of the Group Loan (V/WOCP) portfolio.

AKRSP's savings programme was important in that it demonstrated the significant potential of savings at the village level in an area which was considered well below the national income level. By the end of 2002, a total of Rs 430 million had been generated by the Village and Women's Organisations as savings and Rs 200 million had been extended as credit. By the end of 2002, cumulative credit of more than Rs 1.7 billion had been provided in about 600,000 lending operations since the initiation of the credit programme in 1983.[3] The demonstrated potential for savings also opened the wide spectrum of financial autonomy and innovation at the village level through the internal lending mechanism and informal trading opportunities.

The use of savings to promote empowerment in the AKRSP approach was given considerably more importance than the financial factors for savings discussed above. Indeed, for women, savings provided the first opportunity for owning an asset. This approach can explain much about the way AKRSP's savings programme developed. Savings in AKRSP's conception was an extremely important tool for social intermediation and developing the grass roots capacity for self-help (Bennett *et al.* 1996). Some felt that there was too much emphasis in the AKRSP approach on savings as a tool for social cohesion and felt that AKRSP should consider developing a savings strategy which graduated from savings as a means of empowerment to a demand-driven financial service approach in which individual financial needs were targeted. It was said that this would represent a major philosophical shift in the organisation, requiring a new way of looking at the rationale behind savings and the reasons for promoting savings (World Bank 2002).

There was some ambiguity at the start as to whether AKRSP's original objective of generating a collective capital base implied that the savings were to be used for collective development initiatives with these funds. Even though AKRSP harboured this notion initially through its conception of the long-term comprehensive village development plan,[4] the practical difficulty of implementing this idea did not develop much further and community members did not have a common vision on the allocation and use of savings. In the beginning attempts by the villagers to use collective savings for entrepreneurial activity were discouraged, especially the setting up of shops. The Third Quarterly Progress Report from 1983 stressed that 'attempts were being made to make VOs understand the real use and purpose of equity capital i.e. to attract capital for promotion of agricultural activities because it is in agriculture that the well being of majority lies and not in shop-keeping.'[5] The idea of collective village development planning and implementation through collective loans did not get off the ground because individual farmers did not have a common perception about village development and considered this an individual sphere of activity. The actual outcome of the savings process has thus been collective only in promoting solidarity and empowerment, and only in managing the risk of credit given to individual members. The agglomeration of village savings for use in VO Banking, or Group

Loans as they were later called, also allowed the use of individual savings for collective purposes.

In 1991, the thinking at AKRSP was that the 'villagers had gained tremendous experience and have also generated a large amount of capital. The objective was to ensure village autonomy in development finance as the formal credit structure is unlikely to revise its rules, procedures and attitudes towards the small farmers. If the small farmers are to access credit for agricultural needs, as well as for other purposes, in a sustainable manner, then they will have to use their capital to create and manage their own financial institutions. This is the only way to ensure autonomy in development finance and to preserve the sovereignty of the village level participatory institutions in Northern Pakistan.'[6] Sadly this vision was never discussed with villagers to assess their views about it and no attempt was made to assess its feasibility or to operationalise it.

Where is the savings programme today? The VOs continue with their savings with or without AKRSP. Some VOs and WOs also lost much of their savings as a result of AKRSP's policy to deduct loan defaults from collective savings which villagers had pledged in order to access the group loans. AKRSP was not very mindful of the fact that within the same organisation the borrowers may have been different from the savers—and often were. Many of the VOs and WOs have learnt from this experience and have stopped borrowing from AKRSP and only lend money from their internal lending programme. Other organisations have stopped giving out loans altogether and focus only on savings. The main thing is that the savings programme continues unharnessed and unabated. AKRSP in one sense has lost control of the savings programme and has unleashed an energy which is now being guided by the villagers themselves.

What has happened to these savings after the establishment of the First Micro-Finance Bank (FMFB)? While the villagers are still saving through the VOs, it is unclear how effectively the FMFB will be able to generate and collect savings from the Northern Areas. The FMFB currently has five branches in the Northern Areas and two in Chitral. The potential opportunity to use the members' savings as equity capital for the bank or to buy the members an ownership in the FMFB was never assessed or used. The conception of the bank as something which would emerge from the grass roots and be a natural progression of the savings programme was severed by the decision to generate equity capital from other sources to establish the Bank. How this could have been achieved and whether the members would have agreed to this option is another matter. The option was never fully explored. It is unlikely that the VOs and WOs would even have invested in the bank had they been given a choice, especially in view of the projections of its sustainability. The FMFB has to compete with other banks to attract member savings. Villagers have become very smart in assessing rates of return on savings and carefully consider their options. Interviews with both men and women reveal an incredible knowledge about the rates of return that they can earn from different banks, and VO and WO savings are invested with a wide range of banks in the north. The fact that the FMFB has to struggle for attracting the VO and WO savings is a testament to the autonomy and empowerment the savings programme has imparted to the people of the Northern Areas. This might perhaps be AKRSP's greatest contribution.

Some attribute AKRSP's success in persuading a large number of people to save with the VOs and WOs as a phenomenon peculiar to its perception as an Ismailiya Organisation. The large differential in savings growth between the Ismaili and non-Ismaili areas in the Northern Areas and Chitral is pointed to in support of this contention. While it is true that the greatest development in terms of savings and the internal lending programme happened in upper Hunza which is completely Ismaili, it is also true that it is upper Hunza which offers the greatest potential in terms of tourism and trade with China. Nevertheless, how an organisation is perceived locally is important because it implies that other organisations encouraging savings among their members may not be as successful. In fact, some of the other Rural Support Programmes (RSPs) have not been very successful in generating savings and no other NGO is pursuing savings as vigourously as AKRSP did or has had the success of AKRSP in this regard.

Some of the key lessons that can be highlighted from AKRSP's experience of savings include the following:

- A well developed social mobilisation strategy is required to mobilise savings on the scale that was made possible by AKRSP.
- It is possible to develop an effective model of generating savings from the rural poor.
- A two-tiered savings system is required to preserve the distinction between individual and collective savings.
- Savings provide an effective entry-point for organising women and generating savings from them and can be an important means of empowerment for women.
- The key preferences of clients should be kept in mind while shaping the features of a savings programme such as safety, liquidity, returns and cost.
- The returns on savings are an important feature of the savings programme and strongly influence the motivation and trend in savings.
- Members will capitalise on the opportunities for financial arbitrage and develop strategies which will help them take advantage of these opportunities in their financial decisions.
- AKRSPs use of savings as a tool for social cohesion kept it from developing innovative savings products and there has been virtually no change in the savings product offered by AKRSP's portfolio in the last twenty years
- A well conceptualised savings programme with a clear vision about its future allows the development of institutional arrangements that can help support this vision.

What Lessons Can be Learnt from AKRSP's Credit Experience?

When AKRSP first initiated its operations it had not systematically planned a credit programme for its clients. AKRSP entered the credit market when it realised that its clients needed loans for agricultural production and investments. Addressing itself to this need, AKRSP in its Third Quarterly Progress Report stated that, 'in order to enable the VOs to undertake development projects, AKRSP has decided that it will help arrange loans from commercial banks. Such loans will also partially help to satisfy the expectation of VOs for further help once the first PPI [Productive Physical Infrastructure] has been completed'. However, the existing supply of credit from the formal sector banks could not be easily tapped due to high transactions costs, minimum loan size, cumbersome disbursement procedures and lengthy processing periods. Thus while the formal financial sector disbursed a large amount in loans, only a relatively small segment of the population was reached by this sector. It is instructive to note that when AKRSP initiated its operations an interest-free production loan scheme was available from the commercial sector which entitled small holders to a loan of Rs 6,000 per crop. However, not a single such loan had been advanced to the potential 28,000 farm households in the Gilgit region due to the difficulty in accessing these loans and the small size of loan required by the people in the Northern Areas. There has been rapid growth in AKRSP's credit disbursements from Rs 1 million in 1983 to a high of Rs 276 million in 1997 and Rs 175 million in 2002. There has been a gradual decline in credit disbursements partly due to reduced demand and partly due to AKRSP's attempt to reduce its portfolio at risk. The reduction in demand was due in part to the increasing tendency of internal lending. In 2000, at least one-third of the V/WOs had been provided with loans through internal lending.

AKRSP first ventured into offering loans to its clients through the intervention of established formal banking sector institutions, as it had made no provision for a revolving fund for credit from its own sources and had not developed a policy on interest rates either. In early 1983, AKRSP embarked upon a loaning programme with the approval of its Board of Directors and the availability of a sum of Rs 200,000 from the Habib Bank Limited from its interest-free production loan portfolio on the surety of AKRSP. In February 1983, AKRSP extended its first fertiliser loan to 46 VOs. The average loan size per borrower was only Rs 174 and the total loan amount disbursed was Rs 621,086. In 1984 AKRSP provided medium term credit through the National Development Finance Corporation (NDFC) which provided a soft loan of Rs 5 million to AKRSP. Since then, AKRSP donors have also provided grant funds for credit in the shape of a revolving fund. This early success of AKRSP acting as a social intermediary for wholesale commercial credit and its quick disbursement of this credit was a path-breaking development and was later emulated by many other banks such as the First Women's Bank, the Khyber Bank and the Khushali Bank.

AKRSP's credit chronology illustrates its dynamic and innovative nature. AKRSP has experimented with many types of different loan products since its inception in 1983. In designing its loan products, AKRSP appears to have struggled with balancing several different motivations. Chronologically, its main motivation at first was to try and address the needs of the small farmer through short-term and medium-term loans which were initially extended from anywhere between 12 to 60 months. The utilisation of the medium-term loans indicates that except for loans utilised for agricultural machinery, a period of 12 months was sufficient for medium-term loans, and that even people who had taken loans for five years for land development generally exceeded their targets within two years. As such the medium-term loan was discontinued.

Table 7.1. AKRSP's savings and loan products 1982–2001

Financial Product	Year introduced	Year withdrawn	Interest rate (f) flat, (d) decl. balance
Community savings	1982		
Short term loans	1983	1999	0
Medium term loans	1984	1999	8%
Village Banking or Group loans to VOs (V/WOCP)	1989		15%
Enterprise credit loans ECP	1992		16%, raised to 24% in 1998
Corporate Credit loans	1996	1999	
Business Committee loans	2000		

AKRSP realised that some progressive VOs were experimenting with a village credit system that met not only the agricultural needs of its members but also other credit requirements. AKRSP also noted that the credit needs of the VO did not exceed the current volume of its savings in 1989. Therefore, under the guidance of Dr Akhtar Hameed Khan, AKRSP tried to use the institutional device of the VO for the introduction of Village Organisation Banking in 1989. The VO banking idea marks an important conceptual beginning in AKRSP's thinking about the VO's role. The manner in which AKRSP's short-term and medium-term credit operated meant it was the VO which had primarily shouldered the responsibility of the management and disbursement of its loans. AKRSP soon realised that it was the VO which had determined the quantum of loan for each member, managed disbursements and recovered the loan from individual members It was felt, therefore, that the VO had proved its competence in handling the entire loan operations without reference to the Regional Programme Office of AKRSP. The only function that the Regional Programme Officers (RPOs) and the Social Organiser (SO) were performing was monitoring and account-keeping. As a consequence, AKRSP developed a package of Village Banking under which an amount equivalent to VO savings was advanced to VOs for onward loaning to members. The VO savings was invested in Deposit Certificates and other high interest bearing accounts held jointly in the name of the VO concerned and AKRSP.[7] The VO paid a 7 per cent interest rate[8] as a service charge on the money advanced and the VO was asked to charge 15 per cent to individual members, which was equivalent to the profits VO members were earning on their savings at that time. In addition, AKRSP developed guidelines and provided training to VO representatives. Later, the VO Banking was renamed Group Loans due to reservations by the State Bank on terming this activity VO Banking. However, some of the problems with internal lending pointed to the need for some sort of supervision and regulation of the programme.

Box 7.1. Issues and problems with VO banking

- VO capital was instantly disbursed and there was little element of planning.
- The equity element was often ignored.
- Variability in service charges that were being levied.
- In some VOs the Credit Committee established to oversee the loan disbursements and recoveries was bypassed.
- VO accounts and records were not being maintained in some VOs.
- Lack of clarity regarding the recovery of the capital, its value-added and renewal.
- Loans were given for commercial purposes often for use outside the village.
- No reserve funds were maintained to meet unforeseen losses and contingencies.
- Loans were given for 12 months which did not allow for a high turnover.
- AKRSP relaxed its requirement for recovering the VO capital at the end of twelve months and only service charges were paid to AKRSP at the end of twelve months, which meant that AKRSP did not know what was going on within the VO.

The year 1996 marked the start of a new period for AKRSP in which it became mindful of financial sustainability and moved towards the identification of loan products with high returns which could justify the levying market interest rates. AKRSP acquired a more enterprise development orientation and tried to capitalise on off-farm opportunities through the introduction of a small enterprise development loan and a corporate credit programme. These were important products for AKRSP as it was trying to deepen an existing market in which possibilities of geographic expansion were limited due to the self-imposed delimitation of its area of operation.[9] In the last few years, AKRSP has been particularly driven by its objective of developing high yielding products that would enhance its financial sustainability. This led to experimentation with products that had high risk and targeted a sector that was not part of AKRSP's original target group. AKRSP learned important lessons from the introduction of these products. One of the most important was that the skewed debt-equity ratio in the small enterprise loan was such that it was difficult for the borrower to service the loan. There was need for AKRSP to invest in equity rather than service a loan which it was beyond the capacity of the small business to repay. AKRSP had no policy for equity investments. This was a critical finding for AKRSP as the product which was projected to make its micro-finance operations sustainable was the enterprise development loans and not group loans. In the feasibility projections prepared for the new bank, the fastest growing product from which the profits were projected were the Small and Medium Enterprise (SME) loans. Thus it has grave implications for micro-finance that the potential for this product appeared limited in the Northern Areas.

In recent years, AKRSP has placed itself under enormous pressure to introduce products to increase its sustainability. In the process, AKRSP has been under pressure to expand its credit portfolio rapidly without proper appraisal procedures and has also experimented with poorly performing products, and those that may not be entirely appropriate to its objectives of social and economic development. While AKRSP has been very active in evaluating its loan products and quick to terminate poorly performing products and review its internal policies and procedures, it has lost some of its early focus on the needs of its main target group and has deviated somewhat from its overall mandate of providing micro-finance services to the rural poor. This has happened even more after the establishment of the FMFB, as the main focus of the Bank is on urban areas.

There has been a marked difference in the rate of growth of different loan products. Part of this can be attributed to the difference in the features of the loans, and part to an internal policy that prefers group loans to individual loans and stipulates that a ratio of 70:30 be maintained between the two types of loans. The group loans reduce the transactions cost of AKRSP, place a higher transactions cost on the members, carry greater risk for members who are net savers but have a service charge of between 15 per cent to 18 per cent[10] and are cheaper than the individual loans. The individual loans place a higher transactions cost on AKRSP, are riskier as they are not collateralised but are higher yielding as AKRSP levies a service charge of 24 per cent. The ratio of group loans to individual loans stood at 76:24 in 2000. An analysis of the cumulative loans disbursed in the three regions shows a marked difference in the proportion of the two types of loans. At one stage the proportion of individual loans in Baltistan was as high as 62 per cent as a result of the runaway expansion of the individual loan portfolio in Baltistan District between 1996–1998. Subsequently, there was a high default rate in individual loans and in Baltistan large amounts had to be written off.

AKRSP's policy on interest rates was not very well considered at the start of its operations. Even in 1983, interest-free loans were not considered best practice in rural finance. Yet AKRSP began with a policy of a zero interest rate and only slowly graduated to a policy of charging market rates. The policy on interest rates in the beginning was patterned on the formal sector policy of providing interest-free agricultural production loans and was partly based on the belief that poor farmers would not have the capacity to pay market rates. Later AKRSP decided to impose a 10 per cent per annum service charge, starting with the marketing loans. This policy coincided with the abolition of the interest-free production loans by the government. The first medium-term loans were given on very soft terms i.e. 5 per cent per annum. However, the service charge on these loans has been progressively increased to the market level and in 1989 varied from a minimum of 10 per cent to a maximum of 15 per cent. AKRSP first began charging market rates of interest in 1992 when it felt it had developed a loan product which was appropriate for the commercially oriented investor and justified the levying of market rates. In its first decade of operation, there was not much notion at AKRSP that interest rates should be based on a careful analysis of delivery costs, recovery rates or sustainability of its micro-finance operations. In this AKRSP acted very much with a rural development orientation and not as a financial institution with sustainability as its objective.

AKRSP's policy on collateral has been very instructive and other organisations can learn from its experience. AKRSP realised that using land as collateral was not possible in the Northern Areas due to the limited availability of land titles. However, AKRSP also realised that even if land deeds had been available it would have been difficult to use them as collateral as this would have enhanced the transactions cost of processing loans without adding much value. Moreover, in case of default, enforcement of repayment through recourse to formal mechanisms would have been difficult and would have eroded the spirit of trust and partnership on which AKRSP's approach was premised. Therefore, AKRSP did not demand collateral for short-term loans. For marketing loans a 100 per cent cash collateral was required. In case of medium-term loans which were given for a period greater than 12 months, the VO had to furnish 30 per cent cash collateral. It notionally treated this savings as collateral for loans. In the case of default these collective savings were used as collateral, which presented a huge problem to the savings and credit programme as the savings belonged to one set of people and the loans had been taken by another.[11] The basic cornerstone of the lending policy was the issue of collective savings as collateral. This policy can be questioned on ethical grounds as many AKRSP clients lost their savings due to no fault of their own but simply because they had given surety for others.

As a result of its collateral policy in which its loans were completely covered, AKRSP's overall record of repayment has been excellent. The programme has disbursed Rs 1.7 billion in different types of loan products between 1983 and 2002 and has recovered 99 per cent of this amount. There is a marked regional difference in the pattern of repayments by region and gender. In 1999 Chitral had the smallest percentage of overdue loans at the end of December 2000, as its overdue loans stood at 18 per cent of total outstanding loans, followed by Gilgit District at 24 per cent. Baltistan with 48 per cent of its loans overdue had the worst record. Women appeared to be much better at timely repayments and in each region the amount of loans overdue by WOs was much lower when compared with loans borrowed by men. An analysis of the credit portfolio of AKRSP reveals that there has not been a marked change in the amount of loans overdue at the end of each financial period in the last six years. The credit portfolio at risk showed an increase in each region at the beginning of 2000. However, the overall portfolio at risk has declined due to the policy of writing off bad loans at the Core office.

Some assert that AKRSP's credit programme became a supply driven programme in some respects. Its policy of giving the VO and WO managers a commission of 2 to 3 per cent for recovery of loans encouraged them to push for large amounts of loans on the recovery of which they would make a substantial commission. This, combined with the system of VO banking in which the VOs took the major decision about who would get the loans, encouraged quick disbursements without proper appraisal, and minimum supervision led to the increase in defaults against which collective savings were pledged and entailed huge losses for unsuspecting savers. AKRSP had successfully transferred the entire risk of its credit programme to the VO and WOS. Weary from this experience many VOs and WOs had branched off on their own and were running their own successful internal lending and savings programme. Thus when the FMFB came along it became just another player on the scene and did not impact these organisations.

The following key lessons emerge from AKRSP's credit operations:

- Product development needs to be closely aligned and balanced with the various objectives of the organisation such as meeting the needs of the target group, efficiency and financial sustainability.
- Interest rate policy needs to be carefully considered from the outset, focusing on sustainability rather than based on notions of the borrower's capacity to repay.
- Policy of collateral should be developed in a manner which helps to retain the advantages of micro-finance without eroding the social basis on which micro-finance lending is provided.
- Local capacity of VOs can be built to undertake on-lending operations by managing, disbursing and putting a system for recovery in place with proper guidelines, supervision and training.

- The autonomous operation of VOs in micro-finance needs to be balanced with some form of regulation to ensure transparency, equity, efficiency and cost recovery.
- The debt-equity ratio in small enterprise loans needs to be balanced in a manner that allows the borrower to service the loan properly.
- Policy of paying commission to local agents for loan recovery needs to be watched so that it does not encourage a supply driven approach to credit.

Did AKRSP by Inclusion of Micro-Finance as a Key Part of its Activities Promote an Unsustainable Model of Community Mobilisation and Organisation?

Did AKRSP's savings programme achieve its initial objective of social mobilisation? At the group level, AKRSP's experience demonstrated that saving through the V/WO can provide a community with a sense of empowerment due to its ability to generate large sums of money from its own sources. However, the sustainability of the savings and credit programme is inextricably linked to the sustainability of the Village and Women's Organisations. AKRSP has been finding it difficult to sustain these organisations in the absence of significant village level activity and investment. The most active phase of a VO's existence is during the construction of the PPI scheme. AKRSP has been hard pressed to find ways to keep the organisations active. From time to time, opportunities such as those presented by the implementation of the physical works under the Khushal Pakistan Programme and others provided a brief spurt of activity and interest. Some assert that it is difficult to keep an organisation alive based on a savings programme alone. While this may be generally true it is not true of many women's organisations. Women in the Northern Areas attach such a high value to savings alone that many of their organisations are not only alive but actively engaged in many activities as a result of their savings programme. Many women's organisations meet either weekly or monthly to collect their savings and are running internal lending programmes with a part of their savings. In some cases they have hired male managers who help them manage their savings and credit programme for a small fee.

The question of whether the inclusion of micro-finance eroded the collective spirit of co-operatives arises because of the tensions inherent in the collective community interest and individual self-interest, AKRSP's policy of using the collective savings as collateral for individual default and the dichotomies implicit in its conception of the village organisation as a hybrid credit union. While one of the objectives of a credit union, like that of the VO, is to encourage its members to save and to obtain a reasonable rate of interest on these savings (promotion of thrift), there is another objective which can be construed as being directly in conflict with this, which is to create sources of credit at a fair and reasonable rate. The lower the interest rate charged on credit, the lower the interest allowable on deposits. Furthermore, the manner in which AKRSP was using collective savings as a collateral for individual default not only had the potential of dividing the village organisation but destroyed the VOs and WOs in many villages where individual default was realised through collective savings. In practice, some of the VOs later fell into disarray because collective savings were used to remit individual debt, members in charge of savings began either to embezzle collective savings or to provide cheap loans on a preferential basis to selected members.

There was some concern within AKRSP that internal lending jeopardised the savings of the V/WO members and that defaults could erode the basis of social organisation at the village level. The social dynamics of each village are different but because of the close personal relations it may be difficult for members to refuse the use of their savings to members whom they have known all their lives. Furthermore, in some villages, a disturbing trend which emerged was that a few powerful borrowers dominated decision-making and could jeopardise the savings of the V/WO members. Apart from the concern for protecting the small savers, AKRSP assessed that many of the organisations did not have the requisite financial management capacity to be able to mange an effective internal lending programme. There is also evidence that some of the organisations are under pressure due to internal conflict and dissension. It is estimated that around 8 per cent of the V/WOs are under social stress because of internal conflict. Moreover, there are also likely to be a growing number of organisations that are unable to deal with the conflicts that may arise as a result of the high risk activities of internal lending that they are engaged in. Case studies conducted by AKRSP of model VOs show that there is rapid attrition in these organisations following problems of loan repayments.

Could AKRSP have learnt any lessons about this issue from the early co-operative history? There are important aspects in which AKRSP's micro-finance programme was similar to the early co-operatives and equally important aspects in which it was dissimilar. For example, if one examines some of the rules drafted by the Third Co-operative Congress held in London in April 1832 which represents the first attempt in the systematic self-regulation of co-operatives, one can make a comparison with AKRSP. This congress decided that 'it was universally understood that the grand ultimate object of all co-operative societies whether engaged in trading, manufacturing or agricultural pursuits, was community on land'. It is interesting to look at some of these rules and compare them with AKRSP's savings and credit model that was designed 150 years later (see Box 7.2).

Box 7.2. Comparison between the third co-operative congress and AKRSP

Third Co-operative Congress (1832)

A weekly subscription, either in money, goods or labour from a penny to any other amount agreed upon, is indispensably necessary to be continued from year to year, until a capital sufficient to accomplish the object of the society be accumulated.

It is the unanimous decision of the delegates here assembled, that the capital accumulated by such associations should be rendered indivisible,

It is deemed more especially essential in all the trading transactions of co-operative societies that credit shall be neither taken nor given as deviation from this important principle has been the sole cause of the destruction of so many previous societies.

Aga Khan Rural Support Programme (1982)

Weekly savings no matter how small which in the initial phase had to be accumulated to achieve the objectives of the VO.

The savings were initially treated as indivisible and no withdrawals were allowed even though members were given individual passbooks for recording individual savings.

There was no credit component in the VO model when it first emerged at AKRSP but very quickly loans were included as a key aspect of AKRSP's model of rural development.

Many of AKRSP's village organisations began operating like credit unions upon the initiation of their internal lending activities in the late 1990s. These VOs fall fairly neatly into the definition of credit unions (Berthoud and Hinton 1989) as they offer loans to their members out of the pool of savings that are built up by the members themselves. The seeds of this were laid by the savings programme and the introduction of the Village Organisation Banking model in 1989 which gave greater autonomy to the VO and provided them a model that eventually led them to use their own funds to initiate their internal lending programme. The VO began using their own funds when they found loans from AKRSP too expensive and once their own savings invested with commercial banks stopped earning high returns.

Did AKRSP Pursue Sustainability as a Key Aspect of its Micro-Finance Programme?

In answering this question, it is useful to divide AKRSP's micro-finance history into two distinct phases; 1982 to 1996 and post-1996. There is no evidence that AKRSP tried to pursue sustainability as a key aspect of its micro-finance programme in its first fourteen years. AKRSP initiated its micro-finance programme with the primary objective to mobilise people and better serve their micro-finance needs. Sustainability was not a factor in this equation. There was no information ever collected in its first decade and a half to estimate the cost of the savings or the credit programme. AKRSP's evolution and expansion is in sharp contrast with programmes like Kashf which begin with a clear analysis of how they could achieve sustainability. In Kashf, for instance, this analysis was undertaken for the branch level and it guided the operations of the NGO from the first day. The Field Management Unit (FMU) of AKRSP which can be considered the equivalent of a branch was never regarded as a separate cost centre at AKRSP until after 1996. AKRSP could also have learnt from the experience of the Lachi Poverty Reduction Project which many years later tried to develop a sustainable model of micro-finance at the Union Council level and undertook a detailed analysis in this regard. A comparison of these two models with AKRSP shows the extent to which sustainability was disregarded at AKRSP.

Figure 7.1. Comparative analysis of AKRSP's model of sustainability with other NGOS

Programme Features	Kashf	Lachi Poverty Reduction Project	AKRSP
Geographical Focus	Urban and peri-urban areas	Rural	Rural
Model of sustainability	The NGO has developed a model under which sustainability is being pursued at the branch level	The project has developed a model of micro-credit that it hopes to make sustainable at the union council level	1982–1996: No model 1996: 2003: Focused on FMU for performance evaluation purposes but no calculations of sustainability
Break-even point or sustainability defined as the branch being able to meet its own costs	For achieving break-even or sustainability at branch level Kashf needs 1100 borrowers per branch	For achieving break-even, the project team estimates that they will need to disburse a minimum of Rs 6.5 million per union council to around 1200 borrowers[12]	No cost calculations for FMU level sustainability Estimated that AKRSP's operations could not be sustainable if they only operated in the Northern Areas and Chitral
Achievement	Of its 16 branches, 10 were currently sustainable and the rest were expected to become sustainable by June 2003	By the end of March 2002, the project had disbursed Rs 4 million to 820 households in Shakardara Union Council	Sustainability was never achieved
Policy on sustainability	Branches are closed if they do not reach break-even within a specified period	No specified policy	No policy of closure

AKRSP staff first became mindful of sustainability issues when they attended the Boulder Course on micro-finance which radically transformed their thinking about the management of micro-finance at AKRSP. At this juncture AKRSP decided to reorient its operations and build a financially sustainable micro-finance programme. The first step they took was to establish a separate micro-finance section which employed specialised micro-finance officers who took primary responsibility for delivering financial services out of AKRSP's FMUs. Day to day decision-making responsibility was decentralised further. Micro-finance Officers in the field were given authority to sanction loans. The micro-finance programme costs, budget, and income were separated from the rest of AKRSP. Excess funds in various AKRSP accounts were allocated to the Micro-Finance Programmes credit pool, and any funds from this pool in excess of the loan portfolio were invested with banks to earn a return. A manual of Credit Policies and Procedures and a monthly Credit Operations Report were established to improve the management of credit operations.

Although AKRSP's operating cost ratio did not change significantly between 1995 and 2000, there has been a significant change in the income and operating costs of AKRSP. The income from service charges increased almost five-fold between 1995 and 2000. This is explained by the increase in the interest rates, improved loan recovery performance and the increase in loan volumes in the intervening period. However, the most significant increase has come from the income from investments. There was no income being generated from investments in 1995. However, by the end of 2000, AKRSP improved its fund management by investing its idle funds in high yielding returns.

In the same period, AKRSP strengthened its Micro-Finance Section with the addition of Micro-Finance Officers at the field level, from 6 in 1995 to 31 by the end of 2000. In addition, a Loan Portfolio Auditor, a Financial Analyst, and a Systems Analyst were added to its Core Staff. AKRSP also created a separate cost centre for the Micro-Finance Programme and all direct and indirect costs were charged to the Micro-Finance Programme in an attempt to estimate the real costs of the programme and help it in its move towards financial sustainability. As a result, the operating costs of the Micro-Finance Programme increased from Rs 2.8 million in 1995 to Rs 19.41 million in 2000. However, AKRSP's micro-finance programme did not achieve sustainability, and the feasibility study for the FMFB projected that AKRSP could not achieve sustainability if it continued to operate only within the Northern Areas and Chitral and that sustainability considerations required expansion into other areas of Pakistan.

It would be fair to recognise that AKRSP's investment in micro-finance entailed a substantial investment in human resource development and in enhancing the financial management skills of men and women managing the savings and credit operations at the village level and the NGO level throughout its twenty years. AKRSP had also devised a very effective system of training at the grass roots level and from the outset focused on the training of a cadre of village activists in micro-finance operations, accounts and audits. One of AKRSPs' greatest achievements has been the awareness it has created about micro-finance operations and the possibilities of financial arbitrage. By the year 2000, AKRSP had a professional staff strength of 63 in its Micro-Finance Section including nine staff members in the Core Office. Each Micro-Finance Officer was responsible for overseeing the accounts of on average 70 organisations. This staff was supported by 178 Village-level Field Accountants (FA) charged with the responsibility of auditing the accounts of Village and Women's Organisations for a fee of Rs 300 per organisation on a six-monthly basis. One FA was on average supervising 21 Village and Women's Organisations. The team of Field Accountants included 23 female accountants. Each organisation had a manager for maintaining the books and record-keeping of village accounts. Where it was not possible to find a literate woman, men were nominated by the women to manage their accounts.

The question is, why did AKRSP not worry about sustainability in its early years? There are several answers to this question. There are virtually no barriers to entry in the field of micro-finance in Pakistan. The Micro-Finance Ordinance does not apply to NGOs. Thus there is no training required, no regulation and no experience required for someone wanting to enter the micro-finance arena. An NGO may get staff with no previous experience in micro-finance and hence no orientation towards sustainability or even understanding of how this is to be achieved. As such, the direction which an organisation takes does not often depend upon an overall vision for the institution but individual proclivities. Furthermore, when AKRSP started its operations, donor funding was readily available at zero per cent interest rate for financing its credit operations. AKRSP eventually put all the grants it had received as revolving credit funds into one high yield account which it used to finance its micro-finance operations. An organisation which has a financial self-sufficiency ratio of over 300 per cent is not going to be overly concerned about sustainability at the field level. Does this imply that cheap donor funds actually impeded the quest for financial sustainability at AKRSP in its first decade and a half?

Just prior to its decision to separate its micro-finance operations in preparation of the establishment of the First Micro-Finance Bank, AKRSP's Subsidy Dependence Index was estimated to be around a negative 130 per cent. This favourable ratio was due to the fact that AKRSP was using its own funds for its credit programme and could borrow at concessional rates of 6 per cent from the Pakistan Poverty Alleviation Fund. Furthermore, AKRSP's income from its investments provided the major source of funds. Its operating cost ratio was 4.6 per cent and its operating self-sufficiency ratio was estimated to be as high as 300 per cent due to the large amount of income it earned from its other investments. AKRSP realised that its scale was not increasing in the sense of both its client base and its volume of lending. AKRSP believes that with the creation of the FMFB it can eventually make its operations sustainable. It plans to cross-subsidise and use the profits from its urban branches to sustain rural areas. The shareholders of the FMFB are not pushing for a profit for the first five years and this gives the FMFB some breathing space.

AKRSP's credit operations are not directly comparable with most Micro-finance NGOs operating in Pakistan[13] due to the very small size of their loan portfolios compared to AKRSP, different implementation methodologies and the limited time for which they have been in existence. However, a comparison of AKRSP with other NGOs in the Micro-Finance Group indicate an overall favourable picture of AKRSP's micro-finance programme. AKRSP's financial self-sufficiency ratio is the highest in the Group due to its large volume of loans and income from other investments. AKRSP's operating cost ratio is among the lowest, but this is due to its large volume of performing assets that may have reached a saturation point while the volume of loans may be growing for other NGOs relative to their costs. Returns on performing assets indicated that while AKRSP was not earning as high a return as some of the other NGOs like Kashf (17 per cent), OPP (19 per cent) or DAMEN (24 per cent), it was earning 15 per cent which was the average return.

Lessons from AKRSP's Model of Institutional Development and Growth

The policy environment for micro-finance underwent rapid change as a result of the promulgation of the Micro-Finance Ordinance in 2001. The enforcement of this Ordinance has opened up new opportunities and challenges for the micro-finance sector in Pakistan. The main benefit from registering as a bank is that the organisation would be allowed to take deposits and use its funds, an advantage that was denied to AKRSP due to the restrictions on NGOs on taking deposits. As a result an NGO's decision to transform itself into a bank is inextricably linked to its savings potential and the cost-efficacy of the model it can develop to generate savings. However, this decision has to be taken very carefully, as the prudential regulations impose a high cost on the establishment of a bank by requiring a heavy equity investment and its requirement of regular audits, branch features, security arrangements, etc. In AKRSP's case, the startling fact is that the savings of AKRSPs VOs and WOs were not automatically saved with the FMFB as most were tied in long-term government bonds and could not be liquidated. The FMFB will be unable to draw upon what was presumed to be one of its principal advantages—the savings of its clients—and will have to begin the long arduous journey of raising a savings base all over again.

While AKRSP has always been very mindful of an exit strategy it has not successfully been able to evolve such a strategy. Encouraged by donors, AKRSP was constantly pressed into thinking about its future institutional growth. It was felt that 'an overarching principle for AKRSP to adopt was to ensure the long-term sustainability of its initiatives and to transfer some of its functions to successor institutions.'[14] It was felt that one function which could be shifted was the credit and banking operations of AKRSP. However, there was not enough thought on how this could be achieved. While there had been a prolific increase in the number of V/WOs, the long-term growth and development of these organisations was always a question mark. Furthermore, even though there was considerable debate on the formalisation of the VOs and the benefits and advantages that would accrue from registering them as formal entities, this discussion never really got off the ground. Regardless of these discussions, one of the most significant aspects that emerges from AKRSP's experience with the community based approach to micro-finance was the institutional development that took place at the village level.

The concept of Village Organisation Banking introduced by AKRSP was a novel concept in that it established a community owned and operated system of micro-finance at the grass roots level. Under the autonomy that was given to the VOs under this component, they determined the quantum of loan for each member and managed disbursements and recovery from individual members. The VO had the freedom to set their own service charge rates, although AKRSP recommended that 24 per cent per annum be charged. In 1989 data from 24 Village Organisation Banks (VOBs) in the Gilgit region indicated that there was a wide range of service charges actually levied ranging from a minimum of 8 per cent to a maximum of 20 per cent with an average of 14.5 per cent.[15] The VOs demonstrated their competence to handle the entire loaning operation without reference to the regional office. This led to the expectation that somehow VOs would play a key role in the future management and ownership of the micro-finance portfolio of

AKRSP. However, this operation also needed some form of regulation in view of the wide divergence in the manner in which some VOs were dealing with the disbursements of loans. Furthermore, the villagers' demonstrated capacity to generate large savings had also led to the expectation that the villagers would have a stake in the institutional development and formalisation of the micro-finance programme.

In the thinking that emerged around 1989 it was felt that there was a need for the formation of a sustainable banking system as a continuation of the present credit and savings programme[16] and that the VO would play a critical role in it. The objective would be to maintain the sanctity of the VOs while being intrinsic to the grass root developments of the whole region. This view was expressed within AKRSP by the Finance Manager who stated clearly that 'one of the long-term objectives of AKRSP was to establish a financial institution which should be subsequently owned, operated, managed and funded by the villagers of the Northern Areas of Pakistan on a self-supporting and self-sustaining basis.'[17] The Finance Manager admitted that a charter did not currently exist but the proposed bank was expected to take the 'form of a public company with its shareholding restricted to AKRSP and its member VOs, and AKRSP's share would eventually be taken up by VOs so that the ownership could eventually be transferred to these VOs.' This thinking was echoed in the report prepared by a team of consultants from the Shorebank Advisory Services[18] at the end of the same year and they also noted a 'strong desire for a member-owned bank that would responsively finance economic activities and operate conveniently located depository facilities.' The Houghton group recommended that VO members must buy ownership of the financial institution and over time, through increased ownership earn a larger voice in its management. This team recommended that a permanent and self-sustaining Investment Organisation (IO) should be established as a separately incorporated institution or a separately managed window of AKRSP, primarily to serve VOs. It was recommended that this IO should be operationally distinct from the non-financial parts of AKRSP's programmes. It was felt that the VOs must put shares into the IO, earning a stake in its management, and VO shareholders should assume eventual management control of the IO. While this proposal established the principal of the VO being an integral part of any future organisation for micro-finance development, it was fraught with misgivings due to its suggestion that all the VOs put their savings in one account from which automatic deductions should be made in case of VO defaults.

In 1990 it was felt that the challenge for AKRSP was to formalise its credit programme so that dependence on AKRSP was minimised, yet ensuring that the genuine credit needs of the small farmers were met.[19] The objective was to ensure 'village autonomy in development finance, as the formal credit structure was unlikely to revise the rules, procedures and attitudes towards the small farmer. If the small farmers were to access credit for agricultural needs as well as for other purposes, in a sustainable manner, then they would have to use their capital to create and manage their own financial institutions.'[20] This was considered to be the only way to ensure autonomy in development finance and to preserve the sovereignty of the village level participatory institutions in Northern Pakistan. There was a strong argument for a key role for the VO in the future institutional model chosen to manage the micro-finance programme. The VOB operation demonstrated a rudimentary model of how this could be achieved and the experience with internal lending demonstrated the fact that VOs were willing to undertake and manage the risk entailed in micro-finance operations. In its early discussion of the Bank, AKRSP presented it as a VOB and the operation of village level banking was a typical example of a semi-formal financial institution. 'As soon as the VOBs fell under the regulation of the State Bank and were therefore legal, they would become formal financial operators.'[21]

While it is very clear that there was strong support for the idea of formalising AKRSP's micro-finance portfolio, it is also very clear that the initial conception of this formalisation was to make the VOs an integral part of the ownership and the management of the micro-finance operations. However, when AKRSP's decision to establish a bank was finally taken it was done without any role for the VOs. It was decided that AKRSP and the Aga Khan Fund for

Economic Development (AKFED) would be the two main stakeholders in the FMFB. Thus the investment in the institutional growth of the VO as a financial intermediary was not capitalised upon and the opportunity to develop a truly village based system of banking with local ownership and management, giving the VOs a role in their own destiny and linking them in a sustainable way with the formal sector, was lost.

The Micro-Finance Section was separated from the other sections of AKRSP with effect from January 2001. This move was made as a first step in anticipation of the Micro-Finance Bank and it was assessed that it would help to reconcile tensions that have existed in some regions to unduly expand the Micro-Finance Programme to reflect well on performance and at the same time run a programme in which portfolio risk is properly managed. At the time, it was felt that while the move towards autonomy was a rational one given the proposed shift to the planned Micro-Finance Bank, it divorced the Micro-Finance Section from the leverage that other programme components could exercise on the credit and savings portfolio. In particular, it was felt that the advantage of securing loan repayments as an incentive for further AKRSP investments at the village level would be lost. There was also an advantage in integrating the credit activities with technical assistance from other programme components and it appears that this aspect would also be weakened.

The feasibility analysis of the FMFB assessed that it was not possible to establish a sustainable bank, if it was restricted to the six AKRSP districts. It was decided that the bank would be a national level bank and it would expand its operations to Karachi, interior Sindh and eventually to the rest of the country. However, it was stressed that the bank would ensure that the commitment to the North would remain, and it was estimated that the FMFB would have to cross-subsidise its operations in the North. The bank would focus on savings mobilisation as well as loan disbursements. In 2002 the micro-finance operations were incorporated into a newly formed First Micro-Finance Bank which started its operations from its head office in Islamabad. It appeared more and more that the micro-finance strategy of AKRSP had been taken over and was being driven by the decision to establish a bank rather than seeing the bank as a means to achieving AKRSP's original objectives. The Fourth World Bank Evaluation also cautioned that while the idea of a bank was useful, in that it would enable AKRSP to accept deposits, provide it legal cover for its micro-finance operations and provide it long-term presence, there was a danger that the need to make the bank sustainable would direct the development of the micro-finance programme and could divert it from its initial mandate of serving the poor.

The following key lessons emerge from AKRSP's model of institutional growth and development:

- AKRSP had a clear vision about its role in rural development. While this overall vision was necessary it was not sufficient to guide the specific development of different programme components, especially micro-finance.
- It is essential to develop a clear vision for micro-finance and to articulate it in a manner that helps in establishing the parameters for institutional growth, guides product identification and diversification, specifies delivery strategy and shapes the management information system.
- While there was broad agreement that micro-finance should help AKRSP's clients enhance their incomes, there were frequent changes in micro-finance policy due to lack of direction on where the micro-finance programme was headed.
- State-of-the-art training and interaction with other practitioners are key in shaping micro-finance thinking and infusing a vision into key aspects of the programme.
- Can you change livelihoods through micro-finance ?

It is difficult to answer the question regarding the impact of AKRSP's micro-finance programme and the extent to which it has enabled the transformation of livelihoods because of lack of empirical evidence. AKRSP has not undertaken credit utilisation and impact studies on the basis that such studies are generally donor-driven and waste resources that could be productively used elsewhere. The average size of the loan was small and insufficient to transform livelihoods but was designed to deal with vulnerability and the small productive investments in the agriculture sector. A question that can be asked is if AKRSP by focusing on loan products designed for the low productivity agriculture sector limit its own impact. An informal assessment of credit utilisation showed that AKRSP loans had helped in enterprise development, in providing loans for investments in the social sectors and housing and in reducing the vulnerability of poor households by helping them meet consumption needs. Women have particularly benefited from diverting loans for consumption purposes. In 1989, an assessment was undertaken of AKRSP as a source of credit in the Northern Areas. This analysis revealed that AKRSP had the greatest outreach in terms of the number of people it had reached and in Gilgit District it had provided 50 per cent of the loans. In terms of loan amounts it had provided 22 per cent of the total loaned in Gilgit District, 44 per cent in Chitral District and 21 in Baltistan District. While overall poverty trends show that poverty in the Northern Areas has declined, it is difficult to demonstrate that this decline is linked to AKRSP's activities and more specifically to the micro-finance programme.

Table 7.2. Analysis of outreach and significance of financial sources for credit (percentage distribution)

Loan Sources	Gilgit		Chitral	Baltistan
	Loan Amount	No of Loanees	Loan Amount	Loan Amount
Government Agencies	1.8	0.4	0.1	0.0
Commercial Banks	45.0	7.1	8.0	6.5
Co-operatives	0.0	0.3	1.2	0.1
AKRSP 21.7	50.6	43.5	21.4	
Friends 6.2	6.0	15.4	43.6	
Village Shop Keepers	25.3	35.5	31.8	28.4

Source: M.H. Khan. 1989.

AKRSP's micro-finance programme has particularly benefited women who have been very proactive in this regard. It was the women of Sherquilla who, in June 1983, formed a Women's Organisation and invited AKRSP to help them initiate a programme even before AKRSP had any plans on how to involve women with project activities. They had saved Rs 4,000 or an average of Rs 59 per member.[22] Traditionally, women do not own land and own few other assets. The savings programme provided women with one of the few opportunities to own something of their own. The savings programme has empowered women by giving them their own accounts and ownership of the accounts. This programme also encouraged women to pursue opportunities of productive employment in the bid to increase their savings. By the end of 2002, about 50,221 women had cumulative savings of Rs 121 million. Interviews with WOs and the experience of women with savings across the Northern Areas and Chitral shows clearly that women have really been empowered as a result of the savings programme and have undertaken many innovative enterprises as a result. Women have valued AKRSP's savings component more highly than the credit component and have continued with savings with or without AKRSP. The large savings of women have changed intra-household dynamics and are helping to tilt the balance in a manner which offers women greater equity in their household interactions. The credit programme has also provided women with the opportunity to access credit in large numbers. About 3,459 women obtained credit of a total amount of Rs 215 million. However, women members received only 15 per cent of the total loans disbursed between 1983 and 2000. There is significant variation in the amount of loans disbursed to women by region and loan types. Women received 20 per cent of the total loans disbursed in the Gilgit District, 12 per cent in the Chitral District and only 5 per cent in the Baltistan District in 2000. These figures are likely to go down further when the loan leakages to men are accounted for, as many of the loans taken by women are passed on to the men in the family. There are also indications that some of the male WO managers may be diverting some of the group loans extended to WOs for their own use.[23] An analysis of the disbursement of different types of loan products by gender shows that women received 19 per cent of the V/WOCP loans, 22 per cent of the group loans, 8 per cent of the individual loans, 4 per cent of the short-term loans, 3 per cent of the medium-term loans and none of the Corporate Credit or the Business Committee loans. This analysis shows that women tend to benefit more from loan instruments that are designed for groups as compared to individual loan products.

The features of AKRSP's micro-finance programme are such that it is generally assumed that it will be of interest to mainly poor households. However, there are some features of the loan and savings programme with the potential for excluding the very poor households. The Group Loans can only be availed to the extent of the savings of individual members and the Individual Loans are not generally available to the very poor households as they require investment in an existing enterprise. A major problem with AKRSP's savings model was that it did not provide easy access to savings when they were required. Poor people tend to require greater access to their savings to manage risks and have a high liquidity preference. Until 1999 individual savings withdrawals were typically managed through an informal system, whereby cash on hand with the manager or savings collected at recent meetings were used to meet the occasional needs for liquidity. According to policy, larger withdrawal demands were permissible (provided that the savings have not been pledged as collateral), but in practice, withdrawals required authorisation from AKRSP's regional management which was a time consuming process.

International Experience and AKRSP

A key aspect of the study was to compare the theory of micro-finance as it was practised by AKRSP with the theoretical knowledge and understanding of micro-finance. There was constant experimentation at AKRSP and the micro-finance programme evolved from a small savings programme that added subsidised loans to its portfolio and gradually bifurcated credit from the rest of its operations and has formalised its operations under the newly established FMFB. The micro-finance environment has also rapidly changed in the period under review and the current study examined the factors in the evolving micro-finance environment that shaped AKRSP's micro-finance policy and procedures. An attempt has also been made to compare AKRSP's experience with other practitioners in the region and elsewhere. The idea was to identify the manner in which other programmes developed, and assess whether AKRSP's micro-finance programme evolved differently or in a fashion similar to other programmes in the region and internationally, and compare common and dissimilar aspects and isolate factors that shape micro-finance policy.

The international comparison between AKRSP and the other micro-finance organisations has been organised around four main themes which are (a) Community-Based Organisations (CBO's) as a basis for micro-finance; (b) savings as a starting point for micro-finance and as a source of funding; (c) the contribution and cost of experimentation and innovation, and (d) the lifecycle of Micro-Finance Institutions (MFIs) and what remains after formalisation.

Community-Based Organisations as a Basis for Micro-Finance[24]

AKRSP demonstrated that CBOs can be a solid basis for efficient and sustainable micro-finance that reaches large numbers of rural poor. AKRSP started basically as a promoter and facilitator, helping VOs and WOs provide their members with financial services by linking them with formal sector commercial organisations. It ended up as a typical provider with the creation of the FMFB, reaching out directly to the clients. In such a process, the role of the CBOs in financial service provision normally declines. The future will show how this choice will affect the attention to the poor.

AKRSP's community based model was successful in reaching a large portion of the rural poor. In developing this model, Shoaib Sultan Khan was inspired by Raiffeisen experience with co-operatives, a century old experience in quite another context. To mobilise the potential of the villagers, he introduced a model based on the three Raiffeisen principles: formation of financial capital through savings, upgrading of human skills through training and organisation of the people. However, there were also clear differences with the co-operative movement. Unlike the co-operatives, the VOs did not become formally established entities. The savings was not meant to be the capital base for on lending, although VOs started diverting a large part of their savings towards on-lending. Additional elements have been adapted from the village organisation and cooperative models that were successfully tried in Taiwan and Korea in the post-1945 era (World Bank 1987: 4).

In terms of CBO based micro-finance, there were few experiences in developing countries from which AKRSP could learn when it first started its operations. One should bear in mind that in the beginning of the 1980s micro-finance was still a largely unexploited field. Although CBOs had been around—particularly in Asia—for a long time, there were no organised and documented experiences of CBO based micro-finance when AKRSP started. Village banking on the other hand had not been developed and a franchise organisation like The Foundation for International Community Assistance (FINCA), now a major promoter of this system, started its operations only in 1985. The financial sector associations are a phenomenon of the nineties. The Association for Social Advancement (ASA) Bangladesh, now acknowledged to be an interesting example of CBO based financial service provision, initiated savings and credit activities in 1992. This was originally based on the Grameen Bank model, but it was later decided to turn to a savings and credit group based model, which was self managed (Srinivasan *et al.* 2000). Looking back at this, AKRSP practically took the only route possible: to start with the commitment and conviction that village based finance had potential and experiment with it. Part of the savings could have been used to form equity for a co-operative model (see e.g. Nepal, Latin America) or AKRSP could have promoted a more active relation between the VOs and their banks, making them into credit clients (e.g. equity Building Society in Kenya).

AKRSP experimented and developed its own model and was very successful in expanding the savings and credit services to the villages. In doing that it combined the role of the promoter and facilitator with that of the provider. Early discussions at AKRSP reveal that the NGO was grappling with how it could use the VOs and WOs for the formation of a banking system (see earlier sections). In other words, AKRSP was looking for the possibility to keep on combining both roles. Staff from within AKRSP as well as several consultants developed ideas for a sustainable banking system as a continuation of the credit and savings programme.[25] The idea of village organisation banking was originally proposed to assist clusters of VOs to take loans for on-lending to members. This would have meant the development of a system of village banking and building upon the more or less spontaneously started internal lending. Another possibility would have been to focus on maturing the VOs (by bringing in efficient administrative systems, by guaranteeing adequate governance and by creating a federation) and linking them directly with banks (the banks that already knew them because of the savings relationship); this was the model applied by the National Bank for Agricultural Research and Development (NABARD) in India.[26] Both options would have required capacity building at the VO level in the field of financial services provision and the promotion of uniform guidelines. By this time, international experience had become available through FINCA and NABARD in India but was not used. Failure to access this experience limited the scope of internal lending which could have been used to guide VOs[27] at this stage.

A comparison of AKRSP's decision to create a bank[28] with international practice, gives a mixed analysis. On the one hand, the evolution into a supervised institution can be considered a natural progression. The Entidad para el Desarrollo de la Pequena y Microempresa (EDPYME) in Peru and the Fondos Finacieros Privados (FFP) in Bolivia illustrate this. On the other hand, there is a 'school' in favour of the idea to base financial services on CBOs and use existing banks to provide them with credit and loan facilities.[29] The latter option can be more cost effective as the CBOs undertake a lot of the ground work, and have a much wider outreach than a formal financial institution limited by its higher cost. In the end this discussion is about how to reach the rural poor.[30] AKRSP could have compared the sustainability and outreach of both models when taking its decision on the establishment of the new bank. The final verdict on this will be based on an analysis of the client profile of the FMFB and its outreach to the poor.

Savings as a Starting Point for Micro-Finance

In a period where supply driven credit ruled the development world, AKRSP distinguished itself internationally by putting savings first. Applying some of the basic principles of the co-operative movement, it managed to mobilise large amounts of savings which contributed to the financial soundness of the credit operations and to the empowerment of the villagers. This pioneering of savings contributed to the now universally accepted knowledge that the poor can save. And very important it set a standard for other Rural Support Programmes throughout Pakistan. However, internal choices and external circumstances made the model hit its limits. Unlike successful international experiences, the formal link between savings and credit was not made.

From a micro-finance best practices point of view, the focus on savings was a very good choice. It is now widely acknowledged that poor people, as part of their effort to manage the little money they have, do want a safe place for their savings (Rutherford 2001).[31] In promoting and demonstrating this, AKRSP has been one of the frontrunners in terms of putting savings at the centre of financial services provision. It was one of the first donor-supported rural development programmes to include savings as an important component. Unlike with the co-operative movement, the savings never became a formal source of funding. The money was deposited at banks that did not provide direct lending to the VO's. The savings however did generate a more or less informal system of village banking when villagers started to do internal lending. In its early years AKRSP did not provide one of the fundamental elements poor people want when they deposit their money: easy access (people save in order to get the money when they need it for emergency, for life-cycle events or when investment opportunities arise). This is one of the factors that influenced savings pattern at AKRSP along with the returns on savings (See Box 7.3). Internationally it is increasingly being recognised that this access is fundamental for the steady promotion of savings. International experience shows that successful savings and credit institutions like the Cajas Municipales in Peru and the Equity Building Society in Kenya offer flexible savings products, with few limits in terms of minimum amounts and withdrawal. These and other non-bank institutions also offer a somewhat better interest rate than the banks. They heavily promote an image of trust to compensate for the traditional distrust people have in non-bank financial institutions. AKRSP did not gain from higher savings, since it did not need the money for its loans as these were externally financed. AKRSP has made no special effort to keep on attracting savings. Little or no innovation took place in AKRSP's savings model in the last twenty years, and after the creation of the FMFB the link between savings and credit was lost. In fact, the Bank cannot use the savings of the AKRSP clients as most of these are deposited in long-term bonds with the government.

Box 7.3. Growth in savings

During the first years of the Programme, average savings per member doubled every two years. Saving money was attractive because it yielded 18%. At the end of the eighties, growth rhythm slowed down, a trend that continued in the nineties. Between 1994 and 1998, average savings per member increased by 50% in Rupee terms. The highest amount in real terms was reached in 1995/1996 with VO members having an average of US$85 in savings and WO members an average of US$52. Between 1998 and 2002 growth practically came to a halt. In real terms (US$) average savings per member have decreased and in 2001 stood at the level of the beginning of the nineties (based on AKRSP statistics).

The Contribution and Cost of Experimentation and Innovation.

The willingness to learn and the availability of donor money have allowed AKRSP's micro-finance programme to grow steadily and to survive crisis and mistakes. The lesson learned is that offering the right financial services to the poor requires knowledge of the clients and their needs and that innovation is needed to keep up with the changing preferences and circumstances. Donor money can be fundamental to finance innovations and experiments.

One of AKRSP's principles has been 'learning by doing' and donor funding has effectively made it possible to apply this principle to all components of the programme, including micro-finance. However it should be noted that this experimentation has not been a planned one. Planned experimentation would for example mean starting group lending with two methodologies and comparing their effectiveness against a predefined set of parameters. Or start with a low interest rate service charge to find out whether it allows the combination of widening the client base with a sustainable operation at institutional level. Consequences of certain choices were not estimated or calculated beforehand. Until 1996 there was not a single projection of loan portfolio. Nor was there a calculation of financial indicators or basic costs of delivering the savings and credit component. The experimental nature of the approach lies more in the fact that the programme tried out different approaches and was quite flexible in changing or bringing in new elements. The same holds true for the reaction when things went wrong. There are indications that the culture of experimentation also allowed for bringing more financial logic into the savings and credit component from 1990 onwards. The component was not so tightly structured that change became impossible. However, there was resistance to certain changes. A typical case is the introduction of interest rates and the subsequent increases. AKRSP continued to charge below market rates until the mid-nineties, apparently unaware of the rapidly shifting views on rural credit and its cost. The negative effects of cheap credit had already been widely documented and in 1984 Adams, Graham and von Pischke had published their book 'Undermining rural development with cheap credit' (Adam *et al.* 1984), which changed the paradigm. It took years for these views to penetrate into AKRSP, and when they were promoted the field staff questioned these changes.[32] There was also opposition at the Board level.

While donor backing allowed for experimentation and learning from mistakes, they brought no clear view on the need for sustainability or non-donor-dependent funding. It was contact with the best practices in micro-finance that brought about a change in the orientation and thinking about micro-credit by inspiring those managing the credit programme in AKRSP. In 1995 two high level staff of AKRSP participated in the micro-finance course in Boulder in Colarado. They brought back home the paradigm of sustainable micro-finance. From 1995 onwards, sustainability, real interest rates, separation of financial and non-financial services and specialisation of staff became real issues. It was at a time that internationally it was already being acknowledged that a sustainability perspective was fundamental. From the beginning of the nineties onwards, it became clear that sustainability and outreach were not contradictory and that 'Micro-finance institutions can and indeed need to be self-sustaining if they are to achieve their outreach potential by providing access to financial services to the poor.'[33]

The Life cycle of MFIs and the Influence of the Drive to Sustainability and Formalisation

Although the life cycle with many MFIs worldwide show comparable patters, each institution walks a distinctive road to becoming a sustainable provider of financial services. With 20 years in micro-finance, AKRSP is one of the oldest players on the Asian micro-finance scene. Although the perspective to become a supervised financial institution has been present almost from the beginning, the road to becoming a bank has been long. As most MFIs embarking upon the road to commercialisation, it has not thoroughly assessed the possibilities of mission drift and has no clear strategy to assure the continued provision of financial services to the original client group.

Micro-finance institutions are very diverse, and so is their life cycle. Many MFIs have been born out of NGOs or development programmes. They start as socially oriented initiatives, often with several components including social and economic sectors and later specialise in financial service provision. This process is being repeated all over the world and its duration can be anywhere from 3 to 20 years. Some MFIs start as specialised and regulated institutions, a typical example being the Grameen Bank or the specialised micro-finance banks set up in the Balkans in the past five years. Others make it to maturity and become regulated institutions after having evolved from a development programme or a multipurpose NGO. FINCA International[34] presents a model with three growth stages that applies to the evolution of its own affiliates and is also representative for the life cycle of many MFIs.[35] International experience shows that, as MFIs move through this life cycle, the principles of sustainability and efficiency get applied in a stricter way. In practice this means cost-based pricing, stricter screening of clients with more weight given to the ability to pay back and other measures that might contribute to cost-efficiency such as concentration of branches in areas with a critical mass of clients. This drive towards commercialisation sometimes misunderstood as the dominance of commercial/profitability goals over development goals can cause mission drift.

Box 7.4. The three stages of MFIs

• During the Start-up phase, the MFI can have different 'shapes' and institutional characteristics. Quite often micro-finance is not dominant at this phase or is being run in a basic way, with little focus on sustainability. NGOs adopt micro-finance because it is a tool to provide the target group with financial means, which in turn is expected to reduce poverty. Or a donor funded rural development programme includes it because the identification has stressed the importance of providing small farmers with loans because they don't have access to banks. The loan product is normally a simple and standard one. Financing is provided by donors. For AKRSP this phase was very long and lasted from 1983 till 1994/5. During this period, AKRSP made no pretension about being a sustainable financial services programme. Industry-wide this phase normally takes from three to eight years. A typical indicator of the shift towards the next phase is the separation of AKRSP into three divisions (1994): Development, Micro-finance and Enterprise Support. This organisational change had far reaching consequences for the micro-finance component. It laid the basis for separate accounting and allowed the development of an orientation towards sustainability. It also allowed the management to select people with a mindset suitable for micro-finance.

- During the Expansion or Self-sufficiency phase, the micro-finance activities become an activity in its own, with sustainability becoming a goal. The poverty alleviation or social objective is still present but board and management know that in order to provide the clients with a sustainable service, the institution has to be run on commercial grounds. Expansion takes place, with an expansion of the branch network and an increasing diversification of the loan products. Financing is still provided by donors, but grants are complemented by funds from subsidised sources and special credit windows. For AKRSP this phase ran from 1996 to 2001. That is in line with the industry standards.
- During the Transformation phase the institution becomes regulated and enters the formalised and supervised financial sector. As it can attract savings, it can start to diversify its funding, thus reducing the dependency on donors and institutional fund provideRs The MFI pays special attention to the market and focuses on client needs, which often results in the development of individualised loan and savings products. For AKRSP this phase had its origin in the eighties (the first discussions about becoming a bank) but formally started in 2002 with the creation of the FMFB.

In Latin America the drive towards regulation has been spurred by the search for funding. In countries like Bolivia and Peru the leading MFIs lobbied successfully for a special licence that would allow them to obtain access to savings and to central bank funds. In East Africa (Uganda, Kenya) several NGOs transformed into regulated institutions or are in the process of doing that. These processes are often characterised by discussions between management, field staff and board members (including donors) on the trade-off between regulation/commercialisation and continued service provision to the original target group.[36] AKRSP was no exception to that standard but managed to come to a clear-cut decision: all the micro-finance activity was brought into the FMFB. In Bolivia the NGOs who constituted one of the first FFPs, had a two-year long discussion about bringing their loan portfolio into the newly established institution. This kept the portfolio growth of the FFP well below its target and finally resulted in the owners selling the portfolio to another FFP.

In the case of AKRSP, the last World Bank report mentions that 'there are significant risks for poverty outcome in the shift toward the Micro-finance Section autonomy, and finally the micro-finance bank' (World Bank 2002: 105). In the case of AKRSP this risk has already materialised in the past years as client selection has become stricter. Loan approvals decreased as loan conditions and screening became stricter.[37] Although there is awareness that the shift away from the poorer clients is a risk, no serious study has been undertaken to estimate this risk or to take actions to control it. A reference is the work done by Robert Peck Christen on Latin America.[38]

Appendix: Co-operative History and Principles

Brief History of the Co-operative Movement in England and Europe

In England the first attempts to organise were made by workers in the factory system where the workers realised the need to organise to improve their working conditions and their economic situation. It was the result of this thinking that as early as 1760 workers organised their own two corn mills in Chatham and Woolwick. This was at a time when the UK government discouraged workers from uniting. The Combination Act of 1824 allowed workers to combine together only to improve wages and for nothing else. In 1834 a group of farmers in Dorset organised a union and were tried for administrating illegal oaths. They had adopted their oath directly from the one based by the Rochdale Weavers to organise their union. The farm workers were found guilty and transported to Australia and became known as the 'Talpuddle Martyrs'. Their case and the severe sentences served on them dampened the spirit of farmers and workers and discouraged them from organising themselves openly for many years. It was only in 1868 that the trade union congress dared to have its first national meeting.

Co-operatives had been in existence in Britain as far back as 1769 when the Fenwick Weavers' Association was formed. However, the first documented co-operative institution was founded in 1844 in Rochdale, England. The success of co-operatives in Rochdale was due to many factors including, the volatile economic and social climate at the time of the emergence of the Rochdale co-operative. This volatility was caused by the industrial revolution. Prior to the industrial revolution, Rochdale had been a centre for the manufacture of flannel using the handloom. The industrial revolution resulted in increased competition as the power loom came into existence, producing more flannel in a faster time scale. In addition, increases in American tariff policies resulted in lost markets. These two events caused the decline of the local flannel industry. The result of this caused the people of the area to suffer from periodic unemployment, low pay and dangerous workplaces. There were no social benefits such as insurance, healthcare or pensions. The common people were dependent on merchants for goods and work. Many of these were unscrupulous, exploiting the helplessness of the poor by selling at high prices, adulterating goods, or trapping the workers with credit agreements (Fairbairn 1994). At this time, the government was not democratically elected and therefore the people had no voice to protect themselves. Their answer to these social problems was to form a kind of mutual self-help through co-operative endeavour.

Some of the factors which explain why Rochdale in particular, was successful in its co-operative movement include the following; first, the town was well known as a centre for co-operative idealism and radical politics. It had a history of strong support for movements, whose ideals supported raising social standards and rights for the ordinary people. These movements included the trade-union movement (violent strikes were recorded in Rochdale in 1808 and in 1829), Chartism (campaign to obtain the vote for ordinary people) and the Factory Act movement for regulation of industry and the protection of employees. In addition, Rochdale had strong links with the Owenite movement. This movement was named after Robert Owen, an industrialist who supported the ideal of socialism, trade unionism, social reform and cooperation. To achieve social reform Owen believed that economic and educational improvement was essential for improving social standards.[39]

While the UK movement was largely the product of industrial workers, similar attempts were made in other parts of Europe. In France, Francis Buchez promoted co-operative associations for cabinet-makers and goldsmiths between 1832 and 1834. During the same period Hermann Schulze and Friedrich Wilhelm Raiffeisen (1818–1888) promoted credit co-operatives in Germany. Although Raiffeisen adopted Schulze Delitzsch's principles of self-help there were fundamental differences between these two types of societies. Raiffeisen insisted on brotherly love and Christian principles for motivating the credit unions, while Schulze was mainly concerned with promoting economic self-sufficiency. Moreover, Schulze concentrated on urban workers and shopkeepers, while Raiffeisen devoted himself to helping farmers. Schulze also believed that membership should come from a large and economically varied area, but Raiffeisen preferred to restrict membership to small district, preferably a parish. The Raiffeisen Co-operative Societies enjoyed much larger growth than the Schulze. The Rochdale movement of UK and Raiffeisen of Germany particularly influenced the Asian co-operative movement.

Key Principles of Co-operatives

International Co-operative Alliance 1937: Seven principles defining co-operatives
The International Co-operative Alliance (ICA) formed in 1895 with delegates from many countries including the UK, Germany, Russia, Holland, Hungary and Serbia. The aim of the list of principles was to provide a benchmark against which entities could be compared, to establish whether they were genuine co-operatives or not. In 1961 these principles were revamped. However, the modified list included most of the principles formulated in 1937. The main change was that the emphasis placed on the promotion of education and the cash trading principle was dropped. An additional principle called 'Cooperation among co-operatives' was inserted.
1. Open membership
2. One man one vote
3. Distribution of refunds on a patronage basis
4. Limited interest payments for the use of capital
5. Political and religious neutrality
6. Cash trading
7. Promotion of education

NOTES

1. This was not an initial requirement but was subsequently added due to the high demand and competition among VOs for PPIs.
2. Just three of the banks with the largest outreach in the Northern Areas, i.e National Bank, Habib Bank and the Co-operative Bank, indicated total deposits of Rs 2.6 billion.
3. Performance Indicators Report: January-December 2002. Report No 6. Pakistan Micro-finance Network.
4. Third quarterly report August to October 1983 AKRSP.
5. *Ibid.* p. 16.
6. Shoaib Sultan Khan, Hussain Wali Khan, Khaleel Tetlay and Mutabiat Shah, *Village Organisation Banking: A Status Report as of December 1990.*
7. AKRSP had the authority to draw the money unilaterally to satisfy VO defaults.
8. Equivalent to the interest earned on Profit and Loss Sharing (PLS) account.
9. A suggestion by AKRSP staff in the mid 1990s that AKRSP should consider expanding to areas outside the Northern Areas was considered premature and ignored.
10. AKRSP's service charge is 15% but the V/WOs on-lend at around 18%.
11. Third quarterly report August to October 1983 AKRSP, p. 40.
12. An average loan of Rs 5,400 per borrower.
13. The National Rural Support Programme (NRSP) comes closest to AKRSP in terms of the maturity of its micro-finance programme, but the Micro-Finance Group's Performance Indicators Report for 2000 does not give figures for NRSP.
14. Khaleel Tetlay and Mutabiat Shah, *A Strategic Review of AKRSP's Micro-finance Programme by AKRSP*, July 1991, p. 7.
15. *Ibid.* p. 46.
16. Du Marchie Sarvaas, E.C: *Creating a sustainable savings and credit facility in the Northern regions of Pakistan* (1991: 26).
17. Javaid Hassan, Finance Manager, 'A Proposal for AKRSP Bank', February 1989.
18. Mary Houghton, Richard Pattern and Ronald Grzywinski.
19. 'Village Organisation Banking. A Status Report as of December 1990', Shoaib Sultan Khan *et al.* AKRSP.
20. *Ibid.*
21. Du Marchie Sarvaas, E.C: *Creating a sustainable savings and credit facility in the Northern regions of Pakistan* (1991: 31).
22. Second Quarterly Report, May to July 1983, AKRSP, p. 9

23. This appeared to be the case in some of the villages visited by the World Bank Team, as members of some of the WOs met were unaware of the loans indicated against their organisations.

24. Worldwide there is discussion about the role and efficiency of CBOs in providing financial services. Different models exist, from informal Savings and Credit Associations to village banks, from the traditional co-operatives to the Financial Sector Associations, a model that emerged in Africa in the nineties. See e.g. the comparative work by Jeffrey Ashe and the Symposium on savings-led micro-finance and the rural poor.

25. Du Marchie Sarvaas, E.C: *Creating a sustainable savings and credit facility in the Northern regions of Pakistan* (1991: 26).

26. More than 300 banks participate in the programme. As for the relation between the banks and the Self-Help Groups (SHGs), NABARD applies three models: 1) bank lends through an NGO to SHGs (9%); 2) bank forms SHGs and lends to them directly (16%); 3) NGO facilitates and SHG borrows directly from the bank (75%). SHGs loan normally on a basis of 1:1 to the savings and gradually increasing to 1:4.

27. Although there is no exact information on the volume of internal lending, contact with the field revealed that internal lending has only developed well in Gilgit, with Hunza taking the lead (35 of the approximately 300 V/WOs do internal lending). In Chitral and Baltistan less than 1% of the VO/WOs do internal lending.

28. As far as we know, the feasibility of a VO/CBO based financial services system was not studied.

29. An interesting experience is being developed in Tanzania where the Co-operative and Rural Development Bank (CRDB) establishes links with ROSCAs to use them as part of the Bank's network, offering in turn financial services to the Associations.

30. Based on the July 2003 internet discussion about micro-finance and the potential of SHGs. Contribution of J. Ashe.

31. See also the research and insights contributed by MicroSave.

32. Interview with Stephen Rasmussen, former CEO of AKRSP.

33. CGAP Focus Note, 'Maximizing the Outreach of Micro enterprise Finance: The Emerging Lessons of Successful Programmes', October 1995.

34. FINCA International (based in the USA) has promoted a village banking model throughout Latin America, Africa, Eastern Europe and Central Asia.

35. FINCA International. Paper presented by Lawrence Yanovitch at the Almaty Micro-Finance Conference in April 2003.

36. Financial Assistance, Consultancy, Entrepreneurship and Training (FACET BV) has carried out several assignments for MFIs at different moments of their transformation. This experience shows that the management and the headquarter staff normally are the stoutest defenders of the transformation. This can partly be explained by the fact that they are responsible for the funding and see the limitations of future access to donor money. Initiatives

to increase interest rates and to rationalise on client attention also often come from this level because they directly relate to the performance indicators that have to be 'shown' to the board and to the outside world (as stated by one of FACET's clients, 'As we all publish our performance indicators, I can not allow our MFI to perform below the industry's benchmark here'). Field staff on the other hand often show a 'protective' attitude towards the clients. Sometimes this reflects fear of losing clients or reluctance to become the carrier of bad news (higher interest rates).

37. Interview with Salim Jiwani, CEO of the FMFB, until 2001 responsible for AKRSP's savings and credit programme.

38. Christen, Robert P.: 'Commercialization and Mission Drift: The transformation of micro-finance in Latin America'. CGAP, 2002.

39. **The objectives of the Rochdale cooperative:** From the outset the overriding concept underlying the purpose of the Rochdale co-operative was that of self-help. The co-operative existed for the benefit of its members and the improvement of their social and household condition. The co-operative was multi-purpose and the founders prepared objects to guide how the co-operative should be developed. Firstly, a store would be opened (Toad Lane, 1844), then housing would be undertaken, next co-operative production would provide employment to the members, from this a utopian co-operative community would evolve. Finally, a temperance hostel would be founded to improve moral standards. To achieve the objects, monies were required. To obtain cash, members could subscribe for shares, which could be paid for by small weekly amounts. These shares formed the capital of the co-operative. This capital was used to purchase goods at low cost and to sell them to its members at retail price. Any surplus made was to be distributed to the members according to their use of the store after paying the capital providers a small fixed sum, retaining some for the development of the society and 2.5% for the education of the members (introduced in the 1854 changes). Education was of vital importance to the founders of the society. By 1850 the society had a library and unlike most modern co-operatives promoted all forms of education. One professor from Cambridge was invited to give a lecture on astronomy!

8

Collective Action: The Threatened Imperative

Geof Wood with Sofia Shakil[1]

INTRODUCTION

In the original meeting (November 2002) to set up this lessons
learned exercise, Collective Action did not feature in either
AKRSP's or DFID's list of papers to be pursued. However the
argument for its inclusion was readily accepted. It is the nature of
that argument that sets out the distinctive intellectual and applied
development space for this chapter. Although the language of social
mobilisation has dominated much of the AKRSP discourse,
alongside other terms such as social organisation, social development
and institutional development, the principle of collective action has
been central to rural development worldwide, and now urban too.
Its significance as a term is that it switches the responsibility away
from external agency towards the social agency of local people in
their pursuit of livelihoods, survival and progress. The other terms,
especially social mobilisation, reflect more the preoccupations of
intervening agencies ('how *we* are organising *them*') rather than the
more balanced perspective of partnership in which, nevertheless,
the ultimate onus for action will lie with local people.

As a term, Collective Action has further significance in linking
the institutional formations already present in a local society with
any new institutional innovations introduced by outsiders. It
reminds us of an essential continuity in forms of community
action, a reminder that whether external development agencies are
present or not, local people especially in the remoter, more

vulnerable parts of the world, have to cooperate with each other for survival, and do not really need to be told or urged on by outsiders to this effect. This is not to deny outsiders a role in this process, but to put 'projects' in their proper perspective in the lives of local people: i.e. a part of their institutional landscape, but never the whole nor major proportion of it. The windows of perception of locals are not the same as those of external programme staff. The irony for AKRSP is that the windows of perception for programme staff themselves vary importantly, with some tendency for the staff from down-country to regard themselves as coming from a more developed, advanced society, thus coming as modernisers and mobilisers of the people in these remote communities. It was outsider, down-country staff who created the image of a post-feudal institutional vacuum which required the introduction of formal organisation. Locally hired staff had and have their origins in these communities, and thus a different perspective and insight on this process. Collective action is a more comfortable term for them—it captures partnership better by reflecting the contribution of pre-existing local institutions to the ongoing development process.

However, transcending these nuances, there can be little doubt that AKRSP has been about the promotion and support of local institutions as the vehicle for development—whether self-development or externally induced. In that sense, AKRSP fits into a wider tradition across South Asia (and elsewhere in large-scale agrarian societies) of attempts to improve local level livelihoods through support for infrastructure and increases in the productivity of the natural resource base both as public as well as private goods. In order to reach this agenda, a range of support functions are required. These have been described in the programme as support for human, financial and social capital. It is the social capital dimension which we are dissecting here. This is a highly problematic and ahistorical term and we should not get too side-tracked about its contested intellectual status at this point, though we will need to return to it. The main issue here is the way in which the AKRSP experience fits into a wider model of rural development which combines the notion of extension with the idea of community: that is the essential partnership.

In that sense, AKRSP is part of a lineage deriving from early cooperative movements in the West, adapted to South Asia by Akhtar Hameed Khan in both Comilla and Peshawar, but also reflecting various colonial experiments with community development in undivided India, which, of course, were also carried on in post-Partition India in various guises. However, it is the assumptions being made by various stakeholders about the idea of community which are so important to the investigation of collective action. Thus the very principle of collective action is itself socially constructed and cannot therefore be divorced from ideology, with ideology itself a reflection of the interests and convenience of dominant classes of the epoch. Thus post-revolutionary Russia had its soviets and post-revolutionary China had its communes, both tightly controlled by the central bureaucratic and political elites. The Indian subcontinent inherited the community ideology of Gandhi into a wide array of incarnations. But even Gandhi's notions of the rural community were fanciful construction: a way of representing the class problem in colonial India as a major alliance between a colonial bourgeoisie and local *zamindari* landlord classes, without choosing to acknowledge the problem of class, power and exploitation below the level of the *zamindari* landlord. Indeed, Gandhi's preoccupations with caste were inadequately transposed onto a critique of community, again choosing to focus only upon the outcaste, the *Harijans*. These legacies have entered the psyche of rural development and assumptions about community and collective action in the sub-continent to this day. They have also had their pragmatic dimension: any celebration of the self-reliant capacities of local communities is usually a policy of resource denial and urban or industrial bias. Community development in India was the counterpart of centrally managed, industrial oriented planning.

However, it would not be fair to tag the AKRSP initiative in the Northern Areas and Chitral (NAC) with this perspective. AKRSP's origins reflected other concerns about a remote, poor, mountain, frontier society, home to the minority sect of Ismailis as well as poor Sunnis and Shias,[2] abandoned by the mainstream development activities of down-country Pakistan due to difficult logistics and the uncertain political status of the Northern Areas in relation to the prolonged dispute with India over Kashmir. The pursuit of a rural development agenda in these socio-political conditions required some concept of local community, albeit one that implied re-construction and strengthening through the introduction of Village Organisations into an existing institutional landscape at the local level. The strong presumption was of village households, all more or less equally poor once the elite layer of feudal families had lost their formal rights and status.[3] Thus, ironically, while Gandhi's romantic ideas about community may not have worked for much of India, they could be more relevant in the remote valleys of the Karakoram and Hindukush. At the same time, these external, socially constructed assumptions about community and collective action need a more anthropological reality check in order to distinguish between the real and imagined collective behaviour of local people in pursuit of secure livelihoods.

Participation, Free-Riding and Inequality: The Collective Action Debate

AKRSP's development efforts in NAC are not only part of a particular institutional lineage in South Asia but also interact with ongoing global discourses about social development and about partnership as a distribution of social agency between stakeholders. Given the centrality of sustainable natural resource management as the basis for secure livelihoods in the NAC, there is a strong convergence between social development concerns and natural resource/common property management. Some of this convergence revolves around the principle of participation, both as a form of collective social agency within the community and in the sense of effective counterpart behaviour to external support interventions, as from AKRSP. This is not the place for a separate extended review of the debates about participation both as rhetoric and reality,[4] but some issues relate closely to AKRSP's philosophy and experience. AKRSP's point of departure (the 'institutional vacuum') contained a more subtle position about the non-participatory practices of prevailing resource management arrangements, left over from the dismantling of feudal authority. It thus sought to deploy the incentive of infrastructure and other grants as a lever to bring about improved participation and democracy of local institutions. The objective was to avoid capture of new resources and opportunities by erstwhile elites and their immediate kin through their domination of local project identification and priority setting. The introduction of Village Organisations reflected a desire to overcome inequalities of power and influence locally: i.e. the rhetoric should triumph over the reality. Here we encounter a widespread paradox of micro-level rural development: communities are made up of kin networks and therefore power structures, and these mediate any new values or principles of working offered by the external agency. By insisting on participation as indicated by attendance at meetings as well as speaking and saving, AKRSP was certainly keen to ensure an awareness of what was going on and what decisions and commitments (e.g. of village counterpart labour as contribution in kind to projects) were being made. Of course, simply being informed is a weak version of participation, if one lacks the power to object or propose alternatives. Perhaps the more profound 'right' in these contexts is choice. The problem with participation in its full version is that it imposes costs on the participants, especially if they are poor, migrant or female headed/managed in an otherwise male dominated social environment.

Certainly the notion of participation embodies also a sense of membership in community level institutions. Family livelihoods are crucially dependent upon the household being regarded as a full member of a range of local institutions with corresponding rights and responsibilities. Exclusion is to be avoided at all costs, thus encouraging conformity to prevailing norms and implicit rules. These norms and rules are partially a function of necessities in natural resource management (i.e. there are only certain ways of managing water distribution), and partially a reflection of local power structure and leadership customs. Power and leadership has traditionally been represented at the local level through a combination of delegated feudal powers to key clans and their dominant families, and other respected elders having quasi-religious authority including mullahs and priests from among such families. Thus there is a complex, indigenous institutional landscape with overlapping membership structured as a set of concentric circles in which some are core leaders and others are followers. Outside the immediate conditions of the family, characterised by its dependency ratio stage in its domestic cycle alongside its asset base, membership of these other institutions are the next determinant of welfare. In this sense, collective action is not an option but an imperative; but it is socially constructed, and is not necessarily achieved through equality.

This is an important observation as it restricts the relevance of much theory (i.e. game and clubs) to an understanding of collective action under these social and cultural conditions. Basically, the question is: what binds people together? Is it the pragmatically perceived mutual advantages of cooperation? Is it a set of moral ties? Is it conformity to traditional customs? Is it respect for traditional institutions of leadership and authority? Is it an overwhelming sense of community? Only the first possible answer ('the pragmatically perceived mutual advantages of cooperation') fits with economics derived game and club theory. There is a basic tension between the explanations of different social science disciplines at this point, with, for example, anthropologists critical of the *in vacuo* game theory of economists. Certainly the rationalist preoccupation with free riding and cheating betrays a methodologically individualist approach to understanding social relationships, and what welfare gains flow from them.

Given the necessity for local collective action as an expression of the strength of local ties, but also the livelihoods dependency upon local level natural resources, any threats to collective action are serious with respect to welfare outcomes. Deploying the language of exit, voice and loyalty (Hirschman 1970), where the prospects for either exit or voice are weak, then loyalty is the only option. And it is the loyalty rather than voice dimension of participation which is the more significant for the sustainability of these institutions. What potentially threatens this loyalty? There are two main sets of explanations: those to do with internal group dynamics; and those deriving from overall socio-economic changes in livelihoods. It is the former set which has preoccupied economists and social game theorists, and the latter anthropologists and sociologists. Both sets of explanations are relevant to a discussion about the sustainability of community forms of development and livelihoods support.

Considering internal group dynamics, the premise is that the motivational basis for collective action is transactional rather than moral, derived from individual or household perceptions of self-interest. It is further presumed that behaviour is not altruistic. Thus people cooperate either because they are satisfied with the equity arrangements, which ensure fairness of input and benefit, or because the fear of sanction is greater than the cost of loyalty. There is a further assumption, associated with self-interest, that people primarily relate to other people instrumentally, and expect to receive instrumental treatment in return. This is consistent with a propensity to cheat and free-ride if it is possible to do so. These arguments have appeared in various guises in the literature. Edward Banfield famously wrote in 1958 about the *Moral Basis of a Backward Society*, where the zero sum game conditions of a low technology, low productivity society induce an ethos of amoral familism, in which loyalty to one's own immediate family overrides all other social calculations. Because this principle applies to all actors, therefore all actors expect others to seek to outmanoeuvre them. Under such conditions, trust collapses and the opportunities potentially to be derived from collective action are lost or foregone. Such 'pessimistic' arguments have been reinforced by the theory of Prisoners Dilemma, in which social actors will not prefer the most socially beneficial outcome since they fear that other actors will act for self rather than collective interest, so that they must do likewise. The Tragedy of the Commons offers a further variant on the theme by arguing that unregulated individuals will seek to free-ride by sharing the costs of overexploiting a natural renewable resource while individually receiving the short term benefits of over-use. Most of these game-based theories of the threats to collective action and common property management rely upon the separate individuality of social actors, leading to mutual assumptions rather than mutual knowledge about each other's motivations (i.e. partial information), operating in single negotiation periods. Furthermore, the free-riding propositions are at their strongest in the context of larger groups where members are more likely to be partial or complete strangers.

Many of these conditions and assumptions have to be substantially modified in the NAC context. Much cooperative behaviour occurs in relatively small groups with significant intimacy between members, often derived from kin relations. Thus self-interest is tempered by a genuine sense of moral care for others: i.e. altruism, within limits, is possible. Also these kin based groups comprise ongoing internal structures with leading families able to gain compliance of other extended kin. Such groups persist over time, so that members are playing multi-period rather than single-period games. In this way, they have knowledge of each other's past actions on which to predict future behaviour and thus discount or account for it. This could be understood as pragmatic trust, based on knowledge rather than moral affinity. Negotiating positions adopted in one time period and in one sector (e.g. irrigation) are always therefore tempered by either the prospect of future negotiations or simultaneous parallel ones in adjacent sectors (e.g. grazing). Thus there is always capacity for adjustment, if first round behaviour is proving dysfunctional. The extent of loyalty to the resource (in the sense of dependency on it) also contributes to an internalisation of the costs of depletion (if loyalty is high) or non-compliance to a sustainable maintenance of the resource (if loyalty is low).

At the same time, the informality of rule setting and small group basis for continuous iterative adjustment can be lost in a larger group context. Mancur Olson (1971) placed strong emphasis upon the inverse relationship between group size and successful collective action. Thus many of the pessimistic arguments about collective action apply as the group size enlarges. In the context of AKRSP, a key question is the extent to which the incentive of Productive Physical Investments (PPIs) brought about the formation of Village Organisations which were beyond the 'natural' size for continuous, non-incentivised collective action. There would seem to be some evidence to this effect with VOs breaking up into smaller, constituent VOs after the completion of the initial PPI. In upper Bagrote, for example, the initial larger VO broke up into a series of new, *haiti* (clan) based VOs, especially for ongoing irrigation and pasture management. However, an alternative explanation for bifurcation has been offered, namely that members were strategically re-defining themselves as a new organisation in order to qualify for further grant support for PPIs. It is interesting to observe that some of these smaller VOs have subsequently re-formed as Village Development Organisations (VDOs, almost like the previous VO) in order to pursue common objectives like a school or community centre. Then the question is whether the new VDO requires the same intensity of cooperative behaviour as for continuous natural resource management, and/or whether the new VDOs reflect dynamic leadership rather than equitable collective action. These are highly relevant questions for the next phase of AKRSP's relationships to the local communities in NAC, since the intention is to rely even more heavily upon the principles of self-reliance and collective action especially at the all-valley level.[5]

Returning to the two types of threat to collective action and the loyalty dimension of participation, the second category of threat, indicated above, referred to changes in the socio-economic basis of livelihoods. It is here that the threats to sustained collective action even at small group level may be the most serious. Clearly part of the criticism of the pessimistic accounts of free-riding and cheating is that local level social actors are not simply self-interested, instrumental individuals or households operating within an amoral familistic ethos. Rather they are bound together by moral ties arising from kinship, neighbour proximity, similar, undifferentiated lifestyles, and a shared reliance upon immediately local, renewable but fragile natural resources. Remoteness is an additional bond, loyalty being a function of reduced exit options. Again, this moral framework for collective action may not be constructed of equal individuals enjoying symmetrical reciprocity but rather reflect strong leadership and hierarchy. So threats to well established leadership as well as to a sense of community as the essential ingredient of survival will undermine that moral framework for social action and collective agency. Again the overarching question is whether we observe a linear process of individualisation and commodification of relationships thus transferring the notion of social capital from local, intimate group based relationships and networks to more abstract, contract based, market ones reinforced by universal statutory rights? In other words, are we observing a set of changes in which the exit options are expanding, and sole reliance upon local natural resources is weakening?

This is a general question, which can still be applied to many parts of the world, especially the poorer, remoter parts. Some might argue that as global integration continues apace, swamping and homogenising local resource management systems, modernisation and hegemony of markets will replace local, 'indigenous', pre-capitalist, community based systems of management. Others would dispute this account of history and future institutional trends. Long (2001) has written of globalisation and localisation, and also of re-localisation. It is the plea to understand not just diversity but the logic of its intensification under certain conditions of non-linearity. To illustrate this logic of diversity, this chapter examines the experience of collective action, supported by AKRSP as an external agency, in this remote corner of the world, the high mountain areas of Hindukush and the Karakoram in Northern Pakistan.

The Demise of Feudalism and its implications for Collective Action

The feudal system of the princely states persisted after Partition up to the early 1970s and its formal abolition under the People's Party government of Zulfikar Ali Bhutto. Of course, remnants of status, property and respect remain, with some members of erstwhile ruling families moving into politics alongside business activity and the holding of other offices. Before examining the significance of abolition, two essential characteristics of the feudal system are highly relevant to the analysis which follows. First, the term 'feudal' is properly used from its European context of control over persons rather than control over land (the term has been frequently misused in other South Asian contexts to describe the latter). Control over persons reflects earlier conditions under which labour was the scarcest factor of production, even in these mountain areas where cultivable land was only a minor fraction of the whole. In any epoch, the dominant mode of production will always be centred on control and management of the scarcest means of production. The political subjects of ruling families would have their movements curtailed, with some valley 'frontier' passes even policed either to prevent actual escape (the origin anywhere of passports and exit visas) or to charge taxes (significantly in kind—i.e. substituting the labour of other family members) for the privilege of leaving (i.e. for trade, education or other purposes). Political subjects might also be posted to settle other villages (as noted above). Second, such control over persons was significant for the creation of public goods under low technology, low efficiency conditions: creation and maintenance of irrigation channels; road and paths; bridges; terracing of alluvial fans; and of course construction of forts and religious buildings. Given the high dependence of all upon irrigation under mountain desert conditions, the feudal mobilisation of labour for this key productive good has been described as 'hydraulic society'. The term has broader application in central, south, east and south-east Asia where both canal and tank irrigation has required similar labour mobilisation beyond immediate social space. In other words, where hydraulic space transcends social space, so principles of wider authority have to transcend local collective action based upon a sense of local community, in order to overcome the fission between such communities. Such systems have also been referred to as 'oriental despotism' (Wittfogel 1957) or by Marx as the 'Asiatic mode of production'. The main challenge to the inhabitants of these societies was how to maintain and create expanded public goods, especially the productive ones and those coming under threat such as forests and pastures, at the same time as these feudal institutions were being abolished throughout the nation-state of Pakistan, including the non-federal Northern Areas. However, the timing of this challenge has coincided with other changes, which have brought the market in various forms into the reckoning as a set of social institutions to compete with non-market principles of collective action.

AKRSP's Institution Building Record

To 'development experts' worldwide, this area of Northern Pakistan has come to attention through the pioneering work of the Aga Khan Rural Support Programme (AKRSP) and its 'parent' network of institutions in the Aga Khan Development Network (AKDN), which includes other specialist sector organisations in education, health, cultural conservation, sanitation and construction. Although education and health sectors have been established from the 1950s (AKES and AKHS respectively), from the early 1980s, AKRSP has deliberately set out to address many of the institutional questions raised above in the management of natural and other newly created resources. With a deliberate programme of creating new institutions at the village level, it has sometimes created the medium through which local communities interact with the other Aga Khan (AK) programmes. It should be noted that the AK institutions have been particularly prominent in the area (especially Gilgit–Hunza and Baltistan) precisely because of the area's special political status in respect of the central Pakistan government as an area whose ultimate political status remains to be resolved as part of the resolution of the Kashmir question. Thus, while the Pakistan government has a presence in the area through the army and local councils, it has been wary of full-scale political incorporation as a signal to the Indian government that this is in effect Pakistan territory with the implication that across the line of control is therefore Indian territory. This can never been conceded without a full plebiscite on both sides of the line of control with a range of options offered. Under these conditions, the AKDN, with AKRSP in the forefront, has been the development catalyst in the region.

All these AK institutions operate under the general leadership of the Aga Khan Foundation worldwide. Although it has a 'development' interest in areas of significant Ismaili presence, it seeks to work, if allowed, with all communities. Thus, AKRSP works among the Sunni communities in lower Chitral, and the Shia communities of Baltistan as well as the Ismaili and Sunni/Shia pockets in the remaining parts of the NAC region. In all of these areas, the erstwhile 'feudal' structures were formally abolished in the mid-seventies, but were not obviously and immediately replaced by other forms of government, as explained above. Thus the rationale for AKRSP can be described in the following terms:

- **Points of departure:** poverty; institutional vacuum; precarious natural resources under threat;
- **Objectives:** improved and sustainable productivity of the natural resource base;
- **Rural development strategy:** enhancement of physical capital via grant and subsidy; levering social capital in the form of Village Organisations and Women's Organisations; supported by human capital investment and financial capital accumulation.

Let us now examine AKRSP's initial experience by looking at: the institutional background for collective action and formation of VOs; the relation between AKRSP leverage and institutional formation; the formation of separate organisations for women; and the evolution of institutional diversity beyond or alongside VOs.

Institutional Background

The present day institutional landscape of the Northern Areas and Chitral is built upon a rich and complex heritage of diverse and strong indigenous forms of organisation. As indicated in Chapter 1, these groups included clans based on kinship, religion, and organised within a framework of feudal authority in remote communities that had remained isolated for centuries, protected from the outside world by the harshness of their own physical environment. This mature institutional landscape was further preserved by the political and geographical nature of isolation of this part of the country. These social building blocks reflected the management imperative to protect its precious, yet precarious, natural resources on which such a high proportion of the population depended exclusively for their livelihoods. The key natural resource conditions for survival in the mountain 'desert' are: sparse river beds and alluvial fans where settlement and agriculture occur; the glacial outlets from which irrigation channels can be constructed; and the hidden high pastures that provide sustenance to the livestock during the summer months. It is thus no surprise that the communities have found that the collective pursuit for survival is far more rewarding than individual or fragmented gain. The spirit of collective action is rooted strongly in these traditions. There are examples of such types of collective action that persist even today— the efforts to conserve the natural high forest is based on, for example, the communities' efforts of the past. Communities continue to be readily organised around these issues.

Living in isolated valleys and agrarian settlements, constantly challenged and threatened by natural disasters, the people of the region have thus developed social mechanisms and folk technology that enable them to cope with their immediate environment. Collective action has been the underlying social force that has allowed the communities to maintain their existence and to thrive in these areas. When the modern day state emerged after Pakistan gained independence, and especially after the demise of the rule of the royal families in the 1970s, slow and steady integration with the rest of the nation certainly led to the view that many of the former cohesive institutions that had existed were in danger of breaking down. This was understood in terms of 'an institutional power vacuum' and an outsider's assumption of the need for 'top-down' development. When AKRSP began its programmes in 1982, there was some element of institutional fragmentation on the ground. But behind the formal institutional changes, there existed a social spirit that had never eroded, a binding force that would be the foundations for collective action.

AKRSP Leverage and Institutional Formation

Since the beginning of its programme in 1982, AKRSP has promoted the organisation of communities and is recognised for its pioneering work in the area of social organisation. Social organisation is the process of mobilising communities to help them form village organisations (VOs) and providing them with institutional support so that they can be effective partners in development. These VOs are based upon democratic principles, requiring the participation of a majority of households in the village.[6] More than 4000 VOs and Women's Organisations (WOs) have been formed during AKRSP's twenty years of work in northern Pakistan. Using what it termed as the **diagnostic process**, AKRSP started its work in Gilgit region, and expanded rapidly into Chitral and Baltistan. The diagnostic process used a three-dialogue approach, which comprised an initial dialogue with the communities that focused upon the identification of a project; a second series of meetings, or dialogue, that included the appraisal; and the third dialogue in which formal agreements were signed (e.g. AKRSP grant and community contribution via labour days) and implementation commenced. As a result of this approach, AKRSP's initiatives have been seen as need-oriented and cost-effective. The community contribution, particularly measured through participation in implementation, management and maintenance remained at the forefront of AKRSP's initiatives. AKRSP built upon the spirit of the local communities by engaging them to be involved in their own development. The aim was to mobilise the people to organise themselves more formally and deliberately than hitherto so that they could identify and undertake projects beneficial to them. AKRSP's staff social organisers were the 'front line soldiers' that took AKRSP to the communities and worked with V/WOs throughout the process. Technical staff such as engineers, agriculturists, foresters, and livestock specialists were later included to provide technical support to the V/WOs.

As an incentive to mobilise communities, AKRSP entered the community with a 'package' of development. Obviously based on the needs of the people and area, this initially included small infrastructure projects known as PPIs. PPIs served as a quick and effective way to engage communities and act as an incentive for them to create organisations that AKRSP believed would remain active to undertake other types of activities. Building upon this, a core essence of the village organisation was mandatory savings by the members that was then linked to a credit programme. Evidence based on numerous studies and surveys within AKRSP[7] shows that many of these organisations did continue to remain active and engaged in other activities (e.g. Natural Resource Management (NRM) and credit) but it has also been the case that upon completion of these PPI activities, many VOs lost their functions and went into a period of 'dormancy.' However, as argued in this paper, dormancy is not something necessarily to be rated as a failure of AKRSP and the VO formation approach. Many communities and VOs re-grouped and emerged again—in different forms and for varying purposes, often with a new profile of leadership and membership. This process proved to be especially so for younger members of the community (particularly the more educated and perhaps even entrepreneurially oriented youth) who did not see the benefits of partnership with AKRSP for activities and inputs such as vegetable farming, poultry farming, or livestock improvement. These younger generation community members opted for different initiatives that would help improve the social status of the community at large—such as through improved social sector services, particularly education for girls, and income-generation activities linked to tourism (e.g. using funds to set up tour companies and small hotels).

V/WOs were initially village-based, later expanding in horizon to involve more supra-village level issues and activities that required coalitions of VOs that were known as clusters. More recently some of these clusters have been brought together by their members as super-clusters, thus becoming even more sophisticated valley-level organisations and local development organisations.[8] This development is closely linked to the earlier argument that where VOs lost the interest of the younger generation, villagers (sometimes men and women together) then re-grouped around different interests that would be better served by means of alternative institutions. With this process emerging, from the mid-'90s, AKRSP also began to change its approach towards social organisation by recognising diversity in the institutional landscape.

AKRSP's approach to social organisation also carried the burden of religious identities and related community responses to its external efforts. While launching its programme in the Gilgit region, AKRSP successfully managed to gain ownership among the Ismaili communities in the Hunza and Ghizer valleys. Although many Sunni communities also located in these areas, such as Ghizer, also accepted AKRSP and began to form organisations and participate in AKRSP-initiated development activities, those Sunni communities that were located in the periphery proved to be a more stern challenge. Areas towards the southeast of Gilgit are still a challenge today. Many VOs that were formed there (in Jaglote for example) did take on activities with AKRSP, especially to benefit from its credit and savings programme, only to default years down the line as the sense of 'ownership' and belonging to the programme dissipated among these communities. The spread of the programme in Baltistan also was very gradual, yet AKRSP did succeed in reaching out to a wide part of this region. In more recent years, however, the fragmented sense of ownership among the Balti Shia communities became apparent when extreme religio-political forces denounced AKRSP and appealed to the communities to de-link themselves from AKRSP. AKRSP–Baltistan emerged intact from this crisis in the late 1990s with great difficulty. Although AKRSP's programme continues in Baltistan, the weak sense of ownership and commitment remains an issue.

The 'Other' Half: the formation of separate organisations for women

Women in northern Pakistan have played strong traditional roles at home, in the community and in society at large. While contributing the majority of the labour at home through domestic chores and carrying out many of the labour intensive functions in farming (including fetching water, livestock rearing, and harvesting of the crops), women have also been an invisible pillar of strength that binds the community together in this remote corner of the world. Despite the important role that women hold in these communities (through kinship links, ritual practices, observing religious events and festivals, and participating albeit indirectly in resource management and common property decisions), their lives can be easily characterised by a large household and farm workload, restricted mobility, and extremely limited access to education and other social services.

AKRSP's institutional approach to working with women and, more relevantly here, with organised women, has gone through variations throughout its two-decade history. At the outset of the programme, AKRSP believed that women's development needs would be included and addressed through the collective base of VOs—a village organisation which would include the meaningful participation of men and women. However, AKRSP was to soon learn that in a society where women's participation and representation outside of the household and in the realm of men was restricted, women could not be meaningful and active participants in the VOs. Women from the communities themselves approached AKRSP to demand a separate platform on which they could join together to take part in issues that were of importance and relevance to them. AKRSP was swift in modifying its approach and began the formation of women's organisations. It recruited female social organisers to help facilitate this process.

Initially, typically and traditionally, the women's programme did not vary much from the interventions that were targeted at 'male dominated' VOs. Women became active participants in credit and savings activities, and especially in packages related to those agriculture and livestock activities that were within their traditional realm, particularly poultry and vegetable production. AKRSP, for the women, was a source of support and impetus to help them formally take on familiar activities for income-generation purposes. The opportunities provided to them seemed endless, and participating women began to experience their entrance into an entirely new social way of being. Men in the same communities generally supported the WOs as they recognised this to be an opportunity to increase the village's overall participation with AKRSP and the packages that it had to offer. Gradually, women began to undertake activities beyond the farm, including innovative packages such as village shops (where women could sell sundry goods to women by taking credit from AKRSP and operating easily accessible shopping for women in the villages), vocational training for skills such as tailoring and embroidery, and literacy centres. However, the process of women's participation through WOs varied from one region to another, and even today many challenges remain in some of the more conservative communities where the formation of WOs has been a difficult task.

However, women's needs exceeded what was being met within the remit of WOs and what AKRSP had to offer through the traditional V/WO approach. Even in the less remote areas, women were still experiencing inadequate access to health and education, and even where the basic services were available (e.g., primary schools for girls and basic health units), access to higher levels of services (i.e., opportunities for middle and higher schooling, and facilities for more complicated cases for women's health) was still missing. By the mid-1990s, more than fifteen years into AKRSP's work, women of northern Pakistan began seeking participation in some of the other activity-specific local development organisations that were emerging in the area.

Similarly, AKRSP's own institutional approach towards women and women's organisation underwent transformation. When AKRSP began working with WOs, it recruited and formed a separate cadre of female professionals to work on the women's development programme. This was to facilitate better access for AKRSP into the conservative realm of women, and to support them in a close manner. Gradually, and keeping up with the development pendulum of moving from 'Women in Development' (WID) to 'Gender and Development' (GAD), AKRSP adopted a generic gender approach and began to merge its women's programme into the mainstream programme from the mid-1990s. This process was not easy, not least for the women employed at AKRSP.[9] In conservative parts of Baltistan, Chitral, and even Gilgit, the spirit of women's participation through WOs suffered some setbacks as AKRSP female staff were having to attend to mainstream VOs as well as WOs. This was particularly difficult in an institutional environment when resources that had been previously allocated specifically to women were no longer exclusively at their disposal, often causing delays in their work programme. This entire process was a struggle for AKRSP as well as for the communities. The semi-autonomous regions of AKRSP[10] responded by reverting back to the 'WID' approach. Thus, in the relatively more conservative Baltistan and Chitral, this was a welcome step for the communities and also provided relief to the female staff. Gilgit region has maintained its gender mainstreaming approach at the organisational level, which has produced mixed results in the diverse and varied communities of Gilgit region.

AKRSP continues to work out what would be the best strategy to work with the women of the north. As a flexible organisation, it has recognised that what might work for women of Hunza does not apply to women of Astore, Baltistan or lower Chitral. The social fabric of women in northern Pakistan is as diverse, if not more, than that of the men and society at large, and this has been the cause of much tension, debate, experimentation and change in AKRSP as an organisation.

Evolution of Institutional Diversity

Like with the women's programme, recognising diversity and different ways of approaching the communities emerged as a key development in AKRSP's institutional history. The area, the communities, and the fabric of collective action have seen tremendous change during these first twenty years of AKRSP. It is relatively easy to measure the amount of tangible, physical change that has occurred by glancing at AKRSP's well-documented statistics: land area brought under cultivation, number of trees planted, numbers of infrastructure projects completed, amount of land developed into forest and so on.[11] However, what is difficult to monitor and measure is the degree of social change that began to take place within the communities. This change has manifested itself in various forms, most obviously by the types of diverse forms of organised institutions that have emerged and even now continue to form. The realisation of the significance of these institutional developments 'crept up' on AKRSP from the mid '90s, and were extensively discussed by staff through the Training and Learning Programme (TLP) in Social Development during the later '90s.[12]

Essentially, in social organisation terms, two dimensions have emerged which have challenged AKRSP's mainstream original approach of concentrating at the village level via the windows of infrastructure development, and productivity improvement in local natural resources especially at the farm level. First, organisational levels beyond and above the VO were re-activated by local communities in order to address the wider (often common property management) issues of pasture and forest management, more extensive and technologically challenging irrigation channels, as well as wildlife conservation and preservation of natural forests. Most of these issues involve 'natural resource' space beyond the 'social' space of the *mohallah* or village. Since these extended spaces require social organisation across and beyond immediate kin and clan identity (and sometimes religious sect also) in the context of increasing demand pressures for use of these resources (with population pressure, fragmentation of farm holdings and so on), formal organisations at cluster and valley levels were required.[13] Secondly, the AKRSP social organisation focus upon its mainstream activities was increasingly bypassing the interests of a significant proportion of the local population.[14] In addition to the problem of bypassing the interests of the poorest households in the NAC who could benefit only to a minor extent from farm level investment (as their holdings were so small), other interests, especially of the youth, were being overlooked. These tended to be interests more aligned to the social sector. Thus an observer might reasonably refer to other parts of AKDN to address these interests. However, the point is that AKRSP had the lead role in social organisation among AKDN, but was following a mode of partnership (V/WOs and clusters) which effectively excluded these interests. It was thus excluding itself in a mobilisation/organisation sense from the emerging social development agenda for its programme area.

Numerous examples can thus be cited which demonstrate this dynamic aspect of collective action in the Northern Areas and Chitral. Nonhihal Development Organization (NDO) is a local NGO in Nagar Valley of Gilgit region. It took root in a locally driven initiative by a group of motivated individuals that sought something else than what AKRSP was offering—the opportunity to promote access to girls' education through establishment of primary and middle schools and mobilising communities to identify young women who could serve as teachers, as well as the promotion of primary health care (including maternity clinics). From its early beginnings in 1995 when AKRSP facilitated and encouraged its development,[15] NDO has developed into an NGO receiving funds from a variety of donors. Slightly later, the Karakoram Area Development Organisation emerged in Hunza (around Karimabad and Aliabad), though this was supported more in its inception by the Aga Khan Cultural Services Programme (AKCSP) and focused particularly upon the commercial production of traditional handicrafts designs and products.[16] Further examples also emerged during the second half of the '90s in Baltistan and Chitral. Thus, across NAC, there are now farmers' associations, fruit marketing interest groups, wildlife preservation groups, educational and welfare associations—all formed within the fundamental social fabric, outlined above, that has held the communities together for centuries.

AKRSP has responded to these different institutions with increasing flexibility yet also with considerable difficulty. As an organisation, AKRSP had been used to an approach whereby V/WOs, formed through its 'mainstream social organisation' approach, were the main mediator between the Programme and the communities. However, as these different groups became more prominent on the landscape, AKRSP recognised the need to alter its approach. In addition to the internal training and learning efforts of AKRSP,[17] the different manifestations of collective action were themselves the greatest learning ground for AKRSP and its staff.

A further dimension to institutional diversity in collective action has been the increasing presence of other external development, conservation and social sector partners in the NAC. Within the AKDN, as noted above, other programmes such as the Aga Khan Education Service and the Aga Khan Health Service have been working in the region for decades longer than AKRSP. Other newcomers such as IUCN and WWF also work vigorously in the area, and with the same communities as AKRSP. Local communities in NAC have been much more aware about the different policy objectives, and management and organisational styles of these various development programmes than even the programmes themselves were. They have become adept at altering their organisational profile to interact through the different organisational windows erected by these potential external partners. Whether they organised themselves as VOs and met with AKRSP staff one day, and the same people re-grouped as a Village Education Committee the next day for a meeting with the Aga Khan Education Service, or presented themselves as a political constituency for a meeting with a local councillor or Government official, the underlying spirit of collective action and local level solidarity persists, at least when dealing with external agencies. However, we also need to recognise the processes of fission and fusion at different levels of 'locality', which can appear as conflict, mutual suspicion and distrust when differentiated local groups are trying to negotiate with each other. Thus although forms of ongoing, unplanned collective action can clearly be identified, the picture is not one of unilinear or even predictable social capital formation, since threats and challenges also arise from other dimensions of socio-economic and cultural change in the NAC.

Key Factors Shaping Collective Action and Social Capital in Northern Pakistan

The impact of AKRSP on the region has been analysed by many insiders and outsiders, including a series of World Bank evaluations, the most recent of which was presented in February 2002.[18]

However, this chapter goes beyond a formal evaluation of impact in its limited sense of whether the institutions introduced by AKRSP have taken root in the society. We are concerned to examine a more subtle process of social capital formation or decline, and the role of an external catalyst in that process. **The crucial test for an organisation like AKRSP is not whether its own institutional models have been adopted and internalised by the local populace, but whether the principle of achieving common livelihoods objectives through associational life has been strengthened and refined.** Overall, therefore, we are considering an argument that a variety of associational forms are evolving which reflect the perceived needs of local populations at particular points in time, but which do not necessarily represent a strict continuation of the AKRSP model of VOs, WOs and clusters, or even valley forums.[19] In this sense, we have to recognise that AKRSP operates in a changing socio-economic context beyond its own influence, so that the analysis of collective action has to reflect a combination of historical and contemporary dimensions. There are four key issues to consider: institutional legacy; micro-diversity; individualisation; and the socio-economic change case for poverty targeting.

Firstly the assumptions made by AKRSP about an 'institutional power vacuum', after the abolition of feudal authority structures, were too strong and over-emphasised. It is clear that many traditional local institutions have continued to perform essential collective management functions in the village. Some of these institutions are religious, performing social functions; some are hierarchical; some are reciprocal. Thus the VOs and WOs formed by AKRSP are part of pre-existing social structures and as such are deeply embedded into the village institutional landscape, consisting of kin relations, clan structures and power configurations. These relationships shape the real social character of 'participation' and 'democracy' in these AKRSP organisations. What appears as full-scale collective action is usually reflecting inequalities in influence and power, with the stronger families dominating. While the basis of that domination may have altered, say from being the appointee of the feudal authority (known as the *numberdar* in some areas) towards being the larger landholder, being more formally educated, and/or receiver of the larger remittances leading to visible positional goods (e.g. housing, 4x4s, and satellite TVs), the erstwhile stronger families have mainly been the ones to capture the new opportunities both inside and outside the village.

Secondly, as has been noted, there was and is considerable micro-diversity across AKRSP's area of operation in terms of: location (growth poles and peripheries); cropping zone; accessibility by road; religious sect; language group; traditional institutions; education levels; migration patterns (down-country education, employment); availability of remittance incomes; extent of reliance on farming and other local natural resources for livelihoods survival; penetration of external markets; and commercial production and trading opportunities. The social significance of this diversity for collective action is that families resemble each other less and less. They have less in common to manage and therefore declining interest in maintaining the integrity of membership, rules, adjudication and sanctions. However, although there is a trend shift away from collective social and cultural forms to individualisation derived from an increasing nucleation of families partly induced by more family specific and diversified livelihood portfolios, in organisational terms, this trend is not universal across all sectors.[20] This is where the subtlety of analysis is required, especially where a continued reliance is necessary upon some local natural resources as well as the necessity for limited welfare exchanges between households for all families, partly as an insurance against disaster in the down-country economy and partly as a feature of general vulnerability connected to fluctuating family fortunes in the domestic life cycle.[21] Thus collective forms of management are retained in natural resource arenas like irrigation and grazing, even if 'management' now only involves respect for rules and the hiring of other labour to perform the family labour obligations. But also, collective forms of social protection, often organised through socio-religious institutions, also remain especially for the welfare of the destitute.[22] We will also see below situations where collective action reappears in various forms, as a reflection of perceived needs and opportunities.

Thirdly, in a more theoretical sense these trends towards individualisation have profound implications for the cohesiveness of the shared sense of 'community' and the prospects for common property management. The whole notion of membership of the local community and of the common property management group is challenged by the socio-economic differentiation between families, with family members developing attachments and loyalties to other institutions, especially through employment but also sometimes through political party allegiances. Back in the local communities of NAC, these crosscutting and often external ties can introduce problems of free-riding and the breakdown of collective economic security as the primary identity. Those who outmigrate, even seasonally, reduce their reliance upon these local, collectively managed resources (natural or welfare ones) but cannot actually detach themselves completely due to insecurities elsewhere. Thus they cannot be complete deserters, while finding it difficult simultaneously to be complete members. Their participation is restricted, so that free-riding is more structural and less voluntary, motivated more by competing loyalties to other parts of their livelihoods portfolio than by cheating and the search for unfair advantage, which so characterises the literature on free-riding (e.g. Ostrom 1990 and Ostrom *et al.* 1994). These trends challenge and set limits to the validity of indigenous, traditional institutions of collective management (i.e. clan, *mohallah*, mosque/*jamatkhana*/ *imambarga*) as well as the VOs and WOs formed by AKRSP as the preferred institutions for natural resource management, infrastructural investment and maintenance, as well as other financial welfare transactions within the 'communities'.

Fourth, the increasing integration of local communities with wider markets and down-country employment opportunities is responsible for more socio-economic differentiation (i.e. inequality) in the villages (Wood 1996).[23] This has introduced a potential irony, with AKRSP tempted to focus more upon poverty reduction through socially targeting its interventions rather than working with the 'whole community'. This notion of targeting is a new departure for AKRSP and has been hotly debated within the organisation and its constituencies, since the whole previous philosophy of its approach has been to underplay internal differentiation at the local level in order to promote community level participation and social capital through institution building. But a more targeted strategy of poverty reduction, partially in response to demands from donors but also a response to the changing profile of poverty, runs the risk of further undermining collective management principles by acknowledging the limitations of the non-poor families to respond to the needs of the poorest in the community. However, again, the picture is not so simple. We have found that poverty targeting can also bring collective institutions of moral responsibility further into play with local safety net and welfare transfer functions being performed by mosque committees or other such *mohallah* level organisations, thereby reinforcing or even rejuvenating collective action and traditional charitable instincts and practices (Wood 2002).

Non-linear development paths: latent social capital

Given the observations above, we cannot presume a simple linear story of the re-formation of social capital away from personalised, localised forms into abstract, 'society at large' de-personalised forms, characterised by formal, statutory rights and binding contracts. While clearly there are some tendencies in that direction, there are also countervailing tendencies consistent with Long's (2001) notion of re-localisation. This conclusion offers the prospect of some unconventional or unfamiliar observations in the context of more 'normal' discourses about AKRSP and other similar external development agencies. Firstly, NGOs with a strong social mobilisation theme are frequently judged, not least by their donors, in terms of institutional sustainability, self-reliance and maturity. Indeed AKRSP itself developed an Institutional Maturity Index to record this process and offer milestones of achievement to its donors, *inter alia*.[24] However, it is argued in this study that this test of the formation of social capital has been over-narrowly conceived and does not reflect an appropriately sophisticated view of any institutional development process. The 'test' restricts valid

observations to the continuation of active institutional forms
derived strictly from the original social mobilisation model—in the
case of AKRSP this refers to VOs and WOs, and their 'cluster'
spin-offs. But this is not a true test of the principle if the emergence
or continuation of other institutional forms are not recognised.
Secondly, given the additional principle of perceived needs and
opportunities, is it valid to conclude that dead or dormant VOs are
evidence of social mobilisation failure? Perversely, dormant VOs
may precisely be evidence of success! Thirdly, how do we account
for the exclusivity of the social mobilisation model in the first
place? It is becoming clear that VOs and WOs have not captured
all the available and latent interest in associational life: i.e. they are
not the only model in town.

We now pursue this argument through the exploration of
associational initiatives in different sectors of activity (and need) in
the rural societies of NAC, Northern Pakistan. But it is important
to acknowledge that any argument about the activation of latent
social capital has to weigh the balance between the realisation of
potential and the constraints to achieving that potential. In other
words, the story is not one-sided and any optimism about the
emergence of depersonalised and disembedded social capital (i.e.
sustainable and independent of particular actors) across the region
has to be tempered by the power of countervailing social forces and
trends as noted above.[25] Perhaps the driving principle for this
analysis is that the kinds of organisations which people create and
sustain arise out of the combination of the quality of social
conditions which might form the basis of successful collective
action (i.e. senses of shared social and cultural experience, interests
and values) and the perceptions of shared need felt by those
members of the local community. These factors would seem to
define both the 'whether' as well as the 'which' of collective action:
will it happen, and if so, in what manner? Thus, we find a tension
between the ambitions for universal, large-scale NGOs covering
large parts of the region and strong local preferences for subsidiarity,
reflecting particular identities and an unwillingness to take
collective action beyond recognisable, intimate social space. This
sets a limit to the formation of depersonalised forms of social

capital associated with modern, market societies, and retains the significance of segmentary groups as the basis of trust and mutual support. A very local re-localisation, in other words.

It is a little difficult to organise the discussion which follows since we are observing forms of collective action which sometimes address a single purpose, like micro-hydels and the provision of electricity, and which are sometimes multi-purpose across many sectors such as the Karimabad Area Development Organisation (KADO) in the Lutko valley of western, upper Chitral. We are pursuing the argument, therefore, through the following themes: the continuing reliance upon NRM; resolutions to the local energy problem through the introduction of micro-hydels; the evolution of welfare associations outside the V/WO framework; and the formation of more extensive valley associations embracing welfare and development objectives, building upon the collective action experience of V/WOs.

Reliance on Natural Resource Management: public goods, personal resources

NRM conceived as the management of forest (natural or planted), grazing areas (high or low), wildlife and fish has both 'public goods' and 'personal resource' properties. Motivations for action vary accordingly. The question is: which actions are consistent with sustainability? There is also the further problem of whether local conceptions of common property are in fact challenged by other claimants thus converting the resource to open access, or common pool status. Without an effective local state, the defining and policing of common property claims can only rely upon a common sense of rights and therefore legitimate exclusion, or upon meaningful threats of sanction to produce the same outcome. These outcomes are also affected by time preference behaviour, which can vary both according to the resource and its public/private property status. Thus forests and pastures, as quintessentially public goods with weak property status and strong open access characteristics, induce high discount rates among users. Indeed the fear of competitive over-use by others can induce depletion behaviour beyond immediate use values or even realistic exchange values. The Upper Basho Forest near Skardu in Baltistan is a good example of the breakdown of collective action under conditions of open access. Until a forest road was constructed in the early 1970s, only local communities in Upper Basho had access to the forest and its use for traditional consumption needs was sustainable. The process of constructing the road involved labour from other, lower villages and this encouraged the practice of bringing down wood for personal household use when returning home after work. This, in turn, established an informal right which *de facto* extended into collecting wood for commercial sale in Skardu market. When the local communities of Upper Basho recognised the depletion of their natural resource base in the early '90s it had become too late for them to challenge the claims of outside communities. Thus the forest had effectively been transferred to open access from common property, with the 'timber mafias' from the lower communities, who had the better access to other markets, undermining the prospects for creating effective collective action to prevent further extinction of the forest on which the upper communities depend. The 'resource-hopping', commercial instincts of entrepreneurs, not ultimately dependent upon a continuation of local resources, effectively overcame the possibilities for deploying the institutional potential of VOs in the area to regulate the use of the natural resource base.[26]

However public goods and personal resources need not always be in conflict. Here we explore dependency on local resources in a comparative context of constraints to resource-hopping, using the forest depletion comparison between Chilas/Darail (south-west of Gilgit) and Chalt/Chaprote in Nagar, upper Gilgit (Gohar 2002). The opportunities for resource-hopping are greater in Chilas/Darail with irreversible depletion already evident due to proximity to down-country markets and the mobility of forest owners to capture entirely different resources derived from forest profits. This contrasts strongly with the Chalt/Chaprote case in the upper, remoter valleys where resource hopping is constrained by lack of alternatives, so that personal use-value interests, low natural resource discount rates and therefore sustainable public goods management have a greater chance to coincide. There are outbreaks of conflicts, but collective action institutions can and are called into play for their resolution. In Ostrom's terms (1990 and later publications by her), the sense of the multi-period, self contract enforcement game is sufficiently shared as to constrain unworthy behaviour in the present, or at least to permit iterative negotiation in a game sequence. In effect this awareness of the possibilities for iterative negotiation is the basis of community and collective action in such a context. By contrast, under the resource-hopping opportunities of Upper Basho or Chilas/Darail, high discount rates are rational along, therefore, with free-riding, a weakened sense of common property as open access conditions take over, with a consequent low investment in either renewing the resource or devising mechanisms of protection. It is not only that collective action fails to prevent this sequence of behaviour with its depletion outcome, but that any ingredients of collective action are positively undermined in the process.

Across the whole of NAC, almost all households have some element of their livelihoods dependent upon farming and therefore channel irrigation. Any application of the resource-hopping principle in this context would refer to a lack of interest in improving a local channel or creating an entirely new, higher one that would bring more cultivable waste land[27] under cultivation. It would also refer to a lack of interest and free-riding in the maintenance of such channels, which involves contributing labour from the household. Over the last 16 years, for example, in Ghanche District of Baltistan, 21,257 acres of barren land have been brought under irrigation for the first time, and 14,534 acres of pre-existing cultivable land now have more secure water availability. This is the outcome of 192 AKRSP-led irrigation projects in the district, with an estimated 17,809 households benefiting. Given the instability of the local mountain environment with earthquakes and frequent landslides and mudslides, and in the absence of an effective government irrigation department, the local communities really have had no option but to participate in continuous maintenance of these channels as a reflection of their resource dependency. Crucially this has required collective action beyond the VO level with hydrological space significantly exceeding social space. This achievement is clearly based upon successful and sustained social mobilisation in which the principles of collective action, participation and partnership are paramount. This contrasts sharply with pre-AKRSP failed attempts by government to complete any of its initiated mega-irrigation projects: Koro Irrigation Channel in 1969, Siksa Irrigation Channel in 1974, Longkha Irrigation Channel in 1974 and the Kanday Irrigation Channel in 1970. Despite committing a total of Rs 300 million to these projects and having appropriate technical designs, the government had failed to set up a partnership with the local communities, engage their voluntary labour for both construction and maintenance, and establish any sense of local ownership derived from these labour contributions.[28]

Management of Energy: Organisational Opportunities and Constraints arising from the Micro-Hydel Experience

It is customary to spread gloom on this sector by referring to exponential demand in the face of limited supply leading to: forest depletion; higher costs of fuel purchases; and the inadequacies of the state in providing appropriate large-scale investment and efficient unit costs of supply. While these observations are largely true as contributing to the breakdown of common property forms of management, we can note a significant non-linear development in which social capital is re-affirmed and strengthened rather then giving way to the pressures of differentiation and individualisation. The case is micro-hydels, specifically from the implementation of many schemes from Chitral. These are small-scale turbines driven by concentrated flows of water diverted from rivers into channels to create a powerful head before sending it shooting down pipes to the turbine. These micro-hydels mainly produce lighting, but those with higher capacity can also power small motors, especially for milling. Generally the capacity, in relation to the priority demand for lighting, prevents any use for heating. Indeed, at present capacities of between 10-50kw for a local community, other uses are expressly forbidden, and fines can be incurred. However the significance of electric lighting cannot be under-estimated and the local demand is very high, though as Lawson-McDowall (2000) has demonstrated, not inelastic. The collective action required to manage these units sustainably is considerable through different phases of construction, operation and maintenance, and cost recovery. If external grant support is required, this can only be obtained with evidence of a partially matching fund raised in the community to cover subsequent maintenance costs. Thus community level funds have to be raised even before anyone has had sight of the installation. Although a grant might support equipment costs and some technical labour inputs, usually the community has to commit unskilled labour. Again this has to be mobilised, keeping various dimensions of equity between households in mind. A management committee has to be created with responsibility not only for mobilising labour but also for raising and sustaining the necessary finance.

With the micro-hydel installed, it has to be operated in a sustainable manner. This is where long term collective action is required for everyone's success. A charging system has to be devised which maximises the take up of available capacity, while avoiding free-riding and the high transaction costs associated with fee avoidance. Over-inclusiveness may only be achieved at a price which is too low to maintain the operation. Exclusiveness at a higher price may be divisive within the community and undermine other forms of parallel collective action (such as forest or grazing management). Exclusiveness combined with means-tested philanthropy can entail high transactions costs, but they can achieve legitimate outcomes in which 'free-riding' by the poor is institutionalised as deliberate policy. Lawson-McDowall (2000) certainly found a higher incidence of such behaviour in Chitral than in his comparative cases in Nepal.[29]

With hundreds of these micro-hydels now installed in the region, especially in Chitral, there is clear evidence of successful and sustained collective management. This can be illustrated by one of Effendi's cases from Toque Village in the Yarkhun Valley of upper Chitral. Using one of their VOs in the village, Hazratabad, the villagers initiated a dialogue process with AKRSP in June 1997 and completed the project in November of that year before the winter. The project is a particularly strong illustration of ingenious collective action since a water source had to be created alongside a power channel, with construction immediately adjacent to the river being the only topographical option. Thus the VO organised the labour of its own members and other villagers to construct a reservoir of approximately eight *kanals* as the water source, fed by underground streams thereby insulating it from icing up during winter, as well as constructing the power channel. In addition to mobilising labour contributions from outside the VO, the micro-hydel management committee has identified five households, which it assessed as being too poor to afford payments for electricity, and which are now provided electricity, free of cost. Kuragh Village, near Booni has also identified four households to which it provides free electricity. These forms of collective action are occurring even in situations where other common property resource management has broken down, and in some instances has played a role in rehabilitating other, parallel forms of common property management as a bonus outcome. This spreading across of social capital does not always occur, however. Effendi's study of Kuragh is pessimistic about further collective action beyond the immediate management of the micro-hydel, seeing the VO as more strategically created to access AKRSP packages like micro-hydel, but otherwise characterised by unequal households with increasingly differentiated interests, competing with each other to purchase status goods such as satellite TV. Finally, the Izh case illustrates the example of VOs joining together in clusters in order to access and maintain a larger capacity micro-hydel (presently 35kw but soon to move to its full potential of 50kw when the power channel is enhanced). Beyond Effendi's study location, clusters above Izh in Begusht valley (Ujog and Begusht clusters) have been created out of constituent VOs in order to set up micro-hydels.[30]

These three clusters in Begusht have now constituted themselves as a super-cluster in order to plan for a larger hydel installation, arguing that only by organising on this scale can 'mega' projects be contemplated to extend electricity capacity to embrace heating and cooking thus contributing seriously to the conservation of other natural resources by reducing demand for forest products. Such enlarged capacity will also facilitate the creation of other business opportunities in the locality. Indeed the leaders of this super-cluster[31] are trying to rejuvenate the idea of the Garam Cheshma Area Development Organisation (GADO) which was actually registered as a welfare association in 1998 and currently has around 200 activist members. The basis of this organisational ambition has been the creation over the last few years of Valley Conservation Committees to manage high pastures sustainably.[32] A reinvigoration of GADO would bring together 14 clusters, 44 villages, 73 VOs, 87 WOs comprising 2,425 households and a population of approximately 18,200. These same leaders indicated that ways would have to be found to engage the next generation in these ambitions for an NGO, since the V/WO institutions are not relevant to their interests and aspirations.[33]

However, the overall conclusion from the examples offered above is that while there may be linear trends in the decline of social capital around the management of key renewable natural resources in some areas such as Basho and Chilas/Darail, there can also be reversals of such trends for some of these resources (like the high pastures in Begusht). And if new, highly desired resources are created (such as micro-hydel sourced electricity) under conditions where resource-hopping to other forms of energy is effectively denied, forms of collective action can re-emerge even from communities which had strategically created VOs to access PPIs and then abandoned them as irrelevant to their needs.[34] For example, coal deposits in Charpursan, upper Hunza-Gojal, have been found though initial estimates of volume were far too optimistic, and there would be many other environmental management problems attached to such an initiative.[35] Oil and gas are too expensive to import into the area on a significant scale, even for the more well-off families, though some families are using gas cylinders for domestic heating. Solar panel technology has not yet reduced its unit costs to make it commercially viable in relation to local effective demand. Larger scale, state run turbines remain risky as a public sector venture in the eyes of local people due to perceptions of corruption and incompetence.

Evolution of Village Welfare Associations outside the V/WO Framework

In Chapter 2, we have argued that with the increasing socio-economic differentiation of the population over the last two decades new forms of poverty and need have emerged. We have also indicated in this paper that the V/WO organisational approach is not the only model in town, and does not embrace all the interests, needs and aspirations of people when they are seeking to achieve welfare and development outcomes through collective action. Thus there are many examples from across NAC of other associations emerging which do not strictly derive from V/WO origins, though an awareness of the advantages to be gained from collective action may have been indirectly stimulated from the V/WO experience. This refers back to our central argument that forms of associational life may be emerging which depart from the V/WO and cluster format, but are nevertheless valid tests of AKRSP's contribution to social capital formation. Any example chosen to illustrate this theme will invite the criticism of selection or sub-regional bias, but this chapter cannot offer an inventory of the total experience in this regard.

The primary example offered under this heading comes from Lutko in Chitral: the Mogh (*sic*) Welfare Society. The village of Mough (*sic*) is situated 11km south of Garam Cheshma, though strictly in the Shogore Union Council, and is 35km north of Chitral town. It comprises about 75 households, mostly joint. Although quality educational institutions have been far away from the village, it is a 'highly educated' village, and its 'graduates' have served in different organisations, including AKDN, outside the village. However, there has been recent concern that education levels are falling, and some of the educated leaders (e.g. teachers and other professionals) considered that the formation of a welfare society would improve both educational and social development generally in the village. The society was established in February 2003, and is clearly an example of the kind of local welfare and development organisation which AKRSP seeks to promote as part of its post V/WO vision. Although initially motivated by education, it has quickly become a multi-purpose organisation. Its leaders are primarily teachers and other serving professionals (e.g. including the Head Teacher of the local Middle School and the Female Social Organiser of AKRSP now serving in Booni). There were also young students (men and women) present at the meeting with Wood (25.8.03). It has created eight sub-committees, whose titles give an indication of its objectives: education; drug control; environment; sports; village cleanliness; construction; social welfare; and fund raising. Each committee comprises a convenor and a small team.

One of its key principles is to support poorer families in the village. The leaders estimate that there are ten 'needy' households out of the 75 total in the village. These families are being supported through fee waivers for their children at the local school, support for the purchase of school uniforms and essential learning materials, financial support at the time of their marriages, assistance with doctor's fees and medicines. This 'cross-subsidy' or welfare transfer element of the Society's agenda is thus a clear example of the safety net and social protection functions which we indicated as a necessary part of local poverty targeting in Chapter 2. Its objectives include those traditionally seen as AKRSP-VO development activities. Thus, its Construction committee intends to support all villagers in the construction of roads, bridges, irrigation channels and the hydel station, and to engage outside professionals to assist with such work. Its Environment committee addresses conservation of wildlife and forests as well as supplying seeds and plants to its members. Its Cleanliness committee is cleaning up the rubbish around the village (plastic, glass and other waste), introducing a fining system for delinquent households, and making arrangements for clean drinking water for all. It has not yet included sanitation, but it probably will with this overall agenda. There is a concern about 'drugs' in the village, and in the society generally. Their concept of drugs embraces tobacco smoking and excessive alcohol consumption as well as opium and cannabis. The concern extends to trafficking, so shopkeepers and other potential dealers (i.e. those who travel frequently) are being contacted to avoid this practice. There is no sense that drug taking is serious or widespread in the community, but clearly a concern that it could become so under

other media influences, or as a result of unemployment of youth
and so on. Thus these measures against drugs (e.g. lectures about
health, counselling individuals) can be seen as preventive at this
stage. The Sports committee is active and had already arranged one
Sports Festival in March 2003, in which traditional games were
promoted.[36] It is clear not only from this example of Mogh, but
from many discussions with AKRSP field staff and activists across
the Gilgit and Chitral regions that young people in the village are
not very interested in the V/WO institutions, but are forming
sports associations in many villages as an outlet for their
entertainment and pursuit of health. The Mogh society has also
established a Nizari library in the village, and will add to its stock
as funds permit. The Social Welfare committee adds to the cross-
subsidy activity of the Education committee by looking at the
prospects of extending micro-finance products to enable poorer
families to offset their vulnerability through open access savings.

Finally, its Fund Raising committee is mobilising internal funds
but also seeking support from external NGOs and philanthropists.
On the day that Wood was meeting the Society, one of its leaders
had just returned from Chitral town where she had met a rich
visiting uncle from Canada, who had promised to support some of
the activities of the Education committee. Each committee
convenor is expected to work with the Fund Raising committee in
the search for financial support. Internally, the leaders estimate that
in addition to the 10 per cent of visible (i.e. non-farm subsistence)
income paid as a 'tax' to the Ismaili Jamat, those who can afford it
are contributing around 5 per cent additional income to the
Society. There is no formal means testing for these contributions
and amounts contributed vary. However, everyone knows each
other's business sufficiently to judge whether a household is being
generous, average or niggardly in its contributions. This is one of
the advantages of small-scale organisations as argued by Mancur
Olsen: the inter-personal knowledge of members limits free-
riding.

Of course, many questions can be asked about an organisation
like this one. To what extent is it an institutional reversion to
traditional, customary forms of local level charity as might be

experienced through the *jamatkhana*?[37] Thus to what extent does it rely upon the voluntary efforts of self-appointed leaders, with limited principles of participation? The jury is still out in the sense that while there are formal management turnover arrangements, will they actually be realised when first tested? There is a General Body of all 'members' in the village, and this General Body will select/elect members of the Cabinet (i.e. an executive of five office-bearers) every two years. But given what we generally know about village power and leadership structures, will this Cabinet ever change, or will the original activists feel that they are the best qualified and motivated thereby justifying a retention of control, and do they have the social power in the village through traditional clan/kin superiority to ensure this? If they are the best educated, then we can be fairly sure that they come from the strongest families. Does a lack of real internal participation and democracy matter, as long as important development and welfare functions are being performed? Is there a case for a continuing external agency like AKRSP, via some form of leverage, simply to reduce discretion and increase transparency and accountability of financial decision-making so that arbitrary charity is regularised as stable, albeit informal (i.e. not statutory) rights? Does the voluntary element of the activism necessarily restrict the ongoing leadership to those who have the professions, income, property and time which permit such voluntarism, while poorer families are necessarily fully engaged in income generation from farm work or migrant employment?

These are hard, possibly over sceptical, questions given that this is precisely an example of post-VO social capital formation, which constitutes the more appropriate test of AKRSP's (or other external catalyst agency) institution building efforts. After meeting with the leaders of the Society, including young teachers (men and women) and students as well as a couple of 'older hands', it is even more difficult to be judgemental about the possible limits to governance in the future. Perhaps the essential point at this stage is that although causation is difficult to establish between AKRSP's past efforts at social organisation and these non V/WO/Cluster initiatives, their emergence is significant as potentially strong counterpart local welfare/development associations to AKRSP's evolving institutional strategy of removing its own operational presence in favour of a more limited role of promotion, facilitation, mediation, technical support and linkages. Certainly for the argument of this chapter, the emergence of such organisations[38] is clear evidence that in some communities at least[39] the perceived reliance for livelihoods upon one's own efforts is producing the conditions for collective action and limited free-riding.

The formation of more extensive valley associations embracing welfare and development objectives, building upon the collective action experience of V/WOs

Again using an example from Chitral, KADO represents a powerful example of the preferred future direction for AKRSP, and perhaps for AKDN more widely. The descriptive analysis which follows is based upon a recent report[40] and direct interviews between Wood and most of its Board members.[41] Although the organisation was formally registered with the Social Welfare Department of the Government of NWFP in July 2000, its origins in collective action go back to the 1960s, and certainly received a boost during the eighties with the formation of VOs and later WOs through AKRSP. Thus in this case there is a causal relationship between the emergence of KADO and AKRSP's own past institution-building efforts. The Karimabad valley also lies in Lutko, tracking initially north-east from Shogore on the Chitral–Garam Cheshma road then bending round more eastwards as it goes up to Susoom village at its upper end. KADO now also embraces the neighbouring valley of Boktuli, near to Shogore. Thus at present it comprises: 7 clusters; 36 villages, 50 VOs, 46 WOs, and 1800 households. Its formation as KADO representing the whole valley was preceded by the formation of a super-cluster of three constituent clusters (Susoom, Breshgram and Herth) in the late 90s, but these were insufficiently representative of the whole valley, hence the later expansion into KADO.

Although having its organisational origins in the VO-Cluster sponsorship of AKRSP, and having the support of an AKRSP Social

Organiser in developing the idea of a wider local development organisation, the formation of KADO was partly inspired by the need to mediate between the competing interests of VOs and clusters in the valley. These institutions had individually scored well in the AKRSP Institutional Maturity Index rating, and it would seem that this strength at the micro level was itself a barrier to further cooperation at a wider, all valley level. Yet there were clearly valley wide interests to be served in terms of high pasture management, forest conservation, irrigation systems, larger scale hydel installations and other social sector facilities such as schools, health clinics and telecommunications (at least, telephone connections). At the same time, the whole valley had and retains a strong sense of common identity. In this sense, the communities represent a classic case of fission and fusion: sometimes cooperating based upon common cultural/sect identity, sometimes in conflict over scarce resources and the location of larger facilities. The 'theoretical' resolution to this fission and fusion is the principle of subsidiarity, recognising that different levels of organisation are appropriate to the achievement of different objectives, with the lowest level of collective action always being favoured where appropriate since the lower the level, the lower the transaction costs of participation, the lower the extent of free-riding, and the higher the sense of ownership and responsibility. Again, like Mogh but on a larger scale, KADO has multi-purpose objectives connected to: quality English medium education; improvement of literacy rates among women; improvement in public health; vocational training to support wider employment opportunities outside of agriculture; conservation of natural resources (including, controversially for some clusters, wildlife by controlling hunting); drug control (in the same sense as Mogh above); preservation and promotion of culture; and improvement of communication facilities. In addition it has sponsored sports events, and used its organisational clout to select (*sic*) Nazims, Naib Nazims and all the councillors of the Karimabad Union Council.

Its Board members, during our meeting, also expressed strong commitments to a broader sense of welfare functions in relation to poorer families in the valley. Intrigued by their sense of the scale of poverty and therefore safety net and social protection needs in the valley, we conducted an exercise in which the nine members present were asked to rank the population of the valley into four economic categories: comfortably wealthy with no vulnerability; coping above the poverty line (whatever their concept of that was) but always vulnerable to major shocks; immediately below the poverty line and chronically vulnerable; and very poor. The median response placed 2% in the first (top) category; 8% in the coping category; 40% below the poverty line; and 50% very poor. Since this was a median response, some were even more pessimistic. The author of the report, from his survey of households, distributed the households 25%, 50%, 20% and 5 % respectively.[42] Whatever the real situation, this exercise revealed that the Board members were concerned to include the principle of safety nets and welfare transfers on the one hand, while having a joint view of the scale of the problem way beyond the capacity of their own collected funds to address. Like the leaders in Mogh, they therefore saw the cross-subsidy priorities as comprising: investment in the education and skills of the poor so that 'while they are poor today, they will be better tomorrow'; therefore fees waivers, assistance with purchase of learning materials and uniform, subsidised support for vocational training; and support for doctors' fees and medicines. In discussions about a broader concept of safety nets, the link between micro-finance or mutual fund societies and forms of social insurance to reduce vulnerability for the transient and churning poor (rather than the chronic poor) was appreciated when introduced into the discussion. However, in addition to the welfare origins of KADO, some Board members were clearly of the view that KADO was in effect a development organisation with an agenda close to AKRSP's mainstream approach in the past, while trying to find ways of stimulating their participation in wider economic development through linkages to other organisations.[43] The members were therefore concerned that they would need to re-register the organisation to enable it to engage directly as a corporate body in business ventures as a Trust (i.e. retaining its non-profit status by distributing profit after re-investment as welfare or start up costs for other ventures which generated further employment and income opportunities).

Perhaps most importantly for this analysis of collective action,[44] is the question of whether KADO evolves into an expanded organisation, embracing other valleys in the Lutko region from Chitral up to Garam Cheshma. It has begun this process by incorporating the neighbouring Botkuli valley, and there are already overtures to the communities in the very poor, remote Arkari Valley where all welfare and development indicators are low. The Board members are clearly ambitious to build upon their early success[45] and to envisage KADO as transformed into at least a Lutko wide development NGO (therefore with a different, all-embracing name—the Khozar Rural Development Organisation has been proposed, as Khozar is the historical name for the entire Lutko valley). At such a scale, they argue, it will be able to: attract more significant external donor funds; employ appropriate technical and professional staff and not rely upon the voluntarism of often absentee professionals;[46] build larger scale facilities such as schools and health clinics; initiate 'mega' projects such as larger hydel systems to move electricity capacity beyond lighting to heating, cooking and other appliances; introduce an adequate telephone network and other telecommunications; manage a wider natural resource environment; and inaugurate social protection/safety net schemes by spreading risk across a wider and more diverse population, thus reducing the co-variance of risk.

However, these 'scale' ambitions raise many other questions. How will other neighbouring communities react to the prospect of an expanded KADO, even with assurances of complete and equal participation in management and policy making? This is where Wood's meetings along the Lutko valley become linked together, and why this area has been focussed on for this part of the analysis. The leaders of the Begusht super-cluster in Garam Cheshma were keen to refer to their own GADO (Garam Cheshma Area Development Organisation) involving, as noted above, other Village Cluster Councils (VCCs) and clusters in the valleys immediately around the Garam Cheshma growth pole. They claim that their GADO was formed as early as 1996, has a membership but has not yet 'taken off'. They look across at KADO with some envy, and argue that: it had the facilitating support of an AKRSP social organiser to create it; more of the KADO leadership have significant links with Chitral town and easier access to other organisations; have among their Board members more professionals who are familiar with designing and presenting proposals (i.e. for external funding); and generally KADO has enjoyed more exposure and attention. Given this wariness, what would be the prospects of a merger between KADO as a functioning organisation and GADO, which remains as a fantasy for an incipient leadership? And where, for example, would a village like Mogh fit in? As a single village sandwiched between the two, would it be rational for its leadership to join forces with one of its conglomerate valley neighbours, since its own scale of activity is limited by the capacity of 65 households (out of the 75, with 10 identified as poor and unable to contribute beyond some labour inputs)? Would such a larger, all Lutko, organisation lose the advantages of cultural unity and homogeneous social identity, and internalise these latent conflicts and jealousies beyond the limited fission already evident between KADO's own clusters and VOs? How does AKRSP's new institutional development agenda engage with these issues? Does it accept the scaling up argument in order to avoid a proliferation of tiny, sub-optimal local development organisations in Chitral District, or does it recognise the potential advantages of a smaller number of larger organisations across the district in terms of developing and concentrating appropriate capacity rather than dissipating it at low level competence across too many organisations? If it accepts the scaling up argument, does the Institutional Development agenda include therefore performing mediating functions between potential collaborating organisations in order to bring about mergers? Does it retain any leverage to bring about such mergers? These are all key questions for AKRSP's new vision and strategy, arising from this collective action analysis within the Lutko valley. The illustration given here clearly has wider relevance across the whole of NAC in relation to AKRSP's strategic institutional choices.

Conclusion

With the Aga Khan Rural Support Programme (AKRSP) as the major post-feudal institutional player in the region, we can remind ourselves that the basis for AKRSP's institutional strategy since 1982 has been the principle of collective action. This has been pursued with a deliberate strategy of leverage and incentives, based upon the assumption that collective action and social capital needed reviving. It is interesting to reflect how far collective action, prior to the abolition of royal prerogatives, was itself induced by strong 'feudal' leadership associated with the idea of hydraulic society. In a sense this justified a replacement 'external enforcer' in the form of AKRSP and its conditional grants for PPI. Nevertheless the historical judgement about the value of 'feudal' institutions to natural resource management and elementary welfare has to be balanced by the evidence of community level, sometimes religious centred, institutions for localised water management, rationing forest products, grazing supervision, mutually exchanging labour services (the *yardoi* system in Chitral, for example) and the distribution of forms of *zakat* during the feudal period itself and not completely lost thereafter.

However, even if there was no institutional power vacuum as such, clear threats to the continuation of collective action now exist alongside evidence of the emergence of new forms of associational life and social capital. Although there is a proper empirical reluctance to accept a simple trend away from collective action, citing, for example, the evidence of resumed collective management around recently introduced micro-hydels and the formation of multi-purpose local welfare and development organisations, threats to collective action have to be acknowledged. Even with micro-hydels, the ownership group may be quite passive in management terms, in effect franchising out the operation (including distribution and fee collection) and maintenance of the installation to a specialist sub-group. Nothing wrong with that if it works institutionally. The point is that full-scale collective action, involving local level participation and democracy, has high transaction costs, and very high opportunity costs for members, especially for those who need to be away from the community for employment and business. We can identify two major forms of social threat, which could undermine present initiatives by activists in local communities as well as AKRSP's current vision and strategy of supporting the development of local development organisations (NGOs) to implement the communities' own projects and welfare functions through partnership with a range of other agencies and through raising necessary financial resources both internally and externally. These two threats are: new patterns of socio-economic differentiation and inequality which affect local level collective action; and an intensification of sectarian identities which can reduce the prospects of larger scale cooperation within and between valleys.

New patterns of socio-economic differentiation and inequality

Fundamentally, the emerging evidence of social differentiation[47] confronts locally cherished concepts of equality, homogeneity and mutual interest around common objectives that will produce equally distributed benefits. Such concepts are, of course, the basis of contemporary aspirations by some local activists and AKRSP to move social capital formation to institutional levels beyond the VO and cluster. Instead, this social differentiation challenges the basis of equal cash and labour inputs into joint projects, when returns to households are differential in impact. For example, the prevailing principle of 'rough equity' in irrigation management (see Wood (1999) for a comparable point about Bangladesh) is difficult to sustain if some households are acquiring land at the expense of others, and/or cultivating it more intensively with high value commercial crops such as potatoes while contributing equal labour input shares as other poorer households.

While not suggesting that we are witnessing classic 'class relations' as experienced down-country and elsewhere in riverine South Asia, the evidence of increasing socio-economic differentiation and inequalities has to be considered in relational terms as well as distributional ones. That is to say, does inequality also represent exploitation, predation, and individualistic (i.e. household) morality as well as 'amoral familism' (Banfield 1958)?

Whereas there has been an earlier image of broadly equal peasants as 'subjects' of various feudal arrangements representing the only form of inequality (i.e. lords and tenants as reflected in Figure 2.2 of Chapter 2), there are now 'surplus value' relationships between educated landowners, tenants and 'landless' labour. Such relations are overlaid by power exercised by strong clans and nuclear families, especially in the deployment of social labour or 'head' levies on 'common interest' projects. In other words, what sometimes appears as fully participatory, collective action is more likely to reflect inequalities of power between clans, extended/joint households and the nuclear elements within them. Meetings are attended, votes cast, funds raised, labour promised—but all under the implicit (second dimension—Lukes 1974) power of the influential local level leaders. Furthermore, there is an interaction between distributional and relational inequality. The former frequently translates into the latter, as successful migrants and market entrepreneurs convert resources and personal capabilities gained in other arenas to exercise relational power locally. A typical example will be returning army non-commissioned officers who have risen up the ranks after many years of service and have accumulated pension entitlements, which constitute a fortune by local comparison. Other examples are educated sons of the past who have entered government or even better paid (though less corrupt) non-government service, thus gaining incomes, wealth and perhaps even more importantly connections and networks which they are able to deploy as new patrons locally. We can expect more of this if market oriented economic development takes off in the NAC.

At the same time, distributional inequality is also compatible with greater individualisation, in which the families moving ahead economically are in effect resource-hopping and weakening their dependence upon local natural renewables. In this way, perhaps reinforced through lengthy absences either in the urban centres of the region itself (for government/army or NGO work) or further away down-country, they are participating less in the village level institutions even though remnants of their families may continue to reside permanently in those settings. But to the extent that those family remnants are increasingly relying upon remittances and perhaps periods of stay in migrant relatives' houses elsewhere (e.g. for education, health or elderly care), their own reliance upon local NRM is also reduced. There is clearly a strong gender dimension to these processes, with males typically migrating more than females, with females perhaps joining husbands and other relatives later if the male has successfully re-located. Families locally who are only represented by females are clearly at a disadvantage in institutions of collective action, where the culture endorses males in the public sphere and excludes women.[48] However, with extended families it is still common for a deserted or temporarily alone female (with husband and/or sons out-migrated) to be represented by another male relative. However the female remains disadvantaged in never being sure that her (or her family) interests are being genuinely represented.

Intensification of Sectarian Identities

Common property management in the region occurs at many different levels of scale. Clearly forests stretch across different communities and are affected therefore by competing rights and claims to use. High pastures have similar characteristics, despite long established customary allocation, which is perpetually in dispute. Likewise water, with irrigation channels extending from glacial sources over long distances to their final, tail-end destinations with numerous distributories to the intervening communities en route. The micro-hydel technologies could add a new dimension to potential conflict if opportunities are denied tail-enders by upstream demand, or if ambiguity exists between electricity sourcing from the Reshun power station (i.e. grid) or local micro-hydels. Thus 'resource' space may not coincide with community or 'social' space in which multi-layered relationships alongside multi-period games contribute, as social capital, towards prospects for collective action. This lack of coincidence between resource and social space, when the resources are distributed over a wider scale, can be exacerbated by sectarian identities in the NAC regions of Northern Pakistan.

The religious aspects of settlement patterns reveal, in sectarian identity terms, some 'mixed' villages, certainly mixed valleys, but also sub-regions dominated by one sect or another. In Chitral, the principal tensions are between Sunni and Ismaili (the latter sometimes are not even accepted as Muslims by the extremist interpreters of Islam among the former). For Ghizer, Gilgit-Hunza, the tensions can be variously between Sunni and Ismaili, and Sunni and Shia, with only insignificant differences as a basis for resource competition between Shia and Ismaili. In Baltistan, the sect identity issue is virtually non-existent with an overwhelming Shia population. There is little doubt that, in mixed areas, sectarian tension is rising, with various 'siege' perspectives intensifying identity and solidarities. This is particularly evident for Chitral, broadly between the Ismaili north and Sunni south, though with some key Sunni dominated valleys in the north as well, such as Turkho and parts of Mulkho valleys. Whereas before (i.e. up to a decade ago), there could be inter-marriage producing 'clans across sects', thus erecting cross-cutting ties which function to offset exclusive identity, sect and clan is now more clearly differentiated as a basis for social identity thus increasing the likelihood of social closure. At village level, where a mix of sects is present, the sub-geographical unit of *mohallah* will usually be identified with a particular sect and thus constitute the basis of collective action for resources which can be managed at that micro level. Thus the institutions of solidarity and identity around the mosque (Sunni), *jamatkhana* (Ismaili) and *imambarga* (Shia) may be intensified and become more functional at a localised level. The problem arises when cooperation is required at higher levels of scale, between differently attached *mohallahs*. The aspirations to form wider organisations could thus be thwarted by these micro identities.

It is important to appreciate that the intensity of these solidarities are not stable. They can lie dormant for long periods of time, enabling inter-sect cooperation to the point where it is simply not an issue. There are numerous examples of mixed Village Organisations (created by AKRSP), with members of different sects sitting together and acting together. However, in the region, the intensity of these solidarities can be affected by events outside the region altogether. Different sects have different religious calendars, so particular events such as the annual Shia Muharram commemoration, which involves public processions, can create tension in mixed Sunni/Shia areas.[49] There are periodic attacks between Sunni and Shia down-country which can also trigger tension. The events of 1988 remain imprinted on contemporary memory when down-country Sunni activists were encouraged by the then government of Pakistan to 'discipline' the Shia community for its disturbing loyalties to Shia identities externally, especially associated with the Iranian religious revolution during the 1980s. The killing of a Sunni cleric in Chitral in August 1999 was widely interpreted as a sect-motivated attack as the guilty party was Ismaili. This caused widespread tension between the two communities and a strong counter-reaction to the AK institutions for being Ismaili in origin. However, a closer examination of the incident revealed that this was, in fact, a family feud over land, with the Sunni cleric actually an earlier converted Ismaili. Nevertheless, it played a strong role in undermining trust in the region, which is only slowly being re-built. This has undoubtedly reduced scope for collective action in the mixed communities and valleys, as well as between the valleys of different sects.

These exclusive identities are also variable, strong or weak, according to other, often quite minor and micro contingencies. Micro-level disputes over grazing which might simply be the result of a non-attentive child, or disputes over irrigation channel maintenance (say, upstream in another village) can easily be understood as a sect based affront and take time to restore. However, a landslide, broken road, or a flash flood might equally bring different sects in a village or valley together in emergency action. These identities therefore have variable and unstable impact upon broader possibilities and needs for cooperation and collective action. It is a picture of fission and fusion, of identities fragmenting and re-forming at different times around different issues. Under such conditions there can never be perfect and complete trust. The social capital is always under negotiation and being re-configured. This fragility certainly affects people's calculations of others' behaviour, introducing a more instrumental, amoral basis to co-operation. This is the social breeding ground for queried membership, for suspicion, anticipatory cheating and free-riding—all based upon the principle that others must be thinking and behaving similarly. But we should not discount the significance of people's continued full or partial dependency upon local natural resources and local systems of safety nets and social protection and a corresponding lack of opportunity for resource-hopping and exiting, alongside the multi-layered relationships and multi-period games at *mohallah* level and sometimes beyond to cluster and valley level, as the set of compensating forces actually supporting collective action.

Agency and Subsidiarity: The Twin Peaks of New Social Capital

The differentiation noted above includes the diversification of people's income portfolios: villagers are no longer peasant clones of each other. The increasing uniqueness of the household in these economic and therefore social terms entails individualisation, and more household-centred calculations of advantage and disadvantage. These socio-economic processes induce cultural shifts in moral commitments and increase the propensity for free-riding and therefore compliance costs for remaining members (who could be the poorest, with higher local NR dependency and reduced opportunity for resource-hopping or spreading their sources of welfare).

There are obvious implications of these threats for social capital spreading across from natural resource management to the organisation locally of other development activity: infrastructure creation, operation and maintenance; enterprise stimulation supported by credit and savings initiatives; and social protection for either the chronically or transitional poor. There may be sectoral and geographical variations in the significance of these threats, with some cyclical reversals (as in micro-hydels), but the centrality of these threats to the core of any organisational strategy for sustained development in NAC cannot be under-estimated. The past is very unlikely to be the future institutionally with basic norms and values on the move.

At the same time, we should also acknowledge local people's agency as expressed through the emergence of many organisational forms, which differ from the original conceptions of the deliberately created village and women's organisations (VOs and WOs) as multi-purpose organisations, albeit levered into creation by the prospect of generous grants for productive infrastructure. The more recent emergence of the single purpose VO, for example, seems to be an example of members perceiving the difficulties of sustaining collective action over a number of parallel objectives, involving complex, interlocked transactions and high degrees of participation. Single-purpose VOs recognise the limits to collective action, with members reducing their intra-transactions accordingly. At the same time, the proliferation of other 'Os'[50] and interest groups, business groups and so on is also testimony to people wishing to experiment with organisations that work better for them against particular objectives and social conditions.

It is interesting in these organisational developments to see to what extent villagers are acting out principles of subsidiarity: creating institutions at different levels appropriate to the scale of the management issue and the numbers of stakeholders to be reconciled. But it is equally important to acknowledge, therefore, that the principle of subsidiarity in this context means that an increased responsibility for personal livelihoods is devolved to the lowest level: namely the household or the individual. This helps to explain the widely observed trend of increasingly nucleated households, with declining responsibilities among brothers for each other's children. In other words, a weakening over time of the moral basis for collective action.

AKRSP has implemented a successful social organisation programme that has been recognised by development policy makers and practitioners around the world. However, this social organisation approach has to date reflected more the preoccupation of the intervening agency (i.e., 'how are we organising them') rather than the more balanced partnership in which the onus for action lies with the people and is based on their organisational preferences and aspirations. To this end, AKRSP has gradually began to recognise, accept and work through the perspectives of the local people and their communities. However, much more needs to be done if AKRSP is to truly align its organisational approach with that of the definitions and parameters of organisation that the communities perceive to be to their best advantage.

This challenge is of special significance as AKRSP embarks upon a new phase of its development work in the Northern Areas and Chitral. As a mature and learning organisation, it is in the process of restructuring its management and operational systems in order to better meet the needs of the area. However, restructuring has to be based on the recognition of the political, religious, social diversity, and institutional maturity of the communities—which is largely what AKRSP's management is doing. What needs to be kept at the forefront is, however, the spirit of collective action—i.e, what the communities deem themselves to be the way that they want to take responsibility and the terms of a partnership that would suit them best. The types of organisation that AKRSP might choose to emphasize and work with should reflect what transformation and processes are occurring among and between the communities.

The collective action 'story' of the people of the Northern Areas and Chitral reminds us that whether external agencies are present or not, local people have and will continue to cooperate and join forces for their survival and progress. The tradition of institutional organisation is strong among the communities of the north, and even without intervention by an agency such as AKRSP, the communities will continue to organise, disperse, and re-group for activities that they perceive to help them in the struggle for their survival. The challenge for an external agency is then to find ways for its own survival by realigning its approach with that of the communities in which it works—or, to find itself a way to gradually withdraw.

NOTES

1. Material for this chapter has also been provided by Shah Makeen, Area Manager, AKRSP, Gilgit as well as AKRSP colleagues from the MER department in the Core Office, Gilgit, as well as Regional and Area Offices from Baltistan, Gilgit and Chitral. In addition therefore to the valuable inputs from my colleague Sofia Shakil, Geof Wood is grateful for all the support he has received from these other colleagues in the preparation of this paper. He also acknowledges the support and key insights of Siraj Ul Mulk, AKRSP Board Member from Chitral, and the hospitality of Siraj and his wife, Ghazala, during the writing of the draft paper for this chapter.

2. See Chapter 1.

3. See Figure 2.2 in Chapter 2.

4. See Cooke and Kothari (2002).

5. There will be some more commentary on this strategy towards the end of the chapter.

6. A majority was expected because a majority was assumed to be poor at the outset of the programme. See Figure 2.2 of the Poverty and Livelihoods chapter.

7. For example, the Institutional Maturity Index and the Institutional Development Exercise.

8. See below for examples of these larger organisations.

9. More complete documentation of the women's programme and approach is presented in Chapter 3.

10. i.e. Baltistan and Chitral, away from the Ghizer-Gilgit-Hunza (i.e. Gilgit region) origins of AKRSP.

11. See Chapter 5 especially 'Natural Resource Management: Sustaining the Stock', as well as the 2002 World Bank evaluation *The Next Ascent*, for details.

12. Gloekler was also commissioned by the Gilgit Regional Office to conduct a reflective study of institutional development in the Gilgit region during this period. A feature of her report was the formation of the Domani Development Association, which brought together VOs and clusters in a valley complex south-east of Gilgit. The TLP process conducted in association with the University of Bath, UK took most of the professional staff from different sectors in AKRSP (and some of the other down-country Rural Support Programmes) through an examination of the principles of social development, using local household and village examples. In total, six batches of about 15 each undertook 6 month courses between 1997–2001. AKRSP holds a full record of its curriculum, learning materials, assignments, and other process documentation connected both to the TLP and strategic implications for AKRSP's approaches to social development.

13. Above *mohallah*/village level resource management and development issues were traditionally organised through the feudal, 'hydraulic society' arrangements, referred to earlier in the chapter.

14 See Figure 1.1 of Chapter 1 on Poverty and Livelihoods, and the supporting arguments for the mismatch between the interests of the poorest households and AKRSP's traditional focus during Period II.

15 There was ambivalence among some staff in AKRSP about NDO during the late 90s, seeing it as a competitor to AKRSP. Clearly the AKRSP staff from Nagar took a different view. This observation is made, since it is now certainly new mainstream policy for AKRSP to unambiguously support such initiatives.

16 This was a more externally induced organisational initiative, though it was certainly able to build upon both traditional as well as AKRSP induced forms of collective action.

17 The TLP in Social Development, referred to above.

18 *The Next Ascent.*

19 Valley forums are being considered as the next stage institutional form for collaboration with AKRSP's new vision and strategy. These forums are not envisaged as long term organisations but more like a *Jirga*—debating the appropriate formation of larger scale, local organisations or NGOs.

20 And spatially, individualisation is more associated with growth pole centres with collective principles remaining stronger in the more peripheral, remoter villages.

21 See Chapter 2 on Poverty and Livelihoods.

22 Again, see Chapter 2. These forms of social protection may be regarded as an extension of the philanthropic traditions prevailing across Islamic society, but intensified in a context where access to other forms of provision (state entitlements, opportunities from labour markets and remittances) are especially tenuous.

23 See again the analysis in Chapter 2.

24 It is interesting to note that Proshika in Bangladesh has been under exactly the same kind of pressure of measuring the performance of its primary groups in a five-point classification system to show the proportion of 'graduating' groups as part of the achievement of Log Frame targets.

25 In addition to the constraints on collective action arising from classic free-riding, game theory analysis discussed in this section, we return to these other countervailing forces in the NAC in the next section.

26 Thanks to Md. Zaman, AKRSP, Baltistan for this case study.

27 Government estimates indicate that 57% of the Northern Areas are cultivable waste, revealing considerable ongoing potential to create cultivable, but currently barren land.

28 Thanks to Syed Ali, Area Manager, AKRSP Ghanche for this example of a widespread story across NAC.

29 This conclusion of Lawson-McDowall is confirmed and reinforced by the three micro-hydel case studies carried out in Chitral by Ali Effendi, Consultant Economist, MER Section, Chitral during March-April 2000. He evaluated Izh Cluster in Garam Cheshma, Lutko Valley; Kuragh Village, 13 km from Booni in Mastuj Sub-Division; and Toque Village in the Yarkhun Valley, North of Mastuj.

30 When Wood visited Ujog cluster some years ago, he noted with interest a logframe for the project in the cluster office, written in Urdu, but still alas retaining its left to right logic, revealing the strength of cultural imperialism!

31 Interviewed by Wood in Garam Cheshma on 25th August 2003.

32 This has been a project of the Mountain Area Conservancy Programme (MACP) of IUCN.

33 The case of KADO will be discussed below, since it is in the process of realising many of the aspirations which remain only as a distant ambition for these Begusht super-cluster leaders.

34 See Effendi's case studies for evidence of both VOs bifurcating to continue further access to PPIs and dormant VOs becoming re-activated when the new micro-hydel opportunities appeared.

35 Many market and environmental pollution questions remain: pricing; subsidies, leakage and exports; correlative infrastructure; transportation; geographical and social distribution of benefits and costs; in-migration of specialist labour; waste disposal and water pollution; growth pole attractions for other industries, including other, more problematic (in environmental terms) mining. All these questions relate to issues of ownership over the process both in an early asset sense as well as entailed social and cultural changes towards individualisation, commercialisation and high discount rates as a deliberate strategy of out-migration.

36 Wood has also witnessed this among the Dom community of Karimabad in Hunza.

37 This is an all-Ismaili village.

38 Wood also has evidence of other examples, though not so formalised or well-developed, of the emergence of such organisations: Village Budalass in Nagar, Gilgit; Village Bargin in Sai-Juglote, Gilgit; Village Orguch in Chitral, practising an extension of the *yardoi* labour cooperation; Kuzh Bala in Yarkhun Valley, Chitral; and several more examples from Khapalu in Baltistan, and Gupis/Ghizer. Each case reveals slightly different issues, especially as some of them are more based upon religious institutions and deploying forms of *zakat* (or equivalent) as their main instruments of welfare transfers to poorer households. The common theme across these cases is that they are not directly derived from the V/WO experience, but draw upon prior social and cultural traditions of local association.

39 Perhaps characterised socially and culturally as an homogeneous minority in the wider society from which limited formal entitlements can be expected.

40 Gul Buhar Khan (2003) 'Contextual and Operational Paper on Karimabad Area Development Organisation', AKRSP, Chitral.

41 In which the author of the report was also present, and able to use the occasion to finalise his report.

42 The overall NAC figure derived from the FHIES compares at 46%, 20% and 34% for the two categories below the nationally set poverty line. See Chapter 2 for further details.

43 Including, for example, single sector organisations like the Chitral Association for Mountain Area Tourism (CAMAT) newly formed and based in Chitral town.

44 Leaving aside internal governance issues, which are discussed in the report cited above.

45 KADO already has one small external grant from the Innovation for Poverty Reduction Project (IPRP) for social mobilisation around the theme of medicinal herbs which are particularly relied upon by poorer families unable to afford modern medicines.

46 Most of the Board members are currently employed in formal organisation in Chitral, such as AKDN programmes, banks and government.

47 See Figure 2.2 in Chapter 2 and accompanying arguments.

48 This was very strongly observed in the Effendi studies of micro-hydel management systems in Chitral.

49 Think of Northern Ireland and the annual marching season.

50 Thus we see Local Development Organisations, Non-Governmental Organisations (but at different levels of scale), and Village Development Organisations which are typically an amalgam of VOs, especially if they split into clan identities soon after the initial grant for productive infrastructure was obtained.

9

Working With Government:
Close but never too close

Adil Najam

For the last twenty years a social experiment of grand proportions
has been taking place in the northern mountains of Pakistan. The
hypothesis behind this much-celebrated experiment in community
development—the Aga Khan Rural Support Programme
(AKRSP)—was that poor rural communities, once organised, can
make dramatic gains in poverty reduction and livelihoods
improvement by unleashing their latent potential for economic
enterprise and innovation. The goal of the experiment was to not
only demonstrate that economic empowerment through community
self-organisation could be facilitated, but to design and test a
'replicable' model for doing so (AKRSP 1984b; Husain 1992). The
broad consensus amongst the many who have analysed AKRSP's
performance over the last two decades is that, in general, it has been
a notably successful experiment both in terms of demonstrating the
poverty reduction potential of community self-organisation and in
developing a model for doing so which is now in various stages of
replication within AKRSP's own areas of operation, across the
country, and across South Asia (Khan, M.H. 1998; Tetlay and Raza
1998; World Bank 1987, 1990b, 1995b, 2002).

Any analysis of the lessons learnt in the first twenty years of the
AKRSP experience is important to development practitioners and
scholars not only because it has become such a widely admired icon
of success and emulation but also because unlike so many other
development interventions, this one lends itself to robust and

useful analysis. From its very inception AKRSP has been consciously structured as an action-research experiment and has recorded a quite detailed account of its various activities and initiatives. Interestingly, however, while the many varied facets of this experience have been studied at great length by AKRSP itself and by others,[1] there is relatively little analysis either in internal AKRSP reports or in external analyses about how AKRSP has 'coped' with government. This is interesting because by virtue of its very mandate—that is, to facilitate the self-organisation of communities—AKRSP has essentially been 'meddling' with the institutions of governance not only of the particular communities but of the larger regions in which it operates. While it is interesting that there is little record or analysis of AKRSP-government relations over the last twenty years, it is by no means surprising. After all, doing so was never part of the experiment's mandate, and recording the ebbs and flows of critical relationships is not always feasible and often not even desirable.

In short, while AKRSP has always had to work in close—even if not always direct—contact with government there is rather little to be found about how this contact has influenced the workings of either AKRSP or government. To the extent that there is an institutional memory of this relationship, it lies not in internal documents or external evaluations but in the institutional memory of individuals within AKRSP and government. This study is an attempt to tap into this institutional memory to better understand, explain and learn from twenty years of experience of AKRSP-government relations. The primary source and reference for this analysis are a series of detailed discussions and interviews with current and former AKRSP staff, current and former government officials at the Federal, regional and local levels, and other civil society practitioners and scholars knowledgeable about the internal details or the ultimate results of this ongoing relationship.[2] In addition a review of relevant AKRSP documents was also made.[3]

Let us be quite clear, at the very outset, about what it does not seek to do. It does not pretend to present the history of AKRSP, or even of AKRSP-government relations. Nor does it seek a definitive evaluation of the relationship over time. Our goals are more circumspect and less ambitious. While the study will attempt to outline key developments in the relationship over time and while it will record the perception of close observers about the nature of the relationship, its ultimate goal is to understand the strategic dimensions of AKRSP-government relations. In particular, it will attempt—in the next three sections—to address three larger questions:

- to understand the nature and evolution of AKRSP–government relations over the last twenty years,
- to explain why AKRSP sought and was able to maintain the particular types of interaction with government, and
- to draw out key lessons from the AKRSP experience.

The bulk of this chapter will deal directly with the first question and the latter two will be answered in light of the insights derived from this first enquiry.

Understanding AKRSP-Government Relations

For those knowledgeable about AKRSP's history and heritage it should be no surprise that the overwhelming perception within AKRSP, within government and within Pakistan's larger civil society is that AKRSP's relationship with government has remained entirely non-adversarial, mostly cordial, and occasionally close. What is surprising, even disconcerting, is how difficult it is to find even the occasional contrary view to this general impression.

This is surprising because for most part civil society-government relations in Pakistan, as elsewhere in many developing countries, tend to be marked with deep expressions of bitterness and hostility on the part of both sides, even amongst—indeed, especially amongst—those civil society and government actors that do work closely together (see Tandon 1989; Sanyal 1994; Garilao 1987). Indeed, there are those within AKRSP who sometimes wish that the organisation had 'taken on' government and its policies more explicitly, and those within government who are resentful of

AKRSP's superior resources, and also those within civil society who wonder whether AKRSP was sometimes too eager to keep the government happy so that it (i.e., AKRSP) could do what it wanted to do. These, however, tend to be small minorities. Strikingly, our interviews found a robust unanimity around the view that the nature of the relationship was generally positive, did not involve a compromise on principles, and served the strategic interests of both AKRSP and government in the regions where AKRSP has operated. Building on the first two, the purpose of this section is to explore the implications of the last of these three perceptions.

AKRSP–Government relations: partnerships of necessity

While the reasons for why AKRSP has been able to maintain generally good relations with government are explored in a later section, it is important to note here that for AKRSP itself, maintaining good relations with government has always been—and remains—a key strategic goal. According to Shoaib Sultan Khan, the founding General Manager of AKRSP, 'the purpose was always to influence government' and it was always stressed that '[government] is to be influenced, not to be opposed.'[4] While the corporate culture within AKRSP has always been one of maintaining good terms with government, an equally dominant strain in the organisational philosophy has been a resistance to getting too close to government. The metaphor one hears again and again from AKRSP staff relates to the desire to maintain a good working relationship with government but to keep government at 'arm's length'. This fits well with the organisation's mandate to influence government while jealously guarding its own participatory ethos and ensuring that it is itself not too open to government's influence.

Within this general corporate ethos which has remained stable through the last two decades, the specifics of AKRSP's interaction with government (both in its operational areas and at the national level) have broadened over time as AKRSP itself has matured and in response to changes in the external framework conditions. Four broad steps in the evolutionary process seem to be easily identifiable:[5]

Inception (the early months and years)

During the very early years of AKRSP, the principal challenge for the AKRSP experiment was simply to be accepted by government; or, at least, not to be actively resisted. Recalling these early days, Shoaib Sultan Khan recalls that the 'greatest support from government was that they did not oppose us.'[6] To get the government's active support—as AKRSP eventually did—was certainly desirable but the challenge in those very early months and years was simply to ensure that local government agencies in the Northern Areas and relevant federal government authorities in Islamabad did not actively deter it from its operations. In retrospect this may not seem like much of a challenge, but at the time the danger of government seeking to thwart AKRSP in the bud was both real and considerable. This was because of the political and security sensitiveness of the region and the ethnic and sectarian sensibilities that could be fanned by an 'Aga Khani' project that sought to organise communities for development action.[7]

Three factors helped AKRSP in maintaining good relations with the government despite the odds. The first was that His Highness the Aga Khan convinced the then President General Zia ul Huq directly of the benefits of the project. This sent a clear message to government functionaries, especially in Islamabad, that the project had support from the highest echelons of national power. Second, at the Gilgit level, the fact that Shoaib Sultan Khan was himself a former civil service officer proved to be a major asset because it gave him direct access to government decision-makers and the ability to directly ally any fears and concerns they might have. Third, a number of the early field staff of the project were themselves former government employees in the region and brought with them good links to local government at the implementation level.

Demonstration (late 1980s)

Once established and accepted, AKRSP soon became a source of support for the government both because of its superior resources and its participatory model. There was a conscious policy within the organisation to be supportive to government, particularly in terms of sharing resources such as the vehicles and the helicopter but also in terms of brokering better community-government relations in areas where AKRSP was working.

With good working relations with government already in place, the challenge now was to move to the greater goal of 'influencing' government. This was a challenge both at the local and national level. During this period, a major focus of AKRSP's work with government was to demonstrate to government officials the efficacy and effectiveness of the AKRSP development model. This was the phase where AKRSP was investing in creating what Shoaib Sultan Khan has called the 'champions for change' within government.[8] This happened at multiple levels. At the field level it happened with officials from line agencies interacting with and often accompanying AKRSP field staff to project activities. Another significant aspect of this demonstration was the regular system of bringing in young government officers, particularly from the Civil Services Academy, to field visits to the project area. At the apex level the demonstrations were for the senior-most government decision-makers who were brought in at regular intervals to see firsthand the fruits of the AKRSP approach.

Flicking through the list of government guests who visited AKRSP offices in this period is a powerful testimony to the efforts that were invested in creating key advocates of the AKRSP model at the various levels of government.[9] The subsequent creation of national and provincial rural support programmes modeled after AKRSP was, in part, a testimony to this process of intense interaction with government decision-makers which not only created goodwill for AKRSP within government at all levels but, more importantly, allowed entire generations of government officials to see the AKRSP philosophy in practice and at close quarters.

Partnerships (early 1990s onwards)

Although AKRSP had been working very closely with government in the 1980s, it was not until that 1990s that it began working directly with government. After a prolonged period of developing a working relationship, the government was now willing to offer, and AKRSP willing to accept, direct partnerships in the implementation of Social Action Plan (SAP) projects. Other direct partnerships have followed, including the community schools (1992), social forestry (1995), community health (1998), and most recently the National Devolution Plan (2000).

According to Steve Rasmussen, AKRSP General Manager from the late 1990s until recently, these partnerships were not as much a source of resource generation for AKRSP as a means of building capacity in government; for AKRSP it was very much part of its larger mission of influencing government and signified a move from 'empowering communities to empowering government.'[10] For government, these direct project partnerships provided hands-on training in the AKRSP model of social mobilisation but the contractual nature of the relationship also highlight the procedural and cultural differences in how AKRSP and government operate.

According to one government official in Gilgit, a decade of working on such direct partnerships has made both government and AKRSP more understanding of each other's operating environments and each has taken on some characteristics of the other.[11] However, familiarity can also breed contempt and working at such close quarters, sometimes under contractual arrangements, has also exposed tensions. Although there is now a history of AKRSP working directly with government, there is also a certain palpable unease within the organisational culture in working in the contracting mode. This unease comes both from a strong desire not to become dependent on government resources and a history of resource abundance where AKRSP has been in the happy position of never needing government resources for its institutional survival.

Policy reform (late 1990s onwards)

With the AKRSP model being generally accepted as both effective and replicable, with the spawning of an 'Rural Support Programme (RSP) movement' not only in Pakistan but in South Asia, with AKRSP field operations maturing in size and spread, and with the AKRSP head office moving to Islamabad from Gilgit, the organisation increasingly found itself being thrust into a new form of interaction with government: policy reform. AKRSP seems to have stumbled into this role rather reluctantly. However, at least in retrospect, and for all the reasons mentioned above, it seems to have had little option but to do so.

Despite a corporate culture that explicitly shies away from aggressive (and certainly adversarial) advocacy, the institutional mandate to influence government necessitated that AKRSP also begin pushing for larger scale systemic change through policy reform. An early example was in the areas of forest management (1995), and by 2000 AKRSP found itself being increasingly pulled into the national policy discourse on policy reform in the areas of micro finance (with the creation of the Pakistan Micro-finance Network and the Kushhali Bank) and on government devolution. Just as forays into project partnerships with government had raised concerns within the organisation about AKRSP and government getting too close for comfort, the arena of policy reform raised concerns about moving on a confrontational path. While such a role does raise the possibility of certain tensions in the AKRSP-government relationship, it may well be a necessary tension at this stage of the organisation's history and influence.[12]

Although necessarily cryptic, the brief historical review of AKRSP's involvement with government suggests that there has been a clear and evident pattern to this evolution. At the very earliest stage, AKRSP saw government as a hurdle to be overcome; certainly not as an adversary but as a contextual parameter that had to be somehow 'managed' so that it did not negatively deter AKRSP's fledgling activities. Quite soon, however, AKRSP began viewing government as an audience, and a key audience, for its activities. The next step in this evolution was for AKRSP to begin engaging government not simply as an audience for what it was doing but as an active, and sometimes contractual, partner. The most recent layer added to this evolving relationship is of government, particularly at the national level, becoming an object of active advocacy. The distinctions and transitions were not always as neat as this schema suggests, but they are perceptible over time. Moreover, these evolving conceptions have built upon, rather than replace, each other. Importantly, then, the evolution of AKRSP-government relations over the last two decades is the story of an expanding relationship rather than a shifting relationship.

AKRSP–Government interactions in the policy space

Although we have argued above that AKRSP has only recently sought to effect policy reform directly, it should also be clear that influencing large scale policy change has always been a key component of the organisation's mandate. To quote Shoaib Sultan Khan again, AKRSP's 'audience was always government' and it was always implicit in the AKRSP model that it could only be a catalyst for demonstrating a model of social mobilisation which could ultimately be taken to scale only by government.[13] Within the framework of such a philosophy, AKRSP has been and remains very much a policy entrepreneur (Annis 1987; Bratton 1990; Najam 1999; Banuri and Najam 2002; Wood, J.C. 2003). In such a conception, policy is seen as a social device to accelerate, decelerate, circumvent, or create particular changes (Najam 1995). The policy enterprise is conceptualised as a dynamic dialectic dialogue between the sometimes competing and sometimes converging notions of the 'public interest' held by the various actors and interests in the larger community—it is in the interaction between these various notions in the policy stream that policy is shaped, reshaped, and reshaped again in a constantly evolving process (Kingdon 1984). Within such a conception of the process, citizen organisations—who, by definition, are agents of change and whose goal is to articulate and actualise a particular social vision—are best identified as being policy entrepreneurs. The normative values they represent and the social visions they seek to actualise are their contribution to what has been called the 'primeval policy soup' or 'policy stream' (Majone 1989; Stone 1988; Kingdon 1984; Najam 1996).

Whether civil society organisations indulge in overt policy advocacy or not—and AKRSP has only recently done so—they remain in the business of influencing policy, through actions, through demonstration, and through the sheer force of changing public perceptions of what 'should be' and what 'can be'. Based on such a conceptualisation of the role of civil organisations in influencing policy (and, thereby government) and building on a wide body of theory and literature on NGOs as well as on public policy processes, the author's earlier research suggests that a 'policy space' in which citizen organisations interact with government can be defined as a space bounded by the three stages of policymaking and the four key policy roles that citizen organisations can play. The three broad stages of the policy process include **agenda setting**, **policy development**, and **policy implementation**. The four possible roles that citizen organisations can play, include: as **monitors**, citizen organisations ensure that government is doing what it is supposed to be doing; as **advocates** they prod government agencies to do what they consider to be the 'right' thing; as **innovators** they suggest how things might be done differently; and as **service providers** they themselves act directly to do what—in their opinion—needs to be done (for an elaboration of this conceptual framework, see Najam 1999).

A 'policy map' constructed by placing the three stages along one axis and the four roles along the other gives us the space within which a citizen organisation interacts with government.[14] Figure 9.1 applies this construct to the last 20 years of AKRSP experience and 'fills in' the policy space with selected examples of AKRSP–government interactions. Although a partial depiction, Figure 9.1 serves to highlight a few key points.

First, we see that *AKRSP's interactions with government have, in fact, been more varied than a more cursory glance at the organisation's history might suggest.* That although these have not been its principal roles, AKRSP has played a significant role both as an advocate of policy reform and as a service provider to government. However, there is no major example of AKRSP playing the role of monitoring over government activities at any of the three policy stages.

Second, and not surprisingly, *the biggest impact that AKRSP has had on national development policy (and thereby on government) is through its development, demonstration and championing of a replicable model of social mobilisation and community organisation.* Indeed, the biggest influence that AKRSP has had on the government is that its model of social mobilisation has been adopted by the government itself and has been translated into a national and various provincial rural support programmes. This has happened not only through the creation of the National Rural Support Programme (NRSP), provincial RSPs and the their counterparts across the region but also through the rather widespread adoption of these ideas by other NGOs and government development programmes.[15]

Finally, *the deeply held institutional view that government is to be engaged but always at 'arm's length' and never in an overtly adversarial matter, manifests itself quite clearly* in the white spaces in Figure 9.1. Unlike many other large NGOs in Pakistan and smaller NGOs in its area of operation, AKRSP has ventured into service provision to the policy machinery only reluctantly and predominantly at the policy implementation stage. This fits in well with the institutional ethos because being a service provider to government at the agenda-setting or policy development stage often requires either getting uncomfortably close to government or uncomfortably adversarial; AKRSP has a stated—and here demonstrated—aversion to either option. The lack of activity on the part of AKRSP as a monitor of policy stems from the very same aversion to adversarial activism, which has been central to AKRSP philosophy over the last twenty years.

Figure 9.1. AKRSP–Government relations: a policy map approach

	Monitor	Advocate	Innovator	Service Provider
Agenda-Setting		Pakistan Micro Finance Network	Formation of NRSP and provincial RSPs	
Policy Development		Social Forestry Wildlife Management	Development of a replicable model for social mobilisation	
Policy Implementation		Government Devolution Plan	Demonstration of a replicable model for social mobilisation	Social Action Programme Community Schools

The overall picture that emerges from this exercise is of an organisation that is, through its actions if not its proclamation, clearly a policy entrepreneur. However, it is also a picture of an organisation that is willing to work with government but always careful never to make the contacts too close for comfort; either by being too chummy or too antagonistic with government.

The demonstrated desire to maintain a decent distance from government comes both from a certain deference for government's legitimate authority and responsibility, but also from a certain disdain for government's very different ways of doing things. In retrospect, this maintenance of distance may well be a key reason for the fact that both have been able to coexist generally well for so long, and have even maintained a mutual respect. After all, as was mentioned before, too much familiarity can breed contempt; and a certain distance can immunise one from that familiarity, and therefore that contempt.

Figure 9.1 does not pretend to present a comprehensive picture of AKRSP's interaction with and influence on government but seeks, rather, to highlight a more nuanced view of the various ways and various levels at which AKRSP has interacted—directly and indirectly, purposely and inadvertently—with government. Such an exercise begins to point us towards a more varied sense of the different ways in which AKRSP has had an influence over local and national government.

AKRSP–Government interactions as strategic choices

We have focused thus far on AKRSP–government relations principally from the perspective of AKRSP. It is understood, however, that any relationship between a citizen organisation and government is ultimately the result of a set of strategic choices made by both sides.

One particular model for this understanding begins directly from a view of governmental and nongovernmental organisations vying within the policy arena for the articulation and actualisation of certain goals or interests (Najam 2000; also see Coston 1998; Fisher 1998; Kumar 1997). On any given issue, these goals will either be similar or not. Each will also have certain preferences for the strategies, or processes, they wish to employ in pursuing these goals. These, too, will sometimes be similar, and at other times, not. In short, it becomes a question of 'ends' and 'means'. Institutional actors—governmental and nongovernmental—each pursue certain *goals* (*ends*) and each have a preference for certain *strategies* (*means*). As they float within the policy 'soup' or 'stream' they bump into one another in one of four possible combinations: a) seeking similar ends with similar means; b) seeking dissimilar ends with dissimilar means; c) seeking similar ends but preferring dissimilar means; or d) preferring similar means but for dissimilar ends.

Figure 9.2. AKRSP–Government Relations: A 'Four C's' Approach

		Goals (Ends)	
		Similar	Dissimilar
Preferred Strategies (Means)	Similar	Cooperation: Occasional Mode	Co-optation: A By-product of Success
	Dissimilar	Complementarity: Predominant Mode	Confrontation: Avoided

The model, as depicted in Figure 9.2, posits that these four combinations—which correspond to a) cooperation, b) confrontation, c) complementarity and d) co-optation, respectively—encompass the realm of possible NGO–government relationships. In the first, governmental and nongovernmental organisations are likely to work jointly towards joint objectives; in the second, they tend to have opposing interests and act to thwart each other's efforts; in the third, they are likely to act separately but towards converging objectives; and in the fourth they may seem like acting jointly, but do so towards different objectives and are likely to attempt to co-opt the goals of the other (for a detailed elaboration of this framework, see Najam 2000).

Applying our earlier discussion of the AKRSP experience to this model, one finds that the predominant behaviour in AKRSP–government relations over the last twenty years has been complimentary, with more occasional examples of cooperative behaviour seen in the 1990s with an occasional direct project partnership between AKRSP and government. Confrontational behaviour has not only not been evident, but has been actively avoided. Co-optive behaviour has, similarly been avoided purposefully. However, it is important to note that an organic and positive co-optation of AKRSP ideas has happened over the years with both government and other NGOs becoming ever more likely to buy into the AKRSP approach, adopt and adapt it to their own activities, and ultimately 'co-opt' those ideas as their own. This co-optation of AKRSP ideas by government and other development actors can be viewed as a vindication and by-product of AKRSP success.

The principal relationship between government and AKRSP has tended to be **complementary** because, as noted, the larger goals (interests) of the two are very similar in developmental terms. But AKRSP has made a very conscious and focused effort to develop and implement a very different model of achieving those goals through social mobilisation. This means that the goals or ends of the two have been generally the same, the strategies or means for achieving them have been very different. For example, in terms of rural infrastructure development, the goals of AKRSP have never been at odds with the goals of government. The differences have been the preferred strategies for achieving them. It is not surprising, then, that the dominant relationship between the two has tended to be complementary. As Shah Maqeen, one of the longest serving staff members of AKRSP, points out, 'government had no interest in opposing what we were doing; we were doing exactly what they had been trying to do for years; we were just doing it differently.'[16] Indeed, at the field staff level, AKRSP activities were liberating for government field staff and local politicians since the goals were aligned and AKRSP brought resources and energy into issues that had earlier been neglected by higher echelons of government.[17]

Interestingly, over time, as the government has begun internalising AKRSP's strategic preferences for implementation— i.e., social mobilisation through community organisation—the ends and means preferred by the two have come into closer harmony and we have begun to see more project partnerships being undertaken in the **cooperative** mode. This process has embedded within it a de facto process of **co-optation** of AKRSP ideas by government, and in fact by other NGOs. As Shandana Khan put it, 'over time, everybody started talking the AKRSP language.'[18] AKRSP staff recount many examples of working together with government once it has bought into (co-opted in our vocabulary) AKRSP ideas. For example, the head of elected local government (Nazim) in District Chitral took on the AKRSP model as the basis of local development. The government program of 'Khushal Pakistan' (translation: 'Prosperous Pakistan') similarly built directly upon the foundation of AKRSP ideas and put communities at the centre of the implementation regime. Even earlier than this, the SAP implementation in the Northern Areas was done in close collaboration with AKRSP because the buy-in of ideas had happened already not only at the level of field workers in government but at the highest echelons of government.[19]

That **confrontational** behaviour has generally been avoided is not really surprising given AKRSP's organisational ethos of staying clear of disputes with government, its tendency to avoid adversarial advocacy, and the simple fact that at their core the development goals of AKRSP and government are very similar (AKRSP has sometimes been called a parallel development agency to government). Indeed, avoiding confrontation with government has itself been a major goal of AKRSP's. Aliya Golker was one amongst the many current and former AKRSP staff who made it a point to stress that AKRSP's 'institutional impulse is not to be confrontational.'[20] This avoidance derived not from a simple desire to keep government 'happy', but rather from a desire to keep government 'out of the way' on the things that mattered most to the organisation, i.e., putting into practice its model of community involvement and development and demonstrating the efficacy of this model. This did, of course, translate into deliberate avoidance of issues that the organisations could have taken on but were deemed too sensitive and likely to breed confrontation with government. For example, on issues such as rights to forest resources, local government, and gender rights, the organisation treaded with great—sometimes excessive—care, since it was quite clear that on these issues there were differences with government related both to what goals were desirable and to what means were preferable. However, AKRSP senior staff view this avoidance of confrontation not necessarily as abdication but as postponement. Over time, it is argued, such issues did begin to resonate more as conditions became more ripe to raise them in an overtly non-confrontational domain, partly because government's own understanding of these issues became more nuanced.[21]

Explaining AKRSP–Government Relations

The goal of the previous section was to understand what the nature of AKRSP–government relations has been over the last twenty years. We started the previous section by noting that AKRSP has sought and been able to maintain a remarkably cordial and non-adversarial relationship with government at the local as well as national level. We then went on to argue that maintaining good relations with government has been a strategic goal for AKRSP which meshes well with its institutional mandate of influencing government to bring about large scale systemic change in the way development interventions are undertaken. In exploring the nature of the relationship between AKRSP and government, we found that AKRSP's interactions have been fairly nuanced and it has acted as an advocate as well as a service provider although its dominant role of influencing government has been as a policy innovator. Moreover, we found that given the nature of its strategic institutional interests it is entirely understandable that the dominant mode of AKRSP-government relations has remained complementary, although over time one has begun to see occasional cooperative behaviour in project partnerships, and there has been a rather widespread and non-coercive co-optation of AKRSP ideas by other development actors, including by government.

In short, we have argued that AKRSP has been, and should be seen as, a policy entrepreneur. Indeed, one might argue that the most lasting impact of AKRSP has come as a policy entrepreneur— what AKRSP has done on the ground is very impressive, but even more impressive is what it has shown can be done. The impact of AKRSP is to be measured not just by what AKRSP has done in these twenty years but also by all the others who have adopted its model and followed its path. It is in this sense that viewing AKRSP as a policy entrepreneur provides a more comprehensive and truer picture of its accomplishments.

This next section builds upon the previous discussion and seeks to explain why AKRSP has been able to maintain generally cordial, positive and non-adversarial relations with government even though so many other civil society organisations in Pakistan have not. We will present three mutually reinforcing explanations—structural, contextual and strategic explanations—for why this has been so.

Structural Explanations

First, AKRSP's unique structure, organisational arrangement and mandate has allowed it to maintain a positive relationship with government. This was largely because for most of its existence AKRSP has neither 'needed' nor 'threatened' government in ways that other nongovernmental organisations do. Hence, it is important to acknowledge the structural explanations for AKRSP's relationships with government.

Tension between NGOs and governments stems usually from threat or from dependence. The absence of both in any serious degree allowed AKRSP a privileged position. Coming in with significant resources to begin with, and more importantly with a generous and sustaining source of future funding and support, AKRSP was able to concentrate fully on its mission and its mandate rather than have to worry about institutional survival as many other NGOs, including those that might start with one-time generous funding, often do. A critical structural element within AKRSP's resource endowment was that it was not seen to be 'taking away' money that would have otherwise gone to government. Resentment is sometimes generated when government functionaries think that the resources going to NGOs are being somehow diverted from them—i.e., that those resources might otherwise have come to, or through, government—has largely not been a factor and was certainly not a factor in the early years. There was a clear sense that the resources coming in for AKRSP were 'net new' resources that would otherwise not have come to the region; in a chronically resource-deprived region, all new resources were welcomed with minimal resentment.[22]

Another key element of the structural explanation was the association of AKRSP with H.H. the Aga Khan and therefore a direct buy-in into the respect that this association afforded both locally and at the level of the federal government. The prestige of this association, coupled with the expertise and institutional safety-net of the wider global network of the Aga Khan network of organisations provided AKRSP with further leverage and independence in its dealings with government, both locally and nationally. In addition, other elements of the Aga Khan Development Network in the region have also contributed to a certain 'heft' that the organisation assumed by always being seen as 'even bigger than it was'.[23]

Contextual Explanations

Second, the nature and extent of AKRSP's relationships with government have tended to vary by issue as well as by location. For example, in Gilgit, AKRSP has been interacting with a 'local' government at the very point of AKRSP's intervention; in Chitral, on the other hand, it is dealing with a provincial government that sits farther away in Peshawar, and therefore, neither reacts to nor understands local issues the same way as the government in Gilgit. Hence, it is also important to understand the contextual explanations for AKRSP's relationships with the government.[24]

It is quite clear that context played an important role in the relationships AKRSP developed with the government. In the Northern Areas, which have been traditionally neglected in the realms of larger national policy, AKRSP brought not only resources but a thrust of national and international interest that the region had long craved for but not received. Moreover, because the Northern Areas do not fall under any Provincial government, the seat of government was much more proximate to the project areas. This meant that not only could the government be approached more easily, but that the government was far better able to see first hand the efficacy of the AKRSP approach. Moreover, the arrival of a 'big' project to a 'small' region was, and remains, big news and a development that could not have gone without notice. Since the government literally 'resided' in the project area, the functionaries of government—who mostly belonged to the region—were also direct 'beneficiaries' of the project—not only in terms of what it did to the region and its micro and macro economy, but often to their own villages. This meant that they have had a far more immediate and personal stake in the development efforts of AKRSP.

The fact that the villages where AKRSP was working were relatively close to the Northern Area secretariat and that those working at the secretariat had more direct and sometimes personal stakes in the development of these villages fostered a certain affinity—or at least a lack of hostility—between government and AKRSP. It is not clear whether this can be expected in much larger, more populous provinces. This might become a significant challenge in the Chitral region where AKRSP has begun working and where the 'levers' of government sit much farther away (i.e., in the provincial Capital of Peshawar), and therefore require a different set of relationships and strategies.

Strategic Explanations

Finally, and not in contradiction with the above, even though the nature and evolution of AKRSP's relationship with the government can be greatly understood by structural and contextual explanations, strategic decisions by AKRSP leadership and staff have consciously sought to maintain a non-adversarial but independent posture towards the government. This includes, for example, a conscious decision by AKRSP leadership to seek to fill gaps in the government's capacity and resources well beyond the call of mandate (for example, through assisting with transport vehicles and helicopter access). Hence, it is also important to understand the strategic explanations for AKRSP's relationship with the government.

Indeed, the structural and contextual conditions that we have discussed are rather difficult to replicate. Therefore, it is difficult to derive prescriptive advice from those explanations, beyond saying that organisations—including AKRSP in the future—should be cognizant of their own structural strengths and limitations and the contextual conditions of the regions they work in. This is not insignificant advice. Indeed, strategy is about responding to the structural and contextual conditions that one finds oneself in and to then make the most of it. It is for this reason that the strategic explanations are of particular interest to us.

In looking at the strategic elements of how AKRSP has worked with the government over the last twenty years, three key lessons seem to emerge; these lessons remain valid for AKRSP in the future as well as for other organisations of its ilk:

Performance matters

The most important lesson, irrespective of what structural and contextual conditions one begins with, is that performance is key. Nothing explains AKRSP's relationship with the government as much as the fact that 'AKRSP worked!'[25] The most powerful argument that AKRSP ever had was the power of demonstration. However, it is also true that performance matters, but it matters most when it is widely seen and widely recognized. It is here that AKRSP's strategy of giving a wide audience to its success, particularly amongst government, was particularly important. Not only has AKRSP consistently worked on bringing local and regional government officials and politicians to its projects but there was a clear thrust, especially in the early years, to share the AKRSP experience with government officials at all levels: from presidents and prime ministers to federal secretaries and heads of international aid agencies, to young bureaucrats still in training. On the one hand, this has built up a lasting network of contacts for AKRSP but, much more importantly, it built a constituency for the AKRSP model which has stood the test of time and has become a key source of sustenance for that model.

Cultivate champions

The story of AKRSP can be told either as a story of specific activities and achievements or as the story of an idea. We have argued throughout this study that the latter story is of particular importance in understanding AKRSP–government relations. If the great harvest for AKRSP is the deep-rooted acceptance of its ideas, then this is a factor of the organisation's consistent strategy of cultivating champions for that idea at all levels. AKRSP has been spectacularly successful in cultivating champions at the highest level of government—for example, [former] President General Zia ul Haq, [former] Prime Minister Nawaz Sharif, [former] Governor Aftab Sherpao. This, of course, has been tremendously important in sending the right message down the 'chain of command'. The higher echelons of the bureaucratic leadership in the country and in the region have been similarly mobilised as champions for the AKRSP idea. However, what is usually not highlighted is the ubiquitous cultivation of champions for the AKRSP idea at lower levels of government, particularly at the local levels. This cultivation of champions came from multiple directions. First, a number of AKRSP field staff came from government itself. Second, government field staff have been consistently invited to maintain close contact with AKRSP and to be involved in relevant projects. Third, active effort has been made to showcase AKRSP successes to government functionaries through targeted programs, trainings, etc. The fact that a very large proportion of AKRSP staff is from the region itself has also contributed because this staff brings with it its own networks of relationships within the region, including in the government. In a relatively smaller region (in terms of population as well as size) these relationships and the goodwill they bring with them can be both deeper and stronger.[26] Finally, an important way in which AKRSP has cultivated champions is by employing some of the very best young professionals on its staff. Over the years these individuals have dispersed across Pakistan and across the world. This very impressive cohort of 'AKRSP Alumni' are all carriers of the 'AKRSP virus', and have generally proved to be very potent ambassadors for AKRSP even after they are no longer working for it directly.[27]

Manage jealousy and do not threaten

Nongovernmental organisations that are well-endowed can very easily cultivate jealousies or become threatening. AKRSP has consciously and consistently employed strategies to manage this tendency. AKRSP's early resource sustainability not only meant that the organisation did not have to worry about creating networks for future resource allocations but also that it now had resources to offer government in a region where resources had been scarce. Given the commonality of a lot of the development goals of local government and of AKRSP, resource-sharing was conceptually justified and built trust and a non-threatening relationship. For example, in a terrain where travel is never easy, the availability of the AKRSP vehicles and helicopter to share with government was useful and was appreciated. The institutional culture of being non-confrontational with government nurtured greater trust within government for AKRSP. The sense within government that resources going into AKRSP were not resources that were being diverted from government was also useful. For its part, AKRSP cultivated cooperation with government even when it did not have to, especially in terms of sharing resources and knowledge. Understanding that by virtue of its size and clout AKRSP could very easily be seen as a threat, the organisation consciously took steps to involve government in its activities and to manage jealousy or perceptions of threat. This was a wise strategic investment on AKRSP's part which allowed AKRSP to create capacities and cultivate champions within government.

AKRSP–Government Relations: Lessons and Challenges

What are the key lessons that AKRSP can draw from its two decades of experience of working with government? The previous section presented three related explanations of why AKRSP was able to develop the type of relationship with government that it did. Some of the factors that were highlighted in the previous section may be replicable by AKRSP and other civil society organisations in the future; many will not. Indeed, many of the conditions that enabled AKRSP to act as it did, no longer exist; others are already in a state of flux. To put it most bluntly, many things that AKRSP could have done in the past, and did quite well, it may not be able to do in the future.

But such are the challenges for all learning organisations. The purpose of this concluding section is to look not at the past but at the future. Looking forward from where we are and building on our experience of the past, what are the key challenges and opportunities for AKRSP in terms of its relationship with government and how can the lessons it has learnt in the last twenty years help it navigate through the challenges and turn them into opportunities. Here we identify three key challenges for AKRSP for the near future.

Devolution of government

The process of devolution of local government has already had a major impact on AKRSP and has dramatically changed a number of framework conditions; it is likely to change more. Two changes are of particular importance to AKRSP's ongoing relations with government. First, if devolution works as planned, the point at which government 'happens' will devolve closer to the ground and closer to where AKRSP works. Although the devolution process is still young and not yet fully implemented in all AKRSP project areas, if it does go ahead as planned it would mean that AKRSP's interaction with government (at least local government) will increase, possibly dramatically. Second, and related to the first, a large proportion of individuals who have been elected in the new local government set-up in relevant AKRSP project regions, are AKRSP alumni; this trend is likely to continue as devolution spreads to other AKRSP project areas. This will not only make it desirable for AKRSP to work more with local government but there is likely to be a demand from local government for AKRSP to work more with it. If both these trends were to become reality, the result will be a need for much more intense involvement with government, at a much lower level, and on a more continuous basis. While it is by no means certain that these trends will actually come to pass, if they do then AKRSP's tried and tested strategy of keeping government generally happy but at arm's length is likely to outlive its utility. Greater interaction with government, at a more local level, and on a more continuous basis will not only make it difficult to keep government at arm's length but will also make it more difficult to keep government happy.

However, there is also the potential for great opportunity. The fact that a lot of individuals who have been trained in community organisation through AKRSP interventions have now made their way into local government could trigger much greater synergy between the mental frameworks and strategic preferences of these local governments and of AKRSP. This might require a new strategy of interaction with government that focuses primarily on local government and seeks opportunities to work closely with local government.

An increasingly crowded field

The emergence of the various Rural Support Programmes (RSPs)—national and provincial—and of other civil society initiatives that build on the AKRSP model of social mobilisation is the most enduring and endearing testimony to AKRSP's success. However, it also poses a unique and rather daunting challenge for AKRSP as it plans its future, particularly in terms of its relations with government. AKRSP no longer operates in the vacuum into which it was launched. Not only have other RSP's emerged to woo the government but in AKRSP's own project areas there is a growth of NGOs, community organisations and development initiatives. Today, the development field in AKRSP's project areas is far more crowded than it was twenty years ago.

Not only is there a more crowded field of civil society initiatives for government and communities to choose from, but government itself has adopted many of AKRSP's principles. While AKRSP needs to celebrate these adaptations of its principles, it also needs to focus its energy on what were always its core strengths to maintain the momentum and impact of its activities. Given that the crowding of the field also comes at a time when AKRSP is unlikely to enjoy the resource abundance it once did, it will most likely have to choose between a geographic broadening of its activities or a thematic deepening. To avoid the risk of spreading itself too thin, it would make sense to do the latter but also return to the original intent and focus on the mandate to influence government as the motor for replication and scaling. The response to the increasing crowding of the field may well be the exact same as the response to the devolution of government; i.e., working more, rather than less, with government but doing so with local government rather than national or regional government.

The call to policy reform

Finally, there is likely to be an increasing and continuing demand on AKRSP to involve itself in policy reform initiatives around micro-finance, poverty alleviation, livelihoods, enterprise development, etc. Given where AKRSP is in its own institutional history, the experience it has accumulated in social mobilisation, and the role it has played in spawning other initiatives that have been modeled after it, it would be very sad if AKRSP were to totally retreat and shy away from policy-related work. Indeed, this would amount to an abdication of its responsibility and of its original mandate.

On the other hand, to be totally sucked into policy advocacy at the expense of its field activities would be equally tragic. AKRSP needs to find a balance between the two and this balance can be found in its original design as an action-research initiative. We began this study by defining AKRSP as an experiment, and it must deny itself the temptation of becoming simply a grand service delivery organisation. AKRSP has always prided itself over world class action-research and it must remain focused on that as the basis of any future policy work it does. While AKRSP should remain engaged on policy reform initiatives that can provide useful multiplier effects to its preferred strategies, it should insist on grounding its policy work in action-research. As we have noted earlier, the greatest policy influence of AKRSP has come not just from the results it has achieved on the field but the ideas that it has harvested from the field. Its influence over government has come from its ability to demonstrate the effectiveness of these ideas to government. AKRSP should continue to perfect these ideas through practice and advocate them through demonstration. This must not mean a retreat from policy work, but a strengthened programme to base its policy advocacy on demonstration in the field, in the best tradition of action-research.

NOTES

1. See companion chapters in this volume.
2. The principal source of information and ideas for this paper are a series of stakeholder interviews conducted during March, June and August 2003. Nearly forty individuals were interviewed in detail, and an additional meeting was held in March 2003 with around 15 field staff members of AKRSP from the various regions where AKRSP operates. These interviews included discussions with current and former AKRSP staff, current and former government officials at different levels (from the Federal to local government), and members of larger civil society in Pakistan who have not been directly associated with it but are knowledgeable about the operations and impacts of AKRSP. Mohammed Saleem of the AKRSP was a critical resource in tapping into this institutional memory and in helping sift out the critical messages from the various interview.
3. The document review included a review of various external evaluation reports, annual reports of the AKRSP, and other internal and project documents that related to AKRSP relations with government. Nadira Khawaja of the AKRSP was particularly helpful with this document review.
4. Interview with Shoaib Sultan Khan (Islamabad, March 10, 2003).
5. The four steps identified here signify what was new (and added to the earlier mix) in each phase rather than what was dominant. So, for example, in the 1990s direct partnerships was a new way in which AKRSP interacted with government but it was never the dominant way of AKRSP-government interactions.
6. Interview with Shoaib Sultan Khan (Islamabad, March 10, 2003).
7. Interview with Tariq Hussain (Islamabad, March 15, 2003).
8. Interview with Shoaib Sultan Khan (Islamabad, March 10, 2003).
9. Interviews with Mujtaba Paracha (Islamabad, March 11, 2003) and with Shundana Khan (Islamabad, March 10, 2003).
10. Interview with Steve Rasmussen (Islamabad, March 14, 2003).
11. Interview with Syed Akbar Kazmi, Assistant Director SAP, Gilgit (June 17, 2003).

12. It should be noted that recent changes within AKRSP make it unclear whether and to what extent the organisation will continue on the policy reform path.

13. Interview with Shoaib Sultan Khan (Islamabad, March 10, 2003).

14. This construct for understanding NGO influences on policy has been applied widely by various scholars, including the author over the last many years; see, for example, Wood (2003).

15. Interviews with Kamal Hyat (Islamabad, March 11, 2003), Pervaiz Hasan (Lahore, March 12, 2003) and Shahnaz Wazir Ali (Islamabad, March 11, 2003).

16. Interview with Shah Maqeen (Islamabad, March 14, 2003).

17. Interview with Mohammed Saleem (Islamabad, March 14, 2003).

18. Interview with Shandana Khan (Islamabad, March 10, 2003).

19. These and many other examples of collaboration with government on the field level come from various interviews with AKRSP staff, particularly from a group meeting with senior AKRSP staff from the regions held on March 10, 2003 in Islamabad.

20. Multiple interviews with various current and former AKRSP staff, March and June 2003. Quote from interview with Aliya Golker (Islamabad, March 15, 2003).

21. On this issue interviews with Steve Rasmussen (Islamabad, March 14, 2003), Aliya Goleker (Islamabad, March 15, 2003), Fareeha Ummar (Islamabad, March 15, 2003) and Shandana Khan (Islamabad, March 10, 2003) were particularly insightful.

22. Interview with Tariq Hussain (Islamabad, March 15, 2003).

23. Interview with Ghulam Mehdi (Gilgit, June 17, 2003).

24. Interview with Masoodul Mulk (Islamabad, June 18, 2003).

25. Interview with Shoaib Sultan Khan (Islamabad, March 10, 2003).

26. Various interviews with Mohammad Saleem and group meeting with senior AKRSP staff from the regions held on March 10, 2003 in Islamabad.

27. Interview with Shandana Khan (Islamabad, March 10, 2003).

10

The Way Forward: Fourth Dialogue

Izhar Hunzai

INTRODUCTION

The title of this chapter draws its inspiration from the well-known project cycle of AKRSP: the three *dialogues*[1]. It is meant to highlight both change and continuity in AKRSP's development approach and engagement in NAC.

The readers will note that this chapter is not a summation of the analytical work contained in the previous chapters, or a commentary on any specific point made in this book, or in volumes of other material available on AKRSP. Having said that, the chapter does refer to general points of perception and tries to provide an explanation where AKRSP feels that an internal interpretation is warranted. It is basically an attempt to describe and share the internal reflections of AKRSP on its own overall experience and to explain to its external audiences and partners the conceptual underpinnings of its new programme. In this sense the chapter is more like 'an insider's story', than an observer's analysis.

The chapter presents broad lessons in key areas that AKRSP has drawn from its own experience, both documented and undocumented, and highlights important issues and challenges that it considers as its 'unfinished agenda'. These lessons, challenges and opportunities in a changing development context of NAC, will define the scope and relevance of AKRSP in the coming years. It must be said that the ideas contained in this chapter do not constitute a 'blue print' for the next phase of AKRSP, which it never had in any case, but only a general direction towards which AKRSP can and will retool to experiment and evolve.

The chapter will also touch upon AKRSP's experience in certain areas of specific public interest and curiosity, especially in Pakistan, that have remained less documented and hence not found adequate comment and reflection in the main body of this book. One such area is the experience of AKRSP as a non-denominational development programme working in a highly charged communal environment. A related theme, which has also remained obscured in this discourse on AKRSP is its role, at least in the context of NAC, in helping to secularize and extend the outreach of its sister institutions in the Aga Khan Development Network (AKDN) to all the communities living in NAC. A third area of 'undocumented experience' is the quiet but unmistakable impact of AKRSP on the system of governance in the area, particularly on the democratic processes and nurturing of a culture of dialogue, accountability and transparency in both the public and private sector institutions.

AKRSP, over the last one year, has made a number of changes in its internal organization and external orientation, demonstrating the characteristic ability of a flexible catalyst, to creatively respond to changing needs and circumstances. It has done so by 'letting go' of a number of 'retail' functions; spinning off selected strategic programmes into separate private companies and, in the process, reducing its field offices and operational budget and substituting its own staff with community-based human resources. At the same time, it has developed plans to expand its role into new strategic areas, such as governance, civil society activism, and supporting democratic processes at the grassroots level. The aim may be similar to managing a large and useful tree with strong roots, allowing it to grow fresh shoots and propagate its seeds into new, fertile ground.

LEARNING BY DOING

Social Mobilization

From its own perspective, the most significant and enduring of AKRSP's legacy has been the renewal of community spirit at the grassroots level through the process of social mobilization. This unique contribution has many facets, including local empowerment through creation and fostering of broad-based democratic institutions at the village level, strengthening of the broader civil society sector; a culture of participatory development and partnership between the state and community sectors, and inspiration to other development actors, notably government, to pursue inclusive policies and programmes. Many of these lessons and outcomes have already been covered under various themes in this book. What remains to be said, however, is how the idea of social mobilization was viewed internally and how it evolved, mutated and took a life of its own, as AKRSP engaged with communities and their issues; in other words, how AKRSP managed the process of 'learning by doing' in this field.

We now know that social mobilization is a dynamic and an open-ended process with potential for a multitude of positive outcomes. Some confusion in understanding has arisen in this area because the process initiated by AKRSP in NAC had a very structured beginning. In retrospect, it appears that this highly structured approach was valid for at least two reasons. Firstly, it helped in translating a complex set of process objectives into a simple communication message; and secondly, it gave AKRSP a solid focus area, which helped in building the initial momentum it needed to produce a runaway phenomenon. Like all dynamic processes, AKRSP-inspired social mobilization outcomes have differed in their shape and form from the original design, which had a fixed structure. This was expected but never fully anticipated and understood by many participants in the process themselves, including some of us within AKRSP.

In the mid eighties, when the first signs of differentiation and individual management styles began to emerge in VOs, reflecting the underlying diversity and autonomy of communities, a debate ensued within AKRSP and across communities, whether or not to preserve the doctrinal purity of the social mobilization concept. The issues, now long settled and may appear trivial, were whether VOs could change their weekly meetings to fortnightly meetings, or meet whenever they need to meet, elect their office bearers for a fixed term, or whether more than one member from the same family could become a member of the VO. The interesting part, and one which offers an important lesson in process learning, is that these issues were not settled in a management forum or through a policy paper by AKRSP staff, but allowed to resolve themselves through sufficient debate and dialogue by the communities in light of their own interest and experiences. One of these old issues, whether or not to seek a legal persona for the institution of VO, is still being debated by some, and resolved by others by creating a separate legal entity out of the VO membership, while still maintaining the VO as an informal forum.

Today, in many areas there are no 'visible' VOs in the shape and form that characterized their original structure. This has caused a debate in some circles about the sustainability of VOs. But this may be a case of 'missing the forest for the trees'. The essential point is that the organizational capacities created through the nursery of VO, have taken a variety of other forms more suited to the changing needs of the area. These institutional outcomes range from committee-based management systems, thematic organizations; area-based structures, coalitions and clusters of VOs, and local support organizations that look like mini replicas of AKRSP. At the end of a long journey, what is visible in these valleys is a more confident and informed civil society with an increased ability to choose its own path to development through a variety of organizational choices and forms now available in the area.

At the policy level, the primary lesson that can be drawn from AKRSP's experience is that social mobilization can be a proactive policy instrument to promote social intermediation for micro-level development. Seen in the light of AKRSP experience, social mobilization models aimed at promoting collective action seem to prove more effective when: a) such models are embedded in the local institutional history; b) when such models follow local preferences for organizational forms, instead of relying on fixed and blue print approaches and, c) infused with democratic norms, renewed with new organizational knowledge, d) backed by broad-based public support and, e) linked to public and private development systems.

The primary lesson for the *practitioner* of rural development may be that social mobilization is a process that works and evolves through experimentation in real time and space; it can be guided and nurtured but can never be imposed. Organizational regimens are necessary for building initial confidence and momentum, but they cannot be a substitute for human ingenuity, creativity and institutional renewal. The best description of this process was provided, years ago, by Dr Akhtar Hameed Khan, the best known philosopher-practitioner of rural development in Pakistan who, settling a debate on the direction of VOs, quipped, 'you need a boat to cross the river, but you don't need to carry it on your shoulders when you have to climb the mountain that is now ahead of you'.

Empowerment of Women

In a *multi-stakeholder forum* recently held in Hunza, one of the more socially *advanced* parts of NAC, the debate on gender equality was disappointing in many respects. The occasion showed glaring gaps in the knowledge and understanding of gender issues among community leaders, even after two decades of relentless efforts by AKRSP. But there were many encouraging signs, too, both in the tone and substance of that debate. Although the debate was still dominated by men, it was happening more on generational, rather than gender lines; older men and women still considered gender equality objectives as disruptive to their values, and liberal minded men tried to defend women's rights as they saw them. The most striking aspect, however, was that those who had an exposure to the knowledge, both men and women, were calm, respectful and having an effect in steering the dialogue in a healthy manner and, above all, getting their message across. The occasion summed up both the scale of the challenge and AKRSP's incremental and non-confrontational approach to unraveling deep-rooted notions about women's and men's place in these traditional societies.

As can be expected of a fairly open and extensively scrutinized programme, AKRSP has attracted its share of criticism for not being more proactive and systematic in championing the cause of women in the area, particularly for not following a vigorous *rights-based* approach and for many of the flip flops in its attempts to evolve a consistent gender and development policy. So, what is the inside story? In fairness, it would be correct to say that AKRSP clearly lacked specific knowledge and tools to address the gender dimension of development when it started its work in 1982. Part of the reason for lacking a specific strategy was a general dearth of, or access to, applied knowledge and expertise in this field in the early 1980s. Could AKRSP have pursued a more vigorous gender equality policy in the intervening years as more knowledge and tools became available? And, was AKRSP overly sensitive to traditional conservative values. The answer may be a qualified, yes!

Viewed in the overall context of its general approach, which was to create options for, and *catalyze* rather than *administer*, development, AKRSP had its own limitations as to how much change it could trigger and at what pace. A more valid point of the criticism may be that AKRSP could have followed a more differentiated approach, at least in the gender sector, allowing more receptive groups within the area to adapt new concepts at a faster pace and thus serve as role models for others in the region. This did happen to some extent, but without a deliberate policy on the part of AKRSP. AKRSP's options in this area were again limited as they conflicted with another central element of its overall approach, i.e., equity.

The criticism about over-sensitivity to local cultural values may also hold true. The pioneering management team of AKRSP and members of its Board—most of whom come from outside AKRSP's programme area and were more inclined to err on the side of caution; AKRSP's affiliation with the Aga Khan Foundation, and funding support, the bulk of which came from international donor agencies, all contributed to some undetermined extent in making AKRSP more risk averse than the real conditions may have warranted.

The difficult starting conditions, lack of initial working knowledge, lack of a differentiated policy and a bit of over sensitivity to local sensibilities may have reduced or delayed the overall impact of AKRSP on women's development, but this effect is likely be only marginal. Based on its own analysis of local conditions and available knowledge at that time, AKRSP thought that it was right on the dot in identifying income generation and social mobilization as the defining features of an effective women's development programme. This strategy was pursued with the conviction that with economic empowerment and the *right of association* through WOs, women in the area can be assisted in making a significant breakthrough in improving their conditions.

In practice, this proved to be an ambitious plan as AKRSP began to confront real constraints. The primary difficulty, which took AKRSP a long time to resolve, was how to reach out to rural women with its message of social mobilization and new productive skills. Without precedence for female employment and the non-availability of suitably qualified local women, AKRSP had to recruit women with the needed technical skills from the south. This option was fraught with its own difficulties, such as linguistic barriers and a clash of cultures, and took a few more precious years and significant amount of resources to produce results. The interface with the main body of rural women still remained a major challenge for a long period of time and still remains an issue in some remote areas. Even though WOs were formed in significant numbers in the first ten years or so, their leadership remained largely in the hands of men, as there were few literate women to transact the business of WOs.

On the economic front, too, there were huge challenges. With no entitlement to land and other assets, restricted mobility, extremely low literacy rates, and under-developed local markets, finding income earning opportunities for women was an extremely difficult and ambitious 'undertaking'. AKRSP tried to confront this problem in a number ways. To redress the lack of assets, AKRSP financed the acquisition of land through long-term leasing arrangements, established fruit orchards to be collectively owned by WOs, and encouraged women to produce and market agricultural and poultry products to earn their own income. This again proved to be a difficult challenge for a number of reasons, including the delayed nature of benefits from orchards, technical difficulties to ensure quality and uniformity in the market-bound produce and a virtually complete exclusion of women from market transactions. Nonetheless, these initiatives opened up new possibilities for women that were previously unthinkable and helped, in some measure, change the attitude of both men and women about their traditional roles.

An important area where AKRSP was too slow to intervene was the social sector activities, such as primary education, basic health and sanitation and drinking water services. Admittedly, this was both a conceptual and strategic misjudgment on the part of AKRSP. Conceptually, AKRSP overemphasized the value of economic interventions and underemphasized the importance of social sector services. Strategically, it was slow in finding a way out of the apparent conflict of mandate with its sister agencies responsible for social sector services. As a learning organization (a slow learning organization may be more fitting in this case, as the women of the area were clear about their priorities from almost day one!), AKRSP corrected its course in early 1990s, when it partnered with the government Education Department and the Aga Khan Education Service in launching a successful Social Action Programme (SAP) funded by the World Bank.

Based on AKRSP's specific experience in this area, it can be said that promotion of gender equality interests in culturally sensitive areas of NAC requires ongoing dialogue with all the stakeholders, including religious and cultural opinion leaders with an objective of building pro-equality constituencies. Further, organizations pursuing gender interests in traditional societies can be more effective by adapting flexible strategies to suit local conditions. A gender agenda can be pursued more effectively when practical and beneficial considerations, such as tangible social and economic programmes, are included in the projects, based on local priorities. Awareness and sensitivity programmes alone are not sufficient. However, AKRSP may have missed another opportunity in this area by not working more closely with more receptive audiences, especially with public sector agencies and local civil society organizations.

Many factors internal to the organization, such as clear understanding of gender concept, senior staff commitment, and strong collaboration among concerned professionals contribute substantially to the promotion of gender equality.

A Flexible Catalyst

AKRSP was conceived as a flexible and imaginative response to the challenges of sustainable mountain development, a field that was largely uncharted in the early 1980s. The main challenge was how to respond to the prevailing conditions of poverty, social fragmentation and powerlessness in much of its programme area. After two decades, we have enough evidence to suggest that AKRSP has succeeded in reversing those trends and accomplished, in significant measure, what it had set out to achieve. Today, we have an active and growing Rural Support Programme (RSP) movement in Pakistan and the experience is being shared with other countries in Asia and Africa.

The creation of a flexible programme like AKRSP was a bold new initiative in the long history of AKDN engagement in NAC. AKDN's operations started in 1940s with the establishment of Diamond Jubilee schools. In the next two decades community health services were established. During 1970s, a renewed focus was given to mass primary education and education of girls. In the early 1980s, AKRSP was launched; during the next decade, housing, culture and heritage management were added to the portfolio. The focus in early 2000 shifted to the quality of education, sanitation and micro finance.

The AKRSP experiment involved several important points of departures from the prevailing norms of governance, management and legal status of AKDN institutions. AKRSP was considered as a special project of AKF under the office of the Director of Special Programmes. Unlike other AKDN institutions, which were registered as voluntary Boards under the Social Welfare Law, AKRSP was created with the flexibility of a public limited company with an autonomous Board of Directors and a professional management structure. It was given a clear mission of *doubling the rural incomes* in the area and *developing a replicable model* for rural development in mountain areas, and was given a broad mandate and flexible resources to achieve this mission.

Within a few years after AKRSP's creation, a clear organizational shift came in which all the main institutions of AKDN were converted from voluntary boards to service companies, separating professional management tasks from governance functions. This was a watershed decision, which led to an explosion in the growth of local professional and management capacities. A parallel effort was initiated to enhance the role and capacity of local people in the governing bodies that has also produced good results. With these changes, the scope of AKDN institutions was extended to serve all the communities living in NAC. The extensive network of VOs and WOs became important vehicles for increasing the outreach capacity of AKDN agencies, especially for the delivery of social sector services, such as primary education, primary health and water and sanitation.

A notable strength of AKRSP was the simplicity of its message and the flexibility of its approach, which resonated well with rural communities and permeated easily into the development culture of the area, including public sector agencies, AKDN institutions and other NGOs working in the area. The message called for building social, financial, physical and human capital for local development. This message had the effect of infusing a new confidence and vitality among rural communities, creating new, more equal and meaningful partnerships with development support systems, and leveraging community resources for local development priorities.

The experience of building social capital, the centerpiece of AKRSP approach, provided a practical answer to the question of creating meaningful partnerships between rural communities and development support systems. Unlike the state and private sectors, there was no obvious mechanism to organize and galvanize a fragmented civil society in rural areas into a 'visible' and credible partner in development, especially under the prevailing conditions of decaying traditional institutions in the area. The social intermediation and capacity building services at the community level, provided an opportunity to work both on the *demand* and *supply* sides of the development equation by extending the outreach and effectiveness of development services available from the formal sectors on the one hand, and adding value in the utilization of these services through active community participation and management, on the other. This was a powerful discovery since development approaches previously known in the area and, indeed, in the rest of Pakistan essentially offered only supply-side alternatives. Under this one-sided approach, rural people had little or no say in their own development, and were made to think of themselves as mere petitioners.

The organized participation of citizens in local and national development had other well-known beneficial effects of making the state and private sector institutions more transparent and accountable, thus triggering a slow but steady improvement in the overall system of governance in the area. Those who have seen the region over the years will notice a perceptible change in the disposition of not only the professional development agencies, but also in the social and political institutions that reflect a level of integrity and maturity unsuspected in a remote corner of Pakistan.

There is a lingering perception in some circles in the Northern Areas that AKRSP may actually have 'disadvantaged' the people of this region by 'blunting' a more vigorous expression of their long-held political aspirations for full constitutional rights. If true, this was certainly not intentional, but these feelings do lend support to the proposition that a culture of dialogue, openness and participatory methods introduced by AKRSP has, indeed, contributed to fostering democratic norms in the area. It may look far-fetched, but an interesting fact—and a sign of political maturity—in this area is the successful working of a coalition government, forged by the Northern Areas Legislative Council (NALC), that is now completing its full term. This may not appear to be so unusual for international readers, but it contrasts the fact that no National or Provincial Assembly has completed its full term in the rest of the country in more than three decades.

Many view AKRSP's approach towards government as an enigma. This is surprising because AKRSP followed a consistent policy of working with the government to promote common development objectives. AKRSP's policy in this area was driven by the recognition that the fight against poverty is a collaborative challenge, requiring a close partnership among the state, civil society and the private sector. Moreover, AKRSP recognized the indispensable role, legitimacy and permanency of the government that could never be substituted by any other actor. For these reasons, it can be said that AKRSP had a 'stake' in the success of the government; therefore, it was neither indifferent nor confrontational to the government, only cordial. As the overwhelming evidence suggests, the relationship between government and AKRSP were mutually rewarding. Throughout its history and through successive governments, AKRSP was viewed as a serious and credible development partner. On its part, AKRSP offered the government policy options in rural development through real action and demonstrated evidence on the ground.

Another apparent 'gray area' has been AKRSP's largely undocumented experience in working with people with diverse cultures and traditions and different religious affinities living in a delicate and often volatile social balance. For those who may not be familiar with the ethno-religious composition of NAC, the region's population is made up of four denominations of Islam, namely, the Sunni, Shia Ithnashari, Shia Ismaili (in roughly equal proportions) and Noor Bakhshi (a small sub-group of the Shia Ithashari sect) traditions, in addition to a small (only in thousands) minority community of the Kalash, a pre-Islamic tribe living in southern valleys of Chitral. The region already has a history of communal discord, which occasionally erupts into outright violence. This polarized communal situation presented a serious challenge for AKRSP, which had a specific mandate to work across communal lines. Naturally, there were varying degrees of expectations, suspicion, enthusiasm, acceptance and internalization of its ideas and programmes by these different groups.

However, AKRSP was quick to establish its non-communal credentials, helped by the fact that its professional team was, and has always been, a mixed bunch, and none of its senior managers and advisors belonged to the Ismaili sect. Still, the communal issue has remained as a 'live-wire' for AKRSP, and taken many turns and twists throughout its history.

Members of the Shia Ismaili community, who follow His Highness, the Aga Khan—the founder of AKRSP—as their *Imam* or spiritual guide, were the most active initial participants in the majority of AKRSP initiatives, though not benefiting more than their fair share of AKRSP resources. The reason for their enthusiasm was two twofold: their allegiance to His Highness and their familiarity with an established institutional development support system through AKDN.

For AKRSP, the issue was not whether it could strictly adhere to its principles of equity and non-partisanship. The challenge was gaining and maintaining the confidence of all the communities at all times, against real risks of miscommunication, deliberate misrepresentation of facts and occasional flaring up of communal strife. As can be expected of any area with a communal problem, there was determined opposition to any idea of change that threatened the existing status quo, which produced a steady supply of discord deemed necessary to maintain separate communal identities.

Having said that, the pitched opposition to AKRSP from a number of quarters, both internal and external to the region, was also motivated by a misconceived but genuine fear that AKRSP may have had a hidden agenda aimed at religious conversion. This fear was played out extensively at different intervals, but eventually faded out for the lack of evidence. In the meantime, confusion and anger prevailed among communities who, on the one hand, understood the benign nature of AKRSP and wanted to participate in its activities, but also needed the reassurance that this was not contrary to their religious obligations. The extent of this confusion can be discerned from the fact that in certain areas, the local mullahs had threatened their followers with such sanctions as the denial of birth and death rites in their families, if they accepted any assistance from AKRSP.

These extreme views had an unexpected effect of precipitating a serious discussion and dialogue within the communities and encouraged people to ask tough questions from their religious leaders. Some bold individuals questioned the qualifications of local mullahs and went to the extent of traveling to higher and more authentic centres of religious guidance, both in the country and outside, and managed to bring religious edits that cleared AKRSP of any malicious intent and wrong-doing. Almost all of this mistrust came from a very small but influential group of mullahs belonging to the Sunni and Shia Ithnashari communities. The Shia Ismaili hardliners had their own ideas about AKRSP. Their view held that AKRSP was an institution established by their *Imam* for the exclusive welfare of his followers, and that AKRSP management was unduly sympathetic to the other communities, who had little appreciation for the generosity of their *Imam*.

These were the odds against which AKRSP worked and keeping its promise of equal access and opportunity. Though difficult and still open to misrepresentation, the neutral and non-sectarian nature of AKRSP is now well established and accepted by the overwhelming majority of people living in NAC. The debate over its intentions has served as a useful purpose of asking tough questions and seeking evidence to determine facts.

A continuing concern of the government and AKDN in the area is a visible gap in the institutional experience and capacity of the Shia Ismaili and other communities, largely because of an early head start advantage enjoyed by the former, through their long association with the AKDN agencies. The growing social disparity in the area was one of the primary reasons for establishing AKRSP as a non-denominational development organization. This also answers a frequently asked question as to why His Highness the Aga Khan has a special concern for this area. AKRSP and increasingly other AKDN institutions, supported by the government, have tried to offset this disparity by offering a full range of economic, social and cultural services. Still, the limitation at least for AKRSP is that most of its investments so far have been in rural infrastructure and agriculture, while the real gaps remain in the social sector services, which require not only adequate resource, but also a real demand from the local communities. The challenge continues.

The Unfinished Agenda

AKRSP has played a unique role in the transformation of NAC and, by example, for other parts of Pakistan and beyond. In terms of its more measurable achievements, AKRSP has made recognizable impacts in poverty reduction and improved livelihood systems of NAC; enhanced professional, managerial and institutional capacities in the area, and created new assets and opportunities for people in the social, economic and rural finance sectors.

Still the challenge of sustainable development in this area is far from over. Resource poverty, isolation, lack of income earning opportunities, energy and other development constraints at the macro level are some of the larger challenges that call for a broader approach and new partnerships with government, civil society organizations, private sector and global initiatives.

The most notable continuing challenge is the persistence of poverty and vulnerability in the area. While poverty levels have come down significantly, there is considerable variation in the incidence of poverty in various parts of NAC. Vulnerability remains an important challenge for even graduating households, owing to the fragility of the local resource base and volatility of incomes from the off-farm sector.

Continued marginalization of women is another serious challenge. As mentioned in a previous section, AKRSP has probably underestimated the scale of this challenge and, in particular, lagged behind in addressing the social development needs of women in the area. In the next phase, this need will have to be addressed in conjunction with other measures to improve economic, institutional and attitudinal environment for women to make a real difference in their lives.

Work is also cut out for AKRSP to bring further improvements in the institutional landscape of the area, with particular focus on the second and third generation of civil society institutions that are rooted in broad-based village organizations, but also working closely with public and private sector institutions, including elected institutions at the grassroots level. A major area of renewed focus and attention would be enhancing management capacities and improving the governance system of public, private and citizen sector institutions.

Bridging productivity gaps in local agriculture, improving natural and other resource management practices, developing strategic sectors based on the region's comparative advantage, finding missing services in local markets and creating opportunities in the off-farm sector are other challenges that require further work and serious attention from AKRSP.

The Way Forward

Retooling AKRSP

AKRSP will continue to respond to evolving development challenges in its programme area. To do this, it will also change its outlook and retool its staff to continue to be effective. AKRSP has developed a new strategy that gives it a clear mission and mandate to address continuing challenges and respond to new opportunities in the next five-years. The strategy has been developed through extensive discussion and dialogue with its key stakeholders and takes into account the knowledge and experience accumulated over the last two decades. The main aim of this strategy is to put a variety of development efforts and initiatives in the area on a more sustainable footing. During the next phase, AKRSP will step back from direct delivery of retail services and reorganize its efforts to enable and empower local communities and their institutions to address local development needs, with a special focus on reducing poverty and promoting gender equality. AKRSP's main role will be to build human and institutional capacities and evaluating and presenting best development options available under different scenarios to local communities. This will include studying institutional frameworks, researching policy options, evolving resource and market development strategies, and assessing risks and rewards associated with the onslaught of globalization in the area.

In the coming years, AKRSP will consolidate its current programs under three major *themes* and start transferring specific components in each *theme* to more permanent, specialist bodies: mature VOs, local CSOs and their networks, as well as formal bodies of the state and market. These themes are:

a) Institutional Development (ID)
b) Resource Development (RD)
c) Market Development (MD)

Institutional Development

The overall purpose and scope of AKRSP's ID strategy is to work for the plurality of competent and accountable institutions, greater local ownership, increased institutional self-sufficiency and institutionalization of the bottom up approach to local development.

To this end, the first objective of this theme would be to foster an array of relevant, effective and broad-based civil society organizations and private sector institutions that can continue and expand, on a permanent basis, the mission started by AKRSP for catalyzing the equitable and sustainable development in NAC.

The second objective would be to improve development policies and practices that are responsive to the needs and priorities of the women and men of NAC through dialogue and partnerships among public, private and civil society sectors.

A third strategic objective is to gradually shift a large number of activities currently performed by AKRSP to permanent partner institutions of the state, private and civil society organizations.

Following will be the focused institutional development areas of AKRSP under this strategy:

a) Civil Society Organizations
b) Elected Institutions
c) Private Sector Organizations

Civil Society Organizations (SCOs): AKRSP's main contribution to the development of the civil society in NAC has been through the social mobilization of rural communities and creation of a network of broad-based V/WOs throughout the region. The VO was meant to serve as a broad-based multi-stakeholder forum to decide and implement development priorities at the primary village level. Today, there is great diversity among VOs in terms of their roles, functions and competencies. While the VOs still have many weaknesses and there are questions about their capacity and relevance to address larger development needs in NAC, they are still the only broad-based local institutions in place in the villages to ensure broad participation in decision-making. The strategy therefore would be to continue AKRSP's partnership with VOs, but in a mature, minimalist and a 'weaning off' mode. The purpose is to enable VOs to enter a new phase in their institutional history in which they are more independent of AKRSP, understand the broader development environment, and are able to forge partnerships and alliances with an array of support systems in the public, private and civil society sectors. In this new phase, VOs will be encouraged to change the portfolio of their activities, giving up some of the old activities and taking on new responsibilities and in the process renew and consolidate their organizational mission and strengths.

The WO forum has provided a critically important platform for collective development of women. In view of the limited possibilities for women to participate in broader village and higher fora in several parts of the region, expanding WO coverage and providing further support to help consolidate the work of existing WOs remains imperative. This work will therefore continue into the next phase with added vigour and focus in view of the still untapped potential to make meaningful differences to the quality of women's lives. Therefore, the strategy for the next phase entails:

- Achieving maximum coverage through new WOs and increasing their membership
- Developing new programmes to ensure the participation of women in a range of social and economic activities as well as increasing their participation in the political and cultural spheres

- Enabling WOs to provide better quality services specific to the needs of sub groups, such as senior citizens, mothers, women without formal education, educated unemployed women, working women, poor and destitute women, through research, linkages, small grants, capacity building and training activities
- Expanding the role of women in emerging sectors, such as information and communication technology, early childhood development, business and professional development
- Building the leadership and increasing participation of women at decision-making and resource allocation fora
- Building networks of WOs in the region and linking them up with the national and international networks and coalitions in areas of rights, welfare, poverty alleviation and protection against violence and abuse

The inspiration and organizational skills now available in the area have led to the creation and proliferation of a second and even third generation of civil society organizations. In greater part, these are organizational forms have evolved from the VO-based cluster organizations or, in some cases, creation of totally new organizations modeled on AKRSP itself. They are either multi-sector institutions serving a particular geographical area, are focused on a theme, or both. Because they are rooted in V/WOs and other community level institutions and represent their interests at higher levels, they can be described as Local Support Organizations or LSOs. The emergence of LSOs and other civil society organizations is, in part, a response to the differentiating and diversifying development needs of the region. In their orientation, these institutions are clearly connected to the larger mission of AKRSP and are, therefore, potentially the logical successors to AKRSP.

In the next phase, AKRSP will work to further enhance the capacity of these intermediary institutions, both LSOs and CSOs, add value to their work, and through them establish a two-way system of aggregating development needs expressed by the grassroots network of V/WOs, as well as a response mechanism that reflects the aspirations of the larger civil society in NAC. AKRSP's support to these institutions will focus on developing their capacity in governance, managerial and technical skills through specifically designed programmes.

The sustainability of LSOs is an important issue. However, as competent intermediaries, LSOs would add value to the work of upstream agencies, such as AKRSP, other AKDN agencies, public sector programmes and donors, it is conceivable that they can meet their operational costs through management overheads provided to them by the larger partners for retailing their services. One sector in which this arrangement can ensure greater financial sustainability is credit retailing.

Public Sector Institutions: The specific objective is to establish processes and mechanisms to improve development policies and practices through partnership arrangements so that public sector programmes and projects are responsive to the needs and priorities of the communities, particularly poor women and men of NAC.

A significant recent development in Pakistan has been the establishment of local government institutions. District, tehsil and union councils have been established in the NAC as part of the current government's plan for the devolution of political authority to local level[2]. At the request of the government, AKRSP has worked with the Northern Areas Department of Local Government and Rural Development in setting up these local government structures that are now directly receiving financial allocations from the government to undertake development work in their respective villages. Many of the members of the district, tehsil, union and village councils are also office bearers of the V/WOs. AKRSP will leverage this overlapping membership of local elected councils and V/WOs to ensure broader public participation in the preparation and implementation of local development plans.

In Chitral, the government's Devolution Plan is fully extended and presents an opportunity to link the local government system with broad-based participatory V/WOs. Already, a number of V/WOs have benefited from its provisions by registering themselves as Citizen Community Boards (CCBs).

The scope of partnership and support will entail the following:

- Capacity and competence building of elected institutions through specially designed training programmes
- Facilitating the formation of the CCBs and building their capacity
- Joint policy research and strategy formulation in specific areas, such as poverty reduction, natural resources management, as well as promoting community based initiatives in economic, social and cultural sectors
- Joint projects through resource pooling and special projects through small matching grants to promote good governance, gender equality and mass participation in the political process
- Promoting public, private and community sector partnerships to develop strategic sectors, such as power generation, tourism and other needed projects

Private Sector Institutions: The private sector is one of the most important pillars of the national economy and, therefore, no sustainable development is possible without the proper involvement and development of this sector. Experience in other parts of the world, particularly in China, shows that the growth of the private sector is an important condition for poverty reduction. The private sector plays a significant role in creating jobs, exploitation of natural resources and provision of general development services. Faster growth is possible only if there are enabling conditions for economic revival and a collective effort by the public and private sector actors to promote economic stability and enterprise development in the region.

The specific ID related objective would be to create conditions for the growth of the private sector by supporting relevant institutions and by fostering public private sector partnerships at various levels. AKRSP can play a catalytic role in fostering these partnerships, supporting the existing institutions and helping to establish new institutions wherever required. Moreover, AKRSP will work to bring positive change, in collaboration with other partners, to the prevailing social context of NAC that has so far limited women's mobility and exposure to opportunities outside their homes, resulting in limited participation and lower productivity in economic activities, thus leading to higher levels of female poverty, vulnerability and insecurity.

Dialogue for Development: AKRSP has pioneered the idea of *dialogue* and developed tools for the promotion of the dialogue process at the village level. The intention now is to expand the scope of the dialogue process in the next phase, by establishing a system of multi-stakeholder fora (MSF) at valley and higher levels. These fora, if properly organized, can bring together all the important stakeholders, including elected representatives, line agencies, civil society organizations, the private sector, intelligentsia and media for addressing common development concerns and developing plans based on the actual needs and aspirations of all stakeholders in each locality. Over time, AKRSP hopes that these fora will become the principal method for participatory local planning and prioritizing local development needs, and serve as an open and transparent mechanism for allocating development resources, whether from government or NGOs.

Resource Development

Over the last twenty years, AKRSP has made sizeable investments in developing economic infrastructure and broadening the economic options for the people of the area. These investments have played a major role in spurring economic growth and securing livelihoods of the poor. Notwithstanding the initial success, our past investment in broadening the resource base in NAC seems less than adequate when we take an inventory of key trends, such as increasing degradation of natural resource, growing unemployment and continuing marginalization of women and the poor. All these trends signify the need for continued investment in key resources with a particular focus on productivity, equity and sustained benefits.

AKRSP's historic investments in physical infrastructure, particularly the land development initiatives and construction of farm to market feeder roads have undoubtedly led to increased production of farm products and their marketability. A simple continuation of these traditional investments alone, however, is less likely to pay higher dividends, especially in the changing context of NAC where non-farm sector is gaining increasing importance in the lives of the people. There is a genuine need to identify and invest in new resources e.g. tourism, power generation, mining, and information and communication technologies that are likely to play a very important role in the coming years.

Besides the need for investing in new forms of infrastructure and resources, an equally important task is to increase the returns from the existing resources. There are still many productivity gaps in agriculture that can be plugged through applying new tools and techniques such as mountain specific research and adoption of better farming techniques and technologies. Similarly, there are many key sub-sectors of comparative advantage within agriculture e.g. seeds, temperate fruits, and eco-tourism that are still under developed. Concerted efforts on the part of public and private sectors are required to develop and promote these key sub-sectors.

It is with this background that a new resource development strategy is being developed. The new RD strategy of AKRSP seeks to develop resources that are of wider relevance and of strategic importance to the people of NAC. At the same time, the strategy also strives to align its approach and interventions with the future direction and outlook of AKRSP.

Diversification and Livelihoods: AKRSP's new RD strategy distinguishes between two sets of resources—support resources and strategic resources. Support resources are basically facilitative in nature and ensure the smooth functioning of economic activities. These include physical infrastructure, e.g., irrigation channels, roads, and bridges; information and telecommunication infrastructure; and financial networks. The other set of resources—strategic resources—constitute those sectors that define the livelihoods and occupation of the people. In the specific context of NAC, strategic resources include selected sub-sectors in agriculture, hydropower, mining, human resources, and tourism industry.

For supporting resources, the primary focus of the RD strategy will be on increasing their outreach, access and consumption in an effective and sustainable manner. As its overall thrust, the RD programme will be required to pay greater attention to increasing the outreach of basic resources to those areas, which still remain cut off from the mainstream development. This will require greater attention to the underserved areas, particularly in the development of traditional resources, such as irrigation channels and roads. As an additional thrust, AKRSP will invest in such enabling infrastructure, as Information and Communication Technology (ICT), which are likely to facilitate and reinforce the development of key livelihood sectors such as human resources, tourisms, and high value agriculture.

AKRSP's thrust for strategic resources will be on promoting diversification, both within and outside agriculture and spur economic growth, while ensuring economic security for the most marginalized and the poorest. This will require a careful investigation into the relative disadvantage of the region and then selection of those areas, which are most suitable and strategic for the people of NAC. AKRSP will follow a total sector development approach under this component to increase the attractiveness of each sub-sector. This will mean initial R&D, piloting, and then scaling up of each intervention, while identifying and developing permanent providers of services at each stage of the value chain.

Through investing in the support and strategic resources, the RD programme aims to achieve the following objectives:

a) Promote diversification within and outside natural resource based livelihoods
b) Secure the livelihoods of poor and marginalized including women

The challenge, however, lies in achieving the objectives described above while doing justice to the resource constraints and future vision of AKRSP. Therefore, AKRSP will focus on identifying and involving institutions from public, private, and citizen sectors to take up most of the activities while intervening in those sectors that remain unattended. The salient feature of new RD strategy will be its increased reliance on public, private, and citizen sector players for the delivery of services required under each resource. In order to make a gradual shift from service delivery to capacity building role, the RD programme will identify and forge partnerships with permanent institutions, such as government line departments and private sector players, particularly those related to natural resource management and infrastructure development. Selection of resources for investment will be based on the assessment of its demand as well as on its comparative advantage. Only those sectors will be selected for investment that are of higher relevance for communities and show good potential in terms of comparative advantage, e.g., seed potatoes, dried apricots, organic farming.

Attention to Poverty and Gender Inequality: Since a market driven and growth oriented strategy may exclude certain segments of the population such as women and very poor, special attention will be given to developing resources that will work to the advantage of poor and marginalized. For instance, a clear strategic focus of RD strategic will be on broadening farming options through identification of high yielding cereal and cash crops in high altitude and marginalized areas. Similarly, affirmative action will be taken to ensure inclusion of women in human resource development interventions, particularly in the emerging sectors such as information technology

A Differentiated Approach: Given the increasing differentiation across regions and valleys in terms of economic growth and development, there is a clear need for a differentiated approach. While most of the subsidy, particularly in infrastructure, will go to relatively underserved and underdeveloped areas within NAC, there is a genuine need to identify ways in which the evolving needs of graduating areas can be addressed. For such areas, greater attention will be paid to attracting private investment for emerging enterprises, e.g., power utilities and Internet service providers (ISPs) with cost recovery mechanisms.

An R&D based scaling up approach is key to reduce risk of failure and to avoid resource wastage. AKRSP's RD programme will ensure the correct sequencing of different steps before scaling up any new interventions. This sequencing will entail doing R&D first, piloting the new intervention in a selected space, incorporating the lessons, and then scaling up.

Support Resources: Investment in support infrastructure is a prerequisite to creating an enabling environment for economic development. Supporting resources facilitate the economic activities through: a) broadening asset base, e.g., irrigation channels and land development; b) through creating the ability to exercise options emerging from larger economic developments, e.g., KKH versus AKRSP financed feeder and link roads; and c) reducing the transaction costs and increasing the effectiveness of development inputs, e.g., information resources, roads. Under the support resources, RD section will focus on physical, information, and financial resources.

Past interventions in physical infrastructure, e.g., irrigation channels, roads, protective works have paid high dividends in the form of increasing the resource base in NAC with a fair distributional effect. There is still an unmet demand to continue such investments, but in a differentiated manner to pay greater attention to underserved areas. Therefore, a grant-based infrastructure development will be continued by AKRSP over the next five years with a special focus on extending this investment to the areas where unmet demand still exists. AKRSP's experience shows that investment in small infrastructure is very effective in internalizing the benefits arising from large projects. The interaction between KKH and AKRSP funded feeder roads is one such example. Therefore, AKRSP will work with government to implement large-scale projects in NAC. At the same time, donor windows that are sponsoring infrastructure projects with a commercial focus will be attracted for investment in those areas where potential for downstream enterprise development exists.

In congruence with the AKRSP's future direction, the Mountain Infrastructure and Engineering Services (MIES) division of AKRSP will be reorganized into a separate private company. This company, using its considerable experience and expertise developed at AKRSP, will provide high quality engineering services to public sector agencies, other NGOs, and the private sector players besides continuing to work for AKRSP on contract. AKRSP will also provide technical assistance to this and other similar professional private sector service providers to make them viable. The value added case for such separate entities lies in the fact that other community organizations, that cannot develop internal capacity to do infrastructure projects will now be able to undertake such activities through professional private sector intermediaries.

In order to harness the tremendous potential of emerging information and communication technologies in increasing effectiveness and reducing transaction costs, RD strategy envisages a proactive approach. Under this theme, the aim would be to promote the use of cost effective conduits for information intermediation. AKRSP will work with relevant government departments and private sector players to extend the geographic coverage of ISPs that have recently sprung up in selected parts of NAC. Like other infrastructure development, the benefits from larger infrastructure developments, e.g., availability of Internet, can only be internalized when the demand for such services is strengthened. Therefore, AKRSP will work with local organizations and private sector players to establish IT resource centers at the village level. These resource centers will work as training centers as well as information hubs for disseminating information.

Compared to other sectors, a functioning network of financial institutions in the form of commercial banks and microfinance institutions already exists in NAC. However, the challenge lies in designing customized financial products to promote key sectors, such as human resources, tourism, and mining. AKRSP will work with the state and private sector financial institutions to identify and design new financial products for emerging sectors. Increasing the outreach and effectiveness of financial products for the poor is a key challenge. The RD programme will systematically identify areas where financial products can serve as safety nets to the poor. One example of such intervention is the designing of group life insurance for earners of poor households by identifying ways in which those poor households can be cross subsidized through the premium from non-poor. Similarly, the challenge lies in designing and delivering financial products to non-traditional sectors such as professional education loans to promote human resource development in NAC.

The continuity of development interventions by different NGOs, particularly at the local level, is dependant upon availability of funding from external sources and this dependence is likely to continue into foreseeable future. Many NGOs often face a financial crunch mainly due to their lack of awareness about different funding windows. There is room for information intermediaries between the donors and recipients of donations. Therefore, RD will also promote resource centers aimed at collecting and disseminating information on funding windows with added services, such as proposal development and impact monitoring.

Strategic Resources: Based on the preliminary analysis of the comparative advantage of NAC and changing market dynamics within NAC and outside, the RD programme will focus on three key strategic resources, namely, natural resources, human resources, and environmental & cultural resources. Investment in these key resources will promote the objective of diversification within as well as outside natural resources. These resources are equally important from the perspective of securing the livelihoods of the marginalized and poorest.

A majority of households in NAC are still associated with farming. Moreover, about half of the total household incomes are drawn from farm-based activities, such as crop farming, livestock keeping and forestry. This important source of livelihood is, however, eroding rapidly owing to increasing population pressure, unsustainable forest cutting and land fragmentation. The challenge for RD is to secure the livelihoods of those who continue to rely on natural resources. AKRSP's past investment in irrigation channels coupled with the introduction of improved technologies in agriculture, livestock and forestry was an attempt at addressing this challenge. The challenge, however, continues to exist. There are productivity gaps in agriculture that can be plugged through research specific to NAC conditions, introducing improved management, farming technologies, tools and techniques. Similarly, there are unexplored niches that offer tremendous potential in terms of producing products under comparatively advantageous conditions.

NAC presents a unique opportunity for the production of farm products under organic conditions. Geographic isolation of many valleys, low diffusion of chemical inputs, and traditional farming practices are some of the key features of farming in NAC that can be turned into competitive strengths to tap into a rapidly growing health food market in the country. AKRSP's past investment in developing high value horticultural products, such as apricots, cherries and apples has paid good dividends to the farmers of NAC. Based on the lessons learned in promoting these three high value fruits, the RD programme will follow a total sector development approach towards investing in other potential fruit crops such as grapes and nuts. This approach will entail the identification and involvement of relevant service providers at each stage from the supply of quality planting material to the post harvest handling and selling.

Quality seed is one of the most important determining factors of productivity in agriculture. The RD programme envisages investing in seed sector primarily to ensure the availability of quality planting material for the farmers in NAC, besides promoting its exports to down country and, in some cases, to adjacent international markets such as Afghanistan. Key seed enterprises both for local use and export purposes include potato, tomato, and onion. Besides this, the participatory cereal development programme will be scaled up address the objective of food security.

The mineral sector in NAC continues to remain highly under utilized, mainly due to underdeveloped physical infrastructure and high capital investment requirements. Large-scale mining is only possible when these barriers are lowered through the concerted efforts of public and private sector. Nonetheless, in the medium term, possibilities of small-scale mining can be explored in partnership with NAC government and external funding agencies.

Investment in human resources is the key ingredient of positive and sustainable diversification. The inadequacy of arable land in NAC only furthers the need for accelerated efforts on this front. In view of this challenge, the RD programme plans to facilitate the entry of youth, particularly women to key marketable skills, such as information technology, nursing, and teaching in specialized fields such as early childhood development. Concerted efforts on the part of AKRSP, other AKDN institutions, public, and private sector particularly financial institutions will be required to devise scholarship programmes and customized loan products to facilitate the entry of youth to these promising disciplines.

Diversity of natural environs and ethnicities in NAC serves as a great attraction for tourists from all over the world. Today, many households in NAC are dependant on this sector for their livelihoods. In order to strengthen this sector, RD will work with other partners to develop facilitating resources such as establishment of information kiosks and increase the attractiveness of NAC for eco-tourism through investing in publicity and advocacy. Major activities under this component will include developing and hosting event calendars in partnership with private and public sector institutions, development of information resources for publicity of NAC, and advocacy for tourism sector development in NAC.

MARKET DEVELOPMENT

The main focus of the AKRSP's MD programme would be on building the capacity of individuals, public and private sector institutions for creating new opportunities for provision of efficient market and financial services. Under this strategy AKRSP will explore market-based opportunities for income, enterprise and employment both within and outside NAC. The strategy also envisages promoting social enterprises and finding market-based solutions to public and community-based service delivery challenges.

A clear objective is to help expand and accelerate private sector participation in the development of NAC. To this end, the strategy seeks to define a systematic and coherent programme of actions to be pursued by AKRSP in the next phase. Under this strategy, the MD programme will utilize the capabilities of public, community and private sector partners to deliver synergistic solutions to problems that impede private sector growth in the NAC.

In the public sector, the strategy will be to support and add value to government policy for creating enabling conditions for public-private partnerships; identify policy and service delivery gaps, and assist in improving and extending available services for business and enterprise development in NAC.

In the private sector, the major thrust of the strategy will be sector-specific research, creation of entrepreneurial skills, particularly among women, and catalyzing private investments and improving financial and business development services.

In the community sector, the focus will be assessing the potential for starting and managing financially viable social enterprises and improving the governance and management capacity of individuals and civil society organizations operating such enterprises.

Adding Value to Public Services: In recent years, public policy has moved rapidly towards a more 'investor friendly' environment in Pakistan. The stated goal of the government is to create a favorable business environment, especially for small and medium enterprises (SMEs), in Pakistan's economy and eliminating unnecessary obstacles. In support of this policy, the government has initiated a number of support programmes, ranging from accessible business finance, training, business development services and tax incentives for new investments. However, because of the remoteness, political marginalization, and generally weak 'starting conditions' of NAC, public sector support systems are still sub-optimal in the region.

Under this strategy, AKRSP will work with both public and private sector partners to streamline the delivery of existing services and advocate for creating new enabling conditions conducive to stimulating growth of the private sector in NAC. This may include research-based advocacy for sector reforms and public-private investment proposals for strategic investment in key infrastructure facilities, such as export processing zones, industrial areas, dry ports, roads, telecommunications, and power utilities needed to enable the private sector to undertake business activity more efficiently. Where found desirable based on benefit-cost analysis, the location of such facilities can deliberately be chosen to influence the flow of private investment to poverty-stricken areas.

Another area of focus would be creating demand for public sector services through training, information dissemination, feasibility analysis, provision of social collateral, and 'good governance' assurances. A third area of interest would be to facilitate the extension of SMEDA, Export Processing Zone (EPZ) Authority and other innovative government programmes and projects to NAC through partnership and collaborative arrangements. A fourth area of interest would be to create capacities for market research and enterprise training at local educational institutions.

Supporting Local Enterprise: As a first step towards devising a workable enterprise support system it is important to have a clear idea of the 'natural habitat' within which small and micro enterprises can flourish. The SME universe or ecology refers to the dynamic interplay of all external financial and non-financial factors that support and sustain micro, small and medium enterprises by contributing to their operational capacity, access to markets, management skills, financial efficiency, and access to marketing and information networks. This environment includes a number of independent, but mutually supportive services. These services are both operational and strategic in nature. Operational services are those needed for day-to-day operations, such as information, communication and financial management. Strategic services, on the other hand, are those used by the enterprises to address medium and long-term issues in order to improve their performance, such as R&D, improving access to market and ability to compete, differentiate, expand and diversify into new areas.

The first part of the challenge for AKRSP's MD strategy is to identify missing links in the SME universe in the context of NAC and develop a plan for the gradual creation and improvement of both operational and strategic services. The second part of the challenge is to do this in a least interventionist manner, involving the private and public sector players themselves in the provision of missing services.

AKRSP's major role in implementing this strategy will include product (e.g., apricots), service (e.g., microfinance, micro insurance) and sector (e.g., tourism, seed & mining) specific research and development, based on the comparative advantage of the area; underwriting risk in selected cases, such as equity participation and market guarantee; skill enhancement and devising innovative investment mechanisms, combining social and financial equity to facilitate the entry of strategic investors.

For AKRSP it is necessary to make a distinction between *operational* and *strategic* interventions and services. This distinction is based on the understanding that operational services, which have a direct bearing on enterprise 'transactions', may be considered as a direct interference in the market system. Strategic services, on the other hand, can be viewed as 'pre-transaction' interventions that essentially facilitate the entry of new actors into what may be under-developed markets. The examples of the former are subsidized credit, business management or marketing services, while the examples of the latter include basic research in industry or agriculture and fiscal incentives for road or power infrastructure. According to this understanding, business development services fall somewhere in between. If AKRSP provides business development services and recovers part of the cost, it may be justified on the grounds that it is not directed at a particular enterprise or group of enterprises. However, if AKRSP facilitates the provision of these services through other providers—developing a market of providers of BDS through initial training, it will fall in the second category.

In providing direct operational services to enterprises, AKRSP will go through this second, 'public goods' route. For example, AKRSP will invest in the creation or capacity building of marketing or producer associations, enabling them to provide production and marketing services to individual members, rather than providing these services directly to individual producers and operators.

An important function of AKRSP would be to promote a range of business development services required for smooth growth of the market by supporting both exiting and new service providers. The economy of NAC is both informal and underdeveloped, therefore, the best approach would be to develop and strengthen informal market-based support systems, such as marketing and business associations and groups. Specific services required for providing business appraisal and management support to existing or new enterprises, such as feasibility studies, business plans, accounting and audit services will also be created in the private sector through support to professional groups. These groups will then provide specialized market and business support services through normal business channels. AKRSP's support role will include the following:

- Identification of services required in the market
- Initial support in training the service providers
- Support in formation of business associations and groups.

Action research is the lifeline of enterprise development. The business related research and development needs of NAC are large and diverse but almost non-existent. The starting point for intervening into any sector and sub sector is through market research. A product, service or sector specific market research and information service is crucial for understanding the market dynamics for both the supply and demand end players. In order to survive in an ever changing and evolving market environment, it is essential that new products be introduced and existing ones modified. Unfortunately existing SMEs are not in a position to undertake new product development research as the risks and cost associated with it are too high. It is therefore the task of the support organizations to conduct research on behalf of the entrepreneurs and share results with the market players. Moreover, in order to increase the trade and exchange in the area it is imperative to access the 'down country' and 'international' markets. This can only be achieved by provision of technical support (product standard and product grading) to penetrate these markets. To increase competitiveness of the products of NAC, a quality assurance service is also essential.

The existence of a specialized and permanent service provider for market research is a vital 'public good' but currently missing in NAC. At the national and provincial levels, there are a number of public sector or public interest originations that provide these services. While searching for a more permanent public sector service provider, AKRSP will work with appropriate local institutions to provide these services in selected areas.

A major constraint on enterprise development in NAC is the absence of an established enterprise culture that has severely inhibited adequate realization of business possibilities and development opportunities. Short and long-term measures are needed to address this important constraint. As a sort-term intervention, AKRSP will train educated potential entrepreneurs, particularly women in starting their own businesses, and include a training module in basic business management skills in its 'functional literacy' programme, aimed at men and women who have had no opportunity to acquire formal education, as well as start a Business Development Newsletter containing business and market information in key areas aimed at the local business community. As a long-term measure AKRSP will work with a reputable national university to design and run a micro enterprise course to be taught at the Karakoram International University (KIU) as part of its MBA programme.

Growing unemployment, particularly among the young, educated men and women is a serious problem in NAC. Given the limited private sector opportunities, this problem cannot be adequately addressed within the confines of NAC, at least in the near term. A potential way out is to look for employment opportunities elsewhere in the country, while making serious efforts to create private sector jobs and self-employment opportunities with the region. Under the current strategy, AKRSP will make a modest start by launching an employment exchange programme aimed at providing information on job opportunities at the national level to local job seekers. On a pilot scale, this programme will be supported with professional, technical and vocational skills. The self-employment part of this programme will be linked to other elements of the Market and Resource development strategies of AKRSP.

Looking holistically, the financial needs of the market in NAC will evolve and need additional financial products, such as insurance, investment and audit services etc. AKRSP will work with the FMFB and other providers to develop appropriate products for local businesses. Some preliminary ideas that need further thinking include the following:

- Exploring the scope and potential for a micro insurance scheme for small business holders and community members.
- Piloting of non-traditional investment avenues as a profitable investment for the underutilized savings of village and women organizations.
- Helping to establish a financial control and auditing services in the area.
- Organizing investment conference and fame-tours for investors in the area.

Addressing Investment Needs: Despite all the efforts at the micro level, meaningful and sustainable business and private sector development in NAC is unthinkable, without macro level investments in key sectors, such as power generation, mining, telecommunications and tourism and tourism related industries. Given the difficulties of physical access and the delayed nature of returns in these investments, private investors and operators are unlikely to be attracted to the region. This is the biggest challenge of development for both the government and the AKDN, the two major, public/private sector partners in the development of NAC.

The potential solution to this problem can be found in the emerging policy shift in Pakistan, supported by international donors, towards a public-private partnership approach that can be applied to addressing investment needs of the type described above.

In brief, investment mechanisms can be developed in which international donors would be willing to provide a large part of the initial capital cost, provided a development-oriented investment fund, such as AKFED, agrees to co-invest and an implementing agency, such as AKRSP mobilizes local human and management resources to undertake operations and management of the resultant enterprise. AKRSP under its new strategy would make a serious effort to explore such avenues, starting with small-scale power utilities. At the same time, AKRSP will explore possibilities to attract investment capital from neighbouring China for value-added activities in NAC.

Promoting Social Enterprises: One of the challenging, but most exciting and rewarding tasks ahead of AKRSP is to study and field test the idea of private providers of social services. This is a difficult challenge, but AKRSP has valuable experience and expertise in both social and enterprise development sectors and stands a good chance of success. Part of the reason for this optimism is that there is a growing demand in the urban pockets of NAC for quality services in education, health and childcare and this demand is rapidly spreading to many rural settlements. Already, a growing number of communities and social solidarity groups are managing private schools and basic health centres, without any significant on-going support from the AKDN or other support agencies.

For AKRSP, the first step would be to study the business models of such local 'good practices', and to suggest ways to improve their performance even further by 'borrowing' from national and international good management practices. One simple but effective method would be to link a number of similar service providers in a valley in a network to achieve economies of scale through standardizing their management, accounting, purchasing, recruitment and training practices or sharing common services, such as audit and personnel management, and even 'trading' their over and under capacity throughout the network to utilize excess capacity at any given time. Based on the positive evidence for the growing scope of sustainable social services through private providers, AKRSP would assist existing and new providers in developing new products and services, such as professional day care centers for early childhood development in rural areas.

CONCLUSION

AKRSP's involvement and commitment to the development of NAC is for the long haul. During the last two decades, AKRSP has added and supported the efforts of the government in bringing about desirable change by investing in local institutional and productive capacities. AKRSP will try to build on the achievements of the past by further strengthening the synergetic links among the public, private and community sector institutions and development support systems. The main focus of AKRSP in the coming years will be to improve the overall governance systems of public and private sector agencies and institutions for addressing the long-term development needs in the area, with particular attention to the needs of the poor and women and other marginalized groups.

NOTES

1. The Diagnostic process comprising a series of dialogues between AKRSP and rural communities involves explaining AKRSP's approach and terms of partnership to the community members in the *First Dialogue.* The *Second Dialogue* involves identification of local needs and priorities in the form of a project, including participatory surveys, technical design and preparation of project cost estimates. The *Third Dialogue* is essentially an open review and formalization of the terms of partnership between AKRSP and the communities, which also included the formation of a Village or Women's Organization, and the inception of a programme of development work.
2. The last local bodies elections in the Northern Areas were held in 1999 and the next election is due in October 2004. NAs has 5 district councils, 103 union councils and 558 dehi (village) councils under its local government system, which is different than the system introduced in the rest of the country in 2001. Chitral, which is part of NWFP, has a local government system with district, tehsil and union councils

ANNEXURES

FIG. A–District-wise Language Composition of Northern Areas and Chitral

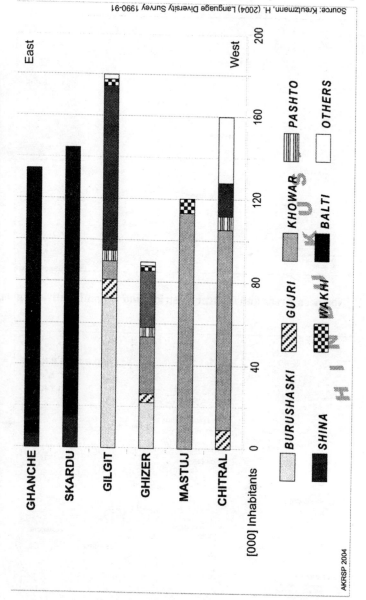

Source: Kreutzmann, H. (2004) Language Diversity Survey 1990-91

AKRSP 2004

Northern Areas and Chitral

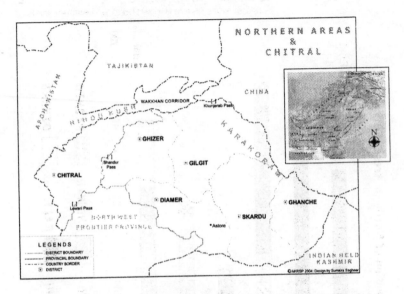

Northern Areas and Chitral (Districts and Administrative Regions)

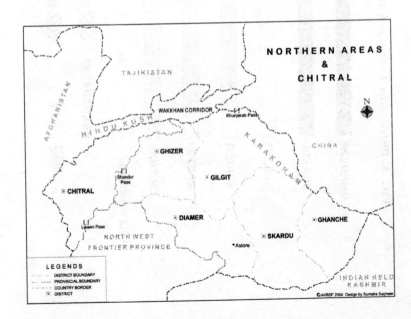

Overview of Linguistic Diversity of Northern Areas and Chitral

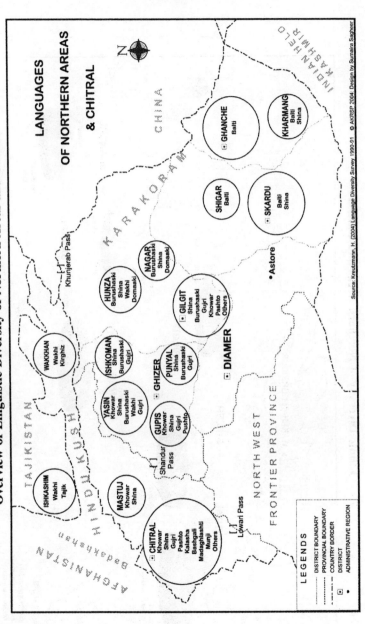

LANGUAGES OF NORTHERN AREAS & CHITRAL

Ethnic Diversity of Northern Areas and Chitral

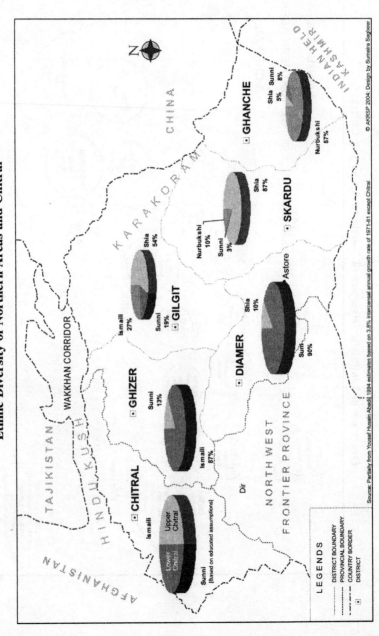

© AKRSP 2004: Design by Sumaira Sagheer

LEGENDS

.... DISTRICT BOUNDARY
--------- PROVINCIAL BOUNDARY
—·—·— COUNTRY BORDER
⊡ DISTRICT

References

Abidi, S. M. (1987), *Pastures and Livestock Development in Gojal*, Gilgit: AKRSP / IUCN.

Adam, D., Graham, D. & Von Pischke, J. D. (1984), *Undermining Rural Development with Cheap Credit*, Colorado: Boulder.

Afzal, F. (2003a), 'Subsidising Business Ambitions, Does it Work? A case study on Shubinak Project', Prepared for the University Seminar Series 2003, sponsored by the Aga Khan Foundation, Canada.

Afzal, F. (2003b), *An Assessment of the Patti (Shu) Market Potential*, Gilgit: Swiss Agency for Development and Cooperation / Naunihal Development Organization.

Aga Khan Foundation (2002), *Gender Equity Strategy 2002-2006*, Islamabad: Aga Khan Foundation.

Ahmad, Z. & Longmire, J. (1990), *Wheat Technologies and the Impact of AKRSP Wheat Development in the Double Cropping Zone of Gilgit, 1988-89*, Paper 90-6, PARC / CIMMYT.

AKRSP (1982), *Annual Report*.

AKRSP (1983), *First Annual Review*, Gilgit: AKRSP.

AKRSP (1984a), *Second Annual Review*, Gilgit: AKRSP.

AKRSP (1984b), *Background Paper on Strategy and Programmes*.

AKRSP (1985a), *Annual Report*.

AKRSP (1985b), *Third Annual Review*, Gilgit: AKRSP.

AKRSP (1986), *Fourth Annual Review*, Gilgit: AKRSP.

AKRSP (1987a), *The Strategy Paper for the Second Phase*, Gilgit: AKRSP.

AKRSP (1987b), *Fifth Annual Review, Incorporating the Twentieth Progress Report*, Gilgit: AKRSP.

AKRSP (1987c), *Project Area Data Book*, Gilgit: AKRSP.

AKRSP (1988), *Sixth Annual Review, Incorporating the Twenty-Fourth Progress Report*, Gilgit: AKRSP.

AKRSP (1989a), *Annual Report*.

AKRSP (1989b), *Seventh Annual Review*, Gilgit: AKRSP.

AKRSP (1990a), *Annual Report*.

AKRSP (1990b), *Eighth Annual Review, Incorporating the Thirty-Second Progress Report*, Gilgit: AKRSP.

AKRSP (1991a), *Annual Report*.

AKRSP (1991b), *Ninth Annual Review, Incorporating the Thirty-Sixth Progress Report*, Gilgit: AKRSP.

AKRSP (1991c), *Joint Monitoring Design Mission to the Aga Khan Rural Support Programme, Pakistan*, Islamabad: AKRSP.

AKRSP (1992a), *Annual Report*.

AKRSP (1992b), *Tenth Annual Review, Incorporating the Fortieth Progress Report*, Gilgit: AKRSP.

AKRSP (1993a), *Reports of the Joint Monitoring Missions*, AKRSP.

AKRSP (1993b), *Eleventh Annual Review*, Gilgit: AKRSP.

AKRSP (1994a), *Reports of the Joint Monitoring Missions*, AKRSP.

AKRSP (1994b), *Farm Household Income and Expenditure Survey in Northern Pakistan: Results for the Farming Year 1991*, Gilgit: Monitoring, Evaluation and Research Section, AKRSP.

AKRSP (1994c), *Twelfth Annual Review, Incorporating the Forty-Eighth Progress Report*, Gilgit: AKRSP.

AKRSP (1995a), *Contextual Study of the Northern Areas and Chitral*, Gilgit, Northern Areas: AKRSP.

AKRSP (1995b), *Reports of the Joint Monitoring Missions*, AKRSP.

AKRSP (1995c), *Thirteenth Annual Review*, Gilgit: AKRSP.

AKRSP (1996a), *Farm Household Income and Expenditure Survey in Northern Pakistan: Results for the Farming Year 1994*, Gilgit: Monitoring, Evaluation and Research Section, AKRSP.

AKRSP (1996b), *Joint Monitoring Mission: Final Report*, AKRSP.

AKRSP (1997a), *Reports of the Joint Monitoring Missions*, AKRSP.

AKRSP (1997b), *MTR Recommendations Action Plan*, Ahmedabad, Gujarat, India: AKRSP India.

AKRSP (1998a), *Annual Report 1998: The Challenge of Poverty*, AKRSP.

AKRSP (1998b), *Strategies to Position AKRSP (I) in the year 2010: A Concept Paper*, Ahmedabad, Gujarat, India: AKRSP India.

AKRSP (1998c), *Annual Progress Report 1998*, Ahmedabad, Gujarat, India: AKRSP India.

AKRSP (1999a), *Annual Report 1999: Joining Hands in Development: Women in Northern Pakistan*, Islamabad: AKRSP.

AKRSP (1999b), *Reports of the Joint Monitoring Missions*, AKRSP.

AKRSP (1999c), *Sustainability and AKRSP: Plans for the future*, Report by the Task Force on Sustainability prepared for the AKRSP Board.

AKRSP (1999d), 'AKRSP's Women's Programme', Proceedings of a one day cross-regional meeting, 18th September 1999, AKRSP, Islamabad.

AKRSP (1999e), *Farm Income Survey*, AKRSP.

AKRSP (2000a), *A Synthesis of the Findings from the Impact Studies on Land Development Projects*, Gilgit / Islamabad: Policy and Research Section, AKRSP.

AKRSP (2000b), *An Enquiry in to Institutional Maturity of Village and Women's Organisations: Results of the Institutional Development Exercise 1998 (A Process Monitoring Approach)*, Gilgit: Policy and Research Section, AKRSP.

AKRSP (2000c), *An Assessment of Socio-Economic Trends and Impact in Northern Pakistan (1991-1997): Findings from AKRSP's Farm Household Income and Expenditure Surveys*, Gilgit: Policy and Research Section, AKRSP.

AKRSP (2000d), *A Synthesis of Findings from the Impact Studies on Communication Projects*, Islamabad: Policy and Research Section, AKRSP.

AKRSP (2000e), *A Synthesis of Findings from the Impact Studies on Power Generation Projects*, Islamabad: Policy and Research Section, AKRSP.

AKRSP (2000f), *A Comparative Cost Analysis of AKRSP's Investment in Infrastructure Project in 1998-1999*, AKRSP.

AKRSP (2000g), *Participatory Variety Selection*, Gilgit: AKRSP.

AKRSP (2001), *Annual Report 2001: From Mountains to Market: Promoting Enterprise Development*, AKRSP.

AKRSP (2002a), *A Strategy for Poverty Reduction Through Enterprise Development*, Islamabad: AKRSP.

AKRSP (2002b), *Reshit Coal Project, Chapursan Valley, Karakorum Himalayas*, Draft Consultancy Report 22, DFID, UK.

AKRSP (2002c), 'Gender Policy', mimeo.

AKRSP (2002d), *Report Prepared for DFID Annual Review Mission*, AKRSP.

AKRSP (2003a), 'Future Options for North South Seeds', Paper presented to the Chairman of the Board of Directors, AKRSP, Enterprise Development Programme, Core Office, Islamabad, AKRSP.

AKRSP (2003b), *Northern Areas and Chitral Integrated Household Survey (NACIHS), Conducted in 2002*, Gilgit: Policy and Research Section, AKRSP.

AKRSP (2004), *An Assessment of the Socio-Economic Trends and Impact in Northern Pakistan (1991-1997)*, Gilgit: Policy and Research Section, AKRSP.

Ali, A. & Tetlay, K. (1991), *Dynamics of Livestock Development in Northern Areas, Pakistan*, Gilgit: AKRSP.

Ali, A. (2002a), *Performance Evaluation of Local Production Centres*, Gilgit: AKRSP.

Ali, A. (2002b), *Participatory Varietal Selection (Wheat) Year 2002*, Gilgit: AKRSP.

Amburgey, T. & Dacin, M. T. (1993), *Evolutionary Development of Credit Unions*, Centre for Credit Union Research, The School of Business, University of Wisconsin-Madison.

Amin, A. (1999), *The Role of Women in Household Decision Making*, Gilgit: AKRSP.

Annis, S. (1987), 'Can Small-Scale Development Programmes be a Large-Scale Policy?', *World Development* 15 (Supplement), 129-134.

Banfield, E. (1958), *The Moral Basis of a Backward Society*, Free Press.

Banuri, T. & Najam, A. (2002), *Civic Entrepreneurship: A Civil Society Perspective on Sustainable Development*, vol.1, Islamabad: Gandhara Academy Press.

Barron, D. N. (1992), *Credit Unions: Density-Dependent Evolution*, 137-160 .

Bennett, L., Goldberg, M. & Hunte, P. (1996), 'Ownership and sustainability: Lessons on group-based financial services from South Asia', *Journal of International Development* 8 (2), 271-288.

Berthoud, R. & Hinton, T. (1989), *Credit Unions in the United Kingdom*, London: Policy Studies Institute, Printer Publishers Limited (UK).

Bibi, S. (2001), *Report on Gender Awareness and Sensitisation Workshop for Senior Staff, 22nd to 24th October*, Chitral: AKRSP.

Bratton, M. (1990), 'Non-Governmental Organizations in Africa: Can They Influence Public Policy?', *Development and Change* 21 (1), 87-118.

Bryceson, D., Kay, C. & Mooij, J. (eds.) (2000), *Disappearing Peasantries: Rural Labour in Africa, Asia and Latin America*, London: IT Publications.

Buvinic, M. (1986), 'Projects for Women in the Third World: Explaining their Misbehavior', *World Development* 14 (5), 653-664.

Byerlee, D. & Husain, T. (1993), 'Agricultural Research Strategies for Favoured and Marginal Areas: The Experience of Farming Systems Research in Pakistan', *Experimental Agriculture* 29, 155-171.

Chambers, R. (1983), *Rural Development: Putting the Last First*, Harlow: Orient Longman.

Chayanov, A. V. (1966), *The Theory of the Peasant Economy*, London: Irwin.

CIDA (1999), *CIDA's Policy on Gender Equality*, Canadian International Development Agency.

Collard, D. (2000), 'Generational Transfers and the Generational Bargain', *Journal of International Development* 12 (4), 453-462.

Conway, G., Mian, A., Alam, Z., Yar, M., & Husain, T. (1987), *Agroecosystem Zoning of the Hunza Valley*, Gilgit / London: AKRSP / IIED.

Cooke, B. & Kothari, U. (eds.) (2002), *Participation: The New Tyranny?*, London: Zed Books.

Coston, J. M. (1998), 'A Model and Typology of Government-NGO Relationships', *Nonprofit and Voluntary Sector Quarterly* 27 (3), 358-382.

Croteau, J. T. (1956), *The Federal Credit Union (Policy and Practice)*, New York: University of Notre Dame, Harper & Brothers Publishers.

Croteau, J. T. (1963), *The Economics of the Credit Union*, Detroit: Wayne State University Press.

Derbyshire, H. (2002), *Gender Manual: A Practical Guide for Development Policy Makers and Practitioners*, London: DFID.

DFID (1997), *Pakistan: Aga Khan Rural Support Programme (AKRSP) Gilgit Region, Northern Areas, Project Memorandum*, London: DFID.

DFID (1998a), *Pakistan: Aga Khan Rural Support Programme (AKRSP) Chitral Region, Pakistan, Project Memorandum*, London: DFID.

DFID (1998b), *Pakistan: Aga Khan Rural Support Programme (AKRSP) Chitral Region, Annual Review Mission Report 1998*, London: DFID.

DFID (1998c), *Pakistan: Aga Khan Rural Support Programme (AKRSP) Gilgit Region, Annual Review Mission Report 1998*, London: DFID.

DFID (1998d), *Project Memorandum: Western India Rainfed Farming Project, Phase 2*, New Delhi, India: DFID India.

DFID (1998e), *Western India Rainfed Farming Project, Report of the Final Annual Review of Phase I (5-9 December 1998)*, New Delhi, India: DFID India.

DFID (1999), *Pakistan: Aga Khan Rural Support Programme (AKRSP) Gilgit and Chitral Regions, Annual Review Mission Report 1999*, London: DFID.

DFID (2000), *Target Strategy Paper (TSP): Poverty Eradication and the Empowerment of Women*, London: DFID.

DFID (2001), *Pakistan: Aga Khan Rural Support Programme (AKRSP) Gilgit and Chitral Regions, Mid-Term Review Mission Report*, London: DFID.

DFID (2003), *Further Progress on a Participatory Approach to Cereal Improvement*, Consultancy Draft Report, Gilgit: AKRSP.

Dreze, J. & Sen, A. (1995), *India: Economic Development and Social Opportunity*, Delhi / Oxford: Oxford University Press.

Ellis, F. (2000a), 'The Determinants of Rural Livelihood Diversification in Developing Countries', *Journal of Agricultural Economics* 51, 289-302.

Ellis, F. (2000b), *Rural Livelihoods and Diversity in Developing Countries*, Oxford / New York: Oxford University Press.

Esping-Andersen, G. (1999), *Social Foundations of Postindustrial Economies*, Oxford: Oxford University Press.

Fairbairn, B. (1994), *The Meaning of Rochdale: The Rochdale Pioneers and the Cooperative Principles*, Centre for the Study of Co-operatives, University of Saskatchewan.

Farman, K. (2000), *New Ideas, New Resources: The Use of Remittances and the Life of Returnees in Local Situation in Village Mehdiabad*, Baltistan: AKRSP.

Fauzia (2002a), *Assessment of the Services of Traditional Birth Attendants (TBAs)*, Baltistan: AKRSP.

Fauzia (2002b), *Assessment of the Services of Adult Literacy Teachers/Centres in Baltistan*, Baltistan: AKRSP.

Ferguson, C. & McKillop, D. G. (1997), *The Strategic Development of Credit Unions*, Chichester: John Wiley & Sons.

FHIES-AKRSP (1991), *Farm Household Income-Expenditure Survey*, Gilgit: AKRSP.

FHIES-AKRSP (1997), *Farm Household Income-Expenditure Survey*, Gilgit: AKRSP.

FHIES-AKRSP (2001), *Farm Household Income-Expenditure Survey*, Gilgit: AKRSP.

Fisher, J. (1998), *Non-Governments: NGOs and the Political Development of the Third World*, West Hartford, CT: Kumarian Press.

Flannery, M. J. (1974), *An Economic Evaluation of Credit Unions in the United States*, Research Report 54, Federal Reserve Bank of Boston.

Freire, P. (1970), *Pedagogy of the Oppressed* , New York: Continuum.

Garilao, E. D. (1987), 'Indigenous NGOs as Strategic Institutions: Managing the Relationship with Government and Resource Agencies', *World Development* 15 (Supplement), 113-120.

Geisler, G., Keller, B., & Norman, A.-L. (1999), *WID/Gender Units and the Experience of Gender Mainstreaming in Multilateral Organisations: "Knights on White Horses?"*, Ministry of Foreign Affairs, Norwegian Government.

Gloekler, A. (2002), *Partners in Empowerment: Ground Realities of the Devolution Plan and AKRSP Chitral's Support Role While Addressing Poverty and Gender Mainstreaming*, Chitral: AKRSP.

Gloekler, M. A. & Hussain, A. (1995), *The Specialist Dilemma: Looking into HRD's Multi-specialist Training and its Implications*, Baltistan: AKRSP.

Gloekler, M. A., Raza, A., Iqbal, M., Zaffer, I., & Hussein, W. S. (1995), *High Pastures - High Hopes: A Socio-Economic Assessment of some High Pastures in Baltistan and Potential for Integrated NRM Activities*, Skardu: AKRSP.

Gloekler, M. A., Zaffer, I., Ahmed, N., Ali, H., Ahmed, K., Wali, R., & Qalandar, Y. (1996), *Grassroot Level Planning: Participatory Resource & Need Assessment at Hassis NRM Pilot Site*, Gilgit: AKRSP.

Gloekler, M. A. (1997), *Project Process Monitoring: Khyber Community Conservation Area*, Gilgit: IUCN.

Gloekler, M. A. (1999), *Project Process Evaluation: Lessons Learned During the PRIF (Pilot Phase 1995 - 1999)*, Islamabad: IUCN / UNDP / Government of Pakistan.

Gloekler, M. A. (2001), *Principles of Social Mobilisation: Social Mobilisation Strategy for Northern Areas Conservancies*, Gilgit: MACP / IUCN / UNDP / GEF / Government of Pakistan.

Gohar, A. (2002), *Problems of Sustainable Forest Management in the Northern Areas of Pakistan*, PhD Thesis, University of Bath.

Gough, I., Wood, G., Barrientos, A., Bevan, P., Davis, P. & Room, G. (2004), *Insecurity and Welfare Regimes in Asia, Africa and Latin America*, Cambridge: Cambridge University Press.

Government of Pakistan (n.d.) *Peyaam-e-Gilgit*, Government of Pakistan, Village Aid.

Government of Pakistan (2002a), 'Legal Framework Order 2002: Chief Executive's Order No. 24 of 2002', *Gazette of Pakistan, Extraordinary*.

Government of Pakistan (2002b), *National Commission of the Status of Women*, Islamabad: Government of Pakistan.

Government of Pakistan (2002c), *National Policy for Development and Empowerment of Women*, Islamabad: Ministry of Women's Development, Social Welfare and Special Education.

Government of Pakistan (2003), *Draft Report on Participatory Poverty Assessment in the Northern Areas*, Islamabad: Government of Pakistan, Planning Commission.

Griffiths, G. H. & Howells, G. G. (1990), 'Britain's Best Kept Secret? An Analysis of the Credit Union', *Journal of Consumer Policy* 13 (4), 447-467.

Guinnane, T. W. (1994), 'A Failed Institutional Transplant: Raiffeisen's Credit Cooperatives in Ireland, 1894 - 1914', *Explorations in Economic History* 31, 38-61.

Guyer, J. & Peters, P. (1987), 'Introduction to *Conceptualising the Household: Issues of Theory, Method and Application*', *Development and Change* 18 (2), 197-214.

Guyer, J. (1997), 'Endowments and Assets: The Anthropology of Wealth and the Economics of Intra-Household Allocation', in Haddad, L., Hoddinott, J. and Alderman, H., *Intra-Household Resource Allocation in Developing Countries: Models, Methods and Policy*, Baltimore and London: John Hopkins University Press, pp. 112-125.

Hardin, G. (1968), 'Tragedy of the Commons', *Science* 162, 1243-1248.

Harper, A. (1996), *Support for Women's Enterprises in the Gilgit Region - AKRSP's Experience*, Gilgit: AKRSP.

Harper, C. S. (2002), *The McGraw-Hill Guide to Starting Your Own Business (A Step by Step Blueprint for the First Time Entrepreneur)*, 2nd edition, New York: McGraw-Hill.

Harris, O. (1981), 'Households and Natural Units', in Young, K., Wolkowitz, C. and McCullagh, R., *Of Marriage and the Market* , London: Routledge and Kegan Paul, pp. 136-154.

Hart, G. (1995), 'Gender and Household Dynamics: Recent Theories and their Implications', in Quibria, M. G., *Critical Issues in Asian Development: Theories, Experiences and Policies*, Oxford and New York: Oxford University Press.

Hart, G. (1997), 'From "Rotten Wives" to "Good Mothers": Household Models and the Limits of Economism', *IDS Bulletin* 28 (3), 14-25.

Hemani, T. & Warrington, S. (1996), *Supplementary Village Profile to Gender Roles in Farming Systems in the Gilgit Region*, Gilgit: AKRSP.

Hirschman, A. O. (1970), *Exit, Voice and Loyalty*, Cambridge, Mass.: Harvard University Press.

HM Treasury (1999), *Credit Unions of the Future*, London: HMSO.

Hooper, E. (1989), *Study of the Women in Development Programme of the Aga Khan Rural Support Programme, Chitral*, Consulting and Internship Report 25, Chitral: AKRSP.

Hunzai, I. A. (1987), *The Political Economy of Forestry: The New Management System of Forest in Chalt-Chaprote*, Gilgit: AKRSP.

Husain, T. (1986a), *Wheat in the High Mountain Valleys of Gilgit*, Gilgit: AKRSP.

Husain, T. (1986b), 'Research, Planning and the Mobilization of Small Farmers for Rural Development: The Reformist Agenda', *Pakistan Administration* 23 (2), 119-133.

Husain, T. (1990), *Conclusions and Generalizations: The Macro Perspective*, Quetta: ICIMOD / AKRSP / Pak-German Self-Help Project.

Husain, T. (1991), 'Condoms, Commerce and Community: Facets of a lively NGO in Thailand'.

Husain, T. (1992), *Community Participation: The First Principle*, A Pakistan National Conservation Strategy Sector Paper, Karachi: IUCN.

Hussain, G. (2002), *Human Resource Development (Process, Progress and Prospects) through Learning Support Initiatives*, Baltistan: AKRSP.

Hussain, G. (2003), *The Status of Continued Education Programme Baltistan (An Initiative in Education Sector as Pilot Project by Learning Support Unit, AKRSP Baltistan)*, Baltistan: AKRSP.

Hussain, H. (1993), *An Impact Case Study on Vegetable Introduction Package in Three Regions of the Programme Area*, Gilgit: AKRSP.

Ibadat, G. *Impact of Ladies' Shop Enterprise on Women's Decision Making Power in Nagar*, Gilgit: AKRSP.

IUCN (1987), *Sustainable Forestry in the Aga Khan Development Programme: A Proposal*, Gland: IUCN, Conservation for Development Centre.

Javed, A. & Khan, S. (1998), 'Investment in People - A Key to Enhance Sustainability: Lessons from Northern Pakistan', in Van der Linde, H. A. and Danskin, M. H., *Enhancing Sustainability: Resources for Our Future*, Gland / Cambridge: IUCN.

Javed, A. & Mahmood, F. (1998), *Changing Perspectives on Forest Policy*, Policy that Works for Forests and People Series 1, Islamabad / London: IUCN Pakistan / IIED.

Jeevunjee, Z. (1996), *A Comparative Analysis of Male Managed versus Female Managed Women's Organisations (WOs) in the Gilgit Field Management Unit (FMU)*, Gilgit: AKRSP.

Joekes, S. (1995), 'Gender and Livelihoods in Northern Pakistan', *IDS Bulletin* 26 (1), 66-74.

Kanji, N. & Salway, S. (2000), *Promoting Equality Between Women and Men*, SD SCOPE Paper 2, London: DFID.

Kaushik & Lopez (1994), 'The Structure and Growth of the Credit Union Industry in the United States (Meeting Challenges of the Market)', *American Journal of Economics and Sociology* 53 (2), 219-243.

Kerr, J. (2002), *From 'WID' to 'GAD' to Women's Rights: The First Twenty Years of AWID*, Occasional Paper 9, Association for Women's Rights in Development.

Khan, A. (1998), *Women and the Pakistan Government: A Brief Policy History (1975-1998)*, Islamabad: Gender Unit, UNDP.

Khan, M. H. (1998), *Climbing the Development Ladder with NGO Support: Experiences of Rural People in Pakistan*, Karachi: Oxford University Press.

Khan, M. H. (2001), *Community Organisations and rural Development: Experience in Pakistan*, Lahore, Karachi, Islamabad: Vanguard.

Khan, M. F. (2002), 'Islam, Law and Culture/Customs Redefinng Muslims Women's Rights in Islam', Paper submitted to a Regional Seminar on Gender Mainstreaming in Social Science Research organised by the Academy of Educational Planning and Management, Islamabad, 2-6 September 2002.

Khawaja, N. (2002), *The Impact of the Women's Organisation on the Household Decision-Making Role of its Members*, Chitral: Monitoring, Evaluation and Research Section, AKRSP.

Kingdon, J. (1984), *Agendas, Alternatives, and Public Policies*, New York: Harper Collins.

Kotler, P. (1986), *Principles of Marketing*, Englewood Cliffs, NJ: Prentice Hall International Editions.

Kreutzmann, H. (1985), *Background Information on Pastures*, Gilgit: Monitoring, Evaluation and Research Section, AKRSP.

Kreutzmann, H. (1993), 'Challenge and Response in the Karakoram: Socioeconomic Transformation in Hunza, Northern Areas, Pakistan', *Mountain Research and Development* 13 (1), 19-39.

Kumar, L. (1997), *State and Nonprofit Sector in India: Reluctant Partners or Willing Collaborators*, Swansea: University of Wales.

Kuriakose, A. T. (1996a), *WO Development: An Investigation of Organisational and Institutional Issues in Chitral Region*, Gilgit: AKRSP.

Kuriakose, A. T. (1996b), *An Investigation of Male Out-Migration, Stratification and Local Institutions in Baltistan: Implications for Equity and Participation in AKRSP-Supported Organisations*, Gilgit: AKRSP.

Kuriakose, A. T. (1996c), *Social Dynamics: An Investigation of Institutional Issues in Gilgit Region*, Gilgit: Policy and Research, AKRSP.

Lawson-McDowall, B. (2000), *Handshakes and Smiles: The Role of Social and Symbolic Resources in the Management of a New Common Property*, PhD Thesis, University of Bath.

Long, N. & Long, A. (eds.) (1992), *Battlefields of Knowledge*, London: Routledge.

Long, N. (2001), 'Recontextualising Social Change', in Long, N., *Development Sociology: Actor Perspectives*, London: Routledge, pp. 214-239.

Lukes, S. (1974), *Power: A Radical View*, London: Macmillan.

MacDonald, M. (2003), *Gender Equality and Mainstreaming in Policy and Practice of the UK Department for International Development: A Briefing from the UK Gender and Development Network*, London: The GAD Network, Womankind, London.

Majone, G. (1989), *Evidence, Argument and Persuasion in the Policy Process*, New Haven: Yale University Press.

Makeen, S. (1999), 'Male Out Migration and Impact on Women: A Case Study of a Small Village in Northern Pakistan', A Major Professional Paper Presented to the University School of Rural Planning and Development, University of Guelph, Canada, June 1999.

Malik, A. & Ahmed, R. (1994), *Gender Sensitisation Training for AKRSP Staff*, Gilgit: AKRSP.

Malik, A. & Piracha, M. (forthcoming), 'Economic Transition in Hunza and Nagar Valley', in Kreutzmann, H., *Karakoram in Transition - The Hunza Valley*, Karachi / Oxford: Oxford University Press.

Malik, A. & Piracha, M. (2003), 'Poverty Trends and Issues in the Northern Mountains of Pakistan', Policy and Research Section, AKRSP, Gilgit.

Malik, A. (1994a), *Review of First RPO-Baltistan RMT Gender Analysis/Training Workshop*, WID and MER Sections, AKRSP.

Malik, A. (1994b), *Review of Management Group Gender Analysis/Training Workshop*, WID and MER Sections, AKRSP.

Miehe, S. & Miehe, G. (1998), 'Vegetation Patterns as Indicators of Climatic Humidity in the Western Karakorum', in Stellrecht, I., *Karakorum, Jindukush Himilaya: Dynamics of Change (Part I)*, Koeln: Ruediger Koeppe Verlag.

Miehlbradt & McVay (2003), *BDS Primer (Seminar Reader: Developing Commercial Markets for Business Development Services)*, Annual BDS Seminar, Turin, Italy (Small Enterprise Development Programme of the ILO).

Miers, H. (1996), *Statement of Assignment, Objectives, Conclusions and Recommendations: AKRSP Chitral October 1995 to December 1996*, Chitral: AKRSP.

Miers, H. & Bibi, S. (1998), *Incorporation of Gender Planning into the Planning Process*, Chitral: AKRSP.

Mock, J. (1990), *Field Trip Report and Discussion Paper on Conservation and Management of the Khunjrab National Park*, Lahore: World Wide Fund for Nature.

Moffat, L. (2001), 'Aga Khan Rural Support Program Baltistan: Organisation Gender Assessment', Prepared for the Aga Khan Foundation, Canada.

Moffat, Z. (1999), *A Qualitative Comparison of Trends in Women's Empowerment between Sherqilla's Vocational Centre for Uniform Sewing (FMU Punial) and Three Vocational Centres in Lower Hunza*, Gilgit: AKRSP.

Moody, J. C. & Fite, G. C. (1971), *The Credit Union Movement: Origins and Development 1850 - 1970*, Lincoln: University of Nebraska Press.

Mosse, D. (1999), *End of Project Report: Social Development (Participation; Poverty Focus; Gender Equity; Local Institutions), Kribhco Indo-British Rainfed Farming Project*, Dahod, India: Kribhco.

Murshed, R. A. (1998), 'Gender Interventions as Applied in BRAC's Organisations and Programmes', in Dolberg, F. and Petersen, P. H., *Women in Agriculture and Modern Communication Technology: Proceedings of a Workshop*, Tune Landboskole: Danish Agricultural and Rural Development Advisers Forum.

Muzaffar, R. (2002), *Assessing the Income Generating Potential of the Vocational Training Package of AKRSP*, Baltistan: AKRSP.

N.M.Sadguru Water and Development Foundation (1999), *Annual Report Year Ending 31 March 1999*, Dahod, Gujarat, India.

Najam, A. (1995), *Learning from the Literature on Policy Implementation: A Synthesis Perspective*, IIASA Working Paper WP-95-61, Laxenburg: International Institute for Applied Systems Analysis.

Najam, A. (1996), 'Understanding the Third Sector: Revisiting the Prince, the Merchant, and the Citizen', *Nonprofit Management and Leadership* 7 (2), 203-219.

Najam, A. (1999), 'Citizen Organizations as Policy Entrepreneurs', in Lewis, D., *International Perspectives on Voluntary Action*, London: Earthscan, pp. 142-181.

Najam, A. (2000), 'The Four C's of Third Sector-Government Relations: Co-operation, Confrontation, Complementarity and Co-optation', *Nonprofit Management and Leadership* 10 (4), 375-396.

Nazir, A., Nyborg, I., & Aqil, G. (1998), *High Altitude Integrated Natural Resource Management, Report No. 5: Gender, Resource Management and Livelihood Security*, AKRSP/NLH.

Nicholas, R. (1963), 'Village Factions and Political Parties in Rural West Bengal', *Journal of Commonwealth Political Studies* 2.

Oehmke, J. F. & Husain, T. (1987), *The Rural Economy of Gilgit*, Department of Agricultural Economics, Michigan State University.

Olson, M. (1971), *Logic of Collective Action: Public Goods and the Theory of Groups*, Cambridge, Mass.: Harvard University Press.

Ostrom, E. (1990), *Governing the Commons: The Evolution of Institution for Collective Action*, Cambridge: Cambridge University Press.

Ostrom, E., Gardner, R. & Walker, J. (1994), *Rules, Games and Common-Pool Resources*, Ann Arbor, University of Michigan.

Overstreet, G. & Rubin, G. M. (1991), *Blurred Vision: Challenges in Credit Union Research Modelling*, Filene Research Institute, Centre for Credit Union Research.

PARC (2002), *The Western India Rainfed Farming Project Seminar and Discussion (at DFID, London, 5 July 2002)*, PARC Document No. 8, Birmingham, UK.

Pervaiz, S. & Rasmussen, S. (1997), *Growth, Poverty and Inequality in the Programme Area: A Comparison of 1991 and 1994 Results based on FHIES Data Summary of some Preliminary Results*, Gilgit: Policy and Research Section, AKRSP.

Pervaiz, S. & Rasmussen, S. (2002), *Sustaining Mountain Economies: Sustainable Livelihoods and Poverty Alleviation*, AKRSP.

Qureshi, S. N. (2002), *Aga Khan Rural Support Programme, Phase IV (AKRSP IV): Monitoring Mission Report, June 2002*, AKRSP Monitors Project No.: A-020522, Islamabad, Pakistan: Stiles Associates Inc.

Rao, A. & Kelleher, D. (1997), 'Engendering Organisational Change: The BRAC Case', in Goetz, A. M., *Getting Institutions Right for Women in Development*, London: Zed Books, pp. 123-139.

Rao, A. & Kelleher, D. (2002), *Unravelling Institutionalised Gender Inequality*, Occasional Paper 8, Association for Women's Rights in Development.

Rashid, M. (2003), 'Why Men? A Shift in Ownership', *Pehchaan Newsletter* 7, 7-8.

Rathgeber, E. (1990), 'WID, WAD, GAD: Trends in Research and Practice', *Journal of Developing Areas* 24 (4), 489-502.

Raza, A., Iqbal, M., Ali, J., Gloekler, M. A., Gloekler, A., Khanum, Z., Ali, A., Raza, T., & Karim, Z. (1996), *NRM Planning Exercises I: NRM Pilot Project Shut*, Baltistan: AKRSP.

Razavi, S. & Miller, C. (1995a), *From WID to GAD: Conceptual Shifts in the Women and Development Discourse*, UNRISD Occasional Paper 1.

Razavi, S. & Miller, C. (1995b), *Gender Mainstreaming: A Study of Efforts by the UNDP, the World Bank and the ILO to Institutionalize Gender Issues*, UNRISD Occasional Paper for Beijing 4, Geneva: UNRISD.

Razavi, S. (1997), 'Fitting Gender into Development Institutions', *World Development* 25 (7), 1111-1125.

Room, G. (2000), 'Trajectories of Social Exclusion: The Wider Context', in Gordon, D. and Townsend, P., *Breadline Europe: The Measurement of Poverty*, Bristol: Policy Press.

Roomi, A., Rehman, M. & Newnham, J. (2000), 'The Commercialisation of BDS through an NGO: Case Study of AKRSP-Pakistan', Paper presented at the International Conference of the Donor Committee on Small Enterprise Development, 'Business Services for Small Enterprises in Asia: Developing markets and measuring performance', Hanoi, Vietnam.

Rutherford, S. (2001), *The Poor and their Money*, New Delhi: Oxford University Press.

Saadi, H. N. & Khan, A. (2002), *Maintenance of AKRSP Assisted Infrastructure Projects in Gilgit Region*, Gilgit: AKRSP.

Sanyal, B. (1994), *Cooperative Autonomy: The Dialectic of State-NGOs Relationship in Developing Countries*, Geneva: International Institute for Labour Studies.

Schech, S. & Haggis, J. (2000), *Culture and Development: A Critical Introduction*, Oxford: Blackwell Publishers.

Seeley, J. (2000), *Consultancy Report on 'Support for AKRSP Gender Strategy'*, October 2000, AKRSP.

Shah, M. K. (1998), '"Salt and Spices": Gender Issues in Participatory Programme Implementation in AKRSP, India', in Guijt, I. and Shah, M. K., *The Myth of community: Gender Issues in Participatory Development*, London: Intermediate Technology Publications, pp. 243-253.

Shakil, S. & Usman, H. (1997), 'Gender, Natural Resource Management and Organisational Development: A Case Study of the Aga Khan Rural Support Programme', Prepared for the International Centre for Integrated Mountain Development in Kathmandu, Nepal, for ICIMOD's Training Programme in Organisational Development for Gender-Sensitive Sustainable Mountain Land Use, Policy and Research Section, AKRSP, Gilgit.

Shakil, S. & Khan, S. (2001), *Back to the Office Report: Visit to AKRSP to Review Women's Programme*, RSP Network.

Shanin, T. (1972), *Peasant and Peasant Societies*, London / Victoria: Penguin.

Sharif, I. & Wood, G. (2001), *Challenges to Second Generation Microfinance*, Dhaka: University Press Ltd.

Sharma, G. K. (1998), *Co-operative Laws in Asia and the Pacific*.

Sharma, U. (1980), *Women, Work and Property in North West India*, London: Tavistock Publications.

Shaukat, A. (2002), *Building Strategies for Effective Gender Training, December 17 2002 - Islamabad, Pakistan*, Islamabad: Aga Khan Foundation (Pakistan) and Human Resource Development Network.

Shrestha, A. (1994), *Eating Cucumbers without any Teeth: Variations in the Capacities of Rural Women to Participate in Rural Development in Nepal*, PhD Thesis, University of Bath.

Siddique, T. S. (1995), *The Women's Movement and Democratization in Pakistan (1977-1988): Opportunities and Limitations for Political Participation*, London School of Economics and Political Sciences, University of London.

Smith, D. J., Cargill, T. F. & Meyer, R. A. (1981), 'Credit Unions: An Economic Theory of a Credit Union', *Journal of Finance* 36, 519-528.

Spencer, J. E. (1996), 'An Extension to Taylor's Model of Credit Unions', *Review of Social Economy* 54 (1), 89-98.

Springfield Centre (2002), *Business Development Service (BDS) Training Manual*, Durham: Springfield Centre.

Srinivasan, G., Biswas, S., & Mirza Najmul, H. (2000), *Ashrai and its Advasi Groups*, Evaluation Report, Bern: Swiss Development Corporation.

Stiles Associates Inc. (2001), *Aga Khan Rural Support Programme, Phase IV (AKRSP IV): Draft Monitoring Mission Report, February-March 2001*, Stiles Associates Inc.

Stone, D. A. (1988), *Policy Paradox and Political Reason*, Glenview, IL: Scot, Foresman & Co.

Streefland, P. H., Khan, S., & Van Lieshout, O. (1995), *A Contextual Study of the Northern Areas and Chitral*, Gilgit: AKRSP.

Tandon, R. (1989), 'The State and Voluntary Agencies in Asia', in Holloway, R., *Doing Development: Government, NGOs and the Rural Poor in Asia*, London: Earthscan.

Taylor, R. A. (1971), 'The Credit Union as a Co-operative Institution', *Review of Social Economy* 54, 89-98.

Taylor, R. A. (1977), 'Credit Unions and Economic Efficiency', *Revista Internazionale di Scienze Economiche e Commercaili* 24, 239-247.

Taylor, R. A. (1979), 'Demand for Labour by Credit Unions', *Applied Economics* 11, 333-340.

Tetlay, K. & Raza, M. A. (1998), *From Small Farmers to Sustainable Livelihoods: A Case Study on the Evolution of AKRSP in the Northern Areas*, Baltistan: AKRSP.

Tinker, I. (1990), 'The Making of a Field: Advocates, Practitioners and Development: Gender Analysis and Policy', in Tinker, I., *Persistent Inequalities*, Oxford: Oxford University Press.

Ummar, F. (2000), *Women's Movement in Pakistan: Choice of Strategies, An Analysis of Autonomous Approach from the State*, Dissertation, London School of Economics, Faculty of Economics.

United Nations (1998), *Statement on Gender in Pakistan: From the Heads of United Nations Agencies Resident in Pakistan*, Islamabad: UN Pakistan.

Van Vugt, S. M. (1991), *Application of a Gender Analysis on the Women in Development Programme of the Aga Khan Rural Support Programme: Experience in the Northern Areas of Pakistan*, Department of Gender Studies in Agriculture, Agriculture University, Wageningen, The Netherlands.

Varley, E. (1998), *The Impact of WO Membership, Income Generating Activities and Socio-Economic Variables on Women's Household Decision-Making: A Qualitative Examination of Trends in Decision-Making among WO Members in the Gilgit Region*, Internship Report, MER / AKRSP.

Von Pischke, J. D. (1998), *Strategies for Improving AKRSP Savings and Credit Operations*, AKRSP.

Walker, M. C. & Chandler, G. G. (1977), 'On the Allocation of the Net Monetary Benefits of Credit Union Membership', *Review of Social Economy* 35, 159-168.

Warrington, S. & Hemani, T. (1996), *Gender Roles in Farming Systems*, Gilgit: AKRSP.

White, S. (1992), *Arguing with the Crocodile: Gender and Class in Bangladesh*, London: Zed Books.

Williams, S., Seed, J. & Mwau, A. (1994), *The Oxfam Gender Training Manual*, Oxford: Oxfam.

Wittfogel, K. (1957), *Oriental Despotism: A Comparative Study of Total Power*, New Haven: Yale University Press.

Wood, G. (1996), *Avoiding the Totem and Developing the Art in Rural Development*, Paper prepared for AKRSP Strategy Review, April 1996.

Wood, G. (1997), 'States without Citizens: The Problem of the Franchise State', in Hulme, D. and Edwards, M., *NGOs: Too Close for Comfort*.

Wood, G. (1999), 'From Farms to Services: Agricultural Reformation in Bangladesh', in Rogaly, B., Harris-White, B. and Bose, S., *Sonar Bangla? Agricultural Growth and Agrarian Change in West Bengal and Bangladesh*, Thousand Oaks, CA: Sage, Ch. 11, pp. 303-328.

Wood, G. (2002), *AKRSP Poverty Policy for 2003-8 Phase: Issues, Strategies and Dilemmas*, Paper prepared as part of AKRSP's Poverty Workshop series, 9th March 2002.

Wood, G. (2003), 'Staying Secure, Staying Poor: The Faustian Bargain', *World Development* 31 (3), 455-473.

Wood, G. (2004), 'Informal Security Regimes: The Strength of Relationships', in Gough, I., Wood, G., Barrientos, A., Bevan, P., Davis, P. and Room, G., *Insecurity and Welfare Regimes in Asia, Africa and Latin America*, Cambridge: Cambridge University Press, Ch. 2, pp. 49-87.

Wood, J. C. (2003), *Policy Entrepreneurs: Civil Society and the Policy Press*, London: London School of Economics.

World Bank (1986), *Interim Evaluations*, Washington DC: Operations Evaluation Department, World Bank.

World Bank (1987), *The Aga Khan Rural Support Programme in Pakistan: An Interim Evaluation*, Washington DC: Operations Evaluation Department, World Bank.

World Bank (1990a), *Interim Evaluations*, Washington DC: Operations Evaluation Department, World Bank.

World Bank (1990b), *The Aga Khan Rural Support Programme: Second Interim Evaluation*, Operations Evaluation Department, World Bank.

World Bank (1992), *Participation*, Washington DC: World Bank.

World Bank (1995a), *Interim Evaluations*, Washington DC: Operations Evaluation Department, World Bank.

World Bank (1995b), *The Aga Khan Rural Support Programme: The Third Evaluation*, Operations Evaluation Department, World Bank.

World Bank (2001a), *Interim Evaluations*, Washington DC: Operations Evaluation Department, World Bank.

World Bank (2001b), *World Development Report 2000/2001: Attacking Poverty*, Oxford / New York: Oxford University Press.

World Bank (2002), *The Next Ascent: An Evaluation of the Aga Khan Rural Support Programme*, Washington DC: Operations Evaluation Department, World Bank.

INDEX

A

Accumulated Savings and Credit Association (ASCA), 105

Afghanistan, xiii, xx, xxiv, 33, 35; Northern Alliance, 33, 53, 76, 87; refugees, 35, 62; Taliban, 53

Africa, xix, xxviii, 367, 462

Aga Khan Cultural Services Programme (AKCSP), 390

Aga Khan Development Network (AKDN), 6, 20, 41, 49-52, 59, 83, 89-90, 96, 101-2, 105, 108, 110, 113, 126, 151, 169-70, 380, 389, 391, 404, 425, 444, 455, 462-3, 466-7, 473, 483, 489-90

Aga Khan Education Services (AKES), 13, 41, 49, 79, 88, 126, 159, 169-70, 195, 380, 391, 461

Aga Khan Foundation (AKF), xvi-xvii, xxiii, xxviii, xxix, 140, 170, 175, 189, 286, 380, 459

Aga Khan Fund for Economic Development (AKFED), 348, 490

Aga Khan Health Service, (AKHS), 41, 50, 88, 126, 157, 169, 182, 219, 380, 391

Aga Khan Jubilee Schools, 49

Aga Khan Rural Support Programme (AKRSP), xiv-xvi, 1-6, 13-14; Accelerated Professional Development Programme (APDP), 146-7, 183 ; AKRSP(India) 164-5; Agriculture Valley Specialist, 250; Apna Karobar Scheme (AKS), 309, 314; Collective Action, 369-425; Community infrastructure, 16-17, 196-225; Dry Fruit Project (DFP), 284, 289-90, 293; Enterprise Development, xv, 247, 259-314; Field Management Units (FMU), 147, 340, 342; Heifer Breed Improvement Project, 231; Market Development Programme, 267; Micro-Finance, 315-368; Natural Resource Management (NRM) , 16, 18,

86, 91, 95-96, 99, 146, 226-258, 384, 397, 416; Participatory Plant Breeding (PPB), 248; North South Seeds (NSS) 293-5, 313; Northern Area Conservation Strategy, 171; *Shubinak/Shu,* 290-3, 313-4; Social Action Plan (SAP), 432, 461;South Asian Network of Gender Activists and Trainers (SANGAT), 166; Traditional Birth Attendant (TBA) xvii, 141, 182; Training and Development Centres (TDCs), 229; Village Education Committee, 391; Village Livestock Specialists, 247; Village Organisations (VOs) 4-6, 9, 12, 18, 19-21, 25, 27-28, 60, 77, 94, 109, 121, 132, 138, 142, 145, 171, 203, 205, 207, 210-1, 213, 216, 223, 229-30, 232-3, 235, 241, 249, 251-4, 265-6, 273-7, 280, 312, 318, 320, 322-3, 325-6, 329, 335-9, 342, 346-8, 356-7, 366, 372-3, 377, 383, 385-7, 389, 392, 394, 396, 400-2, 404-5, 407-9, 414, 418, 420, 456-8, 463, 471-3; Women's Organisations (WOs) 12, 27, 77, 94, 121, 123, 129-30, 132-3, 140-5, 148, 154, 159, 168, 171, 179, 182, 188, 203-4, 211, 223, 229, 231-3, 235, 241, 265, 318, 320, 322, 325, 334-7, 343, 352, 356, 358, 383, 387-9, 390, 392, 394, 396, 404, 407-8, 420, 460, 463, 471-3; Working with Government, 426-53

Aga Khan University, 169; Tawana Pakistan, 169

Agriculture, Livestock and Forestry (ALF), 235

Aishi Paen, 242

Almaty Micro-Finance Conference, 2003, 367

Akbar Development Fund, 100

Alexander [the Great], 39

Allama Iqbal Open University, 193

Al-Nusrat Welfare Organisation, 160

Ansari Commission, 179
Asian Development Bank (ADB), xvii, 119
Astore, 35-36, 47, 85, 169, 226, 237, 255, 388
Aurat Foundation, 139, 191
Australia, 363
Ayun, 74

B

Badakshani states, 35, 76
Bagrote, 36, 377
Baltistan, xvii-xviii, 6, 33-34, 36, 40, 47, 51, 85, 121, 123, 133-4, 140-1, 145, 148, 152, 155, 157, 159-60, 169-70, 176, 180, 187, 189-95, 199, 218, 235, 237, 247, 255-6, 275, 312, 332, 334, 351-2, 367, 380-1, 383, 385, 387-8, 390, 398, 417, 422-3, 275; All Baltistan Women's Association, 133; *Baltarang,* , 218, 243; Balti, 36; Baltistan Gems Association (BGE); 304. Ghanche district; 169, 399; Shigar Valley, 257; Upper Basho Forest/Basho, 398-9, 403
Balochistan, 12
Balwantra Commission, 8
Banfield, Edward, 375
Bangladesh, xiii, xvi, xix, 4-5, 9-10, 14, 16, 25, 30, 45, 118-9, 162-4, 189, 192-3, 268, 317, 355, 414, 423; Association for Social Advancement (ASA), 355; BRAC 10, 162-4, 166, 194; PROSHIKA xiii, 5, 10, 16, 423
Bar Valley Project, 235
Begusht Valley, 402, 403, 411, 424
Bharuch District [Gujrat], 164
Bhutto, Benazir, 136-7, 181-2
Bhutto, Z.A., 40, 378
Bolivia, 356, 362
Bombagh, 242
Borogil, 17
Botkuli Valley, 408, 411
British/Britain, 33-4, 36, 186, 363
Buchez, Francis, 364
Buni [Booni], 73, 76,78, 190, 402, 405
Burushuski, 36-37

C

Cairo, 184
Caja Municipales, 357
Canada, xvi-xvii, 406
Canadian International Development Agency (CIDA), xxiv, xxix, 159, 174-5, 179, 185-6, 189, 193-4
Central Asia xxiv, 1, 16, 26, 32, 34-35, 44, 367
Cento Internacional de Mejoramiento de Maiz y Trigo (CIMMYT), 248, 250
Chalt-Chaprote, 235, 239, 242, 251-4, 257, 398
Chambers, 4-5, 9-10
Charpursan, 403
Chatham, 363
Chila/Chilas-Darail, 40, 47, 398-9, 403
China, 10, 16, 26, 33, 40, 44, 87, 198-9, 252, 322, 325, 371, 474, 490
Chitral, xvi, xxvii, xxix, 6, 12, 17-18, 21, 26, 30, 33-36, 38, 40, 47, 51, 62, 64, 73-78, 84, 88, 90, 117, 121, 123, 126-7, 132-4, 140-2, 145, 148, 155-6, 160-1, 167, 169, 176, 180-2, 186, 188-90, 193-6, 203, 218, 220, 222-3, 226, 237, 255-6, 260, 262, 291-3, 304, 308, 312-3, 324, 334, 351-2, 367, 381, 383, 387-8, 390, 400-1, 404, 406, 408, 410, 412-3, 417-8, 422, 424-5, 440, 444-5, 465, 474, 491; Chitral Area Development Program (CADP), 84, 90; Chitral Association of Mountain area Tourism (CAMAT), 304, 425; District Assembly, 192; Gujars, 88; Hazratabad, 401; Kalash, 465; Kators, 38; *Krui Jinali,* 218, 243; Lutko valley, 397, 404, 408, 410-2; Mehtars, 34, 36, 38, 40, 45, 61; NGO Network, 155; *Parsan,* 218; Scouts, 42, 74; Toque Valley, 401; Yarkhun Valley, 17, 76, 401, 424
Christen, Robert Peck, 363
Civil Services Academy, 431
Comilla, 118, 317, 371; Academy 8; model 4; project, 229, 255

Convention on the Elimination of All Forms of Discrimination against Women (CEDAW), 137, 174, 185, 191

Co-operative Movement, 363-5; Asian Co-operative Movement, 316; Chartism, 364; Combination Act of 1824, 363; Fenwick Weavers Association, 363; Owenite movement, 364; Raiffeisen Co-operative Societies, 365; Rochdale Weavers/co-operative, 363-5, 368; Schulze Delitzsh's Principles, 365; Talpuddle Martyrs, 363

D

Daudzai project, 229, 255, 317

Doms, 44, 424

Department of International Development (DFID), xiii-iv, xix-xx, xxiii, xxix, 94, 156, 165, 174, 181, 183, 185-7, 189-90, 192-5, 248, 250, 369

Dera Ismail Khan, 180

Development Action for Mobilization and Emancipation (DAMEN), 345

Diamer district, 35

Diamond Jubilee Schools, 47, 195

Dir, 35-36, 51, 53, 76

Domani Development Association, 422

Drosh, 76

E

East Africa, 362

Entidad para el Desarrollo de la Peqena y Micrempresa (EDPYME), 356

Europe, 316, 363-4, 367

F

Federally Administered Tribal Areas, 190

Federally Administered Northern Areas (FANA), 199

First Micro-finance Bank (FMFB), 15, 23, 324-5, 331, 335, 344-5, 349, 353-4, 358, 368

First Women's Bank, 182, 328

Freire, Paulo 4

Fondos Finacieros Privados (FFP), 356, 362

Food and Agriculture Organisation (FAO), 244, 314

Foundation for International Community Assistance (FINCA), 355-6, 361, 367

France, 364

Frontier Works Organisation, 199

G

Gakuch, 73, 100, 114

Gandhi, 8, 371

Garam Cheshma, 404, 408, 411, 424;Garam Cheshma Area Development Organisation (GADO), 403, 411-2

Gender and Development (GAD), 12-13, 27, 122, 148-9, 162, 166, 175, 184, 193, 387

Gender Quality Action Learning (GQAL), 163

Gender Resource Centre, 163

Germany, 316-7, 365

Ghizer, 33-37, 40, 70, 73, 84, 99-100, 114, 131, 169, 321, 385, 417

Ghulapan, 242-3

Gilgit, xvi, xviii, xx, 3, 33-36, 40, 51, 63, 68-69, 73, 75-77, 84, 118, 121, 126, 131-4, 139-41, 143-6, 148, 151, 176, 179, 181-3, 186, 188-90, 192, 199, 222, 224, 229, 229-30, 237-8, 247-8, 252, 255, 257, 260, 263, 272,283, 306, 308, 310, 312-3, 321-2, 327, 334, 346, 351-2, 367, 380, 383, 385, 387-8, 390, 398, 406, 417, 422, 430, 432-3, 444; Jutal Channel, 224-5

Gircha, 258

Global Environment Facility (GEF), 253, 258

Global Water Partnership, xvii

Grameen Bank, 355

Green Revolution, 9

Gupis; 69. Gamais community, 99

H

Habib Bank Limited, 327, 366
Hatoon Development Organisation/ channel, 146, 224
Himalayan Range, 36, ibex, 242, 253, 258
Hindu Raj/Hinduism, 36, 53
Hindukush 1, 33, 372, 378
Holland, 365
Houghton Group, 347
Hudood Ordinances, 136, 178, 189, 191-2
Hungary, 365
Hunza, xv, 33-34, 36-37, 40, 44, 69, 73, 84, 131, 139, 179, 189-90, 218-9, 230, 240,283, 322, 325, 367, 380, 385, 388, 390, 403, 417, 424; Aliabad, 219, 390, 218; Khyber village/Model , 238, 240-2, 256-7; Threadnet, 190
Haq, General Zia ul, 135-6, 178 -9, 181, 430, 447; Law of Evidence, 136, 178-9
Hyderabad, 139, 179

I

Imperial College, University of London, 230
India, xiii, xvi, xix-xx, 8-9, 12, 21, 161, 164, 194, 356, 371-2
Indus Valley Road, 199
International Centre for Integrated Mountain Development (ICIMOD), xvii, 168
International Fund for Agricultural Development (IFAD), xvii, 168, 190
International Institute for Environment and Development (IIED), xvii
International Irrigation Management Institute (IIMI), xvii
International Labour Organisation (ILO), xiii, 179
International Union for the Conservation of Nature (IUCN), xviii, 83, 113, 126, 167, 171, 226-7, 231, 233, 236, 256, 391, 424; Mountain Area Conservancy Programme (MACP), xvii, 170, 254, 424

International Year of the Mountains, 2002, 120, 176
Iran, 34
Ishkoman, 69; Raja, 36
Islam, 37, 47, 162, 465
Islamabad, xvii, xxviii, 15, 22, 34, 40, 73, 76, 176, 349, 430, 433
Ismaili(s), 5-6, 34, 35-37, 40, 45, 47, 51, 73, 123, 139, 190, 325, 380, 385, 406, 417-8, 466, areas 79, 424, diaspora, 105, Tradition 13, 38

J

Jafferabad, 143
Jagir Basin, 144
Jaglote, 141, 182, 385
Jamalpur Women's Project, 194
Jinnah, Quaid-i-Azam Muhammad Ali, 138

K

Karachi, 30, 34, 73, 119, 123, 349
Karakoram, 1, 33, 36, 372, 378
Karakoram Area Development Organisation, 390
Karakoram Highway (KKH), xxviii, 40-41, 62, 68, 70-72, 75-76, 78, 84, 114, 125, 196, 198-200, 217, 227, 479
Karakoram International University, 488
Karimabad, 44, 390, 424; Karimabad Area Development Organisation (KADO), 397, 408-12, 424; Karimabad Union Council, 408
Kanday Irrigation Channel, 400
Kashf, 340-1, 345
Kashgar, 199
Kashmir, 12, 21, 34, 40,117, 372, 380
Kenya, 355, 358, 362
Khaplu, 157, 192
Khan, Akhtar Hameed, 30, 255, 257, 329, 371, 458
Khan, General Yahya, 40
Khan, His Highness the Aga, 21, 38, 82, 430, 466
Khan, Shoaib Sultan, 3, 224, 253, 354, 429-31, 434, 452-3

Khowar, 35-37
Khozar Rural Development Organisation, 411
Khunjrab Buffer Zone, 235, 253
Khunjab National Park (KNP), 252-3, 257
Khunjrab Pass, 199, 252
Khunjrab Village Organisation (KVO), 229, 239, 251, 253-4, 258
Khushal Pakistan Programme (KPP), 216-7, 225, 336, 440
Khushali Bank, 328, 433
Khyber Bank, 328
Kisan Sabha, 10
Koen Khan University, 10
Koghuzi, 145
Kohistan, 75
Korea, 355
Koro Irrigation Channel, 400
Krishi Samabaya Samitis, 4
Kunar Valley, 35, River, 76
Kuragh Village, 402
Kuwait, 34, 105

L

Lachi Poverty Reduction Project, 340-1
Ladakh, 34
Lahore, 34
Lahore University of Management Sciences, 309, 313
Latin America, 10, 101, 355, 362-3, 367
Less-Developed Countries (LDCs), 103
Local Bodies and Rural Development (LB&RD),.199-200, 216, 223
Local Government Ordinance 2001, 134, 187
Lok Virsa, 308, Silk Route Festival, 308
London, 338
Long, Norman, 4
Longkha Irrigation Channel, 400
Lowari, 76
Lowari Pass, 35-36, 51, 76, 126, 196
Lusht, 17

M

Mastuj, 17, 34, 76, 78
Microcredit, 13-14

Micro-finance; xiii, 13-14; Micro-Finance Bank, 15, 23, 349
Micro, Small and Medium Enterprises (MSMEs), 261, 266, 282-3, 299, 301-2, 306
Microfinance Institutions (MFI), 15, 354, 360-2, 367
Millenium Development Goals, 113
Mogh, 155, 406, 409-10, 412; Mogh Welfare Society, 404, 406; Nizari Library, 406
Mough village, 404
Mountain Women Development Organisation, 132
Mulko [Mulkho] valley, 74, 78, 417
Murfi Foundation, 105
Musharraf, General Pervaiz, 186-7
Muslim League,184-5

N

Nagar, 36-37, 40, 53, 69, 73, 85, 100, 114, 129, 141, 143, 161, 169, 182, 189, 190, 257, 390, 398
National Agricultural Research Council (NARC), 234, 250
National Bank, 366
National Bank for Agricultural Research and Development (NABARD), 356, 367
National Commission on the Status of Women, 137, 179, 184, 187, 189, 191-2, Report 182
National Development Finance Corporation (NDFC), 328
National Devolution Plan, 2000, 432, 473. Citizen's Community Boards (CCBs), 473-4
National Policy for Development and Empowerment of Women, 168
National Rural Support Programme (NRSP), 167, 436
Naunihal Development Organisation, 161, 390
Navinchandra Mafatlal Sadguru Water and Development Foundation (Sudguru), 164-5
Nawa Pass, 35
Nepal, xix, 30, 47, 355

Njer Kori, 192
Nomal village, 256
NORAD, 235
North West Frontier Province (NWFP), 12, 21, 35-36, 40, 111, 117, 126, 180, 193, 223, 312, 408, 491
Northern Areas, xxvii, xxix, 30, 34, 40, 51, 63, 75, 78, 85-86,117, 125-6, 134, 141-2, 168, 189, 192, 195, 199-200, 217, 250, 258, 262, 273, 286, 296,312, 319-20, 324, 347, 351, 366, 430,444-5, 491; Chamber of Commerce and Industries (NACCI), 308; Department of Local Government and Rural Development, 473; Human Rights Committee, 134; Legislative Council, 134, 464; Participatory Poverty Assessment xv; Public Works Department (NAPWD) 199, 223; Schools, 169; Women's Directorate, 134; Women's Development Organisation, 132
Northern Areas and Chitral (NAC), xiv-xv, xxiv-xxv, xxvii, 8, 13-15, 23, 33-34, 38-41, 44, 46-47, 54-55, 57, 62-63, 65-67, 71, 83, 87, 90, 92, 96, 98, 101, 104-6, 111-2, 115, 117, 120-2, 124, 128-31, 131, 134-5, 145, 148, 153, 155, 157,160-1, 169-70, 173-6, 196, 198, 201, 215, 219, 221-2, 224, 226-7, 231, 236-7, 243, 247, 249, 256, 261, 263, 265, 268, 271-3, 281-2, 285, 287-9, 293-5, 298-9, 310, 325, 327, 336,343, 352, 371-2, 376-7, 381, 389-91, 394, 396, 399, 412, 415, 417, 420-1, 423,454-6, 462, 465, 467-8, 470, 473-90; Household Income Surveys (NACHIS), 54, 67, 84, 88
Nuristan, 76

O

OECD, 101
Olson, Mancur, 376
Orangi, 30
Orangi Pilot Project (OPP), 345
Oshikandass, 139, 179
OXFAM, 5

Orix Leasing Limited, 308, 314
Owen, Robert, 364
Oxus River, 33

P

Pakistan, xiii, xix-xx, xxiv, 11, 14, 23, 25-26, 33-35, 37, 66, 85-86, 99, 106, 117, 121,127, 131, 134-5, 137, 139, 150, 154, 164, 166, 168, 171, 178, 184, 188, 191, 199, 206, 243, 247, 251, 260, 292, 296, 310, 316-8, 343, 345, 347, 357, 383, 385, 418, 433, 436, 462, 473; Basic Democracies, 8; Chamber of Commerce and Industry, 265; Consortium, 183; East, 8; Export Promotion Bureau, 265; Family Planning Association, 194; Government [of] xv, 40, 121, 137, 199, 217, 234, 244; Partition, 34; Penal Code, 136, 178; Micro-finance Network (PMN), 366, 433; Micro-finance Ordinance, 318, 343, 345; Ministry of Women's Development (MOWD), 136-7, 168-9, 182, 187-8; Northern, 11, 16, 20, 23-24, 27, 30, 54, 111-2, 124-8, 196, 255, 324, 378-9; Social Forestry Project, 234; State Bank, 329, 348; Supreme Court, 184; West, 8; Women's Development Department, 137, 168, 184; Women's Division, 135-6, 178
Pakistan International Airlines (PIA), 76
Pakistan People's Party (PPP), 40, 181-2, 184-5, 378
Pakistan Philanthropy Centre, 119
Pakistan Poverty Alleviation Fund, xvi, 344
Panchayati Raj, 9
Panjshir Valley, 33
Paris, 183
Participatory Rural Appraisal, 10
Pashtu, 36
Pashtun/ Pathan, 33, 35, 127
Peru, 356-7, 362
Peshawar, 8, 34-35, 73, 76, 84, 193, 371, 445
Phillipines, 10
Productive Physical Infrastructure (PPI), 17-18, 94, 140, 182, 203, 209, 319,

327, 336, 366, 376-7, 384, 413; Grants, 116; Orchard Development Project, 182, 192. Punjab, 12

Punyal, 69, 73, 179, 189

Q

Qisas and Diyat Ordinance, 182

R

Raiffeisen, Wilhelm, Friedrich, 316, 365
Rapid Rural Appraisal, 4, 10
Rawalpindi, 34, 73
Rehankot, 133
Renmushey Stores, 247
Reshun Power Station, 416
Rotating Savings and Credit Association (ROSCA), 105, 109
Rural Support Programme Network (RSPN), 168, 189-90
Russia/Russian, 33, 365, 371

S

Sahaj, 165, 193
Sahara Welfare Organisation, 133
Sarhad Rural Support Programme (SRSP), 90, 167
Sarvodaya, 9
Saudi Arabia, 105
Savings and Credit Association, 367
Schulze, Hermann, 364-5
Serbia, 365
Shandur Pass, 40, 76, 126
Shariat Act, 182
Sharif, Nawaz, 136, 447
Sherpao, Aftab, 447
Sherquilla, 139, 352
Shia, 6, 13, 34-38, 45, 47, 51-52, 85, 105, 127, 189, 381, 417-8, 465-6; Ithnashari, 38, 465; Noorbakshi, 34, 465
Shigri, Afzal Ali, 135, 190
Shirkat Gah, 139, 191
Shina, 36-37
Shogore/Shogore Union Council, 404, 408
Shorebank Advisory Services, 286, 347
Shramdana, 9

Sikanderabad, 100, 114
Siksa Irrigation Channel, 400
Sindh, 12, 135, 349
Skardu, 76, 78, 130, 192, 247, 260, 398
Small and Medium Enterprise (SME), 331, 485-7
SME Bank Limited, 309, 314
Small enterprise movement, 16
Small Infrastructure Projects (SIPs), 141
Social Policy and Development Centre, 119
South Asia, xiii, xxiv, 1, 14, 43-44, 53, 162, 166, 371-2, 414, 426, 433
South-East Asia, 101
Sri Lanka, 9
Srinagar, 34
Sungi, 139
Sunni, 6, 13, 35-38, 45, 47, 51-52, 73, 85, 105, 123, 127, 141, 382, 385, 417-8, 465
Sust village, 252, 258

T

Taiwan, 355
Tajikistan, 33, 170
Tanzania, 367
Thailand, 10
Training and Learning Programme in Social Development, 20
Turkho valley, 35, 78, 417

U

Uganda, 362
United Kingdom (UK)/England, xvii, xxix, 13, 101, 106, 117, 289-90, 314, 363, 365
United Nations (UN), 34
UNDP, xvii, xxi, 137, 168, 181,183, 188, 191, 235, 244; Information-sharing for Women in Development Group (INWID), 181, 183
UN International Conference on Population and Development, 184
UNICEF, 137, 179, 200
UNIFEM, xvii

United States Agency for International Development (USAID), 137
United States of America (USA), 13, 53, 367
USAID, xvii, xx, 179, 183

V

Village Aid, 8
Village Welfare Associations, 404-12

W

Wageningen, 4
Wakkhan Corridor, 33, 36
Wakki, 33, 36
Washington consensus, 23
Water and Sanitation Extension Programme (WASEP), 89, 169
Water Management Institute (WMI), xiv
West Bengal, 53
West India Rainfed Farming Project (WIRFP), 164-5
Women's Action Forum, 178
Women-in-Development (WID), xvi-xvii, 12-13, 27, 47, 122, 136, 140, 147-50, 153, 162, 166, 174-5, 179, 181-3, 185-7, 193, 231, 234-6, 387

World Bank, xiii, xvii, xx, xxiv, xxviii, 10, 30, 137, 159-60, 162, 169, 195, 203, 206, 217, 230, 233, 236, 239, 246, 269-71, 273, 282, 287, 311, 323, 350, 362, 367, 391, 461; Development Report, 118; Joint Monitoring Mission (JMM), 269-70, 282, 287
World Conference on Women, 1995, 137, 185; Beijing Follow-up Units, 137, 185
World Food Programme, xvii
World Trade Order (WTO), 87
World Wildlife Fund (WWF), 83, 113, 126, 235, 253, 391

X

Xingjian, 199

Y

Yasin, 69